Forgotten Scriptures

Forgotten Scriptures

*The Selection and Rejection
of Early Religious Writings*

Lee Martin McDonald

WESTMINSTER
JOHN KNOX PRESS
LOUISVILLE · KENTUCKY

© 2009 Lee Martin McDonald

First edition
Published by Westminster John Knox Press
Louisville, Kentucky

09 10 11 12 13 14 15 16 17 18—10 9 8 7 6 5 4 3 2 1

Scripture quotations from the New Revised Standard Version of the Bible are copyright © 1989 by the Division of Christian Education of the National Council of the Churches of Christ in the U.S.A. and are used by permission.

Book design by Sharon Adams
Cover design by Lisa Buckley

Library of Congress Cataloging-in-Publication Data

McDonald, Lee Martin, 1942–
   Forgotten scriptures : the selection and rejection of early religious writings /
Lee Martin McDonald.
      p. cm.
   Includes bibliographical references (p.   ) and indexes.
   ISBN 978-0-664-23357-0 (alk. paper)
   1. Apocryphal books—Criticism, interpretation, etc.   2. Bible—Canon.   I. Title.
   BS1700.M38   2009
   229'.061—dc22

                                                      2009001923

♾ The paper used in this publication meets the minimum requirements
of the American National Standard for Information Sciences—Permanence of Paper
for Printed Library Materials, ANSI Z39.48-1992.

Westminster John Knox Press advocates the responsible use of our natural resources.
The text paper of this book is made from at least 30% post-consumer waste.

In sincere appreciation for
Professor Helmut Koester
Committed Churchman, Scholar, Mentor, and Friend

Contents

Preface

For some time now, I have been impressed with the story that the ancient biblical manuscripts have left for us to consider. They represent what I have called elsewhere the "operative" biblical canons of antiquity. With few exceptions, if any, they functioned as scripture in the communities that received, copied, and made use of them in their churches. The manuscripts that have survived antiquity reflect the sacred scriptures of early Christianity. Although the vast majority of the surviving manuscripts have come to us from Egypt and from several discoveries in the Judean Desert, they are likely translocal texts, that is, they originated elsewhere, and likely reflect a widespread perspective of the early churches. They essentially tell us what books and texts most informed the early churches, and I find that most useful information. For some biblical scholars, it appears that this information is challenging since the books and texts of the earliest churches are not exactly or precisely like those that inform churches today, although there is considerable overlap. A study of the first four centuries of the church reveals that a number of books that did not eventually receive canonical acceptance nevertheless were welcomed as sacred scripture in the early churches. Likewise, although the majority of texts have considerable overlap, a large number of biblical manuscripts have a different text in important places.

I have said for years now that there is nothing wrong with the church today being informed by the same literature that informed the early church. Indeed, many of the most conservative Christians have urged that we follow the example of the early church, but they often hesitate if the texts and books were welcomed by many Christians before the canonization of the Bible in the fourth and fifth centuries. Unlike some, I am not convinced that orthodoxy is a late notion imposed on the churches because of sufficient power and wealth, but rather that the core of it has its roots in the earliest followers of Jesus, and the New Testament literature reflects earliest Christianity. There was no large movement of followers of Jesus who denied his death for our sins and his resurrection.

In terms of the biblical canon, I have also argued that biblical scholars have frequently addressed issues of canon formation in anachronistic and dated fashion and that we need new approaches to this complex issue not only for scholarship but also for believing communities of church and synagogue. In what follows, I have tried to shed some light on the books and texts that informed early Christianity. To the extent that early Christianity is a model for subsequent churches and the future of the churches, I find some of the diversity in early Christianity very freeing, for it allows the church to think out of the box that far too often characterizes the church in modern society. The church of the future, if it is to have a future, will need to exhibit much more flexibility than what has characterized it in the past. Some of that flexibility is reflected in the oldest known sacred manuscripts and the translations of those Jewish and Christian scriptures.

The first scriptures of the church were the Jewish scriptures that they inherited from their Jewish siblings. Precisely what those scriptures were is highly debatable, and I have argued elsewhere, as well as in this volume, that in the first century that collection was not yet fixed and also not limited to the books that now make up the Hebrew Bible. This will be explored in more detail below.

It is difficult to overestimate the value of looking at the specific sacred manuscripts that have survived antiquity. It cannot be unimportant for students and scholars of Scripture to consider the significance of these primary texts, especially when we see in them a variety of books that were not canonized by the church and textual traditions that are not in the eclectic Hebrew and Greek texts of the Scriptures. I hope that the following study will be of special interest to students of the Scriptures and enhance their understanding of those Scriptures in their formative years. Those in the more conservative church traditions are likely to learn more about why the affirmation of biblical authority must be concerned with the data explored in this book.

I owe my gratitude first to those editors and staff of Westminster John Knox Press. They were most kind to contact me about producing a book for them and encouraging me in my research for this project.

Thanks also are due to Mr. Kevin Edgecomb, who has taken a special interest in my study of the origins of the biblical canons of the church. He has patiently read not only this volume but also my earlier volume, *The Biblical Canon*. His reading and commenting on these chapters along with offering useful suggestions to improve it have been most welcome and have added to the quality of the volume and helped me to avoid several errors in the process. His Web site, www.bombaxo.com/blog/, continues to reflect careful information on biblical and noncanonical sources.

My thanks are also due to the Princeton community, both the university and Princeton Theological Seminary, for making available to me their wealth of resources during my sabbatical there in 2007 and 2008. Some of the ideas in this book were tried out on a class that I taught at Princeton Theological Seminary in the spring of 2008. I was also pleased to be able to interact with many of the biblical faculty at the university and the seminary. My wife and I were deeply enriched by our experience there, and we were given every opportunity and courtesy available to visiting professors, including an office in the Scholars Tower and secretarial assistance for the course I taught on canon formation. The many kindnesses extended to us and the remarkable resources made available to me at Princeton have enhanced considerably the care that went into this volume.

I also want to express appreciation to the members of the Board of Trustees at Acadia Divinity College who graciously gave to me a full year's sabbatical as I retired from my presidential duties at that institution. My year at Princeton and this book would not have been possible without their generosity. My years at Acadia were some of the most meaningful that I have experienced, and they continue to bring many fond memories and my heartfelt gratitude to the trustees who extended this opportunity to me for leadership in preparing men and women for Christian ministry.

Finally, I began examining seriously the complex issue of canon formation during my student days at Harvard Divinity School. At that time I received considerable direction, mentoring, and affirmation from Helmut Koester in the pursuit of this subject. Over the years, I have enjoyed his friendship and many kindnesses extended to me. He has been my professor, mentor, and friend, and while I do not suggest that he would agree with everything in this book, I have learned much from him over the years. More especially, his commitment to scholarship, his Christian faith, and his church are exemplary and commendable. For his kindness, mentoring, encouragement, and friendship, I am pleased to dedicate this volume to Helmut Koester for all his considerable influence both on my academic and Christian commitment.

Abbreviations

ABD	*Anchor Bible Dictionary,* ed. D. N. Freedman. 6 vols. New York: Doubleday, 1992
ANF	Ante-Nicene Fathers
BETL	Bibliotheca ephemeridum theologicarum lovaniensium
BHK	*Biblia Hebraica,* ed. G. Kittel. 3rd ed. Stuttgart: Württembergische Bibelanstalt, 1937
BHS	*Biblia Hebraica Stuttgartensia,* ed. K. Elliger et al. Stuttgart: Deutsche Bibelstiftung, 1967–1977
CBQ	*Catholic Biblical Quarterly*
CRINT	Compendia rerum iudaicarum ad Novum Testamentum
DJD	Discoveries in the Judaean Desert
DSD	*Dead Sea Discoveries*
EDSS	*Encyclopedia of the Dead Sea Scrolls,* ed. L. Schiffman and J. C. VanderKam. 2 vols. Oxford: Oxford University Press, 2000
EncJud	*Encyclopedia Judaica,* ed. G. Wigoder. 17 vols. Jerusalem: Keter, 1971–1972
ErIsr	*Erets Israel*
HB	Hebrew Bible
JBL	*Journal of Biblical Literature*
JSJSup	Journal for the Study of Judaism Supplements

JSNT	*Journal for the Study of the New Testament*
JSNTSup	Journal for the Study of the New Testament Supplements
JSP	*Journal for the Study of the Pseudepigrapha*
KJV	King James (Authorized) Version
LCL	Loeb Classical Library
LXX	Septuagint
MT	Masoretic Text
NHS	Nag Hammadi Studies
NIV	New International Version
NRSV	New Revised Standard Version
NT	New Testament
NTS	*New Testament Studies*
OT	Old Testament
OTP	*Old Testament Pseudepigrapha,* ed. J. H. Charlesworth. 2 vols. New York: Doubleday, 1983–1985
RBL	*Review of Biblical Literature*
SBLDS	Society of Biblical Literature Dissertation Series
SBLRBS	Society of Biblical Literature Resources for Biblical Study
SBLSCS	Society of Biblical Literature Septuagint and Cognate Studies
SDSSRL	Studies in the Dead Sea Scrolls and Related Literature
TDNT	*Theological Dictionary of the New Testament,* ed. G. Kittel and G. Friedrich, trans. G. W. Bromiley. 10 vols. Grand Rapids: Eerdmans, 1964–1976
VTSup	Vetus Testamentum Supplements

PART ONE
CHALLENGES
AND DIRECTION

Chapter 1

Introduction

The early church was quite diverse in its understanding of God, Jesus, its mission, and the literature it acknowledged as sacred scripture. While to some degree this diversity still manifests itself among those who call themselves Christians today, it was even more pronounced during the first centuries of the church. It is possible not only to imagine but also to see to some extent the variety of theologies of those early Christian communities that adopted as their sacred literature what we now call the apocryphal or pseudepigraphal Old Testament texts and the New Testament apocryphal writings. To be sure, many faith communities welcomed not only a number of those writings, but also most if not all of the so-called orthodox books that make up the Christian Bibles today. What we now call orthodoxy was only one of the several competing strands of Christian faith in the first few centuries, and because the orthodox churches eventually won the various debates going on in the early church, orthodoxy is largely the primary survivor even if in a variety of Christian denominations. Because the orthodox Christians had the most compelling arguments to the largest number of Christians in antiquity, today we have *their* Bibles in our churches. Bart Ehrman has made significant contributions to this discussion, and his work has initiated a number of important discussions.[1] While I agree with him on the diversity of early Christianity and the variety of its biblical traditions, including the intentional alterations of the biblical text by those in the orthodox tradition, I do not agree with the insinuation that these changes constituted a major departure from the traditions that were first proclaimed in the earliest churches. Orthodoxy won out not because of its wealth or political power, but because before those things were in place the orthodox had in general—not always—made a more compelling case for their positions, and they rooted them in the church's earliest sacred traditions, namely the Old Testament and the first-century Gospels along with the Letters of Paul.

This point should not be confused with my lack of approval of the documents in our current Bibles, as some have suggested.[2] That is simply not the case. As I will state later on, there are good reasons that orthodox Christians carried the day. The texts that they adopted were *generally* (not always) the earliest ones produced in the church and had a greater claim in representing the earliest traditions about Jesus. The Christians who emerged triumphant in the church, from the many "heretical" movements in it, were those whose message more closely reflected the story and teachings of Jesus in the four Gospels and in the letters of Paul. Had that not been the case, it is difficult to imagine the emergence of their dominance in the churches of the third and fourth centuries. I disagree that they won out because of wealth and political power promoting them, since it is clear that by the third century, and well before the so-called conversion of Constantine and the marriage of church and state, the theological arguments of the orthodox were carrying the day among the majority of Christians. This may not have been the case in much of the second century, but it appears to have gained ground by the end of that century through the arguments of its apologists and teachers.

The ancient collections that have survived in various manuscripts often overlap considerably, but not completely, with the books that now make up the Christian Bibles. Occasionally one or more of the so-called noncanonical writings are also preserved in these manuscripts. Interestingly, many of the early manuscripts contain significantly fewer books than are found in Christian Bibles today. The earliest surviving biblical manuscripts, the papyrus manuscripts, seldom contain more than one or two books. Of the 117 papyrus manuscripts now known, only 14 include more than one book. When the technology of the codex or ancient book advanced to the place where it was possible to include the whole of the biblical canon, namely in the fourth century, the church had largely determined which books it would include in its sacred collections; but before then several books continued to be copied and circulated in churches that were not included in the later editions of the sacred collections. Initially, sacred collections included only one book or small collections of books in one manuscript, and it was unusual for any church to have all of the literature that the larger body of Christians in the second century and later believed to be sacred Scripture in the churches. When sacred collections of Christian writings began to appear, they often contained Gospels, or letters, or some combination of Gospels and letters.

The same could be said about the Old Testament writings. Initially, the book of Deuteronomy was the most popular among Jews. In time the rest of the Pentateuch was added, and later other collections were added, such as the Megilloth and the Book of the Twelve (the Minor Prophets). The collections gradually grew and were in time adopted by Jews and Christians as the relevance and value of that literature became obvious to them. As the technology for book production advanced, it was possible for all of the sacred books to be included in one volume in the middle to late fourth century. Even then, however, all churches did not agree on which books were sacred, and we continue to see some variety on the fringe of the biblical canons that emerged in the fourth century.

The focus of this book is on the sacred literature that was left behind and how it was received initially in the churches. Generally speaking, sacred texts were first acknowledged as authoritative writings in religious communities and subsequently acknowledged as Scripture. Finally, those books acknowledged as Scripture were collected and circulated as collections. We now call those collections a biblical canon, that is, a fixed collection of sacred texts that were used in religious communities of faith for religious instruction, worship, and advancing the mission of the early churches. In other words, they were the collected Scriptures of early churches. What is often confusing to students of the Bible is the discovery that very few of the ancient collections had the same books until the Middle Ages. They often included one or more of the so-called noncanonical writings or excluded several of the so-called canonical writings.

Another troubling feature of Christianity today is the regular use of labels for ancient literature that were not employed initially. Terms like "Bible," "canon," "canonical," "noncanonical," "apocryphal," "pseudepigraphal," and others simply did not exist in the early Jewish and Christian communities, and it is not even clear that the notions behind those terms were ever a consideration at that time. These terms were *later* invented to distinguish writings that were *later* deemed to be sacred from those writings that *later* were considered nonsacred. The contemporary use of those labels often prejudices any careful inquiry of that literature today. As I will point out later, these terms are in need of further consideration if we are to have a nonprejudicial manner of evaluating the ancient religious texts that have survived antiquity and were clearly received by some churches as sacred texts.

By the fourth and fifth centuries, most of the noncanonical writings ceased being circulated in the churches, and as a result there was little motivation to continue to copy them. Thus many of these ancient texts disappeared. Writings that were held in high esteem initially were eventually dropped and ceased being reproduced for churches. Before then, it is clear that primitive Christianity (the churches of the first through the fourth centuries) was informed by several other books that today we call apocryphal and pseudepigraphal writings, both Old Testament and New Testament books. Likewise, many churches were not informed by all the books that are included in the Christian Bibles today. Whether that is a problem for Christian faith will be discussed later, but for now

I will simply state that a number of religious texts that once informed Christian faith in time no longer did. That development leads to the title of this volume: *Forgotten Scriptures*. Whether the churches today should reexamine that literature or even open up the canon questions for this generation of Christians will be discussed below. Did the early churches that determined the scope of the Christian Bibles get it right? The discovery and reemergence of several of the so-called noncanonical writings in recent years, as well as the renewed attention being given to that literature, does prompt many questions for Christians today, including the standard issues raised about what criteria were used in forming the Christian biblical canon and whether a case can be made for including other books in the biblical canons in churches today.

It is interesting that the Jews of the western Diaspora were also informed in their worship and teaching ministries by several of the same books that informed early Christianity. In fact, the early Christians took over the sacred collections of the Jews before they had a fixed biblical canon, and much of that additional religious literature that circulated among them also circulated among early Christians both before and following their separation from their Jewish siblings. I will focus attention on the place of that literature among Jews first, not only at Qumran but also among early Christians, before examining the Christian religious texts that were included in or excluded from the Christian Bibles.

In what follows, I will explore some of this development in the churches and draw some conclusions about it at the end of this volume. I will say up front that I do not believe that the results of my research will necessarily lead us to reopen the biblical canon and either add books to or exclude books from the current canon, but I do believe that the church is the poorer in its understanding of its faith and its own development if it is not informed by the literature that informed early Christianity and also early Judaism.

I will show that *most* of the literature that informed both communities of faith during the early years after the death of Jesus included what we now call the canonical writings of the Old Testament and subsequently the New Testament writings, but also in many instances early Christians were informed by the Old Testament apocryphal (or deuterocanonical) and pseudepigraphal writings as well as the New Testament noncanonical and apocryphal writings. The evidence for this is found partially in the lists or catalogues of scriptures from the fourth and fifth centuries onward, the witness of the early church fathers, and the surviving Old Testament and New Testament manuscripts of the early church, including the various manuscripts of the Hebrew Bible[3] (mostly Masoretic texts), but others also such as those Jewish religious texts discovered at Qumran, Murabba'at, Nahal Hever, Masada, and elsewhere. We will also see this development in later Judaism (both rabbinic Judaism and Judaism of the western Diaspora), and in the various translations of the Christian Scriptures, especially the Septuagint (LXX), Old Latin, Vulgate, Syriac Peshitta, and Coptic versions. The evidence for larger Bibles in some cases, especially in the Old Testament books and some New Testament Apocrypha, suggests that in the earlier years of the church, in pre-rabbinic Judaism, and in the synagogues of the western Diaspora there was less certainty on the scope of their sacred literature.

While the church's Bibles today are not uniform, especially in the Old Testament writings in the Roman Catholic, Protestant, Eastern Orthodox, and Ethiopian churches, there is considerable overlap in them, and the orthodox traditions are represented in all of them. The current Bibles, however, are not exactly like the ones that we find in antiquity. Some churches continued to use as sacred scripture for a considerable period such writings as *1 Enoch*, Wisdom of Solomon, Sirach (Ecclesiasticus), *Epistle of Barnabas*, *Shepherd of Hermas*, *Didache*, *1–2 Clement*, *Letters of Ignatius*, and other religious texts not found in some Christian Bibles today. Many of the writings that now make up the Christian Bibles became the primary texts used in the churches, and the others were eliminated in the fourth century and later when orthodoxy carried the day and was adopted by the Roman Empire through its emperor, Constantine. Orthodoxy, however, was not the sole basis for rejecting some of these writings, since the ones mentioned above fit well within the orthodox tradition and informed many of the early proto-orthodox communities before the triumph of Christianity in the Roman Empire. The other writings that had been used sometimes widely in some churches were for various reasons eliminated from later sacred collections, and in time many were lost. When they were no longer deemed sacred, there was no need to continue to copy and circulate them. Archaeologists have recovered many of these religious texts, and others have been serendipitously discovered, for example, in monasteries or in shops of dealers in antiquities. These discoveries have prompted important new studies of that literature and also raised new questions about their inclusion or exclusion in Christian collections as well as interpretations of New Testament literature.

When the church began, there was, of course, no New Testament. There were scriptures that were acknowledged by Jesus and his disciples, but the precise boundaries of those scriptures are not clear in the New Testament writings or in early Jewish or Christian literature. Because citations of many noncanonical books appear in ancient Jewish and Christian texts, it is not clear what books were in the sacred collections of Jews and Christians during or shortly after the time of Jesus. It is difficult to argue that Christians or Jews excluded any of the books in the current Hebrew Bible in the time of Jesus, but it is also difficult to show that all of the books that were eventually included in the Hebrew Bible and in the Protestant Old Testament were included in their sacred collections. In the literature that has survived, not all the books of the Old Testament were cited by either Jews or Christians. As I have shown elsewhere, those who followed the writers of the New Testament did not cite scriptures from any *fixed* collection of Old Testament scriptures, and they also felt free to cite many texts that were not later included in the Hebrew Bible or the Protestant or Catholic Old Testament.[4]

We only begin to see what emerged as a fixed Old Testament and New Testament for most of the churches in the fourth and fifth centuries, when several lists or catalogues of sacred scriptures began to emerge. When the churches began listing those volumes that should be included in their sacred texts, some churches did not subscribe to those lists, as we discover in the ancient manuscripts that have survived antiquity. These manuscripts have become a strategically important resource for recovering as much as is possible not only the original *texts* of the New Testament writings but also the *books* that were in those manuscripts. Those books are what I call the "operative" biblical canons of early Christianity, namely the books that were used in a scriptural manner in the early churches. In what follows, we will look at some of the oldest surviving biblical manuscripts as well as a number of other resources that tell us which books informed the faith of the early churches. Many of these manuscripts contain both a broader range of books than what is now found in some modern Bibles and also in several manuscripts fewer books than are in our modern Bibles.

It is challenging to find resources for this information, since textual critics generally focus their attention on recovering the earliest possible text of the biblical writings and largely ignore other books found in these old manuscripts. Why is so little attention given to the *other* books in them, books that were not eventually included in the modern text of the New Testament? The primary sources that reveal this kind of information include the ancient papyri, majuscule (or uncial) manuscripts, and minuscule (or cursive) manuscripts. There are some 5,740 such manuscripts, and their full story has yet to be told. We should especially note the very significant and largely ignored lectionary texts that date roughly from the fourth century CE. The lectionaries tell us what sacred texts informed the life and worship of the churches at any given time and place. Because they are regularly considered secondary in importance to the continuous text manuscripts, textual critics generally ignore their contents, but they are highly significant for revealing to us those texts that regularly informed the faith of the early Christian churches.

Since the technology was not yet available in the second and third centuries to bind together in one book or codex all of the writings deemed sacred in the churches, the papyri do not tell us as much as we would like to know about the contents of the Christian scriptures, but in some instances they show us that some of what we now call noncanonical texts were bound together with what we now call biblical texts. This phenomenon has been largely overlooked or ignored in the process of establishing the earliest and most reliable text of the New Testament writings. Why were some nonbiblical texts bound together with biblical texts? Why also are some early collections (of Paul's writings) missing some important books, especially the Pastoral Epistles as in the case of P^{46}, but also others? Most of the earliest known papyrus manuscripts, apart from P^{52} and P^{90} (both second century CE), are third- to seventh-century texts that are mostly fragments of the New Testament writings.

The majuscule manuscripts (upper-case continuous letters without spaces between the words) were copied on parchment and date from the fourth century to roughly the tenth century. They are very important because for the first time, in the fourth century, the technology for producing books or codices had developed to the point where all the books of the church's scriptures could be placed in one volume, including the Old and New Testaments. For the first time a manuscript or codex could contain some 1,400 to 1,600 pages. What is most important for scholars who discuss canon formation is that these manuscripts are primary evidence of what books were considered sacred in the churches and placed in a single volume. They do not always contain the same books as now exist in modern Christian Bibles. What other books are included in (or excluded from) them? Daryl Schmidt showed in his research that before the year 1000 only four manuscripts contain all the books in the current New Testament canon and only those books.[5]

The minuscules (lower-case manuscripts with spaces between the words) date from roughly the ninth or tenth century and reveal a more stabilized biblical text as well as a more stabilized collection of books that make up the biblical canon. But in some cases they also show that other books now described as non-canonical were still circulating in churches and some New Testament books were not being circulated in the same collections.

The earliest translations of the Bible do not generally contain the same books, but rather the core books that informed early Christianity. These various translations were often poorly produced. Some collections are larger than others and some contain several noncanonical writings in them. We will explore these phenomena and offer at the end a response to the question, Did the early churches make the right decisions about the scope of their biblical canons? I hope the reader will appreciate more fully the challenges that the development of the biblical canon poses for Christian faith today and also appreciate how the churches eventually dealt with those concerns. As we will see below, some of the literature that identified Christian faith or Judaism in one generation did not do so later.

Finally, at the end of this discussion I will focus on a more practical matter that for many Christians is already settled, but for many it is not. I will offer a postscript on the notion of biblical inerrancy that I hope will promote discussion and further investigation. As one who regularly uses the word "evangelical" as the best description of my theological position, I also no longer hold to the notion of biblical inerrancy, but preserve the term "evangelical" as the best designation of those who continue to proclaim and teach the good news of what God has done for us in Jesus the Christ. I have found over the years that it is a much more open community than those who are known by such terms as "inerrancy" and "infallibility"; but more importantly, those who are committed to the good news and making disciples (Matt. 28:19–20) are better focused to meet the challenges facing the church in this and the next generation.

Chapter 2

The Problem
of Adequate Language

One of the more significant issues facing those who are concerned about the formation of the biblical canon is coming to grips with the fact that few biblical scholars agree on basic definitions of the common terms employed to describe the phenomenon.[1] As a result, scholars often talk past one another when describing the same issues or concerns. Some of the most confusing terms include: "canon," "canonical," "non-canonical," "biblical" or "nonbiblical," "apocryphal," and "pseudepigraphal"—even "Old Testament," "Hebrew Bible" or "First Testament" as well as "New Testament," or BCE and CE instead of BC and AD. All these are anachronistic terms that *later* Jewish and Christian communities used to describe literature that did or did not eventually find acceptance in the Jewish and Christian sacred scripture collections, or they attempt to speak of a phenomenon present in antiquity, but the language may not have been present when the phenomenon took place, as in the whole canonization process.

Most of what we now call apocryphal or pseudepigraphal writings functioned initially as sacred literature in one or more Jewish and/or Christian religious communities. In this chapter I focus on the meaning and validity of such distinctions for investigative research of ancient religious literature and include examples of writings that functioned authoritatively in early Judaism and early Christianity,

11

but were not eventually included in the biblical canons of either religious community. Bart Ehrman acknowledges that "scholars have never devised an adequate term for their 'Lost Scriptures.'"[2] Because of this widespread confusion, I will attempt in this chapter to clarify some things especially for the reader who is examining these matters for the first time.[3] Students of canon formation may already be well aware of many of the issues here, but probably not all of them. In this chapter I will focus on the problem of defining the writings the church and synagogue left behind; this discussion is essential for understanding the rest of this volume.

INTRODUCTION

Both Jews and Christians have historically treated their Bibles as complete and settled entities and have seldom focused on their origins, development, or scope. Indeed, until recently there has been very little sustained interest in the origin and development of the biblical canon for either church or synagogue. Apart from the actions of the Council of Trent in 1546, there was little serious discussion of canon formation for more than a thousand years. Alexander Souter remarked earlier about this dearth of interest in the origins of the biblical canon.[4] Similarly, Bruce Metzger expressed surprise that so important a topic as which books constituted the Bible had received such little attention in antiquity and even in modern times.[5] The current interest in canon formation may have been spurred by the publication of popular books like *The Da Vinci Code* or *Holy Blood, Holy Grail*, and the plethora of spin-off volumes they have generated, as well as by the annual hype just before Easter in the media presentations such as Mel Gibson's *Passion of the Christ*, the *Gospel of Judas*, or the discovery of the supposed tomb of Jesus and his wife, Mary Magdalene! Many of these publications are shrouded in tantalizing promises of revelations that could perhaps destroy Christianity. It is even implied that there is something the church does not want anyone to know because it could or would damage or destroy the church's faith. These sensational claims not only sell a lot of books but also bring new interest in the formation of the Bible and especially in the books that were excluded from the biblical canons of both Judaism and Christianity.

This renewed interest does take away from the fact that for two thousand years the church still has not agreed on the scope of its Bible—even if there is wide agreement on most of it. Today four different Old Testament canons are current in the Christian church: those in the Eastern Orthodox (both Greek and Russian),[6] Roman Catholic,[7] Protestant,[8] and Ethiopian churches.[9] Likewise, many multiple collections of sacred books in antiquity are similar in content, but not identical. Most of these differences were present before the fourth century, but some came later. Then as now, the books that one religious community calls apocryphal or even pseudepigraphal (and thereby dismisses them), another religious community welcomes as scripture. Only the names of the books in question have changed from time to time.

Current research suggests that the larger collections of Old or First Testament writings containing the so-called apocryphal books were more common in the early churches and in Second Temple Judaism than the more limited collection of biblical books in the later Jewish Hebrew Bible and Protestant Old/First Testament. The diverse opinions about the scope of the biblical canon are no doubt rooted in the complexity of the traditions surrounding the origins of the Bible, and what makes matters even more challenging is that no ancient documents explain when the process of canonization began, when it ended, or even what a biblical canon is. Most scholarly conclusions about this process depend on the inferential evidence stemming from a few well-known ancient texts rather than on explicit statements or discussions in antiquity.

Today no one denies the considerable diversity in early Christianity, but how widespread was what we now call "heresy" in the emerging churches of the second and third centuries? In a highly influential and often controversial book, Walter Bauer claimed that the heterodox communities outnumbered the orthodox in the second century and that they even produced literature opposing the "heretical" teachings of those churches that we now call orthodox![10] Bart Ehrman, who agrees with Bauer, also contends that in the second century "orthodoxy" was more limited in influence than earlier thought—and he may be right, but he is probably overstating his case when he claims that orthodoxy, "in the sense of a unified group advocating an apostolic doctrine accepted by the majority of Christians everywhere, did not exist in the second and third centuries."[11] Neither wealth nor political power in Rome can account for all the factors that led to the so-called triumph of orthodoxy in the greater church in antiquity. Ehrman does not give adequate weight to the antiquity of the orthodox tradition in the churches (it appeals to the writings of Paul and the canonical Gospels, the earliest Christian writings known to the church) and the force of Irenaeus's teaching about apostolic succession in the church.[12] Nevertheless, I concede that there was considerably more diversity tolerated in early Christianity than after the fourth century, but at the end of the second century a proto-orthodoxy appears largely to have won the theological battle and also anchored its theological heritage in the earliest traditions of the church, namely what we now call the canonical Gospels and the writings of Paul.

In regard to the scriptures of the Jews, many have assumed for far too long that the Jews of antiquity were of one mind on the scope and content of their Bible, as if it were a fixed entity no later than the end of the first century CE. Not only have recent studies of the Dead Sea Scrolls shown us otherwise,[13] but also the little-noticed differences between Jews in the east and those in the western Diaspora point to a significant difference in surviving Judaism on the matter. More specifically, we have no evidence that the rabbinic decisions of the east made any significant impact on Jews in the west and their way of life or their views about scripture. Indeed, the opposite appears to be true. Arye Edrei and Doron Mendels have argued convincingly that in their religious devotion Jews in the western Diaspora continued to use the sacred books of the Septuagint, including the apocryphal and pseudepigraphal books. Because for the most part these Jews could not speak or read Hebrew or Aramaic, they were largely unaffected by the rabbinic decisions in the east and the literature that they produced (Mishnah, Tosefta, and the two Talmudim).[14] Was there only one Jewish understanding of scripture and canon in the time of Jesus? That notion was laid to rest long ago, but there has been a continuing notion of unity in Judaism during and after the time of rabbinic Judaism in the second century. This is a misunderstanding of the history of Judaism. Well into the Middle Ages various Jewish sects were still debating the scope of their scriptures. The Karaites and the Samaritans, for example, chided the Rabbanite Jews over their use of the Prophets and having more than the Law of Moses as a scriptural authority.[15] How representative was rabbinic Judaism among the Jews, and were the rabbinic Jews consistent in what they had to say about the Jewish scriptures? I will argue that like the early Christians, a considerable time elapsed before there was general agreement on the fringe areas of their biblical canon.

CLASSICAL AND ECCLESIASTICAL MEANINGS OF "CANON"

"Canon" comes from a Semitic word, *qaneh,* which originally referred to a reed or stalk that grew along a riverbank. In time, these reeds or stalks were marked (sometimes with dots) to measure various lengths, not unlike how a ruler is used today. The notion of a guide that measured up or fit a recognized standard eventually was captured by the term "canon" (see Ezek. 40:5). The Greek derivative of *qaneh, kanōn,* is used in antiquity for classical works such as the *pinakes* at Alexandria to identify lists of classical books. For example, Epicurus (341–270 BCE) used *kanōn* to show the logic and method in thought that stemmed from a collection of principles by which one could determine what was true or false. Later, Diogenes Laertius (200–250 CE) named one of Epicurus's writings as "Of the Standard, a Work Entitled Canon [*kanōn*]" (*Lives* 10.27, 30). The term was used in the Hellenistic world to identify standards whether in the area of art, architecture, music, grammar, or philosophy. Further, Epictetus (ca. 50–130 CE) argued that the goal of philosophy was to determine a "standard [*kanōn*] of judgment" so that whatever needs to be investigated could be measured by and be subject to that standard (*Diss.* 2.11.13, 20; cf. 2.23.21).[16] It is important that those who adopted earlier notions of canons or standards never suggested that they were closed or fixed categories. In time, other important works that rose to an acceptable standard were also added to those lists (or *pinakes*). The same practice took place in Judaism and early Christianity for several centuries: their sacred collections grew, but they became fixed collections in the fourth and fifth centuries.

The notion of well-established but not *fixed* collections of standard writings was widespread in antiquity, especially in Egypt, and may have had some influence on the development of Jewish and Christian notions of a collection of sacred scriptures, even though that is difficult to demonstrate since neither Jews nor Christians claim to have copied this ancient model. Laws, regulations, models, and widely used patterns were common before, during, and after the birth of Christianity and may have influenced the emergence of the notion of a canon or standard of sacred scriptures that identified those writings for Jews and subsequently for Christians that were considered normative in their communities.[17] Such models were present during these formative years for early Christianity and rabbinic Judaism even if neither religious community mentions it. It is difficult to demonstrate that notions of a *fixed* scriptural standard existed before the end of the first century at the earliest (Josephus, *Ag. Ap.* 1.43–47) or mid-second century (*b. Baba Bathra* 14b), but collections of Christian writings and Jewish scriptures can reasonably be shown in both communities (e.g., Psalms, the Twelve Minor Prophets, Paul's Letters). In the early church there appears to be no interest in fixed collections of scriptures much before the fourth century, even though Christians, like their fellow Jews, already welcomed the Law and Prophets (which appears to have included all other sacred texts that were not in the Law), although the Psalms began to find a separate place in the growing scripture collections (Luke 24:44). While Irenaeus himself argued for the acceptance of only four Gospels and no more in the church ("these four alone"; cf. *Haer.* 3.11.8–9), he does not speak about a fixed biblical canon such as we see in the fourth and fifth centuries, and his views that became models in later orthodox communities are not representative of many (most?) of the churches of his own generation. No other writer of his time limited the Gospels to four (Matthew, Mark, Luke, and John), and even Tertullian (ca. 200 CE) gave priority to Matthew and John over Luke and Mark since the latter were not apostles.[18]

Canon (Greek, *kanōn*) is used in the New Testament to describe the limits or boundaries (*kanonos*) of Paul's ministry or another's (2 Cor. 10:13, 15, 16), as well as the "rule of faith" (*kanoni*) or the norm of true Christianity (Gal. 6:16), but it does not describe a fixed collection of scriptures. In the second and third centuries, *kanōn* describes that understanding of the Christian faith that was believed to be normative in the churches (the *regula fidei*). Irenaeus, for example, speaks of "canon" in reference not to a list of inspired books but rather to the Christian faith that he believed had been faithfully passed on in the churches by the apostles—that is, the apostolic tradition (*Haer.* 3.2.2). Irenaeus's summary of "the faith" or "the canon of faith" on which the church depended for its life and witness is found in a well-known text that merits careful scrutiny since its major tenets became the foundation pillars of "orthodoxy" in the church and were a major part of most ancient creedal formulations such as the Apostles' Creed (*Haer.* 3.3.3; 3.4.1). This "canon," or *regula fidei* (rule of faith), was a distinguishing feature in later decisions over which Christian writings were included in or excluded from the biblical canon.[19] Irenaeus writes:

> The Church, though dispersed throughout the whole world, even to the ends of the earth, has received from the apostles and their disciples this faith: It believes in one God, the Father Almighty, Maker of heaven, and

earth, and the sea, and all things that are in them; and in one Christ Jesus, the Son of God, who became incarnate for our salvation; and in the Holy Spirit, who proclaimed through the prophets the dispensations of God, and the advents, and the birth from a virgin, and the passion, and the resurrection from the dead, and the ascension into heaven in the flesh of the beloved Christ Jesus, our Lord, and His [future] manifestation from heaven in the glory of the Father "to gather all things in one," and to raise up anew all flesh of the whole human race in order that to Christ Jesus, our Lord, and God, and Saviour, and King, according to the will of the invisible Father, "every knee should bow, of things in heaven, and things in earth, and things under the earth, and that every tongue should confess" to Him; and that He should execute just judgment towards all; that He may send into everlasting fire all "spiritual wickedness" and the angels who transgressed and became apostates, together with the ungodly, and unrighteous, and wicked, and profane among men, but may, in the exercise of His grace, confer immortality on the righteous, and holy, and those who have kept His commandments and have persevered in His love, some from the beginning [of their Christian course], and others from [the time of] their repentance, and may surround them with everlasting glory. (Adapted from *Haer.* 1.10.1, ANF; cf. *Haer.* 3.4.2.)

The early church did not use the term "canon" as a reference to a closed collection of sacred literature adopted by a religious community. While the term *began* to be used for a collection of sacred writings that made up the church's sacred writings in the fourth century, namely with Athanasius in his thirty-ninth *Festal Letter*, it was not *regularly* used as such until David Ruhnken used it in 1768 in his treatise *Historica critica oratorum Graecorum* to refer to a selective list of literary writings.[20] Rudolf Pfeiffer claims that Ruhnken's use of the term eventually met with worldwide acceptance and more closely resembled a scripture collection rather than the ancient use of the term, primarily focusing on a list of writers rather than books.[21] He argues that while this is common parlance today, it is nevertheless a modern catechesis that originated in the eighteenth century. He further observes that Ruhnken found his model for this use of canon in the biblical tradition rather than in antiquity, where the most common term for a listing or catalogue of writings was *pinakes* (plural of *pinax*). Pfeiffer concludes that if we choose to call a catalogue or collection of Christian writings a canon, we are not using the term in its original sense. G. A. Robbins agrees with Pfeiffer and shows that Eusebius, who is sometimes wrongly assumed to be the first person to use the term "canon" for a collection of the church's scriptures, never used the word in reference to a *fixed* collection of sacred scriptures.[22] Eusebius used the term "encovenanted" (Greek *endiathēkē*) to refer to those texts that were widely received as sacred scripture in the church. Since Ruhnken, however, "canon" has become the term of choice for a closed collection of books that the church accepts as its sacred scriptures.[23]

Later interests in restricting the number of sacred books in both Jewish and Christian communities did not always reflect the interests or concerns of the religious communities that produced, used, and initially circulated those books.

For example, the books in the various lists or catalogues of scriptures in the fourth and fifth centuries are not always exactly the same as those in the biblical manuscripts from the same era, and it is not unusual for other books to be cited as scripture as well. Some of the so-called apocryphal[24] and pseudepigraphal[25] books, both Jewish and Christian, are cited as scripture in the second and later centuries. Generally speaking, the Old Testament Apocrypha are regularly found in the primary uncial manuscripts of the fourth and fifth centuries, namely Codex Vaticanus, Codex Sinaiticus, and Codex Alexandrinus.[26]

The Old Testament Apocrypha did not find a lasting place in the scriptures of the Jewish and later in some Christian communities, but they were used, so far as we can determine, in both communities as sacred literature in Second Temple Judaism and in early Christianity and even until the present in the majority of Christian churches. The Roman Catholics, Eastern Orthodox, and Ethiopian Christians still include these writings in their biblical canons. Some Jews in the east continued to use some of this literature in their places of worship and instruction for several centuries after the birth of Christianity, and they even challenged some of the books that were finally included in the Hebrew Bible,[27] and we have no evidence that the Jews in the western Diaspora rejected them before the late Middle Ages. Eventually all Jews both east and west rejected all of what we now call the Old Testament Apocrypha, but for several centuries those in the west were not limited to the biblical canon that emerged in rabbinic Judaism in the east. Christians, on the other hand, generally embraced much of the apocryphal and pseudepigraphal literature and used it in their worship and instruction in the churches. They inherited it from their Jewish siblings in the first century, and we can see many parallels with the Qumran community's use of this same literature.

The apocryphal and pseudepigraphal writings were neither received nor rejected uniformly in Jewish or Christian communities at the same time or in the same locations. It is seldom clear precisely when religious texts were acknowledged as sacred literature, and that adds to the difficulty of describing the process of canonization of sacred literature. Some Old or First Testament texts were never cited in the New Testament, and they seldom received much attention in early Christianity. For example, Jesus does not refer to or cite Joshua, Judges, Ruth, 2 Samuel, 1 Chronicles, Ezra, Nehemiah, Esther, Job, Ecclesiastes, Song of Songs, Lamentations, Obadiah, Nahum, Habakkuk, or Haggai.

As is well known, Martin Luther rejected recognizing the Old Testament Apocrypha as scripture and acknowledged only the books in the current Hebrew Bible (though not in that sequence), but he nevertheless included the Apocrypha in the first edition of his Bible in 1534 (except 1 Esdras, 3 Maccabees, and the Prayer of Manasseh). He claimed that although they were not equal to Scripture, they were nevertheless valuable reading for Christians. Later, the terms "apocrypha" and "apocryphal" took on the meaning of something spurious and false in Protestant churches instead of that which was secret or hidden. This later use may be directly related to the earlier one.

The New Testament apocryphal books include some eighty writings made up of Gospels and revelatory writings, treatises, apocalypses, acts, letters, and liturgical writings, and they had a readership in early Christianity, even though the majority of churches eventually excluded them. Some thirty-six different apocryphal books (or fragments of them) and logia are preserved in the ancient papyrus manuscripts, and eight of them are preserved in multiple manuscripts.[28] These writings often bear witness to the developing Christian community and the history of early Christianity in the second century, and some scholars also find value in them for understanding the historical Jesus.

Jean Daniélou has noted that a number of references to New Testament Apocrypha and other early noncanonical Christian literature are cited as scripture in the early churches. For example, the *Shepherd of Hermas* was widely known in the African churches. Tertullian comments: "God has instructed (*praecepit*) us to treat the Holy Spirit, since from the goodness of his nature he is tender and sensitive (*tenerum et delicatum*), with tranquility and gentleness, in quietness and peace, and not to distress him by madness, bile, anger and trouble" (*Spect.* 15.2; *Pud.* 7.1). In this text Daniélou notes that the word *praecepit* is reminiscent of the *Mandates* (or *Praecepta*) of the *Shepherd*, in which we read: "The Holy Spirit, who is delicate (Greek *trypheron*) . . . seeks to live in gentleness (Greek *praostētus*) and peace (Greek *hēsychia*)." This passage has most likely also influenced Tertullian's *De patientia* 15.3. Daniélou has observed, "one of the most striking aspects of Latin Judaeo-Christian writings is the tendency to quote apocryphal texts as scriptural."[29]

Sometimes these so-called apocryphal texts are cited as coming from New Testament books, but they come from the New Testament apocryphal writings instead. For example, the author of *De montibus* 13 quotes: "you see me in yourselves as a man sees himself in the water or in a mirror" (*Mont.* 13), which is attributed to Christ and quoted as coming from "the Epistle of John to the people." This is also seen in *De centesima*, where the author quotes a text *as scripture* (*cum scriptum sit*): "All these things were born in the world and will remain here with the world" [*Omnia ista in saeculo nata et hic cum saeculo remansura*]" (*Cent.* 55.5–6). The author of that treatise also cites texts as scriptures that he attributes to Paul, but they are in fact *agrapha*. For instance, he introduces what will follow with the words, "Remember Scripture and doctrine, when it says," and then he quotes: "Happy are those who have wives (and behave) as if they have none" from the *Acts of Paul* (*Cent.* 62.41–44). Similarly, the author (uncertain) of *De centesima* quotes, "If you can carry out all the Lord's precepts, my son, you will be perfect," from the *Didache* (6.1) and introduces it as scripture (*Cent.* 58.10–11). The author of the treatise *De aleatoribus* also provides evidence of this practice and cites the *Shepherd* and the *Didascalia Apostolorum* (4) as scripture that likely developed from the *Didache* (see *Aleat.* 4).[30] Tertullian himself, however, generally rejected all New Testament apocryphal writings, but recognized the value of some Jewish pseudepigraphal writings such as *1 Enoch*, *Sibylline Oracles* (the Jewish but not the Christian oracles), and *Life of Adam and*

Eve for having true teaching that he sometimes cited in his own treatises even if not necessarily as scripture.[31] He does cite *1 Enoch* as scripture, however, and justifies it on the grounds that Jude (Jude 14) did the same (*Cult. fem.* 1.2 and 2.10; *Idol.* 9; *Virg.* 7).[32]

The above discussion highlights the difficulty of continuing to speak about ancient religious texts with the current labels that have been used so long that they appear to be a settled matter among scholars. The use of the Old Testament and New Testament Apocrypha and Pseudepigrapha in both Jewish and Christian religious communities in antiquity shows the difficulty in establishing firm distinctions between Jews and Christians in the early stages of their development following the death of Jesus. The boundaries between them were more permeable in those early years than later, and both religious communities were more open to a broader collection of sacred literature than has usually been acknowledged.

In his introduction to a recent issue of the journal *Henoch*, Gabriele Boccaccini speaks of the importance of removing the barriers between various corpora or canons of ancient literature such as Hebrew Bible, Old Testament, New Testament, Apocrypha, Pseudepigrapha, Apostolic Fathers, church fathers, rabbinic literature, and so on.[33] He is especially concerned that the familiar language that we use to refer to ancient sacred literature of antiquity is religiously motivated and hinders the consideration of the literature in its own right and within its own historical context. He contends further that scripture canons are only understandable "in relation to the epoch and ideology in which they were born and tell us fascinating history of how ancient texts were collected, selected and handed down to us and how religious groups found identity and legitimacy in the process."[34] To understand the canonical processes, we must be familiar with the context in which sacred literature was formed and how it functioned in the earliest religious communities that employed it in defining their identity and mission. Later definitions and categories imposed on this literature often blur their original function in religious communities.

In his Society of Biblical Literature presidential address, Robert Kraft claimed that modern scholarly terminology for ancient religious literature often hinders our ability to examine it without prejudice. He even calls this "the 'tyranny of canonical assumptions' [which] is the temptation to impose on those ancients whom we study our modern ideas about what constituted 'scripture' and how it was viewed."[35] Like Boccaccini, he contends that our ability to investigate this literature without prejudice is hampered by the religious traditions that classify it in what they call acceptable and unacceptable categories. We are so familiar with these categories or groupings that it is easy to forget that they are all later designations based on the theological concerns of later religious communities. Boccaccini acknowledges that religious differences and canonical perspectives have not only isolated this literature but also preserved it through frequency of editions and commentaries on individual documents within these groupings. He bemoans the fact, however, that these artificial walls divide the ancient writings in ways that were not initially intended and isolate these ancient writings from their original religious contexts. Especially because of anachronistic perspectives imposed on ancient religious literature, a clear understanding of canon may continue to be elusive.

THREE CONTEMPORARY MEANINGS OF CANON

One of the more challenging problems encountered with ancient religious literature is finding appropriate ways to describe or define it. At what point can we refer to those documents as "canonical" or "noncanonical," "biblical" or "nonbiblical," "apocryphal" or "pseudepigraphal"? We could easily expand this list and include "church," "Old Testament" and "New Testament," and probably also "rabbinic." Competent scholars examine the same data from antiquity and yet draw different conclusions about its meaning. Much of the confusion in canon research stems from a lack of agreement on what we mean by the frequent terms we use and how much prejudice we bring to our inquiry stemming from anachronistic thinking. As a result, it is not unusual for scholars to talk past one another in this area of inquiry. I will briefly focus on three examples of this in modern biblical scholarship.

Theodor Zahn, whose massive work on the New Testament canon is still worth consulting, argued that the New Testament canon essentially came into existence at the end of the first century.[36] His view is hardly possible to defend today if we understand by it a fixed collection of New Testament scriptures rather than a growing collection, but his understanding of canon had more to do with the notion of authority and influence of several New Testament writings at the end of the first century and beginning of the second. This notion of canon has parallels in antiquity, especially with open collections of standard works, but not of fixed or closed collections. If what we now call a New Testament text was cited or used in a church setting, that text became canon for Zahn. Because there are a number of parallels in word, word order, and thought between New Testament writers and other early church writers of the second century, Zahn believed that he could demonstrate his case through a careful reading of the earliest Christian citations from the end of the first and early second century. He did not argue that there was a fixed collection of twenty-seven New Testament books accepted at the end of the first century CE, but only that the New Testament canon had begun and was well established.

Adolf von Harnack disagreed with Zahn's assessment and argued that the New Testament canon was largely completed by the end of the second century.[37] He claimed that Zahn had failed to distinguish between the citing of a text and its use as scripture. As a result of Harnack's contributions, subsequent scholars of the New Testament canon were more inclined to distinguish between the citing of a text and the citing of a text as an authoritative sacred document (scripture). This criterion has continued in scholarly discussions of ancient religious literature and is a significant contribution to canon inquiry. Consequently, scholars searched diligently to find all the references in the early church fathers to sacred texts that included designations like "as the scripture says" or "as it is written." Harnack himself concluded that the New Testament canon was essentially the church's response to Marcion's creation of what some Christians saw as an abbreviated canon of New Testament scriptures, which included an edited version of the Gospel of Luke and ten epistles of Paul, all of which he edited for his own purposes. According to Harnack, leaders of the church in Rome disagreed only with the scope of Marcion's New Testament canon and therefore constructed its own New Testament canon from a larger selection of Christian writings that were circulating in the churches.[38] He essentially concluded that the church imitated Marcion by producing a larger and more inclusive collection of sacred scriptures, and after that the matter of a New Testament canon was largely settled even if there was some mopping up left to do in determining precisely which books belonged in it.

Another highly significant work on the canon came from Hans von Campenhausen, who, like Harnack, believed that the New Testament was largely settled in the second century, though he extended the time of its definition, concluding instead that the major boundaries of the New Testament canon were set by the end of the second century, largely as a result of the church's response to the Marcionite, Gnostic, and Montanist controversies in the second century.[39] Many discussions of canon formation today follow von Campenhausen's arguments and draw similar conclusions. This is the position, with some modifications, advocated by Bruce Metzger, who produced the most widely read and influential work on the origins of the New Testament canon.[40]

Albert Sundberg offered a third alternative that challenged the widespread consensus that the Old Testament canon was complete well before or by the time of Jesus and that the formation of the New Testament canon was largely completed by the end of the second century with only mopping-up operations left to do.[41] He insisted that the popular notion of an Alexandrian biblical canon in Greek that the Christians adopted instead of the scriptures of the more conservative Hebrew Bible from Judea could no longer be supported. He argued that there is not sufficient evidence to posit the existence of an Alexandrian biblical canon that was different from the biblical canon in Judea (the HB). He argued instead that the Hebrew Bible as we know it did not exist before the second or third century CE and that the collection of scriptures that the early Christians adopted were the commonly accepted scriptures circulating among the Jews in Judea in the first century before the separation of Jews and Christians. His work seriously challenged earlier views about the origin of the Christian Old Testament. He showed that the Jewish sacred literature in Alexandria was even smaller than the later Hebrew canon of twenty-four books that became the scripture canon of the rabbinic Jews in the second and third centuries. Sundberg's view that the early Christians essentially adopted the same scriptures that were current in Judea in the time of Jesus added the notion that this collection was both broader and more fluid than the later twenty-two/twenty-four books that made up the Hebrew Bible in the rabbinic period. What also supports his thesis is that the contemporary of Jesus, Philo of Alexandria, had a more restricted biblical collection, and of his some 1,150 citations of the Jewish scriptures, over a thousand are from the Pentateuch.

Second, Sundberg challenged the traditional dating of the New Testament canon (the end of the second century) and claimed instead that the circumstances of canon formation and most of the available evidence are at home in the fourth century. The Achilles' heel of second-century development of the New Testament canon arguments is the dating of the Muratorian Fragment—which, according to the most popular understanding, was constructed in the late second century in the west (Rome). Sundberg argued that the Muratorian Fragment was a fourth-century list that came from the east.[42] If it did come from the second century and the west, it has no parallels for another 150 years (the fourth century) in either the eastern or western churches. It is still commonly dated at the late second century, having a western (Roman) provenance, with the understanding that the New Testament canon was largely settled in the late second century with only some mopping up to do (dealing with the so-called fringe books such as 2 Peter, 2–3 John, Jude, Revelation, and Hebrews) to put it into its final form. Sundberg concluded that the notion and actual origins of a fixed New Testament canon are fourth-century developments.

Zahn did not distinguish carefully between the authoritative use of a New Testament text in the early church and calling that text "scripture." Likewise, he did not distinguish between calling a text "scripture" and placing it into a biblical canon.[43] Harnack and von Campenhausen failed to appreciate adequately their inability to demonstrate that second-century churches responded to heresy and theological controversies by establishing a biblical canon. Rather, it is clear in the available sources that the churches responded to those theological challenges of that era with a canon of faith (*regula fidei*), that is, the faith that the early churches believed the apostles passed on to their successors in the churches. Sundberg did not focus so much on the *process* of canonization as he did on its end when the biblical books were placed in closed collections. Unfortunately, scholars of canon formation tend to fall into one of the three major understandings noted above, and they agree on important aspects, but they still do not agree on the definition of a biblical canon or when one first appears in the ancient churches. Is it when a text is first received authoritatively in the churches, or when it is actually acknowledged as scripture existing in a flexible collection, or when a book is placed in a fixed collection of sacred books?

If by "canon" we mean a collection of authoritative sacred texts that circulated in either Jewish or Christian communities and that were acknowledged as scripture, there is no question that Judaism and early Christianity had a canon of scriptures; but if we mean by it a fixed biblical collection to which nothing could be added or taken away, then there are problems. What about those several texts that at one time functioned authoritatively as models for faith and repositories for Christian beliefs, but subsequently no longer did? We may need to come up with another term for what happened earlier when texts were cited in a scriptural manner, but did not attain canonical status when the church recognized long-standing authoritative texts in the fourth and fifth centuries. George Aichele speaks of both of these realities and uses the word "canon" for each. He describes canon as "an authoritative collection or list of writings accepted by some community of readers. The canon identifies the accepted texts and fixes the written form of those texts. Canon controls and maintains the understanding and transmission of selected texts, and indirectly all texts (because the canon is authoritative), within that community."[44] He further notes that the canon strongly distinguishes between what is in the canon and what is not, and contends that if the canon is not fully self-explanatory internally and intertextually as well, then external "reinforcements" are needed, namely commentaries or other items that bring clarity to the matter. Since the truth of a canonical text is believed to be inherently different from a text that is external to the canon (noncanonical writings), then that which is external cannot be included in it even if the message of the external text is substantially similar. Aichele states that "the noncanonical text may be true, but it is not True."[45]

This confusion over the meaning of "canon" persists, and it complicates one of the most important issues in current canon research. The confusion of capable scholars in this field led John Barton to conclude that they "chase each other eternally around the unchanging texts . . . like the figures on Keats' Grecian urn, never catching each other yet never abandoning the chase."[46] Inappropriate definitions often lead to inappropriate conclusions about the biblical canon. The first, second, and third centuries constitute a significant time in the process of canonization, but the process was not complete until the church settled the matter of what books constituted its Bible. As we will see below, that process was both complex and drawn out over several centuries; it largely culminated in the fixed biblical canons first catalogued in the fourth and fifth centuries but not settled until centuries later.

"DECANONIZATION" OR "TEMPORARY CANONIZATION"

Scholars of canon know that in their worship and instruction ancient synagogues and churches received and used several ancient religious books that functioned scripturally or authoritatively in those communities long before they were actually called "scripture" and placed in a fixed collection to which nothing could be added or taken away. Later, even after being called "scripture," some of those books ceased functioning as sacred scripture in those same communities. When the later churches considered a writing to be heretical, they understandably saw no need to continue manufacturing copies of it and so they were lost, destroyed by Christians, or turned over to the authorities during the Decian and Diocletian persecutions.[47] Some books that were not considered heretical were nevertheless dropped or rejected because they were unable to address the continuing needs of the churches. Rearranging a thought from James Sanders, one could say that these books were no longer adaptable to the changing needs of the church and therefore they were dropped.[48] Whatever the hermeneutics were for that time, they were unable to rescue a continuing value of this literature. The notion of scripture predates the notion of canon and the latter always assumes the former, but the reverse is not historically true. This widespread reality of some religious books falling out of favor with the majority of churches has been dubbed "decanonization,"[49] which suggests that some literature was only *temporarily* received in the churches as sacred literature, and generally but not uniformly rejected later. Souter identifies this practice thusly: "One of the most interesting parts of this subject [canonicity] is that of books which had canonicity, or something very like it, in a particular church for a particular period, but were afterwards dropped." He goes on to list examples of New Testament books that were earlier received and later rejected, including the *Didache* (or *Teaching of the Twelve Apostles*), *Epistle of Barnabas*, *1* and *2 Clement*, *Shepherd of Hermas*, *Apocalypse of Peter*, and *Acts of Paul*.[50] Metzger acknowledges that some ancient texts attained a "temporary canonicity" or "local canonicity," and one recent volume actually carries the name "decanonization" in its title, but it is nevertheless unusual to hear scholars speak of this reality today.[51] The tendency is either to adopt the notion of largely fixed canons at the end of the second century with some mopping up to do, or to focus on the end of the process in the fourth and fifth centuries to which nothing could be added or taken away. Is there an appropriate term to describe the reality of transient authority in antiquity?

At one time, especially in the second and third centuries, the *Shepherd of Hermas* was cited more frequently than several New Testament books (2 Peter, 2–3 John, the Pastorals) and, along with the *Epistle of Barnabas*, was even included in a major Bible of the fourth century—what we now call Codex Sinaiticus. Indeed, the *Shepherd of Hermas* is the most cited book in the early church that was not included in the New Testament.[52] The problem of decanonization, if that is an appropriate way to describe this phenomenon, cannot be ignored. If "canon" can refer to authoritative writings that were at one time called scripture before they were placed in a fixed collection of the church's scriptures, then we have to find a term to identify those books that were so regarded initially but later dropped from the sacred collection. If we more appropriately speak of the biblical canon as a fixed entity to which nothing more can be added, then canonization occurred in the fourth century at the earliest. Even in the fourth and fifth centuries, we are talking about biblical canons (plural). Although all the surviving canonical lists had a certain core of undisputed books, especially the four Gospels, Acts, the Catholic Epistles, and the Letters of Paul, there continued to be differences in the literature that we may call "fringe" books of the New Testament. These so-called fringe books most often were 2 Peter, 2–3 John, Jude, Hebrews, Revelation, and even the Pastoral Epistles, but sometimes also popular books that did not make it into the eventual New Testament used by Christians today such as *Shepherd of Hermas*, *Didache*, *Epistle of Barnabas*, and *1* and *2 Clement*, not to mention the very popular *1 Enoch*. The matter of a fixed biblical canon that was universally adopted in the churches and included only the twenty-seven books of the New Testament was first fixed by the Roman Catholic Church in 1546 at the Council of Trent. The Orthodox tradition appeals to the Council of Chalcedon in 451 as the time when the church ratified the twenty-seven books of the New Testament to form a closed collection of Christian scriptures. As recently as Luther, however, the full acceptance of all twenty-seven New Testament books was problematic. He relegated James, Hebrews, Jude, and Revelation to the end of his Bible and numbered all the others except these. He likewise left a blank line before them indicating that they were marginalized, not writings of full canonical authority. He favored especially the Letters of Paul, the Gospel of John, 1 John, and 1 Peter.

I have used Gerald Sheppard's distinctions elsewhere to identify the two realities in the canonical process, namely those texts or traditions that functioned authoritatively in their communities ("canon 1"), and those texts that were eventually placed in a fixed tradition in the churches ("canon 2").[53] Before Sheppard made use of these distinctions, James Sanders had recognized the two realities of canon, namely authority and invariability, and he used *norma normans* for texts of stories in a believing community that *functioned* canonically or authoritatively, and *norma normata* for those sacred texts with a fixed shape, that is, unchangeable, to describe these realities of canon formation.[54] While Eugene Ulrich is certainly correct that there is far too much confusion over the meaning and use of "canon," he does not sufficiently address the temporal authoritative status of ancient writings.[55] As we will observe below, "decanonization" has been used to describe temporary sacred writings, but decanonization may not be an adequate way to identify that reality, for it suggests that something was once fixed and then the status was changed. That would be difficult to demonstrate and also confusing.

"Canon" continues to be a useful although often confusing term, but if used for a complete and fixed collection of scriptures, then it is a technically and chronologically inappropriate term for any writings before the fourth century, during which the greater church largely defined the parameters of its sacred literature. But what do we call writings in the second and third century that had a temporal sacred authority in the church? "Scripture" was used in the late second and third centuries to identify or describe much of the literature that is now called apocryphal or pseudepigraphal, but that eventually ceased. While I prefer to distinguish the temporary scriptural status by canon 1 and the later fixed or closed collections as canon 2, I am mindful of the limitations of all such language.[56]

WHEN DO BIBLICAL CANONS EMERGE?

One of the debated questions among scholars of the canonization processes has to do with the dating of conscious canonical activity in Judaism and early Christianity. As I have acknowledged above, the early churches widely accepted the authority and influence of the canonical Gospels as well as several other New Testament writings (especially several of Paul's letters) almost from the time they were first written. Acknowledgment of their scriptural status appears to take place late in the second century for the most part, though only some of the New Testament documents were so recognized at that time. Their authority and influence were felt and accepted before they were acknowledged as sacred scripture, and there is no evidence that the churches in the second century ever considered or discussed the notion of a closed New Testament canon—not even Marcion did. His aim was rather to reject the Jewish influence on the churches and also the Jewish scriptures (Law and Prophets and whatever constituted them) that the churches considered sacred. He eliminated from the writings that he did select all Jewish influences and citations of the Law and Prophets in Luke and Paul (see Cyril of Jerusalem, *Catechetical Lectures* 6.16).

If Marcion had designed a fixed collection of sacred scriptures, however, it is strange that his followers welcomed verses from Matthew, Mark, and John. Ephraem Syrus notes that the Marcionites had not rejected Matthew 23:8 (see *Song* 24.1).[57] Likewise, according to Adamantius, the Marcionite Marcus quoted John 13:34 and 15:19, and he accuses the Marcionites of corrupting Matthew 5:17 (Adamantius, *Dialogue* 2.15, 18). Origen also quoted a Marcionite interpretation of Matthew 19:12 in his *Commentary on Matthew* (5:17). Geoffrey Hahneman appropriately concludes: "if Marcion and his followers added verses to their accepted texts, then they may just as well have added additional sources to their collection of scriptures."[58] It is also likely that the so-called Marcionite Gospel Prologues came from either Marcion or his followers.[59] In the early churches, Irenaeus appears to be the first to speak of a limited number of Gospels (only four). He says nothing about a closed collection of Paul's Epistles, the Catholic Epistles, or any other literature that made up his New Testament canon. In the fourth century, Eusebius lists such a collection, but this list may be Eusebius's invention based simply on Irenaeus's citations of New Testament books.

When did someone *first* say that the church should have a *fixed* list of sacred books? There are no clear statements from second- or third-century writers themselves on limiting the number of sacred books for the church. Eusebius gives a tradition about Melito of Sardis going to the east (Judea or even Jerusalem, probably) to discover the books that made up the Old Testament at that time (*Hist. eccl.* 4.26.13–14). He also apparently noted all the references that Irenaeus, Clement of Alexandria, and Origen made to the New Testament writings and compiled their New Testament collections accordingly (*Hist. eccl.* 5.8.2–8; 6.14.107; 6.25.3–14), but again these are likely Eusebius's inventions developed by simply listing the references each of these persons cited.[60] Nothing in their extant literature shows a list of sacred scriptures that any of them produced or adopted, even though they all regularly cite many of the Old and New Testament scriptures.

When did the notion of a fixed sacred collection begin in ancient Judaism and when was the matter first discussed either by the Jews or the early Christians? Are we certain that the notion appeared in Judaism first? Such discussions among the Jews seem to take place when they first begin talking about the books that do and do not "defile the hands" (see *m. Yadayim* 3:2–5). Rabbi Johanan ben Zakkai (*m. Yadayim* 4:6; ca. 40–80 CE) evidently invented this description in the last part of the first century CE, but it was not a common description for Jewish sacred literature until the second century, probably with Rabbi Judah or Rabbi Jose (both ca. 135–170), who used it to identify sacred Jewish texts—they defiled the hands (*m. Yadayim* 3:5).[61] As Barton explains, there were books in the first century that some believed were not sacred books, that is, they did not defile the hands, and so a selection process had begun to distinguish the sacred from the ordinary. Noting also the fluidity of the Jewish biblical canon, he concludes, "*more* books than the present list [twenty-four in the HB] were serious contenders for canonical status, not that any of the existing ones were candidates for exclusion."[62] As noted above, however, and contrary to Barton's last word, there was some doubt among Jews over the status of several books in the Hebrew Bible during the rabbinic era.

There is no question that the notion of sacred writings appears in Judaism long before the term "scripture" was applied to sacred texts. The words of God were sacred and their sacredness was not diminished when those words were written down (Exod. 19:5–7; 20:1–17). This is also clear later (Deut. 4:2, Ps. 119), and the many admonitions to keeping the Law of Moses that came from God function in a scriptural manner among the Jews before the word "scripture" in Hebrew or Greek was introduced to define a specific sacred text (Exod. 24:12; 34:1–7; 31:18; Deut. 4:2–13, passim). As far as we know, the first time that the word "scripture" (Greek *graphē*) was used in reference to sacred written documents (the Pentateuch) is in *Letter of Aristeas* 155 and 168 (ca. 130 BCE)—and the author of that document is not likely to have been the first to use it since he does not explain it but assumes his readers know what he is saying. Again, it is clear that the notion of sacred writings predates considerably the employment of the various terms to describe it.[63] Christians inherited the notion of sacred writings from the Jews and regularly refer to the Jewish sacred writings throughout the New Testament. The notion of scripture, however, is different from the notion of canon if by canon we mean a fixed or complete collection of scriptures. The notion of a fixed canon does not appear before the fourth century. There is no language in the church for a closed collection of scriptures before the fourth century, and all of the examples of fixed lists of sacred writings come from the fourth century and later, with the only possible exception being the Muratorian Fragment, if one can demonstrate its second-century origin; but as discussed above, that is not likely. A growing number of scholars now accept a fourth-century date for the Muratorian Fragment since that is where it has its first parallels, and, as noted above, several of the peculiarities of the Muratorian Fragment only have parallels in the fourth and fifth centuries. For several reasons that I have noted elsewhere, we first begin to find fixed collections and catalogues of sacred scriptures in the fourth century.[64] The processes that brought Jews and Christians to the place where they needed to identify their sacred literature for their members included widespread use of that literature in worship, instruction, and for apologetic purposes; belief in prophetic and/or apostolic origin; conformity to the prevailing notions of ortho-doxy at the time of selection for canonicity; the believed early dating of that literature; and the processes of decanonization or delimitation.

THE PROCESSES OF CANONIZATION: SOME IMPORTANT REMINDERS

The final authority in early Christianity was Jesus (Matt. 28:19), and when the early Christian preachers began their mission the gospel about Jesus took center stage in their proclamation (Gal. 1:1–3, 6–8; 1 Cor. 1:21–24; 2:1–2). In a short time the focus of Christian preaching moved from proclaiming the kingdom of God, as Jesus himself had preached, to preaching about Jesus himself. The story of Jesus was shared widely and a new community was formed of those who put their faith and trust in him. The identity and fate of Jesus as well as his mission was at the heart of the story of God's love and grace for humanity, and this message was the treasure, according to Paul, that was entrusted to the Christian community (2 Cor. 4:7). In time the church's sacred story was perpetuated also in sacred texts. As James Sanders has shown in reference to the First Testament of Scripture, the sacred story of God's love and mission for ancient Israel moved from an oral transmission to sacred texts.[65]

Why did the Christians, who depended so heavily on the Jewish tradition for their scriptures, not follow the Jewish three-part biblical canon? Why did the early Christians accept the Jewish scriptures but not the Jewish categories with them if they were available to the Christians when they separated from Judaism? The answer is that they did not know about them before their separation from Judaism, and they did not exist in Judea in the time of Jesus. The many attempts to make Jesus' reference in Luke 24:44 into a reference to a tripartite biblical collection falls down at this point. The early Christians did not see this refer-ence to "psalms" as a distinct collection of books equal to the later Ketubim (or Writings) that formed the third part of the Jewish Tanakh. The later tripartite canon had no impact on the Christians who welcomed the Jewish scriptures before their separation from them, but they developed a four-part Old Testa-ment canon and showed no awareness of the later Jewish groupings of their scriptures.

Besides the difficulty of finding suitable definitions for the common terms used in canon research, for several other reasons scholars are divided over the meaning of canon and canon formation, and seem to have little ability to resolve these matters: (1) There is significant ambiguity in the remaining ancient tradi-tions, and none of them tells us how or why the biblical books came to be canon-ized. (2) Scholars commonly assume that the circulation of lists or catalogues is always the circulation of *closed* or fixed canons of Scripture, but because there are several such lists in the fourth and fifth centuries and yet several ancient manuscripts of that time do not reflect these lists exactly, it is time to reexamine this assumption. Only in 1546 do the Catholics for the first time declare universally the scope of their sacred scriptures. (3) Scholars tend to make the ancient lists or catalogues that emerge in the fourth century also normative in the first century, but there is no compelling evidence to support that. This is simply an anachronistic assumption and it is still with us. (4) Scholars tend to ignore or minimize the significance of the larger ancient collections of Jewish sacred texts discovered in the Judean Desert. They allow us to see what texts informed the faith of one of the Jewish sects living in the time of Jesus. (5) Many tend to ignore the differences between the Jews living in the western Diaspora and those in the east. The Jewish communities in the western Diaspora continued to use apocryphal and pseudepigraphal writings through the seventh and eighth centuries.[66] (6) There is the important question about why Melito, the bishop of a large church in Sardis, which was also the home of a large Jewish population, did not know how to answer the one who asked him what literature was sacred and what was not (Eusebius, *Hist. eccl.* 4.26.13–14). After his trip to the east, he produced a list of sacred books that overlaps considerably with the current Hebrew Bible, but his list is not identical to it, as Esther and Nehemiah are missing from it (it is possible that Nehemiah was combined with Ezra) and Wisdom of Solomon is included. Likewise, Melito's list is not organized the same way as the Jewish Tanakh. This suggests that notions of a fixed Hebrew Bible or Old Testament canon in the churches were not yet firmly established. These issues or concerns all add to the complexity of our investigations today.

In terms of the formation of the New Testament canon, it is not yet clear what the early presence of the codex in church transmissions of their Christian books means. Was the Christian preference for the codex an admission that its own literature was not initially viewed as Scripture, or the Christians decide to shift away from the scroll or roll uniformly used by Jews to distinguish their writings from Jewish writings? In time, of course, all Christian Scriptures, both Old Testament and New Testament, were circulated in the codex. Harry Gamble draws attention to the practice of Christians putting their writings on notebooks because of the ease of transportability, which was a practice that the apostle Paul himself may have instigated (2 Tim. 4:13).[67] Can anything about their sacredness be discerned from this aspect of their transmission?

Is a biblical canon simply a loose collection of books that functioned authoritatively in the church, even if only for a brief period of time? Is it a fixed collection that functioned authoritatively or scripturally in local settings, as appears to be the case at the synods of Hippo (393 CE) and Carthage (397 CE)? Are canons temporary or permanent, local or universal, or all of the above? It is difficult to show that the universal church ever agreed completely on this matter, and that makes final decisions about it more difficult. There is more disagreement on the scope of the Old Testament scriptures, but clearly the majority of churches favored a larger collection of Old Testament scriptures than did the Protestants, who favored the books in the Hebrew Bible, though in a different sequence. In all cases in antiquity there is broad agreement on the majority of the books in the Old and New Testaments, but not on all of them. Some books that did not make it into the Protestant Bibles are well attested in the Orthodox, Catholic, and Ethiopian Bibles. Before the triumph of orthodoxy in the churches, the matter was much more complex. The churches of the second century were trying to establish the identity of Jesus and also their own identity, and the orthodox Christians wrote against the heretics of their day. It is also interesting that the Gnostics wrote against the orthodox and the Docetists as heretics as well![68]

It is not likely that the early churches would have been able to create a New Testament biblical canon before they had determined who Jesus was and what they believed about him. There is considerable evidence of theological controversies in the earliest churches in the first century concerning those judaizing Christians who wanted to impose Jewish law and traditions on Gentile Christians (Gal. 1:6–9; 3:1–14; passim) and others who were causing trouble in the church at Colossae (Col. 2:20–23), as well as the early Docetists who denied that Jesus had a real or fleshly body (1 John 4:1–3). Later, Ignatius also condemned both Docetists (*Eph.* 7.1–2; *Trall.* 10.1; *Smyrn.* 2.1) and Judaizers (*Magn.* 10.3; *Phld.* 6.1). Nevertheless, few significant theological discussions address these problems in depth until after the middle to late second century. Robert Grant posits that a fixed biblical canon was hardly possible for the church before it had dealt with the theological issues facing it in the second century. It first had to determine the faith and identity that it proclaimed and taught.[69] Justin, Irenaeus, Theophilus, Hippolytus, and Tertullian all addressed some of these controversial issues in the late second century, and it would be difficult indeed for the church to determine the scope of its biblical canon before it addressed these issues. There was an emerging understanding of orthodoxy, or as Bart Ehrman calls it, "proto-orthodoxy," in many second-century churches,[70] that is, the antecedents to the orthodox traditions that later became firmly entrenched in the late-third- and fourth-century churches.

Because of the ongoing theological debates, and the growth and development of the church's teachings, the canonical process was both slow and not always clearly focused over a long period of time, beginning with the writing of the New Testament literature. Robert Kraft correctly concludes: "There was no 'Bible' as we know it—that is, a set of sacred writings organized into a single physical object, the codex book—until well into the fourth century of the common era."[71] He adds that the special status given to works protected by canonical assumptions often blinds us to the actual situations in which that literature was produced.[72] I agree with James Dunn, who argues in one essay that we see this process *beginning* in the first century, even though it was not completed much before the fourth century, if then. Dunn concludes his essay with the claim, "The *de facto* canon of Jesus and Paul, gospel and epistle, was already functioning with effect within the first thirty years of Christianity's existence."[73] The *process* of canonization was not invented or concluded in the fourth century, even if the final product is more clearly in sight at that time. The biblical canon did not take shape in a moment in time, but developed over several centuries in the churches. At the end of the fourth century, some church synods met and made decisions about the scope of the Bible, especially the Synod of Hippo Regius in North Africa in 393 CE with Augustine present and supporting the New Testament canon of Athanasius, followed by the Synod of Carthage (397) and the Council of Chalcedon (451), all of which established a fixed twenty-seven-book New Testament canon. There is little variation in the collections of books that make up the New Testament after that time, though there is some, as we see in the surviving biblical manuscripts (e.g., Codex Alexandrinus). I should add that Athanasius, though highly influential in his day, did not have the full support of his own churches in Egypt on the scope of the New Testament canon, let alone of all the churches of his own day.

CONCLUSION

When catalogues and lists of religious texts began to emerge in religious communities, the processes of canonization were nearly complete, but what did such collections include and when did they become recognized and normative scriptures for Judaism and for Christianity? Collections of sacred texts can be seen in several places in late-first-century Jewish literature (Josephus, *C. Ap.* 1.43–47 and *4 Ezra* 14:44–48). The author of the *Letter of Aristeas* refers to Eleazar the high priest in Jerusalem sending scrolls of the Law to Egypt to be translated into Greek (see 172–81; see also 308–11), and Josephus refers to a sacred collection of "volumes" that he requested from Titus the Roman general after the fall of Jerusalem (Josephus, *Life* 418–19). In the mid-second century, and for the first time, a specific Jewish listing of the books of the Hebrew Bible in a tripartite collection was prepared in Babylon (*b. Baba Bathra* 14b), but we have no evidence that it was widely circulated in Judea or elsewhere for several centuries. The lack of its awareness in Judea may be the reason it was not included in the Mishnah. These ancient sources reflect not a universal belief among Jews about the scope of their Bible at the end of the first century, but the initial steps in the process of canonization of their scriptures.

I have argued that the processes of canonization of the New Testament writings began fairly early—especially in the case of the Gospels that were welcomed as authoritative texts probably immediately after they were composed (canon 1)[74]—but the notion of a fixed collection of scriptures (canon 2) that we see clearly for the first time in the fourth century is difficult to establish at an earlier time. The oral tradition about Jesus no doubt functioned authoritatively in the churches well before the evangelists put it in writing, but we need to be cautious about what we call it and how we define it. As many scholars agree, the Gospels were received as authoritative documents in the churches well before they were called "scripture." They were also placed into an expanding collection of scriptures in the church before that collection was fixed. When a fixed collection was finally decided, some earlier books that had received a scriptural status were excluded (*1 Enoch, Shepherd of Hermas, Didache, Epistle of Barnabas*, and others). The final fixing of the sacred collection was not the same in all churches even in the fourth century. Local churches had texts that were special to them, and they continued to use them even after canonical decisions had been made and sacred lists were produced (for example, see the additional books in Codex Sinaiticus and Codex Alexandrinus). A core of books (Gospels, most of the letters attributed to Paul, 1 Peter, and 1 John) had gained widespread recognition in the churches and were not in doubt in the fourth century, but churches disputed some writings for several more centuries (Hebrews, James, 2 Peter, 2–3 John, Jude, and Revelation; cf. Eusebius, *Hist. eccl.* 3.25). Some of these New Testament writings were not universally acknowledged as having sacred authority in the second century, but were by the fourth century. Other ancient religious texts, now called apocryphal or pseudepigraphal, were also cited as scripture in the second and third centuries. In time, some of those authoritative texts ceased to function in that role and were not included in most of the fourth- and fifth-century manuscripts (e.g., *1 Enoch*), but some continued to be cited as scripture in the churches.

Scholars of canon inquiry occasionally draw inappropriate conclusions based on citations. For example, just because an ancient writer cites a text does not mean that the text was considered sacred, authoritative, or scriptural, let alone canonical. Likewise, just because one writer believed that a text was sacred does not mean that the whole church at the same time thought the same way about it. As noted above, Irenaeus's arguments about the scriptural status of the four Gospels (Matthew, Mark, Luke, and John)—and only those four—were not shared by all Christians of his day. Had they been, Bishop Serapion twenty or more years later would not have initially allowed his churches to read the *Gospel of Peter*, which he later rejected only after having read it (see Eusebius, *Hist. eccl.* 6.12.3–6). Contrast this with Eusebius's reference to the canonical Gospels as the "holy tetrad" in the fourth century (*Hist. eccl.* 3.25.1), and the simple listing of these Gospels by the author of the Muratorian Fragment later in the fourth century. Other Gospels, for example, the *Gospel of Peter* and the *Gospel of James*, were still being read in various other churches at the same time that Irenaeus wrote, and even later. *First Enoch* was also popular in early Christianity in the first three centuries as evidenced by allusions to it in the New Testament,[75] the copies of it found at Qumran, its inclusion in the Ethiopian biblical canon (a canon that most likely dates back to the fourth or fifth century CE), and the many citations of it in the early church fathers. This suggests that a number of Jewish and Christian books were quite popular at the end of the second century, and that they were beginning to form a core of sacred literature even though there was no unanimity at that time on the scope of those collections that eventually became the Old and New Testaments of the early churches.

As we can see from the ancient biblical manuscripts that have survived to the present, the Gospels by far outnumber all the other contenders in popularity, followed by the Pauline Letters, Acts, the Catholic Epistles, and Revelation, in that order.[76] No ancient council decision settled these matters for all time and for all churches. The biblical manuscripts themselves demonstrate this. For example, many of the ancient papyrus manuscripts of Jewish and Christian religious literature contain apocryphal and pseudepigraphal books.[77]

Although it may be correct to say that all first- and second-century religious texts that functioned scripturally in the early churches are "uncanonized temporal scriptures," it takes too long to explain, and most scholars prefer to use the acknowledged anachronistic designations to make sure that readers or students are clear on what texts they have in mind. We may also call these religious texts "recognized inspired literature" or even "scriptures" (where applicable) at the beginning stages of their use in religious communities. Finally it may be wise in practice to reserve the term "canon" for the result of the final stages of canonization in the fourth and fifth centuries, when various books were identified as a "canon" and catalogues of sacred books appeared. This allows for the reality that in some cases there was uncertainty in the church for centuries over some ancient books that were either dropped (*Eldad and Modat, Shepherd*, etc.) or eventually included in the biblical canons of the churches (Pastorals, 2 Peter, Hebrews, 2–3 John, Jude, and even Revelation). If we do use the word "canon" when we speak of authoritative and influential writings that are sometimes called "scripture," it is important to remember that this often does not yet mean that they were placed in a closed collection of sacred scriptures until much later.

We will now turn to some of the manuscripts that were left behind and what was in them. This has considerable significance for understanding the operative biblical canons of early Judaism and early Christianity.

PART TWO
THE FIRST
TESTAMENT SCRIPTURES

Chapter 3

The Lost Scriptures of Early Judaism

INTRODUCTION

Many ancient Jewish religious texts that were part of the life of the Jewish and Christian communities were not included in the Jewish and most of the Christian Bibles. Some of the books left behind or not included are well known today to biblical scholars, but several of them are not currently recoverable. In what follows we will examine some of the ancient texts that were lost or simply ceased being recognized as sacred writings among the Jews. The first collections of these books are referred to in the Old Testament itself, and they seldom receive much attention since all we know about them is that a few writers refer their ancient readers to them for further information about the various kings or what a prophet had said. The other collection of books left behind by the Jews date from roughly 200 BCE to roughly 100 CE and are regularly referred to as Old Testament Apocrypha and Pseudepigrapha. Some of these writings may date earlier than 200 BCE, as in the case of parts of *1 Enoch*, and some may date later than 100 CE, as in the case of some of the *Odes of Solomon*. What can we make of this literature? When did it cease functioning as authoritative religious resources for Jews and later for Christians? As most of those who are familiar with the various Jewish and Christian Bibles in use today already know, much of that literature has continued in several Christian communities as sacred literature, and the titles commonly used by Protestants and Jews to describe it are not the way that other Christians in the Catholic, Orthodox, and Ethiopian churches describe it. What writings were left behind by these religious communities and why? We can more easily identify the books left behind, but the reasons why they were left is the greater challenge.

Some of this literature has been found in monasteries, archaeological sites, libraries in Europe, and elsewhere. As a result of the discovery of Dead Sea Scrolls, these ancient texts have been reexamined with considerable benefit for biblical scholarship and the church as a whole. Not only biblical texts were discovered among the Dead Sea Scrolls in the vicinity of Qumran, but also significant numbers of what we now call noncanonical writings. In fact, of the some 960 documents found there, only a little over 200 or 22 percent of them have books of the Hebrew Bible and Protestant Old Testament in them. Precision here is difficult since many of the manuscripts are fragmented, and some fragments may be part of the same manuscript or from different manuscripts. The manuscripts are mostly nonsectarian Jewish religious texts that were brought to the Essene community at Qumran from elsewhere. The impact of those discoveries has led canon scholars to reexamine some of the popular assumptions about canon formation that were widely accepted earlier. A growing number of biblical scholars are now beginning to accept that there was no firmly established biblical canon in the time of Jesus. It was a long and slow process of formation that took place for some Jews by the end of the first century CE, but for other Jews, especially those of the Diaspora, it took much longer.

Because of the enormous impact of those finds not only on biblical interpretation but also on canon formation, I will summarize some of the more important factors that have led scholars to their recent conclusions. I will examine first the lost books mentioned in the Bible and then the books that were consciously excluded from the sacred collections by Jews and Christians.

LOST BOOKS MENTIONED IN THE BIBLE

Several Old Testament/Hebrew Bible books refer their readers to a number of books that did not survive the ancient screening processes of the religious leaders in Israel and so were excluded from continuing usefulness in the religious Jewish communities. They are important because they are mentioned often in the biblical text as authoritative texts that tell a certain story about Israel. Because several of them are identified as "Annals of the Kings" or some catalogue of the history of the Jewish people, it may seem that they could not have been considered sacred scripture to the Jews; they appear to be something like historical records of activities among the Jews. But since the books of Samuel, Kings, and Chronicles are of a similar genre and they were included in the Jewish Scriptures, it is likely that a high regard, if not an inspired status, was also attached to these earlier writings. Several of these writings are attributed to prophets, and that suggests sacred writings. The list below identifies some of these books, those that are known through the Hebrew Bible/Old Testament witness. There were probably more books than those that are listed below, but the following names and categories have survived:

A. In the Law or Torah: Book of the Wars of the Lord (Num. 21:14)
B. In Joshua, Judges, 1–2 Samuel, 1–2 Kings:
    1. Book of Jashar (Josh. 10:12–13; 2 Sam. 1:18–27; 1 Kgs. 8:12–13 = 3 Kingdoms in LXX)
    2. Book of the Annals of the Kings of Judah (1 Kgs. 14:29; 15:7, 23; 22:45; 2 Kgs. 8:23; 12:18; 14:18; 15:6, 36; 16:19; 20:20; 21:17, 25; 23:28; 24:5)
    3. Book of the Annals of the Kings of Israel (1 Kgs. 14:19; 15:31; 16:5, 14, 20, 27; 22:39; 2 Kgs. 1:18; 10:34; 13:8, 12; 14:15, 28; 15:11, 15, 21, 26, 31)
    4. Book of Acts of Solomon (1 Kgs. 11:41)
C. In 1–2 Chronicles, Ezra, and Nehemiah:
    1. Book of the Kings of Israel (1 Chr. 9:21; 2 Chr. 20:34)
    2. Book of the Kings of Judah and Israel (2 Chr. 16:11)
    3. Book of Kings of Israel and Judah (2 Chr. 27:7)
    4. Annals of the Kings of Israel (2 Chr. 33:18)
    5. Records of the seer Samuel (1 Chr. 29:29)
    6. Records of the seer Gad (1 Chr. 29:29)
    7. Records of the seer Nathan (1 Chr. 29:29)
    8. History of the prophet Nathan (2 Chr. 9:29)
    9. Prophecy of Ahijah the Shilonite (2 Chr. 9:29)
    10. Visions of the seer Iddo (2 Chr. 9:29)
    11. Records of the prophet Shemaiah and the seer Iddo (2 Chr. 12:15)
    12. Annals of Jehu the son of Hanani ("which are recorded in the Book of the Kings of Israel"; 2 Chr. 20:34)
    13. Records of the seers (2 Chr. 33:19)
    14. Story of the prophet Iddo (2 Chr. 13:22)
    15. Commentary on the Book of the Kings (2 Chr. 24:27)
    16. A book written by the prophet Isaiah son of Amoz containing the history of Uzziah (2 Chr. 26:22)
    17. A vision of the prophet Isaiah son of Amoz in the Book of the Kings of Judah and Israel (2 Chr. 32:32; cf. Isa. 1:1)
    18. Annals of King David (1 Chr. 27:24)
    19. Annals of your ancestors (Ezra 4:15)
    20. Book of the Annals (Neh. 12:23)
    21. Additional book: "Laments" in 2 Chr. 35:25 is a reference not to Lamentations, but rather to a book produced by or for Josiah that is now lost.

While we have no evidence that in worship the Jews ever read the above writings, we have no reason to think that all Jews rejected reading them as sacred texts. Until someone finds them in a cave or archaeological site, however, they remain a mystery to us. But we should not ignore them when considering ancient literature that influenced the religious life of the Jewish people. Most of these books are mentioned in Kings and Chronicles and, as Shemaryahu Talmon has noted, they tend to fall into two categories: the historiographical accounts and prophetic genres.[1] In the first category, one should not disparage their sacred significance among the Jews, since the books of Samuel, Kings, and Chronicles were all included in the Jewish sacred literature. The prophetic books referred to are more likely to have carried a greater sense of sacredness, but we cannot be certain. What we can say is that among the Jews of antiquity some earlier writings that have been lost were a source of religious authority at an earlier stage or stages in the history of the Jewish people.

JEWISH APOCRYPHAL AND PSEUDEPIGRAPHAL WRITINGS

Recognition of the sacred nature of the Jewish scriptures was a long and slow process.[2] The Law of Moses (perhaps initially only the book of Deuteronomy) was welcomed as sacred scripture among the Jews no later than the time of Josiah's reforms (2 Kgs. 22–23; 2 Chr. 34–35; ca. 620–619 BCE). This commitment was reaffirmed by Ezra in Judah following the decree of Cyrus, the Persian king, who permitted many Jews, including Ezra and Nehemiah, to return to the Jewish homeland.

When the Jewish scriptures were first translated into Greek (ca. 281–280 BCE) to meet the needs of the Jews who were living outside Judah and whose mother tongue was not Hebrew or Aramaic but Greek, it is worth noting that initially only the Pentateuch was translated. The Prophets were only beginning to be accepted in the category of sacred literature around 450–400 BCE (see 2 Kgs. 17:13); widespread recognition of their value as sacred texts for religious faith took longer. This recognition had apparently taken place by the time Jesus son of Sirach wrote his book of wisdom (ca. 180 BCE),[3] as we can see in Sirach 44–49, which celebrates the great prophets.

By around 130 BCE the grandson of Sirach translated Sirach's book of wisdom into Greek and noted in his prologue that other sacred books, namely the Law, Prophets, and "others," had already been translated into Greek. The additional writings were accepted as sacred scripture among the Jews certainly no later than when they were translated into another language to serve as a vehicle for advancing the mission, worship, and instruction of the Greek-speaking Jews living in lands where Hebrew and Aramaic were not spoken. There can be little doubt that sometime between the fourth and second century BCE other writings besides the Law were included in Jewish sacred collections. What was in those emerging sacred collections is not precisely known in the initial stages, but the term "prophet" or "prophets" began to identify an additional collection of sacred writings among the Jews. While the name was later used to identify only the second collection of the books of the Hebrew Bible, initially it seems to have covered most everything that was considered sacred besides the Law. As we will see below, some used the terms "Law" and "Prophets" interchangeably for centuries. As early as the writing of 2 Kings, another phase of sacred writings appears to be emerging. The text in question states: "the LORD warned Israel and Judah by every prophet and every seer, saying, 'Turn from your evil ways and keep my commandments and my statutes, in accordance with all the law that I commanded your ancestors and that I sent to you by my servants the prophets'" (2 Kgs. 17:13).

Later and in the context of celebrating Israel's heroes of faith, Sirach writes: "It was Ezekiel who saw the vision of glory, which God showed him above the chariot of the cherubim. For God also mentioned Job who held fast to all the ways of justice. May the bones of the Twelve Prophets send forth new life from where they lie, for they comforted the people of Jacob and delivered them with confident hope" (Sir. 49:9–10 NRSV). One can see here a clear indication that other writings besides the Law of Moses were present and influencing Jews in the early to mid-second century BCE, but specifically which books besides Job, the Twelve (Minor Prophets), Ezekiel, and the Law cannot be determined with precision, even though recognition of several (not all) of the classical prophets of Israel as persons, not titles of books they produced, suggests that many if not most of the classical prophets were recognized as sacred scripture at that time. The term "prophet" was not restricted to a fixed list of prophetic writings at that time, and, as we see in the New Testament, all books that were not identified as the Law were apparently acknowledged as "prophets."

Many other religious texts circulating among the Jews were also deemed worthy of translation into Greek, including Sirach itself, 1–2 Maccabees, and several other books that are frequently identified by Protestants as "apocryphal" and "pseudepigraphal" writings. There is no way from the words in the prologue to Sirach to distinguish what we now call canonical writings from noncanonical writings.

The author of 2 Maccabees (sometime between 104 and 63 BCE) tells how Judas Maccabee collected all of the sacred books of the Jews that had been lost, and this included different categories of sacred texts:

> The same things are reported in the records and in the memoirs of Nehemiah, and also that he founded a library and collected the books about the kings and prophets, and the writings of David, and letters of kings about votive offerings. In the same way Judas [Maccabee] also collected all the books that had been lost on account of the war that had come upon us, and they are in our possession. So if you have need of them, send people to get them for you. (2 Macc. 2:13–15 NRSV)

Much is often made of this collection by Judas Maccabee, and many assume that he collected what the Jews later canonized and what now forms the Hebrew

Bible. We do not know, however, what sacred texts he collected, since the text does not say. It refers only to categories of sacred texts. More especially, we cannot say that what he collected was a *fixed* scriptural collection. It is difficult to imagine that the so-called apocryphal and pseudepigraphal writings would have had much currency among the Jews or even been able to have a hearing among them if the matter of the Jewish biblical canon had been settled well before the time of Jesus and even before the time of the production of much of this literature. What makes it unlikely that his collection was exactly like the collection that came to constitute the Hebrew Bible is that other books received considerable attention and veneration among Jews and early Christians.

We may reasonably assume a similar fluid collection of First/Old Testament scriptures among the earliest Christians, a Jewish sect who saw themselves as faithful to the Jewish scriptures in the first century and read them regularly in their worship, missionary activities, and catechetical instruction. The same is true for those in the next few centuries of the church, except that in many cases some of the same so-called noncanonical books were also called "scripture" or cited as scripture in their churches. In the New Testament writings we see that the early Christians acknowledged as scripture the sacred Jewish writings that were acknowledged as scripture in the first century before the separation of early Christianity from Judaism. Since in the Gospels and the rest of the New Testament the writers were informed by the sacred writings of the Jews, one would expect to find similar texts appealed to by Christians, and this can be demonstrated by a comparison of citations both in the New Testament and early church fathers with those of first-century Jews, especially those at Qumran.

While we are unable to determine with any precision what was in those collections, it is clear that the "prophets" had an established place among the scriptures of Israel. At that time, it appears that any sacred text that was not part of the Law of Moses was considered part of the "Prophets." All of Israel's scriptures were so designated until the second century CE for most Jews and Christians. There is only one place in the New Testament (Luke 24:44) where a third category, "psalms," appears to be emerging among the early followers of Jesus; different categories also appear to be emerging among Jews around the same time.

Philo (ca. 10 BCE–40 CE) does not clarify which books he considers sacred, though he significantly favored the Torah or Pentateuch in his writings, and the vast majority of his citations of Jewish scriptures are of the Law. Of his some 1,150 citations of the Jewish sacred literature, all but 47 are from the Pentateuch. Of the pentateuchal citations, fully one-third are from Genesis, followed by Exodus, and not that many from Leviticus, Numbers, and Deuteronomy. Of the 47 references to the other Jewish scriptures, 17 are from the Psalms, 12 from Kings, 11 from the Prophets, 4 from Proverbs, and 1 each from Joshua, Judges, and Job.[4] That Philo has no citations of apocryphal writings supports the conclusion that apocryphal writings, such as we find at Qumran in the first century BCE and CE, first circulated in Judea and were part of the sacred collections passed on to the Christians by their Jewish siblings before their separation from Judaism. It also is a challenge to the notion of an Alexandrian biblical canon that was larger than the collection circulating in Judea at the time of Jesus and later. That larger collection reflects the books that circulated first in Judea before the later Jewish rabbinic collection was established. Philo refers to a group of Jews in his vicinity known as Therapeutae (*Contempl.* 25–29) who have many similarities with the Essenes, though Philo distinguishes them.[5] In the case of the Therapeutae, he indicates that their sacred writings include ("laws and oracles delivered through the mouth of prophets and psalms and anything else which fosters and perfects knowledge and piety" (*Contempl.* 25). Precisely what is meant here is not known, though one can imagine that whatever was included in the collection of prophets at that time was among them and also the reference to "psalms" is likely a reference to a collection of psalms, though which ones is not clear.

The well-known Qumran text, 4QMMT (or 4Q394–399), *Miqsat Ma'aseh ha-Torah* (Some Works of the Law), also identifies collections of sacred texts, but not with precision. The considerable fragmentation in this manuscript makes it difficult to translate, and the portion of this text that canon scholars focus on most has to do with the books that are identified in it: "the book of Moses [and the words of the] prophets and of David [and the annals] [of eac]h generation."[6] While some scholars try to make this a reference to the three parts of the Hebrew Bible—Law, Prophets, and Writings—it is not clear what books or psalms are in the categories of "prophets" or "David" and the possible "[annals of eac]h genera-tion." There are some obvious parallels to this text in Luke 24:44, which speaks of the "law of Moses, the Prophets, and the psalms," but again questions follow these references—we do not know which psalms were involved and we do not know what books were involved in "the prophets" at this time. We will explore this more below. What is also not clear is that "psalms" or "David" refers to the whole of what later became known as the *Ketubim* or Writings (Greek *Hagiographa*) in the Hebrew Bible. By and large, those distinctions (Law, Prophets, and Writings) were not in view in the first century CE, though this passage may well suggest a growing interest in a three- or four-part Hebrew Bible, but this does not mean that they looked like the current three-part Hebrew Bible. Also, the early church opted for a four-part Old Testament canon, even though the Christians accepted all the Jewish scriptures as well as several that the Jews left behind in forming their biblical canon. Nothing in the 4QMMT text identifies the writings the author has in mind in either the prophets or David, but it is clear that Law or Torah was primary among them. There may have been a fourth cat-egory related to generations that was intended in this passage (Chronicles?), but that is uncertain. Of the scriptural citations in this document, however, the Law is cited almost exclusively and given the place of priority.

The prologue to Sirach, Philo, and 4QMMT all suggest movement in the second category of sacred Jewish writings before the time of Jesus, but still the most common way to designate all of Israel's scriptures was with the labels "law," "law and the prophets," or "prophets" (see, e.g., Matt. 7:12; Luke 4:17; John 1:45; Acts 13:27; 28:23; Rom. 3:21). At other times "law" and "prophets" seem interchangeable. For example, see how Psalm 82:6 is referred to as "law" (John 10:34), and Paul refers to a series of quotes from the Psalms as "law" (Rom. 3:10–19). It is also interesting that in his *1 Apology* Justin describes a Christian worship service and states that in the service "the memoirs of the apostles *or the writings of the prophets* are read as long as time permits" (*1 Apol.* 67, emphasis added).[7]

By the fourth century CE several pieces of literature that had been initially welcomed in various churches were rejected as spurious. There was widespread scholarly neglect of much of this literature for centuries, but in modern times there has been a resurgence of interest in it because scholars have rightly recognized that it helps us interpret difficult texts of the New Testament and illuminates the context of early Christianity. These writings also greatly enhance our understanding of the notions of Scripture and canon in antiquity.[8] It is difficult to know precisely why the Jewish Pseudepigrapha and some of the Apocrypha fell into disrepute in the Christian communities[9] and why the rabbinic sages rejected these writings altogether beginning in the second century CE and later. The textual tradition in the Christian communities, however, was far more fluid in the second through fifth centuries. After that, the church used hermeneutics—instead of a fluid textual tradition—to adapt its sacred Scriptures to its ever-changing circumstances. This fluidity in the canonical tradition was also present in rabbinic Judaism in roughly the same period. As late as the fourth century CE, for example, some Amoraim were both citing authoritatively and discussing the authority of Sirach (see *y. Hagigah* 77c; *b. Yebamot* 63b; *Gen. Rab.* 8:2b; *b. Baba Qamma* 92b); and earlier several fragments of Sirach were found both at Qumran (Sir. 6:20–31; 51:13–19, 30) and at Masada (Sir. 39:27–32; 40:10–44:17). It appears also in several important early Christian Old Testament manuscripts, including Codex Vaticanus (mid-fourth century), Codex Sinaiticus (fourth century), and Codex Alexandrinus (fifth century). In time, Sirach was withdrawn from the collection of books that made up the Hebrew Bible, but it was still read in an authoritative manner throughout much of the rabbinic period by a number of rabbis. Its exclusion or "decanonization" was a long and slow process.[10]

Since reading a text in worship and teaching it in a religious community imply a recognition of its sacredness and authority by a believing community, conversely forbidding a congregation to read a document in public worship suggests that it is not or is no longer viewed as Scripture. The primary exception to this may be *4 Ezra* 14:43–47, where readers are permitted to read twenty-four books in public, but seventy other books are to be read only by the spiritually wise. Those books were more private and not read in a public place.

Perhaps because these apocryphal and pseudepigraphal writings were written later than the books of the Hebrew Bible and perhaps because some were written not in Hebrew but in Greek, some Jews from the east began to exclude them from their sacred collections sometime near the end of the first century CE and subsequently by most Jews by 800–900 CE. They may have been excluded because their usefulness, adaptability to the communities, and even suitability for worship and instruction were no longer recognized. It is also possible that some Jews excluded the apocryphal and pseudepigraphal books because of the notion that God had withdrawn the role of the prophet and only writings that existed before then were deemed worthy of inclusion. This view may have its roots in Zechariah 13:2–6:

> On that day, says the LORD of hosts, I will cut off the names of the idols from the land, so that they shall be remembered no more; and also I will remove from the land the prophets and the unclean spirit. And if any prophets appear again, their fathers and mothers who bore them will say to them, "You shall not live, for you speak lies in the name of the LORD"; and their fathers and their mothers who bore them shall pierce them through when they prophesy. On that day the prophets will be ashamed, every one, of their visions when they prophesy; they will not put on a hairy mantle in order to deceive, but each of them will say, "I am no prophet, I am a tiller of the soil; for the land has been my possession since my youth." And if anyone asks them, "What are these wounds on your chest?" the answer will be "The wounds I received in the house of my friends." (Zech. 13:2–6 NRSV)

Echoes of the sentiment of this passage no doubt influenced many Jews in the time of the Maccabees when Simon Maccabee was established as "leader and high priest forever, *until a trustworthy prophet should arise*" (1 Macc. 14:41 NRSV, emphasis added). The notion that the age of the prophets was gone but would one day return is found in the concluding chapter of the book of Malachi, when Elijah was expected to return and turn the hearts of the parents to the children and the children to the parents so that God would not bring punishment on the people (Mal. 4:5–6). Josephus also reflects the view that the succession of prophets had ceased and that only the writings before that time could be included in the collection of twenty-two sacred Jewish books: "From Artaxerxes to our time the complete history has been written, but has not been deemed worthy of equal credit with the earlier record because of the failure of the exact succession of the prophets" (*Ag. Ap.* 1.40–41, LCL).

Perhaps for these and other reasons, the Jews eventually excluded the writings that are now identified by the terms "Apocrypha" and "Pseudepigrapha." Later some Christian communities also separated these writings from their sacred collections, but not initially and not for the same reasons. The Christians did not believe that the Spirit was absent from their community, but that the Spirit had returned and filled them with the power to be witnesses of the risen Christ (Acts 1:8; 2:17–36). Had there been a widespread view that all prophecy had ceased when this literature was created, it is difficult to imagine that there would have been any acceptance of it in either the Jewish or later Christian communities. Indeed, Jesus ben Sirach obviously did not think that the sacred collection of writings was closed and even believed that he was continuing the prophetic/ wisdom tradition of the Jews: "I will again make instruction shine forth like the dawn, and I will make it clear from far away. I will again pour out teaching like prophecy, and leave it to all future generations. Observe that I have not labored for myself alone, but for all who seek wisdom" (Sir. 24:32–34).

It is obvious that Sirach's grandson felt the same about his work since he translated Sirach's book of wisdom teachings for the Greek-speaking Jews and included it among other sacred writings that were translated into Greek for the Jews. He explains this in his prologue to Sirach:

> So my grandfather Jesus, who devoted himself especially to the reading of the Law and the Prophets and the other books of our ancestors, and had acquired considerable proficiency in them, was himself also led to write something pertaining to instruction and wisdom, so that by becoming familiar also with his book those who love learning might make even greater progress in living according to the law. (Prologue, NRSV)

The grandson saw his grandfather's work as highly significant for those who wished to gain learning and were disposed to live according to the law. Whatever views were circulating among the Jews regarding the cessation of the succession of the prophets in the second century BCE, they had little effect on Sirach's grandson or earlier on his grandfather. All Jews did not believe that the age of prophecy had ceased, and so the production of other books continued for a considerable time until the notion of a closing of the succession of the prophets took root in Judaism. Sirach was one of the more popular writings discussed in the rabbinic literature and the most cited text that was not eventually included in the Hebrew Bible.[11] Nahum Sarna indicates that the need of the rabbis to emphasize that Sirach's book did not "defile the hands," that is, that it was not canonical, shows that the collection of Ketubim, the third part of the Hebrew Bible, also known as the Writings or Hagiographa, was still fluid in the second century and that Sirach had already acquired a "measure of sanctity in the popular conscience." He further notes that even after its ban by the rabbis (*t. Yadayim* 2:13), some of the *Amoraim*[12] continued to quote it.[13]

Initially, the word "apocrypha" referred to writings that were not to be read in public worship, but rather to be read in private, generally by the more mature believers. For example, 2 Esdras (= *4 Ezra*) tells the story of how Ezra and five scribes recovered the lost scriptures of Israel by divine action and that God instructed them to make twenty-four books known to all persons, but seventy others were private and to be read only by the wise among them: "'Make public the twenty-four books that you wrote first, and let the worthy and the unworthy read them; but keep the seventy that were written last, in order to give them to the wise among your people. For in them is the spring of understanding, the fountain of wisdom, and the river of knowledge.' And I did so" (2 Esd. 14:46–47 NRSV). This is not unlike how many Christians regarded the apocryphal Old Testament texts, as we see in Athanasius's listing of them for private reading and similarly Luther's inclusion of them for reading but not for doctrine.

In regard to the so-called pseudepigraphal writings, James Charlesworth cautions that not all of this literature is cut from the same cloth, in that it does not all originate from the same sources or the same motives (i.e., deception).[14] It appears that there were several kinds of pseudepigraphal writings in the Greco-

Roman world and they likely had an impact on the producers of the apocryphal and pseudepigraphal texts. There was a tendency among some classical writers (1) to ascribe anonymous pieces to well-known authors of like or similar genre, as in the case of the *Epic Cycle* that was ascribed to Homer. (2) It was also not uncommon for followers of a philosopher to ascribe their works to the master (several short studies made by members of the Academy bear the name of Plato, e.g., *Problemata*, which are Peripatetic and are attributed to Aristotle). (3) There were also deliberate forgeries that were made with the aim of selling their works (see Galen, *In Hipp. de nat. hominis* 2.57.12). (4) Some writers of a later time wanted to ascribe their work to an earlier writer in order to show the antiquity of their particular teaching or doctrine and consequently to give more credibility to it, as in the case of the numerous Neopythagorean treatises attached to the earlier Pythagoreans, including Pythagoras himself. The *Sibylline Oracles* are a notable example of this, as are the *Clementine Recognitions and Homilies* that are not by Clement of Rome. Similarly, several works attributed to Dionysius the Areopagite were produced several centuries after his death. There are five loosely defined categories of the pseudepigraphal writings as follows:[15]

1. Apocalyptic literature and related works

1 (Ethiopic Apocalypse of) Enoch (Jewish, ca. 200 B.C.E.–50 CE)

2 (Slavonic Apocalypse of) Enoch (Jewish, ca. 75–100 CE)

3 (Hebrew Apocalypse of) Enoch (Jewish, present form ca. fifth–sixth century CE)

Sibylline Oracles (Jewish and Christian, second century BCE–seventh century CE)

Treatise of Shem (ca. end of first century BCE)

Apocryphon of Ezekiel (mostly lost, original form ca. late first century BCE)

Apocalypse of Zephaniah (mostly lost, original form ca. late first century BCE)

4 Ezra (Jewish, after 70 CE, with final Christian additions later)

Greek Apocalypse of Ezra (present form is Christian, ca. ninth century CE, with Jewish and Christian sources)

Vision of Ezra (Christian, fourth–seventh century CE)

Questions of Ezra (Christian, date uncertain)

Revelation of Ezra (Christian, sometime before ninth century CE)

Apocalypse of Sedrach (present form is Christian, ca. fifth century CE, with earlier sources)

2 (Syriac Apocalypse of) Baruch (Jewish, ca. 100 CE)

3 (Greek Apocalypse of) Baruch (Christian, ca. first–second century CE, with Jewish sources)

Apocalypse of Abraham (primarily Jewish, ca. 70–150 CE)

Apocalypse of Adam (Gnostic, ca. first century CE, with Jewish sources)

Apocalypse of Elijah (Jewish and Christian, ca. 150–275 CE)

Apocalypse of Daniel (present form ca. ninth century CE, with Jewish sources from ca. fourth century CE)

2. Testaments

Testaments of the Twelve Patriarchs (present form is Christian, ca. 150–200 CE, but Levi, Judah, and Naphtali are Jewish, before 70 CE and probably second–first century BCE)

Testament of Job (Jewish, ca. late first century BCE)

Testaments of the Three Patriarchs (Jewish versions of Abraham, Isaac, and Jacob, ca. 100 CE, linked with Christian versions of Isaac and Jacob)

Testament of Moses (Jewish, ca. early first century CE)

Testament of Solomon (Jewish, present form ca. third century CE, but earliest form ca. 100 CE)

Testament of Adam (present form is Christian, ca. late third century CE, with Jewish sources from ca. 150–200 CE)

3. Expansions of the Old Testament and other legends

Letter of Aristeas (Jewish, ca. 200–150 BCE)

Jubilees (Jewish, ca. 130–100 CE)

Martyrdom and Ascension of Isaiah (first section is Jewish from ca. 100 BCE; second section is Christian from ca. second century CE; and third section, the *Testament of Hezekiah*, is Christian from ca. 90–100 CE)

Joseph and Aseneth (Jewish, ca. 100 CE)

Life of Adam and Eve (Jewish, ca. early to mid-first century CE)

Pseudo-Philo (Jewish, ca. 66–135 CE)

Lives of the Prophets (Jewish, ca. early first century CE, with later Christian additions)

Ladder of Jacob (Jewish, late first century CE; chap. 7 is Christian)

4 Baruch (Jewish original edited by a Christian, ca. 100–110 CE)

Jannes and Jambres (present form is Christian, ca. first century BCE, with Jewish sources)

History of the Rechabites (present form is Christian, ca. sixth century CE, with some pre–100 CE Jewish sources)

Eldad and Modad (now lost, before first century CE; quoted in *Shepherd of Hermas*, ca. 140 CE)

History of Joseph (Jewish, difficult to date)

4. Wisdom and philosophical literature

Ahiqar (Jewish, late seventh or sixth century BCE; quoted in Tobit)

3 Maccabees (Jewish, ca. first century BCE)

4 Maccabees (Jewish, ca. before 70 CE)

Pseudo-Phocylides (Jewish maxims attributed to sixth century BCE

Ionic (poet ca. 50 BCE–100 CE)

Sentences of the Syriac Menander (Jewish, ca. third century CE)

5. Prayers, psalms, and odes

More Psalms of David (Jewish, ca. third century BCE–100 CE)

Prayer of Manasseh (Jewish, ca. early first century CE; sometimes listed in Apocrypha)

Psalms of Solomon (Jewish, ca. 55–50 BCE)

Hellenistic Synagogal Prayers (Jewish, ca. second–third century CE)

Prayer of Joseph (Jewish, ca. 70–135 CE)

Prayer of Jacob (Jewish, mostly lost, ca. fourth century CE)

Odes of Solomon (Christian, ca. 100 CE, influenced by Judaism and Qumran)

Some of these documents are cited in a religiously authoritative way in early Judaism and early Christianity and were included in the ancient collections read by the Essene community at Qumran and later in some of the Christian catalogues and several Christian manuscripts. Their presence at Qumran and in early Christianity suggests that these apocryphal and pseudepigraphal writings were widely used in Judea in the time of Jesus. The earliest example of their use among Jews is found at Qumran. We will now look briefly at this Jewish religious sect and then their collections of sacred texts. Most of the religious texts discovered at Qumran were not sectarian, that is, they were not written or produced by the Essenes at Qumran, though several texts were produced there. After a brief description of the residents at Qumran, I will consider the religious literature discovered there and also list some of the more prominent religious books that were cited authoritatively in Jewish and later in Christian sources.

THE ESSENES AND THEIR SACRED LITERATURE

Among the various renewal movements in Judea in the time of Jesus, a group of religious Jews known as the Essenes lived on the northwest shore of the Dead Sea in a place today called Khirbet Qumran and also in other towns both in and outside Judea.[16] Josephus has carefully identified this sectarian group of religious Jews (*J. W.* 2.119–61; *Ant.* 18.18–22),[17] but so have Philo of Alexandria (*Good Person* 75–87; *Apology for the Jews*) and Pliny (*Nat.* 5). Josephus claims that there were about four thousand Essenes living in various locations (including Jerusalem), but the Essenes may also have been in Asia Minor between Colossae and Ephesus during Paul and John's ministries in those locations and also in Egypt. The best-known place for their activity and their scriptures is Khirbet Qumran on the northwest shore of the Dead Sea. This location is where the famous Dead Sea Scrolls were discovered. Not only were most of the books of the Hebrew Bible/Old Testament discovered in these scrolls, but other books not included in these sacred collections were also found there.

Until recently, scholars focused almost exclusively on the text of the canonical books at Qumran with the goal of establishing the earliest text of the Hebrew Bible. That focus has more recently broadened to include the other documents found at Qumran, and, as a result, new questions have been raised about the other books that were not later included in the Jewish or Christian Bibles. As we will observe below, while textual considerations have loomed large in terms of the Dead Sea Scrolls, not much consideration has been given to them thus far in producing translations of the Bible, especially in the more conservative traditions of the church.[18] I will say more about this in chapter 4.

Strangely, the Essenes are not mentioned by name in the New Testament or in the rabbinic writings of the second to the sixth century, but their presence was certainly known in Judea and elsewhere in the time of Jesus as we see in Josephus, Philo, and Pliny the Elder. At the end of the first century CE, Josephus produced a lengthy and generally positive description of the Essenes, observing that there were several orders of Essenes and offering descriptions of their daily activities and how they practiced their religious piety (*J. W.* 2.119–61). Philo and Josephus have considerable overlap in their descriptions of this religious sect, but Josephus adds much more detail, as we see in the following example:

The doctrine of the Essenes is wont to leave everything in the hands of God. They regard the soul as immortal and believe that they ought to strive especially to draw near to righteousness. They send votive offerings to the temple, but perform their sacrifices employing a different ritual of purification. For this reason they are barred from those precincts of the temple that are frequented by all the people and perform their rites by themselves. Otherwise they are of the highest character, devoting themselves solely to agricultural labor. They deserve admiration in contrast to all others who claim their share of virtue because such qualities as theirs were never found before among any Greek or barbarian people, nay, not even briefly, but have been among them in constant practice and never interrupted since they adopted them from of old. Moreover, they hold their possessions in common, and the wealthy man receives no more enjoyment from his property than the man who possesses nothing. The men who practice this way of life number more than four thousand [the same number mentioned by Philo]. They neither bring wives into the community nor do they own slaves, since they believe that the latter practice contributes to injustice and that the former opens the way to a source of dissension. Instead they live by themselves and perform menial tasks for one another. They elect by show of hands good men to receive their revenues and the produce of the earth and priests to prepare bread and other food. (*Ant.* 18.18–22, LCL)

Philo of Alexandria observed the Essenes in his area and summarized their virtues as follows: (1) they do not sacrifice animals; (2) they live in villages; (3) they work industriously at a variety of occupations that are neither military nor commercial; (4) they keep no slaves; (5) they study morals and religion, especially the allegorical interpretation of their scriptures; (6) they pursue and practice virtue; (7) they refuse to swear oaths and reject ceremonial purity; (8) they hold all goods and clothing in common; (9) they care for the sick and elderly; (10) they admit only adults to their order; and (11) they reject marriage and have low opinions of women.[19]

These Essenes copied, transmitted, and also produced literature that sheds considerable light on Jewish beliefs before and during the time of Jesus. Before the discovery of the Dead Sea Scrolls, the New Testament writings were among the primary Jewish sources on Jewish life in the first century. The literary activity of the Essenes tells us a great deal about the books that many Jews in the first century CE, along with the Essenes, acknowledged as sacred and authoritative texts for their communities of faith. Although other Essene communities existed in Judea, Egypt, and elsewhere, the only Essene literature available to us today comes from the Qumran community. Some of the noncanonical writings at Qumran were also discovered in an ancient *genizah* or storage place for old sacred documents, at an ancient synagogue in Cairo, Egypt (dating ca. eighth to ninth century) best known as the Cairo Genizah. However, the large number of documents found in the vicinity of Qumran is the most impressive and significant collection discovered thus far that have advanced our understanding of the text of the biblical books, the scope of the sacred collections in the time of Jesus, as well as the Jewish people in the time of Jesus. These ancient texts have also had a considerable impact on our understanding of the origin of the Jewish and Christian biblical canons.[20]

The parallels between the scrolls and the New Testament help us understand several difficult passages in the New Testament.[21] They also help us understand Judaism in the first century and the books that many Jews believed were normative for faith at that time. The Dead Sea Scrolls were discovered in eleven caves near the ruins of the Qumran community.[22] Some of the literature discovered at Qumran was sectarian and generated either there or in their various communities, but much of it was common Jewish religious literature of that day and was brought to the Essene communities rather than being created there.

The first caves were discovered near Khirbet Qumran in the winter of 1946–1947, and the remaining scrolls were found in other caves throughout the early 1950s. The community at Qumran dates from approximately 150 BCE to 68 CE. The scrolls contain thousands of small and large fragments and also complete books from about nine hundred documents. There are around two hundred fragmentary scrolls of the biblical books, five of which include more than one biblical book, that is, books that are part of the current Hebrew Bible. It is difficult to be more specific on the number of biblical books since many of the small fragments of biblical books could be a part of the same biblical book or of another manuscript of the same book. Also, some of the fragments found could be part of either a lectionary or a continuous text manuscript. The smaller texts are difficult to identify since many are only the size of a thumbnail, and it is a special challenge to fit them together in their original position; but many of these fragments come from larger documents, and scholars have been able to identify most of them. Some of the documents have multiple copies, and some represent only a small portion of a larger writing. The 220 biblical texts represent about 22 percent of the total, not counting the tefillin and mezuzot.[23] No significant differences between the biblical and nonbiblical scrolls have been established regarding the beginnings and endings of the scrolls, nor the style of writing used in them. Unlike in rabbinic circles, there is also very little if any distinction between the writing of the biblical and nonbiblical scrolls.[24] According to Tov, the scribes there copied approximately only 20 percent of the scrolls discovered at Qumran; 80 percent were imported from elsewhere in Judea.[25]

Many of the manuscripts at Qumran were apparently wrapped in linen and placed in jars by the Jews prior to their impending Roman capture in 68 CE. The documents may have been stored or hidden over a period of time much like worn-out and unusable copies of the Scriptures were placed in a genizah.[26] Another explanation why the Essenes placed these documents in caves is that the community was on the verge of dying and so they hid their most precious and sacred documents to preserve them as long as possible. The caves have been numbered 1 through 11, and a cave number plus Q plus another number and/ or letter or name usually identify the manuscripts or fragments found in each cave.[27] The number of biblical books discovered at Qumran is considerable, including all the books of the Hebrew Bible except Esther and probably Nehemiah. The number of copies of these books also suggests which ones were more used by the community at Qumran, which approximates the use of sacred books in the New Testament. Emanuel Tov has listed them as follows:

Genesis	19–20
Exodus	15
Leviticus	11, possibly 12
Numbers	6
Deuteronomy	30
Joshua	2
Judges	3
Samuel	4
Kings	3
Isaiah	21
Jeremiah	6
Ezekiel	6
Minor Prophets	8
Psalms	36
Job	4
Proverbs	2
Song of Songs	4
Ruth	4
Canticles	4
Lamentations	4
Qohelet/Ecclesiastes	2
Esther	0
Daniel	8
Ezra	1
Nehemiah (possibly)	0
Chronicles	1[28]

From this list, it is obvious that the Psalms collection has the most copies, is the most frequently cited at Qumran, and must have informed the worship of the community. It is also clear that Deuteronomy is the most cited book of the Law and Isaiah the most used and frequently cited prophet. Again, this is similar to the most frequently cited texts in the teaching of Jesus and the rest of the New Testament and early Christianity.

BIBLICAL, NONBIBLICAL, AND SECTARIAN TEXTS AT QUMRAN

A growing number of biblical scholars are convinced that the Essenes did not have a fixed collection of sacred scriptures, but rather a more fluid collection that was in process of definition. Since the early Christians received their scriptural heritage from the Jews of the first century, it is also likely that they made considerable use of the larger collection of Jewish religious texts circulating in the land of Israel in the time of Jesus. I make some observations below that support this suggestion.

The Dead Sea Scrolls exhibit similarities with the New Testament writings, the most important being the apostle Paul's notion of works righteousness (Rom. 4; Gal. 3–4; 2 Cor. 6:14–7:1) and 4QMMT. Other Essene parallels with Paul's terminology include "mystery," "flesh and spirit," "perfect," "truth," and "justification." Qumran parallels with the Gospel of John include "sons of light" and "the spirit of truth." It may also be possible that the heresy mentioned in Colossians was an Essene-type theology, but that is not certain. These similarities do not suggest any dependence of Christians upon the Essenes, but rather reflect the shared characteristics of first-century Jewish sects.

The biblical[29] manuscripts found at Qumran are fully one thousand years earlier than the Leningrad Codex (ca. 1008/9 CE) and the Aleppo Codex (ca. 925 CE), which are the chief witnesses of the Masoretic Text of the Hebrew Bible. Most of the scrolls are in Hebrew, but a hundred of them are in Aramaic, and several from Qumran cave 7 and Nahal Hever (south of Qumran) are in Greek. Some 40 percent of the biblical manuscripts are of the Pentateuch, which points to the primary scriptural authority of the Essenes. Of the rest, thirty-six manuscripts (or thirty-seven) are of the Psalms and thirty-three from the Major Prophets (Isaiah has either nineteen or twenty-one, Jeremiah and Ezekiel have six each). If Daniel is placed into the Major Prophets, then eight more are added to this list.[30]

Among the some 960 documents found at Qumran and that vicinity, about 650 are nonbiblical scrolls or manuscripts. The noncanonical writings have been conveniently classified as (1) rules and regulations, (2) poetic and wisdom texts, (3) rewritten Scriptures[31] (e.g., *Genesis Apocryphon*), (4) commentaries (e.g., *Pesher* on Habakkuk), and (5) a miscellaneous section that includes a variety of other writings that do not fit the above categories.[32] The range of Qumran texts includes the following.[33]

Old Testament Texts

All of the Old Testament books, with the possible exception of Esther and Nehemiah, have been found at Qumran, but this is not the same thing as saying that the canon of Qumran is equal to the biblical canon of later rabbinic Judaism or the Protestant Old Testament canon.[34] For example, the psalmic texts at Qumran exhibit significant variation from the later Masoretic Text, which became the fixed text of the Hebrew Bible.[35] According to Sidnie Crawford, it is unlikely that Esther was ever considered Scripture by the Jews living at Qumran since no portions of it have survived at Qumran, it is never cited or alluded to in any of the other Qumran texts, and the Feast of Purim is not mentioned in any calendar texts at Qumran where calendar events (when to celebrate the Passover, etc.) were especially important.[36] Although some argue that a small fragment of a manuscript discovered at Qumran is from the Gospel of Mark, this view is largely discredited, and scholars generally agree that no New Testament texts were found at Qumran.[37]

Sectarian Literature

The following texts are generally recognized as peculiarly Essene literature.

- *Damascus Document* (abbreviated CD) was found in Cairo in 1895. The Qumran manuscripts appear to be later versions of the *Community Rule*.
- *Community Rule* or *Manual of Discipline* (1QS or Serekh) consists of rules of life for the community: (a) aims and ideals; (b) annual census instructions, including moral outlook (humility); (c) treatise on the spirits of good and evil; (d) regulations regarding obedience; (e) oath of allegiance; and (f) a hymn with reference to calendar details and secrecy of doctrine.
- *Rule Annex* or *Messianic Rule* (1QSa) consists of supplementary provisions for instruction that describe the treatment of the aged and mentally ill, plus offering more council rules.
- *Book of Blessings* (1QSb) is a handbook of benedictions for members and officials.
- *War Scroll* (4QM or *Milhamah*), a nineteen-column document, contains instructions on the preparations for the great eschatological battle when the universal dominion of God's holy race will be established (cf. Ezek. 38–39 and Daniel).
- *Hymn Scroll* (1QH or *Hodayot*) contains some thirty hymns, many of which are thanksgivings for salvation and knowledge. It is somewhat similar to the canonical Psalms, but more individualistic.
- *Halakic Letter* (4QMMT or *Miqsat Ma'aseh ha-Torah* ["some works of the law"]) is a collection of rules for behavior or law codes derived from a particular interpretation of the scriptural law codes (similar to the *Temple Scroll* and *Jubilees*). It has considerable relevance for the study of the canonical process in that it speaks of the kinds of literature about which the community was especially concerned, namely, the Law of Moses.
- Liturgical and astrological fragments.
- *Florilegia* (or testimony books) include three fragments from cave 4 with assembled selections from Old Testament passages.
- *Genesis Apocryphon* (1QapGen or *Lamech Scroll*) is similar to *Jubilees* and contains a rewritten and modernized version of parts of Genesis in Aramaic.
- *Temple Scroll* (11QTemple), a scroll over thirty feet long that was highly influential in the Qumran community.

Biblical Commentaries

The commentaries found at Qumran consist of passages from the Old Testament accompanied by *pesharim*, literalistic and eschatological interpretations of the scriptural books in light of the life and history of the community at Qumran. For the residents of Qumran these constituted the true meaning of the Old Testament.

Late Jewish Apocryphal and Pseudepigraphal Works

Several apocryphal and pseudepigraphal writings were found at Qumran, including a Hebrew version of Sirach and of Tobit, an Aramaic version of Tobit, a Greek version of the Epistle of Jeremiah, a Hebrew version of *Jubilees*, an Aramaic version of *1 Enoch*, and Aramic fragments of *Testaments of the Twelve Patriarchs*—all of which are of special interest because they indicate the theological outlook in Judea in the time of early Christianity. Several of these works were also welcomed and cited as authoritative documents in early Christianity. These were listed and briefly discussed above.

JEWISH SCRIPTURES IN THE FIRST CENTURY CE

Among the writings that are not now in the Hebrew Bible, but which found considerable favor in the Essene community at Qumran, clearly *1 Enoch*, *Jubilees*, the *Temple Scroll*, and others were highly valued. Of the canonical writings discovered at Qumran, the Psalms, Isaiah, and Deuteronomy are cited most. On the other hand, the Psalter at Qumran differs considerably from the one found in Jewish and Christian Bibles today, especially after Psalm 89. The parallels with Luke 24:44 here are obvious, but again, it cannot be shown in the first century that "psalms" meant anything other than psalms and we cannot be certain which psalms were intended. Of the 150 psalms in the biblical Psalter, 126 of them are found in the forty collections of Psalms at Qumran, and of the canonical Psalms 90–150, only five are not represented in the Qumran Psalms, but again, there are many differences. Also, Psalm 32 in the canonical Psalms is missing from the Qumran Psalms, and several of the psalms are in a different order. At Qumran Psalm 31 is followed by Psalm 33 and Psalm 38 is followed by Psalm 71.[38] Abegg, Flint, and Ulrich conclude from their study of the Psalms, "It thus seems clear that the 'book of Psalms' was viewed as Scripture at Qumran; but it is not easy to determine which specific form(s) of the Psalter were regarded as such." They cite as evidence from 11QPs^a-Psalter ("David's Compositions") the statement: "And David, the son of Jesse, was wise, and a light like the light of the sun, and literate, . . . And the total (of his psalms and songs) was four thousand and fifty. All these he composed through prophecy which was given to him from before the Most High."[39] Any insistence that this passage is a reference to the clearly defined third part of the Hebrew Bible, however, cannot be established from the available evidence in the time of Jesus or before. I have presented this case elsewhere.[40] The Orthodox churches have included Psalm 151 in their sacred collection, but more puzzling is how some scholars gather the whole of the third part of the Hebrew Bible, the Writings, into "psalms" or "David."[41]

Many argue that the Scriptures of the Hebrew Bible were settled well before the time of Jesus for all Jews in Judea. In a manner almost condescending, some argue further that only those Jews outside Judea accepted the much wider collection of books that included the apocryphal and pseudepigraphal texts that existed in Greek and circulated in the Septuagint, the Greek translation of the Hebrew scriptures. The collection of sacred or religious texts discovered at Qumran and elsewhere in the Judean Desert dispels the notion that only the books of the Hebrew Bible were circulating as sacred texts in the time of Jesus. The discovery of the Dead Sea Scrolls also lets us know that this so-called noncanonical literature was also circulating in Israel among the Jews both before and during the time of Jesus. The Greek Bible, which also contains much of that literature, was not the only sacred text containing the apocryphal and pseudepigraphal writings. Even though most, if not all, of the books that now make up the Hebrew Bible were acknowledged as Scripture in the time of Jesus, there was no notion of a fixed biblical canon circulating in the time of Jesus either among Jews or among early followers of Jesus who accepted as sacred the books they inherited from their Jewish roots, which included more than the books of the later Hebrew Bible.

DIASPORA JUDAISM

Both before and during the time of Jesus, most Jews throughout the Roman Empire spoke Greek and were familiar with the Hellenistic customs prevalent in the areas where they lived. They would also have been pressured to reconcile their Jewish faith with these customs. Philo, for instance, not only spoke and wrote in Greek but also was quite familiar with Hellenistic culture, including athletics. To some extent, this culture was also experienced by the Jews in the Land of Israel, and the differences between Jews in their land and those in the *Diaspora*[42] was more one of degree than of substance. For our purposes here, the regular Jewish practice of reading the Scriptures in Greek in their diaspora synagogues is more important. While it is not precisely clear when or how the translation of the rest of the Jewish scriptures took place—certainly no later than the first century BCE and probably in the second century BCE—the translations of the Jewish scriptures were united into a whole and widely received by the Jews in the Diaspora as their sacred scriptures. Various Greek translations of the Jewish scriptures were used in Jewish worship in the Diaspora, and the implications of this are quite significant since the Greek scriptures contained more books than did the later recognized Hebrew Bible.[43]

As is well known, the Greek scriptures contained more books than did the *later* Hebrew Bible canon, and the use of these scriptures, which included apocryphal and pseudepigraphal books, continued in use among Jews not only in the first century BCE and CE, but also in the western Diaspora at least up through the ninth century CE. While the initial translation of the Hebrew scriptures into Greek included only the Pentateuch, in time, and certainly by the time of the translation of Sirach by his grandson (prologue, Sirach, ca. 130 BCE), the Law and the Prophets and other books were also included in this collection. It is not clear what was included among the Prophets since that appears to have included all scriptures that were not classified as Torah in the first two centuries among the Jews and also the Christians. In the New Testament only one passage has a separate category beyond Law and Prophets for the Jewish scriptures (Luke 24:44) and this practice of identifying the Jewish scriptures as either Law or Prophets or Law and Prophets continued in the Christian community for centuries, and for several centuries as well as in rabbinic Judaism.[44]

Along with the reading of the Law and the Prophets, Jews in the Diaspora were observant of the Sabbath and of Jewish holidays, and they maintained contact with the Jews in the Land of Israel, including the payment of the annual temple tax required by law.[45] The overwhelming majority of epitaphs in their synagogues are in Greek or Latin; only a few are in Hebrew.[46] According to Schürer, of the various known ancient synagogues only Rome had inscriptions in Hebrew, but the majority were in Greek. This is also true in the east, where Greek inscriptions were found at Dura-Europos. Most of the Hebrew inscriptions date after the sixth century CE, and even then most inscriptions were in Greek and Latin.[47]

E. P. Sanders poignantly and correctly concludes: "diaspora Jews were capable of interpreting the Bible, and they did not sit, patiently waiting for the Houses of Hillel and Shammai to send them their disagreements."[48] This raises the question of how much dependence the Jews of the Dispersion had on their fellow Jews in the Land of Israel or those in Babylon, the two best-known places for the study of the Law in the first century and following. After the destruction of Jerusalem, however, what was the relationship between the Jews in the Dispersion and those in the Land of Israel? That the Jews in the western Diaspora did not speak Hebrew or Aramaic, and the rabbinic traditions—the Mishnah, Tosefta, and the two Talmudim—were all composed in Hebrew and Aramaic and not translated into Greek, suggests that the rabbinic traditions had little effect in the western Diaspora communities. Also, since there is little evidence of visits by rabbinic teachers or the establishment of rabbinic schools in the west, it is likely that the rabbinic traditions, from which came the Hebrew Bible, had little effect on Jews to the west. After the destruction of the temple and the consequent (though delayed) cancellation of the temple tax by Roman authorities (Roman law 30) in 363 and 399 CE with the approval of the Diaspora Jews, the sacred traditions and sacred literature important to the Jews in the west were those known to them before the destruction of the temple in 70 CE.[49]

Arye Edrei and Doron Mendels have made a strong case that the scriptures of the Diaspora Jews are those that were passed along to them in the Septuagint, including the apocryphal and pseudepigraphal books, at least until the eighth century CE.[50] What strengthens their case in part is the discovery of the books of Tobit and Sirach in both Hebrew and Aramaic in the Cairo Genizah that dated from the ninth and tenth centuries. Clearly Jews in the Cairo region did not follow the lead of the rabbinic Jews in Israel or in Babylon. What appears evident is that there were few strong or binding connections between Jews in the east and those in the western part of the Roman Empire especially after the destruction of the temple in 70 CE. Whereas the temple was the center of·connectedness for the Jews in the east and west as well as in Israel, after the destruction of the temple in 70 CE, the center became the text of the Oral Torah that was written only in Hebrew and not translated into Greek. To a large extent, those in Israel looked down upon those who lived in exile, and exile was viewed as a judgment from God.[51]

It is an overstatement to say that the Jews in the Land of Israel had no effect on the Jews living in the Diaspora, but Jews in the Diaspora also had relative independence from their homeland. The Jews of the Dispersion were well aware that the Dispersion was seen in their scriptures as a punishment for sin (Lev. 26:33; Deut. 28:63–64; Jer. 5:19; 9:15). Those who were taken from their land by force and compelled to live elsewhere would be seen as judged by God. This view is seen in the *Letter of Aristeas* in which the king of Egypt asks one of the wise men how one could express love of country (be a patriot), and the response to the king clarifies how banishment from one's country was seen "by adopting the view that it is a noble thing to live and die in one's own country. A foreign country produces for the poor contempt, and for the rich disgrace, as for men exiled for crimes" (*Ep. Aris.* 249, *OTP*). It was also not unusual for Jews in the Diaspora to be judged for the sins of their fellow Jews in their homeland (see Tob. 1:18; 3 Macc. 2:21–24; and see how Cicero justified confiscation of Jewish money in Asia Minor because their fellow Jews in Judea went against Pompey in battle, *Pro Flacco* 28.69).[52]

While matters of circumcision, observance of the Passover meal, observance of the Law, and the practice of prayers were common features of the Jews in the east and west, the sacred texts that they recognized were considerably different after the destruction of Jerusalem. Edrei and Mendels claim that two different Judaisms emerged after the destruction of the temple in 70 CE, the western "Written Torah Judaism" and the eastern "Oral Torah Judaism."[53] The Jews in the west continued to celebrate Passover but differently from those in the east. They also continued their prayers, but not the prescribed ones (e.g., *Eighteen Benedictions*) from the Mishnah and Talmudim.

When we compare this information with the writings of the New Testament, we see similar echoes of priority, namely the high value attached to Deuteronomy,

Isaiah, and the Psalms. This is also similar to the rest of the New Testament writings and also the writings of the early churches. There is no question that the Jews in the time of Jesus and also the early Christian community were informed by the same sacred writings at their core, but what about these other writings that are now identified as apocryphal or pseudepigraphal? Remarkably both Jews of late antiquity and the earliest followers of Jesus appear to have been informed by the same sacred writings, which also include what we now call noncanonical writings, even if they are not in the majority of texts cited.

The Hebrew Bible appears to have been something of an abbreviation of the scriptures adopted by the Essenes at Qumran, although one can argue that only with caution. It is not certain that there was any fixed biblical collection at Qumran like the one that was adopted later in the rabbinic tradition. Many other religious books at Qumran seemed to function as scripture among the Jews there, namely *1 Enoch*, *Temple Scroll*, Sirach, Tobit, Epistle of Jeremiah, and *Jubilees*, among others, and many were found in multiple copies.

Multiple copies of books at Qumran suggest the value placed on them by the Jews in that community. Some books were obviously more favored than others at Qumran since we have multiple copies of Isaiah (21), Deuteronomy (30), and Psalms (36), but only one of Ezra and Chronicles, two of Joshua and Proverbs, and three of Judges, Kings, and Ecclesiastes. On the other hand, multiple copies of so-called nonbiblical books were also found at Qumran, such as the *Temple Scroll* (3 copies), *1 Enoch* (12 copies), *Jubilees* (14 copies), Tobit (5 copies), and Sirach (2 copies). In the case of the *Temple Scroll*, we see from 11QT[b] that significant attention was given to this book well into the first century CE.[54]

In my discussion of the text of the Hebrew Scriptures/Old Testament, we will see that the text of the Hebrew Bible/Old Testament was even more fluid than that of the New Testament, but fluidity can be seen in the origins of both collections of sacred texts. There is considerable variation in the books that make up the ancient manuscripts, and the texts of those books are also very mixed. As we will also see below, the text of the Hebrew Bible at times differs considerably from the text of the Greek Bible (the Septuagint, or LXX), and the Latin Old Testament is likewise different especially in the so-called fringe areas of the Old Testament (the Writings and the apocryphal books). Until the nineteenth century, the Protestant Old Testaments were frequently published with the Apocrypha included. These books were often separated in some Bibles from other Old Testament literature only after the early sixteenth century with the emergence of Protestantism and its rejection of these books. Before then, as in the cases of the three major uncial manuscripts of the fourth and fifth centuries (Vaticanus, Sinaiticus, and Alexandrinus), they are mixed within the Old Testament collection and without distinction. I should also note that the texts of the manuscripts discovered at Qumran and elsewhere in the Judean Desert vary considerably, and the text of Greek Esther is significantly different from the Hebrew form of Esther.[55]

CONCLUSION

Collections of Jewish religious texts were circulating among the Jews in the time of Jesus and before. These collections were not yet closed or fixed in the sense of being a closed scripture canon, and the notion that no more inspired writings would or could emerge, though present among some Jews, was not held by many in the time of Jesus. The popularity of some of the so-called apocryphal and pseudepigraphal literature among Jews and early Christians suggests that the volumes of sacred literature were many more than what eventually came to make up the Hebrew Bible or the Christian Old Testaments.[56] Indeed, for centuries writings now described as apocryphal and pseudepigraphal were in use in the Jewish and Christian communities and recognized as sacred scripture. The presence of many of these writings at Qumran and in a number of Christian manuscripts suggests that their popularity among Jews in the first century BCE and later also among Christians for at least several centuries was considerable.

This raises the obvious question about the stability of the Bible and whether other books should be added to it or even taken away. I am not anxious to do either, but rather to be informed by the same religious texts that influenced early Judaism (the matrix of early Christianity) and early Christianity and that gave rise to the formation of the Christian Bible. We can see in Jewish and Christian communities a core of writings that were received as sacred by both faith communities and also a collection of books that may have been acknowledged as sacred or inspired writings but had little obvious impact upon either community of faith (e.g., Samuels, Kings, Chronicles). The core writings among Jews of the first century BCE and CE were the books of the Torah and some of the prophets. The collection of prophets was fluid and "prophets" was a catchall term for everything else considered sacred. As we see elsewhere, non-Torah books are sometimes referred to as Torah, and sacred texts that did not find a place in the collection now identified as prophetic writings in the Hebrew Bible were called "prophets" (the Psalms). This was true also in the writings of the New Testament, which favors "law" or "law and the prophets" throughout with only one exception (Luke 24:44). We do not know which books were included in the list of the prophets until the second century CE for some Jews and even later for the Christians. The collections of sacred books that were circulating among Jews and Christians in the first century were apparently still open, and other writings (1 Enoch, Wisdom of Solomon, Sirach) not later included continued to serve in a scriptural manner among the Jews and Christians at that time.

But again, does this mean that the Jews or the Christians established the "wrong" Bible or fixed an inappropriate biblical canon? No! It appears that they had something of a canon within a canon that functioned in their respective communities, just like Jews and Christians today have in their synagogues and churches. While a large number of texts were widely recognized as scripture, a narrower collection tended to inform their religious faith and activities. Christian ministers favor the

Prophets, especially Isaiah, Jeremiah, Hosea, Micah, and Malachi, over Leviticus and Numbers or Kings and Chronicles. African American Christian preaching today seems to favor more of the Exodus stories along with issues in Samuel, Kings, and Chronicles that speak about bondage and freedom. Such texts are not as popular among Asian American churches. The texts that speak to our immediate needs and circumstances are the ones that we tend to favor in our preaching and teaching in religious communities. This has always been the case in the church, and there are periods in which some sacred texts receive little more than acknowledgment that they still belong in our Bibles—there is little focus on them in the church's life. As times and circumstances change, certain books become more popular in religious communities. Over the years I have chided congregations that professed acceptance of the authority and inspiration of the whole Bible but made little use of many parts of it. Very few Christians are aware of the message of Leviticus, Nahum, or Haggai, and in the New Testament, the message of Hebrews, 2–3 John, Jude, or Revelation (and probably others), apart from a few favorite texts in these books. Likewise, no lectionary that I know in any church tradition includes all the books of the Bible.

I hope these comments and the study above will open us to the idea that God still speaks in remarkable ways in the books of the Bible and probably also in other writings in the history of the church. I am always impressed with the number of Protestants as well as Catholics who cite St. Francis of Assisi, Mother Teresa, Martin Luther, John Calvin, Martin Luther King Jr., and Billy Graham, with an obvious appreciation and respect of authority in matters that are intended to settle questions. I have been asked from time to time for a rationale for the closing of the biblical canon, and in a recent favorable review[57] even chided a bit (kindly) for not telling more how the church moved from a fluid canon of sacred texts to a fixed one. I have said on more than one occasion that there is no theological or scriptural rationale that I am aware of in the early church that sets forth such a position, and it is difficult today to make such an argument.

Surprisingly, I have been cited in a Mormon publication in a way that supports the inclusion of some of their sacred books in the biblical canon, namely the *Book of Mormon*, *The Doctrine and the Covenants*, and *The Pearl of Great Price*. I have had very good and collegial exchanges with some Mormons on this matter who have not only cited my work frequently at places that would advance their perspective on an open biblical canon, but they also cited my qualifications in several e-mails I had with David L. Paulsen about their work.[58] While I do not agree completely with their specific theological enterprise, I do agree with them in principle that the notion of inspired literature within the community of faith is still open. In practice, however, it will be very difficult to make any changes to the biblical canon, and it would also create many problems and lead to further divisions in Christian churches. It will take a long time for Christians to consider including more or fewer books in their sacred Scriptures.

I would add that the criteria that were consciously or unconsciously employed in establishing the current collection of Christian texts, if applicable still, should be employed in establishing any new considerations: Does what is being considered for inclusion conflict with or support the sacred traditions and faith that were passed on in the churches? Does it cohere with the traditions we already hold sacred, and does it advance our understanding of the God who calls us into faith and obedience through Christ? If not, I would encourage a reconsideration of the additions being entertained. I personally do not think that adding or deleting any ancient books to the current Old Testament canons circulating in churches will do anything good for the Christian churches, and could well bring chaos and division in the churches. As a word of caution to those wishing to add or subtract from the sacred collections already in the churches, at no time has there been or will there be anything close to universal agreement on what should be added or deleted. Interestingly, in the mid-1990s, I was a plenary speaker for the Jesus Seminar in Santa Rosa, California, and from what I was able to discern after three days of discussions, most of those at the meeting were quite open to the notion of adjusting or modifying the current biblical canons in the churches, but they could not agree on how to do it or on what books to admit or to exclude in forming a new biblical canon. I suspect that this continues to be the case, and it would be the case in whatever group that meets to discuss such matters.

The above notwithstanding, I believe that it is a good idea for Christians to know about the additional books that informed the Christian churches over the centuries, especially in their formative years. Some of these writings clarify many obscure passages in the biblical text, bring out information not known earlier, and add to our understanding of the context of early formative Judaism and the ancient churches, as well as to our understanding of the Bible itself. Knowing how such writings were received and functioned in various Jewish and Christian communities is important for understanding both religious communities today. I do not believe that the church today has anything to fear from being informed by those same sources that informed many of the earliest Christian communities.

In the next three chapters, I will focus on the Old Testament/Hebrew Bible manuscripts that have survived antiquity and what is in them, the text of the biblical books, and the various translations of the Hebrew Scriptures.

Chapter 4

The Ancient Manuscripts: What They Tell Us

INTRODUCTION

The central biblical literature for the Jews in antiquity, and even the present, is the Law of Moses. For the Jews at Qumran, for Philo at Alexandria and for the Jews of his region, and for all Jews everywhere in the ancient world, the Torah was the core of Jewish sacred literature. This is seen in the frequency of citations. Along with Deuteronomy, the Psalms and Isaiah were the most cited texts not only at Qumran but also among the early Christians.

Craig Evans has observed that in the Synoptic Gospels, Jesus was informed by the same books that are frequently quoted or cited in the Qumran scrolls, namely he refers to Deuteronomy some fifteen (or sixteen) times, Isaiah some forty times, and the Psalms some thirteen times. Jesus apparently favored these books the most, but he also frequently cited Daniel, Zechariah, and a few other books. Evans concludes: "Jesus' usage of scripture was pretty much in step with what we observe in similar circles, circles that took the Law very seriously, understood the Prophets eschatologically, and had some regard for the Writings, though this last division was very open-ended."[1] Of the some 650–670 nonbiblical scrolls discovered at Qumran and elsewhere in the Judean Desert,[2] several have some

65

verbal parallels with the New Testament literature. Besides the New Testament's use of the Old Testament/Hebrew Bible writings, there are a number of New Testament citations of or allusions to several of the so-called nonbiblical writings discovered at Qumran, including manuscripts containing *1 Enoch*, *Jubilees*, possibly the *Apocalypse of Moses*, *Testament of Levi*, Tobit, and Sirach, as well as others that have no parallel in the New Testament and are not alluded to or cited either by the New Testament writers, or by the early church writers such as the *Temple Scroll*, 4QMMT, and the *War Scroll*. These parallels citations or allusions do not suggest, however, that Jesus recognized a fixed collection of sacred books.

There is considerable evidence in the Gospels that Jesus regularly cited the Jewish scriptures, but no evidence that he cited any particular *form* of the various biblical texts. As Evans observes, Jesus regularly "appealed to words, phrases, and sometimes whole passages—whatever their textual origin—in an ad hoc, experiential fashion."[3] What can we say about the ancient collections of Jewish religious texts that Jesus cited or made use of in his teachings? His practice was apparently in keeping with the practices of his fellow Jews in the first century. In the following sections we will look at the various Jewish sacred manuscripts that have survived antiquity, and then focus on the texts of those manuscripts to determine if there was a fixed biblical text in the time of Jesus, and finally examine the differences in the sacred collections in the surviving translations of the Hebrew Bible/Old Testament.

ANCIENT MANUSCRIPTS: WHAT IS IN THEM?

I have argued earlier that Jesus did not have a biblical canon in the traditional understanding of canon, that is, not like the one that emerged in rabbinic Judaism and ultimately in most Protestant churches. While his teachings were rooted in the widely accepted books of Moses and several other books among the Prophets, he was also informed by other Jewish religious writings that were later called noncanonical texts, especially 1 Enoch; Wisdom of Solomon; Sirach; Epistle of Jeremiah; 1, 2, and 4 Maccabees; and probably more. In several instances, he shows more awareness of some of the so-called noncanonical writings than he does of some of the so-called canonical books. As noted above, Jesus made no known reference to many Hebrew Bible books, and his early followers appear to have followed his example and cited authoritatively both what we now call canonical and noncanonical literature. Scholars would do well to consider this additional literature as part of the religious heritage that informed the historical Jesus.

As already observed, Jews in the Second Temple period and the earlier followers of Jesus (through the third century CE) made use of a number of Jewish religious texts that were not eventually included in the fixed biblical canons that emerged in both Judaism and Christianity. I will note below some of the less familiar books that are in the ancient manuscripts that have survived antiquity and those that are referred to but have not survived. I drew attention to some of the better-known apocryphal and pseudepigraphal books earlier. Most of these so-called noncanonical books are in single volumes, but some books, especially the books of the Law of Moses, were commonly placed in one volume or scroll, though not always in the same sequence. Students and church members often ask why this literature did not survive in the history of Judaism or the church, and the answer can be rather simple initially, but it does not answer all the questions about canon formation of the Old Testament writings. Initially, since the literature that was left behind no longer met the worship and catechetical needs of most Jews and most Christians, those in the synagogue and church no longer considered them part of their sacred scriptures. In time, the copies that were present either wore out or were discarded and not replaced. A number of the manuscripts that contain these writings were found accidentally in buried locations such as the Cairo Genizah or in a garbage dump in Egypt, or found among misplaced and ignored collections over the centuries such as Codex Vaticanus and other biblical manuscripts. The considerable number of manuscripts or fragments of manuscripts that have survived give us a glimpse of the faith of the early Christians who made use of them. The most popular of these ancient texts were included in the biblical canons of the Roman Catholic and Eastern Orthodox churches,[4] but other ancient texts less known and less quoted have all but vanished—at best only a few surviving fragments exist—and yet in the centuries of Judaism before the end of the first century CE and then in the early church, they did serve a purpose before they fell into disfavor and were rejected or discarded. Many of these books were developed around the names of famous Old Testament characters, such as Adam, Moses, Melchizedek, and the patriarchs. Some of these writings are included in the three well-known ancient lists provided below, but the lists are not exhaustive. Some of these writings are listed along with the manuscripts in which they are found in the standard work of Joseph van Haelst and the subsequent additions to his work now posted on the Web.[5]

In the well-known work commonly referred to as the *Stichometry of Nicephoris* (ca. 806–815 CE),[6] the author lists the following titles of Old Testament apocryphal books along with the lines of text in each book:

Enoch	4,800
Patriarchs	5,100
Prayer of Joseph	1,100
Testament of Moses	1,100
Assumption of Moses	1,400
Abraham	300
Eldad and Modad	400
Of Elias the Prophet	316
Of Sophonias the Prophet	600
Of Zacharias the father of John	500

Pseudepigrapha of Baruch, Ambacum (Habakkuk), Ezekiel, and Daniel (no lines indicated)

Besides this, the *Sixty Books*,[7] which refers to the canonical books, lists the apocryphal books without the *stichoi* (or lines) as follows:

Adam

Enoch

Lamech

Patriarchs

Prayer of Joseph

Eldad and Modad

Testament of Moses

Psalms of Solomon

Apocalypse of Elias (Elijah)

Vision of Esaias (Isaiah)

Apocalypse of Sophonias (Zephaniah)

Apocalypse of Zacharias (Zechariah)

Apocalypse of Esdras

Along with these two lists of ancient apocryphal and pseudepigraphal books is the Latin list that is best known as the *Gelasian Decree* (or *Decretum Gelasianum*, ca. 492–496) "concerning books to be received and not to be received" (Latin *De libris recipiendis et non recipiendis*). Attributed to Pope Gelasius, this decree states which books are approved for reading in the churches and which are not. It omits mentioning Enoch and adds several other uncommon names:

The book, concerning the daughters of Adam, of Leptogenesis

The book which is called the Penitence of Adam

The book concerning the Giant Ogias who is stated by the heretics to have fought with a dragon after the Flood

The book which is called the Testament of Job

The book which is called the Penitence of Jannes and Mambres

The writing which is called the Interdiction (or Contradiction) of Solomon

Besides these three collections of apocryphal books, the Armenian lists collected by Theodor Zahn in 1893 have three other shorter collections:

A. Samuel of Ani (ca. 1179) speaks of books brought to Armenia around 591 CE by Nestorian missionaries, and they include *The Penitence of Adam* and *The Testament* (probably of Moses or Adam).

B. Mechithar of Airivank (ca. 1290 CE) lists writings similar to those in Greek under the title of *Secret Books of the Jews*:

> Book of Adam
> Book of Enoch
> Book of the Sybil
> The Twelve Patriarchs (= testaments of the twelve sons of Jacob)
> The Prayers of Joseph
> The Ascension of Moses
> Eldad and Modad
> The Psalms of Solomon
> The Mysteries of Elias
> The Seventh Vision of Daniel[8]

C. A second list under the same writer's name and dated 1085 CE mixes some of the apocryphal books with the canon of the Old Testament in the Roman Catholic and Orthodox churches, as the following shows:

> The Vision of Enoch
> The Testaments of the Patriarchs
> The Prayers of Aseneth (takes the place of the *Prayer of Joseph*)
> Tobit, Judith, and Esther
> Esdras Salathiel (= 4 Ezra)
> The Paralipomena concerning Jeremiah in Babylon (= the Rest of the Words of Baruch)
> Deaths of the Prophets (a version of the Pseudo-Epiphanian, *Lives of the Prophets*)
> Jesus son of Sirach

Besides the above, other writings have occurred in later lists under the names of Moses, Eve, Seth, Noah, Ham, Melchizedek, Hezekiah, and the ancient Persian king Hystaspes.[9] Along with the ancient books that we know about through various ancient sources, including the early church fathers, especially through the fourth century, there were probably many others of which we are unaware that were produced and functioned as sacred literature in one or more Jewish and Christian communities.

QUMRAN MANUSCRIPTS

With the discovery of the Dead Sea Scrolls, knowledge of the biblical text has been moved back almost a thousand years, and at Qumran just over half of the biblical manuscripts follow a proto-Masoretic consonantal text. One of the reasons why the Masoretic Text survived, in the words of Emanuel Tov, is because "those who fostered it probably constituted the only organized group which survived the destruction of the Second Temple."[10] The scrolls discovered at Qumran let us know, however, that a number of ancient texts of the Jewish scriptures were circulating in the first centuries BCE and CE. What is the significance of these finds? The apparent absence of Esther and Nehemiah from the Qumran collection may not be as important as earlier thought, for only one small fragment of the larger book of Chronicles was found at Qumran.[11] What was discovered in and around Qumran cannot be affirmed to be a complete library of what was actually stored there, for the residents made no list of what they stored, and we do not know if one day another cave will be discovered with many more ancient manuscripts. Therefore, a certain amount of caution is necessary before making strong statements about the contents of the Qumran library. Because of this uncertainty, it is wise to soften conclusions about what was not found there.

Even though all but two Hebrew Bible/Old Testament books were found at Qumran, this does not mean that the Qumran community had the same biblical canon as the Pharisees and the later rabbis in the second century CE who were responsible for fixing the number and contents of the biblical books in the current Hebrew Bible. As noted already, other religious manuscripts discovered at Qumran outnumber the manuscripts that were later included in the rabbinic Bible, the Hebrew Bible. F. F. Bruce incorrectly argues, "It is probable, indeed, that by the beginning of the Christian era the Essenes (including the Qumran community) were in substantial agreement with the Pharisees and Sadducees about the limits of Hebrew scripture."[12] Roger Beckwith similarly argues that the presence of all the Old Testament canonical books at Qumran, save Esther (he does not mention Nehemiah's absence), points to the acceptance in that community essentially of the same biblical canon as the one found in Pharisaic Judaism and later identified and promoted in rabbinic Judaism.[13] However, the discovery of parallels with Pharisaic Judaism in some of the books found at Qumran does not support the conclusion that they utilized the same biblical canon. The Qumran texts include considerably more than the Old Testament canonical books, and this suggests that the Essene collection of sacred texts was considerably broader than the current Old Testament biblical canon. In fact, more nonbiblical writings were discovered at Qumran than biblical ones.[14] Beckwith concludes that the Qumran community accepted as Scripture only the canonical writings of the Old Testament, though he concedes that the Essenes excluded Esther for reasons related to the Jewish calendar. Oddly, however, he claims that essentially all the other books found at Qumran, whether books dealing with legal matters or prophetic texts, were simply commentary or interpretations of Scriptures—and even "revealed interpretation" of the biblical books. VanderKam challenges Beckwith's view that *Jubilees* and *1 Enoch* were simply commentary or interpretation of canonical books and argues that they were presented as new revelations. For example, *1 Enoch* 72:1 states that the contents of *1 Enoch* 72–82 (the so-called Astronomical Book or Book of Heavenly Luminaries) were revealed to the writer by the angel Uriel, and in *Jubilees* 6:29–35 a special calendar is traced to "heavenly tablets":

> And they set them upon the heavenly tablets. Each one of them in thirteen weeks from one to another of the remembrances, from the first to the second, and from the second to the third, and from the third to the fourth. And all of the days which will be commanded will be fifty-two weeks of days, and all of them are a complete year. Thus it is engraved and ordained on the heavenly tablets, and there is no transgressing in a single year, from year to year.[15]

VanderKam appropriately asks of Beckwith which Old Testament texts the author of *Jubilees* or *1 Enoch* is citing or alluding to in these passages.[16] While these books make some allusions to the Old Testament Scriptures, the majority of their contents have no discernible reference to biblical books. This leads VanderKam to ask: "What is the writer of the Astronomical Book interpreting?"[17] Again, I must underscore that at Qumran nonbiblical texts were discovered right beside the biblical books with no discernible way of distinguishing between them.

A recent publication, in all other ways an excellent piece of work, illustrates my point about misleading information about the Dead Sea Scrolls. Abegg, Flint, and Ulrich's *Dead Sea Scrolls Bible* contains a useful translation of a select number of writings found at Qumran, but it is not exhaustive of the literature found there, nor does it offer an adequate rationale for the literature selected—or omitted. The title of the book is misleading and simply hype, since the volume in no way represents a "Bible" at Qumran.[18] The term "Bible" suggests both a selected and limited collection of books that were placed side by side to form the stabilized scriptures of a religious community. The title of this volume suggests that contrary to all the evidence that the authors themselves supply, a "Bible" was discovered at Qumran, namely, the books identified in their volume and no others. That is not the case, however, for though Abegg, Flint, and Ulrich do include *Jubilees, 1 Enoch*, some noncanonical psalms, Sirach, Epistle of Jeremiah, and Tobit, they omit without explanation *Temple Scroll, Rule of the Community, Damascus Document, Book of the Giants, 4 Enoch, Book of Noah, Books of the Patriarchs*, and many others. The authors are rightly more comfortable with the term "scriptures" than with "Bible," but the reader might overlook the brief comments in their introduction.[19] In any case, the title is misleading, for it ignores that little or nothing distinguishes the books that eventually became part of the Hebrew Bible from the books that did not. No evidence of canonical activity at Qumran justifies the word "Bible" in their title. Elsewhere, Ulrich clarifies his views on the "Bible" at Qumran, and I agree fully with his position on the status of the biblical canon during the time of the Qumran community's existence: I do not think that "the Bible" in our modern sense (whether Jewish, Protestant, Catholic, or any other) of a complete, fixed, and closed collection of books of Scripture existed as such in the Second Temple period. There is sufficient and sufficiently broad reference to "the Scriptures" or "the Law and the Prophets" to ensure that there were certainly sacred scriptures at the end of the

Second Temple period, but the point would have to be demonstrated that "the Bible" as such was an identifiable reality at that time.[20]

Neusner also claims that the Essene community had a much wider collection of sacred scriptures than did other Jews in Israel. He acknowledges that the Essenes' library at Qumran encompassed a diverse group of writings, surely received as authoritative and holy, that "other Jews did not know within their canon." We have no evidence that the relation to the canon of Scripture of the *Manual of Discipline*, the *Hodayot* (Hymns of Thanksgiving),[21] the *War Scroll*, the *Damascus Covenant*, or others perplexed the teacher of righteousness and the other holy priests of the Essene community. To the contrary, these documents at Qumran appear side by side with the ones we now know as canonical Scripture.[22]

Some of the apocryphal and pseudepigraphal literature influenced early Christianity, and in several cases was acknowledged as Scripture. Whether or not one acknowledges this literature as sacred Scripture today, it is important that the church have some understanding of it. Besides their frequent witness to the authority of the Old Testament books as well as their frequent imitation of them, the use of this literature demonstrates the early church's interest in the major Old Testament figures (e.g., Adam, Enoch, Moses, and Elijah) and also the continuity of faith between the Testaments. M. de Jonge is certainly correct when he claims that "because Christians were convinced of the continuity in God's revelation through the great figures of the 'Old Testament' and through Jesus Christ and his apostles, the distinction between 'Jewish' and 'Christian' was for them only of relative importance."[23]

The above comments and observations argue for various notions of scripture and canon in the Judaism sects of the first century CE that differed from those that existed in later rabbinic and Christian traditions. There is no direct evidence that Christianity borrowed any Essene view, but some Essene influence may be detected in Jesus' understanding of poverty and divorce.[24]

A number of religious texts not included in the HB or most Christian biblical canons were quoted, alluded to, and even referred to as having considerable religious authority among the Essenes at Qumran. These include the book of *Jubilees* (cf. reference to it in the Damascus Document, CD X, 9–10 = *Jub.* 23:1; cf. also CD XVI, 2–4, and elsewhere in 4Q228).[25] In 4QTestimonia there are quotations not only of Exodus (20:21b), Deuteronomy (5:28b–29; 18:18–19; 33:8–11), and Numbers (24:15–17), but also of the *Apocryphon of Joshua* (4QTest 21–23 = 4Q379 22:7–15). In 4Q247 (= 4QPesher on the Apocalypse of Weeks) there is a commentary on the Apocalypse of Weeks (*1 Enoch* 93; 91:12–17). The Damascus Document also alludes to the Book of Watchers (CD II, 17–19). In 1QSa I, 6–7; CD X, 6; XIII, 6–8 there is a reference to the vision of Enosh (4Q417 I, I 16).[26] It is also worth noting that half of the large scrolls at Qumran are nonbiblical.[27]

What to make of all of this is complex, but Armin Lange goes so far as to say that the Qumran covenanters "recognized, in addition to the Pentateuch, the Former and Latter Prophets, the Psalter, Proverbs, Job, Lamentations and Daniel, the following compositions as authoritative: Enochic writings, the Aramaic *Levi Document*, the *Book of Jubilees*, the *Apocryphon of Joshua*, and the *Book of Hugo*." He adds that he does *not* think that the Essenes at Qumran viewed Canticles, Qohelet, Ruth, Esther, Ezra, Nehemiah, and 1–2 Chronicles as scripture.[28] The collection of sacred scriptures of the Essenes at Qumran differed considerably from those finally adopted by the rabbis of the second century and later who decided the scope of the Hebrew Bible.

EARLY CHRISTIAN OLD TESTAMENT MANUSCRIPTS

Of the various Christian biblical manuscripts discovered in antiquity, those most valuable for establishing the earliest text of the biblical books are papyrus manuscripts that date from the second to roughly the seventh century CE. Only two for sure date as early as the second century (P^{52} and P^{90}), both of which are small portions of the Gospel of John, and most of the manuscripts are fragmentary, but they do show the earliest form of the biblical text circulating in Christian churches. For our purposes here, namely discovering the books in these manuscripts, the papyri manuscripts are not as valuable as the later (fourth–ninth centuries CE) uncial manuscripts produced on parchment. These manuscripts were developed when it was possible to include all the books of the Bible in one volume; consequently they allow us more certainty on which books informed the faith of the churches at that time. There is still considerable value in examining the contents of the papyrus manuscripts, and we will consider them first to see what books are in them, and then we will look at some of the best-preserved uncial manuscripts that often include the whole of the Christian scriptures. The papyrus manuscripts are much more valuable in establishing an earlier form of the biblical text than in showing which sacred books informed the early Christian churches. Remarkably, very few of these *Christian* Old Testament manuscripts predate the fourth century, despite the fact that the Jewish Scriptures formed the core scriptures of the earliest Christian churches.

Early Papyrus Manuscripts

We will now focus on the text of the Jewish Scriptures, the Hebrew Bible. Bastiaan Van Elderen has referred to some early collections of Christian scriptures that also included the Old Testament scriptures of the early Christians. Their value has to be tempered by the fact that these collections are quite fragmentary and do not tell the whole story from their generation. The first of these collections that includes both Old Testament and New Testament books is the famous Chester Beatty papyri that were found in the Nile Valley and purchased by Chester Beatty in the 1930s. Most of this collection is housed at the Chester Beatty Library and Museum of Oriental Art in Dublin, but some pages of the collection (thirty leaves from P^{46}, the earliest collection of the Letters of Paul) are located at the Hatcher Library of the University of Michigan in Ann Arbor,

Michigan. They were found in the vicinity of At'fih (ancient Aphroditopolis) on the east side of the Nile near Fayyum. Citing C. H. Roberts, Van Elderen indicates some shared parallels with another collection of ancient manuscripts, the Bodmer papyri (see below). Among the various books in the Chester Beatty collection are several Old Testament books, including Genesis, Numbers, Deuteronomy, Isaiah, Jeremiah, Ezekiel, Esther, Daniel, as well as Sirach, *1 Enoch*, and a homily by Melito.[29] Van Elderen observes that these various manuscripts are combined in a single codex dating around 200 CE and that they predate by almost 150 years the earliest known uncial parchment biblical manuscripts of the middle to late fourth century.[30]

While he mentions the Nag Hammadi papyri, Van Elderen observes that there are no biblical texts in this collection, even if those who made use of these writings acknowledged them in an authoritative manner. Because all of the texts in this collection had their origin in a sect of the Christian community, they will be included later in our discussion of the collections of Christian manuscripts.

The other more significant collection of ancient Christian Old Testament manuscripts is the Bodmer papyri collection. In the early 1950s a large and impressive collection of Greek and Coptic manuscripts were discovered in Upper Egypt and acquired by Martin Bodmer. They are now housed in the Bodmer Library, which in 1954 published two rolls (scrolls) containing the *Iliad* (books 5 and 6), then the rest periodically over a number of years. They are now housed in six locations (the Chester Beatty Library in Dublin, the Palau-Ribes Collection in Barcelona, Duke University, the Vatican Library, the University of Mississippi, and the University of Cologne, Germany). It is not clear that all of these papyri are from the same collection since they include many non-Christian and non-Jewish ancient texts. The biblical texts may come from one single collection that was later grouped with the rest, but that is not certain. It is likely that they were discovered in Panopolis (Achmim), but James M. Robinson has suggested that the find was actually in Wadi Sheikh Ali near Abu Mana, some seven miles east of Jebel et-Tarif. This suggests that the Bodmer papyri were found in the same general location as the Nag Hammadi Library. Van Elderen lists the following among the Old Testament books, or fragments of books: Genesis, Exodus, Deuteronomy, Joshua, Psalms, Proverbs, Song of Songs, Isaiah, Jeremiah (plus Lamentations, Epistle of Jeremiah, and Baruch 1–5), Daniel, Jonah, Susanna, Tobit, 2 Maccabees, and the 11th *Ode of Solomon*.[31]

Uncial Biblical Manuscripts

The most important ancient biblical manuscripts that emerge in the fourth and fifth centuries are the codices Vaticanus (02), Sinaiticus (01), and Alexandrinus (03).[32] What makes them highly significant is that for the first time in the fourth century the technology for producing books or codices was advanced sufficiently to include more than 1,600 pages in one parchment volume. This allowed the church to include both its Old or First Testament scriptures and those of the

New Testament. While there is much that we do not know about these earliest uncial manuscripts (precise date, place of origin, and function in early Christianity), they are still our oldest witnesses to the state of the biblical text at that time, and the books that they contain also inform us about the scope of the earliest Christian Bibles. They contain not only the so-called biblical books (HB), but also some apocryphal or nonbiblical books, and these volumes served as sacred scripture in the communities that had them. Each of the manuscripts is important in shedding light on the collections of sacred texts that informed the faith of some Christian communities in the fourth and fifth centuries.

> Codex Vaticanus (ca. 350 CE): Genesis, Exodus, Leviticus, Numbers, Deuteronomy, Joshua, Judges, Ruth, 1–4 Kingdoms (1–2 Samuel and 1–2 Kings), 1–2 Chronicles, 1–2 Esdras, Psalms, Proverbs, Ecclesiastes, Song of Solomon, Job, Wisdom, Sirach, Esther, Judith, Tobit, the Twelve (Hosea, Amos, Micah, Joel, Obadiah, Jonah, Nahum, Habakkuk, Zephaniah, Haggai, Zechariah, Malachi), Isaiah, Jeremiah, Baruch, Lamentations, Epistle of Jeremiah, Ezekiel, Daniel. Note also the order of these books.

> Codex Sinaiticus (ca. 350–400 CE): Genesis, . . . Numbers, . . . 1 Chronicles, 2 Esdras, Esther, Tobit, Judith, 1 Maccabees, 4 Maccabees, Isaiah, Jeremiah, Lamentations, . . . Joel, Obadiah, Jonah, Nahum, Habakkuk, Zephaniah, Malachi, Psalms, Proverbs, Ecclesiastes, Song of Songs, Wisdom of Solomon, Sirach.

> Codex Alexandrinus (fifth century CE): Genesis, Exodus, Leviticus, Numbers, Deuteronomy, Joshua, Judges, Ruth, 1–4 Kingdoms, 1–2 Chronicles, Hosea, Amos, Micah, Joel, Obadiah, Jonah, Nahum, Habakkuk, Zephaniah, Haggai, Zechariah, Malachi, Isaiah, Jeremiah, Baruch, Lamentations, Epistle of Jeremiah, Ezekiel, Daniel, Esther, Tobit, Judith, 1–2 Esdras, 1–4 Maccabees, Psalms, Odes of Solomon, Job, Proverbs, Ecclesiastes, Song of Solomon, Wisdom of Solomon, Sirach.[33]

THE SAMARITAN BIBLE

Many of the Jews who survived the 721 BCE Assyrian invasion of the northern tribes of Israel and the capture of its capital, Samaria, subsequently intermarried with the Assyrians and became known as "Samaritans." They were generally despised by the Jews, who tended to view them as despised disloyal half-breeds and rejected their participation in the life of the nation and its temple cult. After the devastation of the nation that began in 596/595 BCE and concluded with the subsequent destruction of the temple and deportation of the people in 587/586, the only thing that remained for the Jews who returned to Judah after more than fifty years of exile was a story about their heritage, including their experience with Yahweh.[34] They had concluded that the destruction of their homeland and temple was due to their own failure to keep their covenant with Yahweh.

The school of interpretation that began with Ezra added a new focus on the Law and its practical implications in the lives of the Jewish people. After renewing their covenant with God (Ezra 10:1–5; Neh. 7:73–9:38), they rebuilt the temple under Zerubbabel by around 515 BCE (Hag. 1–2; Zech. 1–8) and then rebuilt the walls around the city no later than approximately 445–443 BCE. During the rebuilding of the walls, the Jews met with opposition from Sanballat, the governor of Samaria (Neh 4:1–7; cf. 2 Kgs. 17:29).[35] This is the first time the Samaritans are mentioned by name. Later, by the first century BCE, the Jews generally viewed the Samaritans with disdain (John 4:4–12, 19) and as natural enemies. The point of Jesus' parable of the Good Samaritan (Luke 10:25–37)—that his disciples are to be good neighbors even to their natural enemies—is emphasized by long-standing Samaritan-Jewish antagonism. The Samaritans built their own temple on Mount Gerizim around 330 BCE, but John Hyrcanus, the Hasmonean king (ca. 128–125 BCE), destroyed the temple, although not the Samaritans' devotion to Mount Gerizim. The period of Persian domination of Palestine (ca. 532–330 BCE) was often turbulent for the Samaritans, but in comparison with the time of the Seleucid domination (198–142 BCE) it was relatively peaceful. Evidence for the upheaval during this period may be recorded in Zechariah 9–14, which some scholars place between 330 BCE and 150 BCE since in 9:13 the rise of the Greeks had already occurred.

What is most important for our purposes is that the Samaritans adopted as their scripture what became known as the Samaritan Pentateuch, which has many variations not found in the Masoretic Text (MT). Some 1,900 similarities between the Septuagint and the Samaritan Pentateuch are not found in the MT. There is no specific information that they ever adopted as Scripture any other books of the Hebrew Bible. It is likely that the limited biblical canon of the Samaritans was adopted in the fifth–fourth century BCE, when the Jews themselves acknowledged as scripture only the Pentateuch. Immediately after the reforms of Ezra and Nehemiah, only the Law of Moses functioned as scripture among the Jews, and the Samaritans had a version of the Pentateuch when they separated from the Jews. This is not to suggest that the Samaritans copied and modified the Jews' scriptures. On the contrary, it is likely that they had an earlier version of the Law than what was eventually accepted by the Jews in their scripture collection. Eugene Ulrich observes remarkable parallels between several texts in the Dead Sea Scrolls Pentateuch and the Samaritan Pentateuch against the MT, and this, he claims, argues for an earlier and separate text of the Pentateuch.[36]

While these two forms of the Pentateuch have much material that overlaps, several textual variations may indicate two literary editions of an earlier Pentateuch. Certainly, the Samaritans considered their Pentateuch to be the authoritative form of the text. For example, the MT of Deuteronomy 27:4–5 says that after the Jews cross the Jordan River, they are to build an altar to the Lord on Mount Ebal, but the Samaritan Pentateuch of the same passage, which may well be the earlier text, says that it is to be built on Mount Gerizim.[37]

On the other hand, the Samaritan Pentateuch adds to the Decalogue a command to build an altar on Mount Gerizim. The Samaritans did not see themselves as a sect of Judaism, but rather as the community that interpreted the Mosaic tradition more accurately, unlike the other Jewish sects that wrongly promoted Jerusalem as the religious center of God. According to J. D. Purvis, the Samaritans may be understood as a "variety of Judaism," since both the Samaritans and the Jews saw themselves as the faithful "carriers of Israel's sacred traditions."[38] The division between Jews and Samaritans so well known in the New Testament was discussed later among the rabbinic sages, who saw the Samaritans as ritually unclean (*m. Niddah* 4:1), and asserted that they made unacceptable offerings to God (*m. Berak* 7:1), did not observe the holy days properly (*b. Rosh Hashanah* 22b), and could not be relied on to give a reliable witness (*m. Gittin* 1:5). A question about when the Samaritans would be acceptable to the Jews is answered in the Babylonian Talmud: "When they renounce Mount Gerizim, and confess Jerusalem and the resurrection of the Dead," which is the conclusion of the *Masseket Kutim.*[39] Although other writings are found in the Samaritan collection of ancient literature, only the Pentateuch is canonized and read in all services of worship. B. K. Waltke says that one of the important features of the Samaritan Pentateuch for canonical criticism is that it bears witness to texts being adapted to meet the needs of the living community and "assisted the Samaritans in preserving themselves as a unified community for over two millennia."[40] Emanuel Tov observes that while acknowledging the antiquity of this biblical text—it was in many cases earlier than the MT—the Samaritans also modified the text for their sectarian purposes in various locations.[41]

SACRED BOOKS IN THE RABBINIC TRADITION

While writing an apology on behalf of Jews in the late first century, Josephus spoke of a limited number of twenty-two sacred Jewish books, which is also the number of the letters of the Hebrew alphabet:[42] "it follows, I say, that we do not possess myriads of inconsistent books, conflicting with each other. Our books, those which are *justly accredited* (Greek *dikaios pepisteumena*), are but two and twenty, and contain the record of all time" (*Ag. Ap.* 1:37–38, LCL, italics added). What he meant by "justly accredited" may be close to the notion of a recognized biblical canon. How widely recognized his, or any other scripture collection, was at the end of the first century is unclear. I have argued elsewhere that Josephus's collection is difficult to identify since he only names types or genres of writings in his collection and the specific books he refers to were not as widely recognized as he claims. Several scholars agree that Josephus was speaking apologetically and that he overstated his case.[43] There is no evidence that his views were widely held by fellow Jews in his own generation or for a considerable time thereafter. There is more hyperbole in his arguments than the known facts of that time warrant.

The criteria that were consciously or unconsciously used to establish the Jewish biblical canon are unclear, and there is no unanimity among scholars on the matter. Some ancient Jewish texts teach that writings were excluded because they were written after the time when some believed prophecy had ceased in Israel, namely after Artaxerxes (ca. 350–330 BCE). The author of 1 Maccabees, for instance, claimed that no prophetic ministry was present in Israel (1 Macc. 9:27; 14:41). Josephus, writing near the end of the first century CE, used the dating of a book as a criterion for including or excluding it from his scripture collection. He contended that any books written after the time of Artaxerxes, more precisely after the time of Ezra, are not included in the sacred Jewish writings (*Ag. Ap.* 1.39–41). Similarly, in the rabbinic tradition Sirach was rejected because "the books of Ben Sira [Sirach] and all books written thenceforward do not impart uncleanness to hands" (*t. Yadayim* 2:13, Neusner trans. 2:1907; cf. also *t. Shabbat* 13:5).[44] In Tosefta we read: "When the latter prophets died, that is, Haggai, Zechariah, and Malachi, then the Holy Spirit came to an end in Israel" (*t. Sotah* 13:3). The notion that prophecy had ceased in Israel, however, was not uniformly held in the time of Jesus, even though some ancient texts make the claim.[45] It is important to remember here that the sacredness of several Hebrew Bible books was questioned later, and other religious books, especially Wisdom of Solomon and Sirach, that were not later included in the Hebrew Bible were used and cited as scripture in the rabbinic tradition for a time.

Some ancient Jewish writings were apparently rejected because of the language used in their production. Some rabbis contended that only those writings originally composed in Hebrew and Aramaic were approved. While it was permitted to translate the Torah into another language, Hebrew and Aramaic were always preferred. Some Jews even argued that the Torah could not be translated adequately. For example, there is a negative reference to the translation of the Torah into Greek: "It is related that five elders wrote the Torah in Greek for King Ptolemy. And that day was as intolerable for Israel as the day the golden calf was made, for the Torah cannot be translated adequately" (*Massekhet Soferim*, 1). In the second century CE, translations of books of Scripture, other than the Pentateuch, were not to be used. For example, "Rabbi Judah said: Even when our masters allowed the use of Greek, they allowed it only for the scroll of Torah, and that came about because of the action taken by King Ptolemy" (*b. Megillah* 8b–9a; see also *Gen. Rab.* 36:8; *Deut. Rab.* 1:1). Notice the following permission: "Sacred writings, even if written in another language, must be put away properly [when they become unfit for use]. . . . *Even if they are written in any language, though they may not be read [publicly]*, yet he [the *tanna*] teaches that they may be saved" (*b. Shabbat* 115a, Soncino trans., emphasis added). This preference for the Hebrew language eventually isolated Jews in the western Diaspora from the religious traditions of their fellow Jews in the eastern Diaspora.

The regular practice of the Jewish religion in the Diaspora to read their scriptures in the Greek language is more important here for our purposes. While the initial translation of the Hebrew scriptures into Greek included only the Pentateuch, in time, and certainly by the time when the grandson of Sirach translated his book (see Prologue, Sirach) around 130 BCE, the Law, the Prophets, and other books were also included in this collection. While it is not clear exactly when or how the translation of the rest of the Jewish scriptures took place, the translations were united into a whole and generally received by Jews in the Diaspora as their sacred scriptures. The various Greek translations of Jewish scriptures were used in Jewish worship in the Diaspora.[46] The implications of this are quite significant in terms of the scriptures that they read in their synagogues. The Greek scriptures contained more books than did the later Hebrew Bible, and the use of these scriptures, including the apocryphal and pseudepigraphal books in the Greek scriptures, continued among the Jews for centuries, especially among Jews in the western Diaspora.

What scriptures informed the faith of early Judaism, namely the faith of Second Temple Judaism (roughly from the decree of Cyrus to allow the Jews to return to Judah from Babylon in 538 BCE to the destruction of Jerusalem and the Jewish temple in 70 CE), sometimes called "formative Judaism," and the first two centuries CE? There is evidence that from the beginning of Second Temple Judaism there was a resurgence of commitment by the Jews to live in accord with the Law of Moses (Neh. 8:1–8; 2 Kgs. 17:13). In time, many Jews were also informed by other sacred texts that came to be called the "prophets," which may or may not be equivalent to the collection now known as the Prophets. There is evidence that the collection of the Twelve (the Minor Prophets) were circulating together by around 200–180 BCE (Sirach).

Some writings were initially and in some cases permanently rejected by the Jews because they were regarded as heretical documents (see *m. Sanhedrin* 10:1; *t. Yadayim* 2:13; *t. Shabbat* 13:5 A-F), or secular in nature (Song of Songs and Esther, the only two biblical books where the name of God does not appear, and Ecclesiastes; cf. *m. Yadayim* 3:5; 4:1–3). According to Rabbi Aqiba, the one "who reads apocryphal books, such as the books of Ben Sira and the books of Ben Laanah, has no portion in the world-to-come" (*y. Sanhedrin* 10:1, 28a).

The oldest mention of a three-part canon among the Jews that specifically identifies the scriptures that constituted the Hebrew Bible comes from Babylon and dates around 140–150 CE. It is in a *baraita*, that is, an *external* text presumably produced by the Tannaim but not included in the Mishnah. It is worthwhile presenting this famous though lengthy text.

> Our Rabbis taught: the order of the Prophets is, Joshua, Judges, Samuel, Kings, Jeremiah, Ezekiel, Isaiah, and the twelve Minor Prophets. Let us examine this. Hosea came first, as it is written (Hosea 1:2): *God spoke first to Hosea*. But did God speak first to Hosea? Were there not many prophets between Moses and Hosea? R. Johanan (250–290), however, has explained that [what it means is that] he was the first of the four prophets who prophesied at that period, namely, Hosea, Isaiah, Amos and Micah. Should not then Hosea come first?—Since his prophecy is written along with those of Haggai, Zechariah and Malachi, and Haggai, Zechariah and Malachi came at the end of the prophets, he is reckoned with them. But why should he not be written separately and placed first?—Since his book is so small, it might be lost [if copied separately]. Let us see again. Isaiah was prior to Jeremiah and Ezekiel. Then why should not Isaiah be placed first?—Since

his book is so small, it might be lost [if copied separately]. Because the book of Kings ends with a record of destruction and Jeremiah speaks throughout of destruction and Ezekiel commences with destruction and ends with consolation and Isaiah is full of consolation; therefore we put destruction next to destruction and consolation next to consolation. [Our Rabbis taught:] The order of the Hagiographa is Ruth, the book of Psalms, Job, Proverbs, Ecclesiastes, Song of Songs, Lamentations, Daniel and the Scroll of Esther, Ezra and Chronicles. Now on the view that Job lived in the days of Moses, should not the book of Job come first?—We do not begin with a record of suffering. But Ruth also is a record of suffering?—It is a suffering with a sequel [of happiness], as R. Johanan said: Why was her name called Ruth?— Because there issued from her David who replenished the Holy One, blessed be He, with hymns and praises.

Who wrote the Scriptures?—Moses wrote his own book and the portion of Balaam and Job. Joshua wrote the book which bears his name and [the last] eight verses of the Pentateuch. Samuel wrote the book which bears his name and the book of Judges and Ruth. David wrote the book of Psalms, including in it the work of the ten elders, namely Adam, Melchizedek, Abraham, Moses, Heman, Yeduthun, Asaph, and the three sons of Korah. Jeremiah wrote the book which bears his name, the book of Kings, and Lamentations. Hezekiah and his colleagues wrote . . . Isaiah, Proverbs, the Song of Songs and Ecclesiastes. The Men of the Great Assembly wrote . . . Ezekiel, the Twelve Minor Prophets, Daniel and the Scroll of Esther. Ezra wrote the book that bears his name and the genealogies of the book of Chronicles up to his own time. This confirms the opinion of Rab (220– 250), since Rab Judah (250–290) has said in the name of Rab: Ezra did not leave Babylon to go up to Eretz Yisrael until he had written his own genealogy. Who then finished it [the book of Chronicles]?—Nehemiah the son of Hachaliah. (*b. Baba Bathra* 14b–15a)[47]

Nothing before or during the time when this text was constructed suggests that its contents were popular or welcomed among Jews in the mid-second century CE. That it was not included in the Mishnah suggests that either it was not known or that it was not widely received by the end of the second century CE. Nevertheless, its list of sacred books is what was eventually accepted as the sacred books included in the Hebrew Bible. For that reason, it should not be dismissed as irrelevant even though it did not have a strong influence in the second century or before. It does suggest, however, that the notion of a fixed collection and the shape of that collection originated in Babylon.[48]

THE INFLUENCE OF NONCANONICAL BOOKS

The New Testament writers were clearly aware of these books and alluded to or specifically cited several of them in their discussions or descriptions. For instance, the author of John 10:22 refers to the "festival of the Dedication," which is found not in the Hebrew Scriptures but only in the Greek text of 1 Maccabees 4:59 and 2 Maccabees 10:18. Similarly, the author of Hebrews 1:3 uses precisely the technical terms for "wisdom" found in Wisdom of Solomon 7:25. Whatever else one can say about the apocryphal writings, it is clear that several of them informed the faith of the early Christian churches. There are many examples of parallels and even citations of this literature in early Christianity.[49] Hippolytus of Rome (ca. 180–200 CE) included sections of Susanna and the Song of the Three Jews in his *Commentary on Daniel*.

In early Christianity homilies, meditations, and liturgical forms were often based on the apocryphal books, which also provided inspiration for poets, dramatists, composers, and artists. It is interesting that although they did not accept the apocryphal writings on the same level as the canonical writings, Athanasius, Jerome, Martin Luther, and later Reformers continued to include them in the various translations of the Bible. They were initially included in the KJV, but subsequently dropped. The Westminster Confession of 1646 eliminated them from the Bible as did leaders in other Protestant groups, but this was not usually the case throughout most of church history to the present. The Church of England included them in their Bibles and made use of them in their lectionaries. The Roman Catholic Church included most of the Apocrypha as canonical Scripture, but eliminated 1 and 2 Esdras as well as the Prayer of Manasseh.[50] There has been a significant renewal of interest in the books that were eliminated in antiquity and also in the various criteria used to make the decisions.

In his introductory material to the NRSV translation of the apocryphal or deuterocanonical books, Bruce Metzger observes that even the discovery of the New World by Christopher Columbus in the late fifteenth century came from his reading a passage in 2 Esdras (6:42). Columbus reasoned that if only one-seventh of the earth's surface was covered with water, the distance between the coast of western Europe and the coast of eastern Asia could not be too distant. With a few good days of sailing, he thought that he could reach the eastern coast of Asia. After citing this text before Ferdinand and Isabella of Spain, he was granted financial support to begin his historic journey.

Metzger adds specifics on how this literature also affected English literature, including Shakespeare and Longfellow. In music, some of the words of the exalted hymn, *Now Thank We All Our God*, depend on Luther's translation of Sirach, and ideas that are included in *It Came upon the Midnight Clear* derive from the OT Apocrypha (observe that nothing is said in the NT writings about the exact time of Jesus' birth). Traces of the apocryphal names of Susanna (legendary figure from the time of Daniel), Judas Maccabee (fl. 165–160 BCE), as well as Alexander Balas (fl. 151–145 BCE), are found in Handel's famous oratorios. Similarly, significant numbers of Renaissance paintings display themes from the Apocrypha.[51]

While Luther rejected the apocryphal books as a basis for Christian doctrine, he did not eliminate them from his Bible. He strongly rejected 2 Maccabees since it was cited to support the Roman Catholic doctrine of purgatory (see 2 Macc. 12:39–45). The same seems true of most early Reformers and those who followed them. Those who constructed and those who accepted the Westminster Confession of 1646 appear to be the first Christians to explicitly reject them as part of their Christian biblical canon.

CONCLUSION

The manuscript evidence noted above shows that there was considerable over-lap in the texts that informed the faith of the early Jews of the Second Temple period as well as the early Christians. The Jewish scriptures were the sacred texts of the early Christian church. While there is considerable overlap in what is found in the various manuscripts and collections of books from antiquity, there are also a number of differences. A number of the noncanonical books that were widely used and circulating among the Jews also did the same among the early Christians. This is to be expected since the earliest Christians were one of the surviving Jewish sects who continued to frequent the Jewish synagogues until they were forced out following the Bar Kokhba rebellion against Rome (ca. 133–135 CE). In the following chapter I will focus on the text of the Jewish Scriptures in both Jewish and Christian manuscripts. I will show that there was considerable fluidity in the text of the Hebrew scriptures for centuries.

As Jewish sectarians, the early followers of Jesus would naturally be drawn to the Jewish scriptures as they were understood in the time of Jesus and until their separation from Judaism. Since we have no discussions before or during the time of Jesus on the scope of the Jewish scriptures, it is all the more important to consider the surviving evidence from antiquity to determine as best we can what writings were considered sacred among the Jews. This can be accomplished to some degree by examining the various texts that appear to have functioned as scripture in the various Jewish and Christian communities of the first century. Also, this is seen in the citations of various texts in the New Testament and the early church fathers, and from references to sacred texts in Philo, Josephus, the rabbinic tradition, and other Jewish traditions from the first century CE.

From all of these sources, we can see that collections existed prior to the time of Jesus and were loosely identified as Law and Prophets and in one New Testament text, "the law of Moses, the prophets, and the psalms" (Luke 24:44). What was in those collections is never spelled out precisely, so it is important to see what ancient texts are actually cited as scripture or sacred texts and what books circulated together among Jews and early Christians. As we will see below, there are many variations in the surviving Jewish and Christian collections. For example, the Jewish religious texts discovered at Qumran and elsewhere in the Judean Desert vary from those affirmed in the later rabbinic traditions, but also from those texts that circulated in the Septuagint, the primary Greek translation of the Hebrew scriptures.[52] There were also Christian texts that influenced early Christianity right from the beginning, and later additional texts were joined to the Gospels and Letters of Paul. Some of those additional writings were left behind and others were incorporated into the New Testament biblical canon.

It is common among scholars to discuss Judaism after the destruction in monolithic terms assuming that all Jews everywhere believed whatever was taught them by the rabbinic sages. This assumption lacks documentation, however, and it is not clear that only one strand of Judaism survived the destruction of Jerusalem and the Bar Kokhba rebellion of 132–135 CE. It is simply not the case that Josephus's claim that "no one has ventured either to add, or to remove, or alter a syllable" to the twenty-two-book collection that he espoused (*Ag. Ap.* 1:42). That was hyperbole enlisted to confute Apion's charges against the Jews in Alexandria. Likewise, although Josephus limited his collection to twenty-two books, reflecting the Hebrew alphabet, other Jews at the same time had a different perspective. While most Jews from the Land of Israel to those in the east as far as Babylon generally accepted the later rabbinic traditions that limited the sacred collection to the books that now make up the Hebrew Bible and the Protestant Old Testament canon, this was not the case among all Jews in the Land of Israel or in the western part of the Roman Empire for centuries to come. Indeed, there appears to have been a continental divide between the Jews in the east and those in the west, namely those Jews living in the Land of Israel and going east to Babylon versus those in the western Diaspora (west of the land of Israel with the exception of Jews living in Egypt). Indeed, it is difficult to demonstrate that those Jews living in the west even knew of the rabbinic traditions, including the Mishnah, the various midrashim, and the two Talmudim. There is no known rabbinic school in the west, and all the rabbinic traditions were produced in Hebrew and Aramaic but were not translated into Greek or Latin, the languages of Jews in the west.

It is not certain that the Jews in the western Diaspora regarded respectfully the decisions of the *nasi* or patriarchs in leadership over the Jews in the Land of Israel following the destruction of the temple in 70 CE. Later the Karaites, who may have been influenced by Jews in the west, did not accept the Mishnah or two Talmudim prepared by the rabbis in Babylon and the Land of Israel. Those Jews in the west generally could not read Hebrew or Aramaic, and since the Mishnah and Talmudim were not translated into Greek or Latin, those in the west would not have known those writings. There were no schools or yeshivot in the west that taught the traditions of the rabbinic sages or the *nasi*, and there is little evidence that the leaders in the east made more than sporadic and infrequent trips to visit Jews in the west. Those in the east were committed to the oral traditions (or Oral Torah), and those in the west were committed to the biblical traditions that derived from the Septuagint Bible that contained not only the books of the Hebrew Bible, but also the apocryphal and pseudepigraphal books that were rejected by the Jews in the Land of Israel and generally by those in the east, especially Babylon.

Further, all the books in the Hebrew Bible are not cited either by Jesus or the early church, or by the residents at Qumran. While the implications of this are a matter of debate, since Jesus and the writers of the New Testament cite texts in an ad hoc manner addressing specific situations, this is largely an argument from silence; the specific texts that most influenced them and were cited by them do not include all the books of the current Hebrew Bible. As I will show below, the books that Jesus cited in his ministry are essentially the same sacred books that the Essenes at Qumran cite. It is clear, however, that they would not have needed to cite all the texts that they believed were sacred if they were not considered relevant to their current topics of discussion, but this does suggest that certain books received priority among Jews in the time of Jesus.

In the following chapter I will focus more specifically on the scriptures or books that Jesus cited as well as those that were cited in the rest of the New Testament and early Christianity, and briefly discuss the various manuscripts that survive antiquity and what is actually in them. How did they function in the communities that had them? To what extent did the local churches follow the recommendations or decisions of the various council or synod meetings about lists or catalogues of sacred scriptures? What were some of the more popular books among the Jews that were *not* finally included in the Jewish biblical canon or the Protestant biblical canon, but are in other church canons? Since the church looked especially on a handful of sacred books more and essentially ignored other texts, did the early church have a canon within the canon in operation? Finally, what text was considered sacred among Jews and early Christians? Was it some proto-Masoretic text or the Septuagint or some other?

Chapter 5

Ancient Translations
of the Jewish Scriptures

INTRODUCTION

The Hebrew Scriptures were first translated into Greek, but subsequently into various other languages, especially after the birth of the church. An important question here is, what books were included in those early translations? As we have seen in our discussion of the Qumran community, there was more variety in the use of Jewish religious literature among Jews in the first centuries BCE and CE than what we find later in the rabbinic Hebrew Bible. This broader collection of Jewish religious literature that informed the faith of the Jews in the Land of Israel during late Second Temple Judaism (200 BCE to 100 CE) also appears to have informed the faith of the early Christians. This is especially true before the fourth-century move toward stabilization in the sacred collections of Jewish and Christian religious texts, but also after this time. The early fluidity in the biblical tradition in Second Temple Judaism was also common for several centuries in the early church. In what follows, I will focus on the translations of the Hebrew Bible/Old Testament Scriptures where this variety of sacred books is also found.

Religious communities in antiquity were reluctant to translate their sacred texts into another language since, as all biblical translators know, it is next to impossible make an exact equivalent translation of another language and there was concern over what might be lost in translation. Leaving sacred texts in their original languages was the norm, and significant interest in translating sacred texts into other languages was unusual. On the other hand, the Christian community seemed unconcerned if the words of Jesus were communicated in Greek, Aramaic, Syriac, Latin, or Hebrew. Indeed, they appear to have had little concern for conveying the exact words of Jesus (Latin *ipsissima verba*, "the very words").

Keeping sacred texts in a language that was no longer the lingua franca of the people for whom the sacred texts were produced was quite common not only among the Jewish people but also later among the Christians, as in the use of Latin in churches when most of the people no longer spoke that language. This practice allowed a limited number of persons (priests normally) to be the primary interpreters of those texts for the people, and this gave such persons a level of control over the religious activities of the people.[1] For a long time, the Catholic Church also maintained that all readings of Scripture in the churches would be in Latin, and the Orthodox churches did the same with Greek. Generally speaking, however, the early Christians zealously translated the teachings of Jesus and other Christian literature into various languages to enable their Gospel to spread more rapidly. It may also be that from the beginning the followers of Jesus wanted to distinguish themselves from their Jewish siblings and so they produced very little literature in Hebrew or Aramaic. In fact, almost no Christian literature in those languages has survived antiquity.[2]

THE SEPTUAGINT

By the early third century BCE (ca. 281–280 BCE), the Torah or Pentateuch was translated into Greek in the vicinity of Alexandria, Egypt. The *Letter of Aristeas*, while certainly legendary at many points regarding the supernatural nature of the translation, may well preserve some reliable information about the origins of this translation. I have noted elsewhere that while other Jewish literature may have been counted as authoritative among the Jews when the Torah was translated into Greek, it is instructive that the Pentateuch is all that was translated at that time, and this suggests that the other writings that were eventually recognized as sacred among the Jews had not reached that status by the beginning of the third century BCE.[3] The Septuagint[4] (LXX) was probably not the first Greek translation,[5] but was certainly the most prominent, and it became the standard Greek translation of the Jewish scriptures through the first century CE and even longer for Christians.

The oldest report of this translation is preserved in the legendary document known as the *Letter of Aristeas* (ca. 127–118 BCE[6]). It is clearly Jewish propaganda. The document may, however, retain some historical features surrounding the origin of the translation, namely that the translation was only of the Pentateuch, that it was produced in Alexandria, Egypt, and that it was based on Hebrew manuscripts and produced by translators from Jerusalem. The high priest Eleazar in Jerusalem may have sent them to the pharaoh, Ptolemy II Philadelphus (282–246 BCE), as the legend goes, because the pharaoh wanted to have a copy of every book in the world in his famous library, including a copy of the Jewish Law.

It is interesting that Alexander established a cult of Homer in Alexandria, and a recension of Homer's works were produced there under the direction of Zenodotus, Aristophanes of Byzantium, and Aristarchus, who compared the various versions of Homer's works and commented on the text with annotations that appear in the margins (scholia). Earlier Peisistratus, the "tyrant from Athens," reportedly employed seventy-two editors to produce a corrected edition of the works of Homer (*Iliad* and *Odyssey*) with the goal of putting them in perfect condition. Until that time (ca. 550–525 BCE), Homer's works were lost or destroyed by fire or victim of some other disaster,[7] so they were largely circulating orally in song and by memory. This tradition is generally cited by the citizens of Pergamum to advance their standing in the ancient world, but several scholars contend that this tradition was legitimate; it was largely ignored by the grammarians in Alexandria mainly for rivalry reasons, namely to lay claim to the authoritative text of Homer.[8]

The Greek translation of the Pentateuch is more consistent than the rest of the books in the LXX, and it is likely that a different translator or group of translators translated each book of the Pentateuch, since the style varies considerably from book to book.[9] Outside the Pentateuch, no two books appear to have been translated by the same person. While some of the books are more literal in translation, Ernst Würthwein observes that Daniel and Job are among the freer or less literal translations. The Greek version of Jeremiah lacks some 2,700 words that are in the Hebrew Bible and the order of the text varies as well. This may also support the view of some that the Hebrew *Vorlage* of the LXX is older than the proto-Masoretic text of the Hebrew Bible. He concludes that the LXX is not a single version, but rather a "collection of versions made by various writers who differed greatly in their translation methods, their knowledge of Hebrew, their styles, and in other ways."[10]

We should add here that collections of scriptures among Jews and Christians differ in terms of their titles, number of books, and arrangement or order, even though there is considerable overlap in the text of the books themselves. The text of the Hebrew Bible varies considerably also from the chapters and verses found in Christian Bibles. Jews have a three-part biblical canon (Law, Prophets, and Writings); Christians have at least four and sometimes five major parts in theirs (Pentateuch, History, Poetry, Wisdom, Prophets). Protestants who recognize the value of the Apocrypha generally include these books between the Old Testament and New Testament books in a separate collection, unlike the Roman Catholic and Eastern Orthodox, who include the apocryphal/deuterocanonical books among the other Old Testament books.

Scholars have observed the parallels between the legendary origins of the LXX according to the *Letter of Aristeas* and the Peisistratus (or Peisistratean) Recension of writings of Homer (*Iliad* ca. 750 BCE, and *Odyssey* ca. 725 BCE). The latter is described in the Scholia to Dionysius Thrax (ca. 170–90 BCE), a student of Aristarchus who edited this recension.[11] The legendary scholia probably date from the third or fourth century CE and may depend in several details on the *Letter of Aristeas* and the tradition of the LXX. For example, the number of elders appointed as editors of Homer (seventy-two) is the same as the number of translators of the Hebrew scriptures into Greek. But scholars are not clear which tradition came first. Peisistratus commissioned some "seventy-two" grammarians, later guided by Zenodotos of Ephesus (ca. early third century BCE) and Aristarchus of Samothrace (ca. 216–144 BCE), whose apparatus of critical signs for reconstructing original texts were later used by Origen (ca. 185–254 CE) in his famous Hexapla. Origen produced a synopsis of parallel columns of texts of the Old Testament scriptures to try to show the variants in the current Hebrew and Greek texts of the Old Testament with the goal of correcting the many textual traditions current in his day. Zenodotos, Aristophanes, and Aristarchus all lived in Alexandria centuries after Peisistratus and in succession took responsibility for the library at Alexandria. They produced an authoritative text of Homer.

The challenge of Peisistratus appointing seventy-two grammarians to edit and produce an authoritative text of Homer's *Iliad* and *Odyssey* earlier adds to the legendary nature of the tradition. Nevertheless, the tradition of a corrected collection of the writings of Homer in the Alexandrian library primarily under the direction of Aristarchus in particular may well have been a model for the author of the *Letter of Aristeas* who wanted to show the relationship between restoring the lost text of Homer to that of the construction of a perfect Greek text of the Torah in Alexandria—or vice versa. In its current form, the legend of Homer appears to depend on the *Letter of Aristeas*, but some elements of that tradition may have influenced the legends surrounding the origins of the LXX. Earlier translations of the LXX were likely deemed inferior and were in need of revision.[12] Is this an important source for the origin of the *Letter of Aristeas,* or could the story of the seventy-two grammarians at work on restoring Homer depend on the legend of Aristeas? The number of these grammarians (seventy-two) is admittedly late in origin and is in an apologetic context, so the story is undoubtedly legendary, but this is not the case in regard to the Alexandrian editorial activity on the works of Homer. The question here is what part of the two legends came first, the one attributed to Aristeas or the one attributed to the grammarians entrusted by Peisistratus? Could the answer be that both legends were informed by each other?

Because of the legend of the *Letter of Aristeas*, this collection came to be known as the Septuagint (regularly abbreviated LXX).[13] By around 130 BCE (perhaps 127–118 BCE), many of the prophetic books were added to that collection of translated sacred texts, though it is not clear which books were included. Certainly by about 250 to 200 BCE many of the prophetic books were circulating as sacred literature among the Jews in the Land of Israel and many of them were translated into the Greek language by around 130–100 BCE; but some translations of Jewish religious texts in Greek are likely as late as the first century CE. While it is not possible to date with precision the recognition of the Prophets as sacred scripture among the Jews, antecedents to that acceptance can be seen as early as 400–350 BCE. For example, see 2 Kings 17:13, to "keep my commandments and my statutes, in accordance with *all the law that I commanded your ancestors and that I sent to you by my servants the prophets.*"

It is not clear when the apocryphal and pseudepigraphal books were included in the Old Greek collections of sacred books, but they were eventually included, and subsequently the Aristeas legend was applied not only to the Torah but also to the rest of the books of the Hebrew Bible/Old Testament, including the apocryphal or deuterocanonical and some pseudepigraphal books. In other words, the Greek translation of all the Jewish sacred books was believed by some Jews to have originated from God, who inspired the translators and preserved them from any variations in their work. It was believed that nothing was lost in the translation and that the LXX was a perfect, divinely inspired translation of all that God intended in the scriptures of the Hebrew Bible. This legend of Aristeas is also quite prominent in early Christianity and several early church fathers, including Justin (*Dial.* 78; *1 Apol.* 1.31), Irenaeus (*Haer.* 3.21.2; preserved also in Eusebius, *Hist. eccl.* 5.8.11–15), Clement of Alexandria (*Strom.* 1.22.148; 1.149.3), Tertullian (*Apol.* 18.5–9 and 19.5–9), Pseudo-Justin (*Cohortatio ad Graecos*),[14] Eusebius (*Praep. ev.* 8.1.8 and 8.2.1), and Augustine (*Letter* 71) welcomed the *Letter* as evidence of the inspiration of the Greek Bible. Origen and Jerome appear to be the first early church scholars—and for a while the only ones—to doubt the claims of the *Letter of Aristeas.*[15]

The LXX translation, more accurately known as the Old Greek, was the Bible of the Jews in the Dispersion as well as the Bible of the early Christian churches. An indeterminate collection of Jewish prophetic books was circulating in that translation among the Jews both in the Land of Israel and among the Jews of the Dispersion for some time before the emergence of early Christianity, but for Jews the Law of Moses was always prominent among the sacred texts and always at the core of Jewish teaching among all the Second Temple Jewish religious sects. As noted earlier, Philo cites the Old Testament scriptures over 1,150 times, and in some 1,100 of those times he cites the Pentateuch. As the Old Testament closes in the Christian biblical canon, Malachi admonishes his readers to "remember the teaching of my servant Moses, the statutes and ordinances that I commanded him at Horeb in Israel" (Mal. 4:4). At that time (perhaps ca. 400–350 BCE), there is little reference to the other writings, namely the Former or Latter Prophets, but they were beginning to circulate among the Jews (2 Kgs. 17:13). Several prophets are referred to by name in Sirach's celebration of great persons (ca. 190–180 BCE), which suggests the ascendency of their writings by that time, but which books comprised this emerging collection of sacred books is not clear. The book of Ezekiel, along with the collection of the Book of the Twelve, is certainly known by the time of Sirach (49:8–10), and later in the second century BCE as we see in 2 Maccabees 2:13, and later in the first century CE (ca. 30–50 CE), as well as at the end of the first century CE in *4 Ezra* 14:1–47. In the first century CE there was as yet no three-part Old Testament collection of Scriptures for either Jews or Christians. Regularly in the New Testament the scriptures are referred to as "the law and the prophets." With the exception of Luke 24:44, which is a unique reference in the New Testament to a three-part collection of scriptures, only the Law or the Law and the Prophets are mentioned in the New Testament in reference to the Jewish scriptures (e.g., Matt. 5:17; 7:12; Luke 24:27; and Acts 28:23, where "the law and the prophets" appear to make up all the sacred scriptures). There are no such divisions in the LXX or in early Christian biblical manuscripts. Sometimes the whole of the sacred writings is referred to simply as "law" (e.g., John 10:34 cites Ps. 82:6 as "law," and 1 Cor. 14:21 introduces Isa. 28:11–12 with "in the law it is written"). Other designations for the Jewish scriptures include "scripture" (John 13:18; Gal. 3:8), "old covenant" (2 Cor. 3:14), and "Moses and all the prophets" (Luke 24:27; John 1:45).

It is widely recognized that the scripture of the earliest Christians was the LXX, the Old Greek scriptures. Among the Jews in the Diaspora, the same is true especially for those in the west, where Greek was the mother tongue. Scholars recognize that the Greek scriptures contain more books than the Hebrew Bible, but often assume that this collection was settled well before the time of Jesus and constituted the sacred books of the Jews in that era and later. It is much more likely that the LXX reflects the books that were circulating as sacred texts among the Jews of the Diaspora and in the Land of Israel during the time of Jesus and later. Indeed, the first known restriction of the collection of sacred books in the Hebrew Bible to the twenty-four books that it now contains is about the mid-second century in the now famous Babylonian *baraita* (*b. Baba Bathra* 14b), even though this limited collection may have been known by some Jews at the end of the first century CE (e.g., Josephus). There is no evidence, however, that the Jews had adopted a *restricted* or fixed collection of sacred texts in the time of Jesus or before the time when Christians were still part of the Jewish community and attended the synagogues and the temple (before 70 CE).

OTHER ANCIENT TRANSLATIONS

Besides the Greek translation of the HB/OT Scriptures, other Jews in the Diaspora and Christians made use of other translations, especially Syriac, Latin, and Arabic.[16] Also, it is likely that Greek translations earlier than the LXX existed in the Diaspora, though we do not have any remaining portions of them. The *Letter of Aristeas* indicates that earlier attempts had been made at translating the Law, but that they were not careful translations and were not well received. The complete report in this legendary account about earlier and faulty translations of the Torah into Greek is as follows:

Scrolls of the Law of the Jews, together with a few others, are missing (from the library), for these (works) are written in Hebrew characters and language. But they have been transcribed somewhat carelessly and not as they should be, according to the report of the experts, because they have not received patronage. These (books) also must be in your library in an accurate version, because this legislation, as could be expected from its divine nature, is very philosophical and genuine. (*Let. Aris.* 30–31)[17]

While we are uncertain of the dating and location of the earlier Greek translations, it is likely that some were circulating, but evidently did not have credibility among Jews. Besides the old Greek translation, the LXX, other Greek translations emerged in the second century CE that were more loyal to the Masoretic Text text than the LXX was. These were the translations of Aquila, Symmachus, and Theodotion, all of which were used by Origen in his Hexapla in the third century. Besides these, major Jewish translations of the Hebrew Bible books deserve mention.

Targumim (or Targums)

When the Jews returned from Babylon under the leadership of Ezra and Nehemiah (ca. 450–400 BCE), the language they spoke was Aramaic, but their sacred scriptures, the Law of Moses, were in Hebrew. When the Law of Moses was read to them, it needed to be translated from Hebrew into Aramaic and its meaning made clear: "So they read from the book, from the law of God, with interpretation. They gave the sense, so that the people understood the reading" (Neh. 8:8 NRSV). At first the targumim were performed orally by a *meturgeman* ("translator"), but by the second century a written Aramaic translation was produced (see *y. Megillah* 1:11), and in the synagogues the Hebrew text was read twice and the Aramaic read once (*b. Berakot* 8a). The Aramaic word *targum* (Heb. *trgm*) roughly means "to translate" and, by extension, "to interpret." The Jewish targumim range from careful Aramaic translations of the Hebrew Scriptures (*Targum Onkelos*) to interpretive paraphrases and even commentary as in the Targum of the Song of Songs. They date as early as the first century BCE (those discovered at Qumran), but most are from the rabbinic period (second to late sixth century CE). Targumim were prepared for all the books of the Hebrew Bible except Ezra–Nehemiah and Daniel, but since large portions of those texts are already in Aramaic, it may not have been deemed necessary to translate them. Some examples of targumim were discovered at Qumran among the Dead Sea Scrolls (4QtgLev, 4QtgJob, 11QtgJob, and perhaps 6Q19, possibly on Genesis) that date quite early (first century CE), but most of these are after the separation of Christians from Jews in the early second century CE. Scholars are divided over the relevance of these works for understanding the New Testament, but there is a growing interest in them and the tide may be shifting in terms of their relevance for biblical research.[18] It is possible that the earliest targumim from Judea (often called Palestinian targumim) may help reconstruct the Aramaic dialect of Jesus. Also, like the targumim, the New Testament writings avoid speaking of God anthropomorphically and anthropopathically (ascribing human form and human emotions to God), and they frequently share a common view of a number of important theological issues in the New Testament such as "Father in heaven," this world and the world to come, Son of Man, resurrection, the day of judgment, Gehenna, and paradise.[19]

There are five primary targumim on the Hebrew scriptures: (1) Targum Onkelos (or possibly Aquila, second century CE, possibly from Babylon), the official targum of the Pentateuch; (2) Targum Yerushalmi, a translation of the Torah (also known as Targum Pseudo-Jonathan); (3) Targum Jonathan on the Torah (attributed to Jonathan ben Uzziel; *b. Megillah* 3a), which covers the Prophets and part of the Writings or Hagiographa; (4) Targum Neofiti 1, which covers part of the Torah; (5) Fragmentary Targum on the Pentateuch. There are also targumim on the Five Scrolls (the so-called *Megillot*: Ecclesiastes, Ruth, Song of Songs, Lamentations, and Esther) and Targum *Sheni* on Esther. Most of the Palestinian targums are periphrastic and include homiletical interpretations, while Onkelos is more literal.[20]

The targumim have different styles of translation, and most of them, especially the targumim on the Writings, date from the Middle Ages and probably after the time that Onkelos became the dominant targum on the Pentateuch. The targumim provide little help in establishing the text of the Hebrew Bible scriptures because they emerge for the most part after the establishment of the Masoretic Text and because they are so free in their translations that they are generally not useful in pointing to a Hebrew *Vorlage* (prototype).

Although all but three books of the HB are translated and interpreted in the targumim, no single targum translates all the scriptures in the Hebrew Bible. This cannot be accounted for by arguing that the various attempts at producing targumim were coordinated somehow and each covered a designated portion of the Hebrew scriptures. The implications of this information for the status of the biblical canon among the Jews during this period are not clear, except that the Torah took priority in Jewish notions of sacred scripture during the rabbinic period.

Syriac Versions

While the Greek translation of the Old Testament/Hebrew Bible began as translations of sacred texts for Jews and subsequently were adopted by Christians, several other translations were prepared largely by and for Christians. The partial exception to this was the Syriac version of the Old Testament writings that was probably begun by Jews for their community, but in time it was taken over by Christians—or those Jews who prepared it eventually became Christians and it became the scripture of the Christians in the region of Syria first and then in surrounding areas. Antioch, Syria, was the third largest city in the Greco-Roman world, and it had a very large Jewish population and eventually a fairly significant Christian community. When Christians came to Antioch as a result of their persecution in Jerusalem and Judea, their ministry of evangelism was initially only among Jews, and many of them became followers of Jesus. Subsequently, a large number of Gentiles also responded favorably to the early Christian message and a sizable number of them became part of the Christian fellowship/church there. There were some conflicts between Jews and those Gentiles who were followers of Jesus (Gal. 2:11–21), but in time Jews became a minority in the church, as the numbers of Gentiles in the church increased considerably. In the second century CE, and possibly earlier, Jews translated the Hebrew scriptures into Syriac, and these scriptures became known as the Syriac Peshitta.[21] Eventually those Jews who began this project were converted to Christianity, and following that time (ca. 200 CE) many of the Christian scriptures were added to the collection.[22] The conversion of the Jews may have come as a result of the rift between the Jews in Syria and the leaders in rabbinic Judaism in the second and third centuries. The whole of the Peshitta was not completed much before the fourth or fifth century.

Metzger states that the origin of the Syriac Bible is "shrouded in uncertainty," but adds that the affinities to the Aramaic Targumim suggests a strong Jewish influence on the translation of the Pentateuch.[23] The surviving manuscripts today show considerable variety in the books and their order in the Old Testament portion of the Syriac Bible. In some manuscripts, after the Pentateuch the order is Joshua, Judges, Job, Samuel, Kings, Proverbs, Sirach, Ecclesiastes, Ruth, and Song of Songs. In other Syriac biblical manuscripts Ruth, Esther, Judith, and Susanna are placed together in the Book of Women. I will discuss the New Testament books in their collection later, but for now I will simply say that their New Testament included only twenty-two books, initially (until ca. 500–510 CE) omitting 2 Peter, 2–3 John, Jude, and Revelation.[24] At the beginning of the sixth century, the Philoxenian version, named after the bishop Philoxenus from Mabbug (Hierapolis), was made; it included the omitted New Testament books. In 616 CE Thomas of Harkel significantly revised the Philoxenian version to form the Harclean version. At roughly the same time, Paul, the Jacobite bishop of Tella in Mesopotamia, also made a translation of the LXX following the fifth column in Origen's Hexapla. Subsequent to that, another version of the Syriac Bible emerged called the Christian Palestinian Aramaic version, using the Aramaic language common in Palestine in the early Christian centuries.[25]

Latin Versions

At around the end of the second century, Latin versions of the Old Testament and some New Testament writings began to emerge especially in North Africa (Carthage?). In time Jerome's Latin Vulgate took priority over all the other Latin translations, but not for several centuries. It is known that Tertullian at the end of the second century quoted from both the Old Testament writings and some New Testament writings in Latin. There was no single Latin translation of the Old Testament and New Testament scriptures that garnered widespread support, and it appears that more were on the way. As Metzger observes, these early

Latin translations were not merely translations of the Greek into Latin, but often gave scribes opportunities for considerable freedom in expanding the text.[26]

These Latin versions followed the LXX until the fifth century, when Jerome translated the Old Testament from the Hebrew text and rejected the apocryphal writings that were current in the LXX, though he included some of them in his translation, but without giving careful attention to them. The earlier expansionist tendencies of these translators is made clearer in one of Augustine's frustrated comments about the diversity of texts in the Latin Bible. At the close of the fourth century, he wrote: "Those who translated the Scriptures from Hebrew into Greek can be counted, but the Latin translators are out of all number. For in the early days of the faith, everyone who happened to gain possession of a Greek manuscript [of the Scriptures] and thought he had any facility in both languages, however slight that might have been, attempted to make a translation."[27] Scholars today have discovered some three families of Latin translations, represented by Cyprian (the African text), Irenaeus (the European text), and Augustine (the Italian text). As a result of this confusion in the Latin texts, Pope Damasus asked Jerome (Hieronymus) in 383 to produce a uniform Latin text of the Scriptures. He was reluctant at first but then proceeded to translate from the Hebrew text for the Old Testament and the Greek for the New Testament. This work between 390 and 404 CE was carried out largely in Bethlehem and with the linguistic (Hebrew) aid of a converted Jew from Syria and later a Jewish rabbi in Bethlehem. As he had expected, his translation met with considerable opposition initially, and it took several centuries before it became the standard text for all Latin churches, but it remained that way for nearly a thousand years. He largely ignored or rushed through the translation of the apocryphal books (Tobit and Judith) since he was not interested in them and did not give them the same recognition or time as he gave to the books in the Hebrew Bible.

Coptic Versions

In the continuing development of the Egyptian language, Coptic emerged. The Egyptian Christians wrote this native language using the twenty-four letters in the Greek alphabet as well as the seven signs taken over from the Egyptian language to express sounds that were not present in the Greek language. The literature that emerged in Coptic is almost exclusively religious and includes versions of the Bible as well as the Apocrypha of the Old Testament and New Testament, as well as legends of the apostles, lives and martyrdoms of saints, and other so-called noncanonical texts. These additional texts were not put in a separate location, but were mixed among the rest of the sacred scriptures of the Egyptian churches.

Around the beginning of the fourth century, possibly sooner, Coptic translations began that eventually included some six dialects (Sahidic, Boharic, Achmimic, Sub-Achmimic, Middle Egyptian or Oxyrhynchite dialect, and Fayyumic).[28] It appears that most if not all of the Old Testament books were included in these translations as well as other noncanonical books, including

Psalm 151. Sometimes the Coptic versions show a preference for the Latin versions, which is not unusual since the Greek scriptures were first translated into Latin in the North African churches.

The Armenian Version

The Armenian people are known for their pride in being the first "Christian nation." When Christianity was introduced in Armenia near the end of the third century by Gregory the Illuminator (257–331), who was of royal lineage, he was able to convert Tiridates III, king of Armenia, who subsequently sent out a herald to call for all his subjects to adopt the Christian faith and to be baptized. By the early fifth century, the Christian scriptures, both Old Testament and New Testament, were translated from Syriac into the newly established Armenian language. Mesrop (ca. 361–439) created the thirty-six-letter Armenian alphabet around 405–406 using also twenty Greek letters. He also set out to translate the Scriptures with the help of others that he recruited for the task. The first book translated was the book of Proverbs. The New Testament or Christian writings followed this, and then the rest of the Old Testament, which was finished between 410 and 414 CE. The earliest dated Armenian biblical manuscript is from 887 CE. From the many surviving manuscripts, it is clear that the Armenians included in their Old Testament the *History of Joseph and Aseneth, Testaments of the Twelve Patriarchs, Book of Adam, History of Moses, Deaths of the Prophets, Concerning King Solomon, Short History of the Prophet Elias, Concerning the Prophet Jeremiah, Vision of Enoch the Just,* and *3 Esdras* (= chaps. 3–14 of 2 Esdras). The New Testament included the *Epistle of the Corinthians to Paul* and a *Third Epistle of Paul to the Corinthians*. This canon is similar to the early Syriac biblical canon. Metzger has noted that the Armenian manuscripts also include many colophons with notes on a broad range of topics that are especially interesting to biblical and text-critical scholars.[29]

Ethiopic Version

The Ethiopian translation of the Bible is one of the more fascinating and puzzling versions. The translation includes "81 books" but it is not clear which "81" are intended since the surviving manuscripts vary in terms of their content. The one constant feature seems to be the number 81. The notion of a biblical canon, that is, a fixed collection of sacred books, was more fluid in the Ethiopian churches than elsewhere, and as a result the Ethiopian Christians have the largest biblical canon known today.

Rufinus (ca. 345–410), church historian and translator as well as monk, in his *Ecclesiastical History* (1.9) claims that the mission to Ethiopia began during the reign of Constantine (ca. 330 CE) with two young men, Frumentius and Aedesius, who preached the gospel in Aksum, the capital then of Ethiopia. The principal resources of the biblical canon in Ethiopia are the *Sinodos* and *Fetha*

Nägäst. Sinodos is a collection of material attributed to the apostles and early church councils and contains lists of its sacred scriptures. *Fetha Nägäst* is the canon law of the churches and cites *Sinodos* as its primary source. Both sources have the same list of books.

There are two main lists of sacred scriptures in the *Sinodos*, and in terms of the Old Testament it includes besides the books in the Protestant biblical canon also the books Judith, Tobit, 2 books of Maccabees, Wisdom, Sirach, and Pseudo-Josephus. There appear to be two primary Old Testament canons in this translation:

The *broader* Old Testament canon includes: besides the Octateuch—Pentateuch, Joshua, Judges, and Ruth (8 books)—Judith (1), Samuel and Kings (2), Chronicles (2), 1 Esdras and the Ezra Apocalypse (2), Esther (1), Tobit (1), Maccabees (2), Job (1), Psalms (1), books of Solomon (5), Prophets (16), Sirach (1), Pseudo-Josephus (1); *Jubilees* and *1 Enoch* are to be included in the number. This comes to a total of 46 books in the Old Testament collection.

The *narrower* Old Testament canon is listed in the *Prayers of the Church* and is printed in the large Ge'ez and Amharic diglots; it includes: the widely accepted Protestant Old Testament books and separates into two books Proverbs 1–24 (*Messale*) from Proverbs 25–31 (*Tägsas*), so the number here is forty and then adds fourteen other books that include *1 Enoch*, *Jubilees*, Wisdom, 1 Esdras, Ezra Apocalypse, Judith, Tobit, Sirach, Baruch, "the rest of Jeremiah," Susanna, "the rest of Daniel," and 1 and 2 Maccabees. This comes to a total of 54 books.[30]

The earliest Ethiopian biblical manuscripts that have survived date from the fourteenth century.[31] Because the Ethiopian Christians were separated from the rest of the Christian world for almost a thousand years following the triumph of the Muslim faith in that part of the world, they have a fair claim to an early Christian collection of sacred books, and we should take their collection seriously if we are interested in the church's scriptures in antiquity.

CONCLUSION

The preceding survey of ancient translations is not complete, of course, and there were a number of other translations of the Old Testament and New Testament scriptures, but the above-mentioned translations have had a significant impact on our understanding of the scriptures of early Christianity. Most of these translations were of poor quality, except for Jerome's Latin Vulgate, and even he was not consistent in the quality of his translation, especially in the apocryphal books. The books included in these translations vary, but several have some apocryphal and pseudepigraphal books in them. Unlike the Jews or other ancient religious communities, the Christians seemed anxious to put their sacred scriptures in other languages to advance their mission of evangelism; but as a consequence of their rush, most of the translations were of inferior quality and there was no widespread agreement on the books that were included in them. While most of the churches accepted the Old Testament scriptures, namely the thirty-nine books of the Protestant Old Testament (with the exception of the Goths, who rejected the Samuels and Kings), they also included more books in their translations than are current in most Christian Bibles today, with the exception of the Ethiopian churches. In the next chapter, we will look more closely at the issues related to the text of the Old Testament scriptures as well as focus on the stability of the books and text of the early church's sacred scriptures.

Chapter 6

The Text and Stabilization
of the Jewish Scriptures

INTRODUCTION

The search for the earliest text of the Hebrew Scriptures involves a careful investigation of a number of ancient sources, including what is called the "proto-Masoretic Text," Masoretic Text (MT), Septuagint (LXX), Samaritan Pentateuch (SP), the Aramaic Targumim (T), Old Latin (L), Latin Vulgate (V), Syriac Peshitta (S), the Dead Sea Scrolls (DSS), and several other ancient translations or versions, especially Coptic, Ethiopic, Armenian, and Arabic.[1] Establishing the earliest and most reliable text of the Hebrew Scriptures is a significant challenge that very few scholars have the expertise to accomplish, but fortunately several capable scholars have paved the way for a more reliable biblical text than was possible earlier and that allows for more careful translations in the future. The most important texts of the Hebrew Bible are the *Biblica Hebraica*, edited by Rudolf Kittel (known as *BH* or *BHK*) first published in 1905–1906, then in 1912, 1937; subsequently that text was revised and published as *Biblica Hebraica Stuttgartensia* (*BHS*, 1969–1977, and subsequent editions and printings through 1997). *BHS* reflects the last hand of the Leningrad Codex (1008 CE), the oldest manuscript fashioned after the Aleppo Codex (see comments about this below) that was seriously damaged and partially lost in 1947, and *BHS* is currently the most complete Hebrew biblical text available.[2]

A new text is being prepared in Israel by the Hebrew University called the *Hebrew University Bible* (HUB) edition, which is still in process, though thus far only the books of Isaiah and Jeremiah have been published.[3] This text is based on what is left of the earlier Aleppo Codex. The Hebrew script of that manuscript was produced in 930 CE by Shlomo Ben Boya'a, and the vowel pointing, cantillation marks, and the masoretic textual notes were supplied by the famed Aaron Ben Asher. He was not the only or the first Masorete, but was universally acknowleged by the Jews as the best expert on the Hebrew text, the recognized "Master." The Ben Asher family produced biblical texts that included the vowel pointing and various scribal notes. The best known of these texts are the Cairensis Codex, the Aleppo Codex, and the Leningrad Codex (Codex Leningradensis, L). The Aleppo Codex, however, was the most important of all Hebrew manuscripts and was seriously damaged in an anti-Jewish riot on November 29, 1947, that destroyed the synagogue where it was stored and numerous sacred manuscripts in Aleppo, Syria, in reaction to the United Nations' decision to partition Palestine to form the Jewish state. It was the most cherished manuscript of the Hebrew Bible, produced in Tiberias, Israel, in 930 CE, along with invaluable notes on the text. This text was known as the "Crown of Aleppo" and was equivalent to the New Testament *textus receptus* (the standard "received text") for the Hebrew Bible. Although the manuscript was feared lost, and it was significantly damaged, 294 pages of the original codex have survived, and it is now in Jerusalem.[4] It is currently missing Genesis 1:1–Deuteronomy 28:26 (i.e., all but the last eleven pages of the Pentateuch) and from Song of Songs 3:12 to the end, as well as Ecclesiastes, Lamentations, Esther, Daniel, Ezra, and Nehemiah. It was not available to the editors of *BHS*, but is being used in the emerging HUB edition, along with the Leningrad Codex, the Dead Sea Scrolls, variants of the LXX, rabbinic literature, medieval manuscripts, pointing, accents, and other helps for those wanting an accurate and up-to-date biblical text.[5]

THE TEXT OF THE JEWISH SCRIPTURES

Of the thousands of biblical manuscripts that have survived antiquity, no two are exactly alike. There was clearly no focus on textual stabilization for several centuries, but even when that began to emerge first of all in the rabbinic tradition and subsequently in the church, there still were no two biblical manuscripts exactly alike until the invention of the printing press. I will examine the implications of this presently, but for now I will focus on the shape of the biblical texts that were used in antiquity.

Eugene Ulrich raises important questions that one must answer before one can make any conclusions about the fixing or stabilizing of the biblical text in its modern canonical sense. While these questions focus on the standardizing of the biblical text, they also apply to the standardized books that go into the biblical canon:

1. What are the data available for determining the nature and characteristics of the scriptural texts in the first centuries BCE and CE?
2. Even if we have the proper data, are we looking at them through the correct interpretive lenses?
3. Since "a standard biblical text" normally refers to the MT, what was the MT? What would be an adequate description of it? Was there such a thing as "a/the standard text"? If so, was it in reality the MT that was the standard text?
4. Was there an identifiable group of leaders in the first centuries BCE and CE that knew of the variety of texts, was concerned about the diversity of textual forms, selected a single form, had the authority to declare a single form to be the "standard text," and succeeded in having that standard text acknowledged by a majority of Jews? Was there sufficient cohesion in Judaism in the first centuries BCE and CE and sufficiently acknowledged leadership to make it conceivable that a majority of Jews recognized and used a "standard text"?[6]

Perhaps the best-known example from Qumran is the *Rewritten* (or *Reworked*) *Pentateuch* (4QRP[a-e] [4Q158; 4Q364–367]). As noted briefly in chapter 3, the term "Rewritten Bible" has been seen rightly as an anachronistic term that assumes some form of a fixed Bible circulating among the Jews in the first century BCE and CE, but it is now widely being replaced with "rewritten Scripture" to show that notions of a fixed biblical text or even fixed Bible came after the times of the Qumran community.[7] Such other terms as "reworked Bible" and "parabiblical texts" are also commonly used to address the same practice at Qumran, namely, an "extending" of the sacred scriptures to more recent and relevant texts through their rewriting or reworking.[8] Kristin De Troyer has shown that the rewriting of sacred texts extended not only to what we now call nonbiblical books, but also to the biblical books such as Esther, Joshua, and 1 Esdras, where extensive rewriting took place.[9]

Yigael Yadin argues convincingly that the *Temple Scroll* was venerated as the Essene Torah and held it to be equal in importance to the traditional Torah.[10] He observes that the so-called Tetragrammaton, the four letters Y-H-W-H that form the unpronounced name of God (Yahweh) in the Hebrew Scriptures, is replaced in the *Temple Scroll* with the personal pronouns "I" or "me." For example, Numbers 30:3 in the *Temple Scroll* states: "When a woman vows a vow to me," which replaces the traditional Torah: "When a woman vows a vow to the LORD."[11] Yadin's point is that the author presents the Law as if it came directly from God himself rather than through Moses. The author of the *Temple Scroll* has rewritten or reworked the original text of the Torah, and the result is the production of another text equal in sacredness with the earlier Torah. Yadin has observed that the square Aramaic script is used in the *Temple Scroll* to write the name of God, just as it is in the other biblical books, which is a further indication that the people at Qumran viewed this scroll as sacred literature. Again, this lengthy scroll was copied several times at Qumran, indeed, more times than Isaiah. This leads Yadin to conclude that "the Temple Scroll was, for the Essenes, a holy canonical book on a par, for them, with the other books of the Bible."[12] There also existed at Qumran a common practice of altering and changing the biblical text, which did not seem to violate their understanding of the sacredness of the texts that they were examining, copying, or editing. At Qumran the sacred texts were apparently on the way to being perfected, and it was deemed appropriate to alter or clarify the meaning of the sacred texts to bring them more into harmony with what was believed in the Essene community.

The Mosaic command forbids adding to or taking from the text. The command was clear: "You must neither add anything to what I command you nor take away anything from it, but keep the commandments of the LORD your God with which I am charging you" (Deut. 4:2). The command is repeated later with essentially the same admonition: "You must diligently observe everything that I command you; do not add to it or take anything from it" (Deut. 12:32). This prohibition became the standard for how Jews (cf. *Let. Aris.* 311) and Christians (cf. Rev. 22:18–19) acknowledged the sacredness and inviolability of their religious literature. The Essene community, however, frequently changed or altered sacred texts.

This reworking or rewriting of sacred texts is evidence that the process of the formation of Scripture was still under way at Qumran. Those who were involved in this process likely did not think that they were doing anything inappropriate; they were, of course, unaware of the methods of textual criticism practiced today. Rather they were anxious to clarify the message of a sacred text; and as they made it more clear and relevant to their community, they did not see this as distracting from the holiness of the text.[13] That the *formation* of scriptural texts was in process at Qumran (and even later) makes the discussion of this practice complicated, but it is helpful to see what was taking place at Qumran. Daniel Falk provides a careful introduction to the variety of ways that scholars have identified the various texts at Qumran and also the difficulty in using such terms. After explaining them, he opts for the more general term, "parabiblical," to describe what was taking place. Because there is little distinction in the sacredness of the writings later called biblical and those rewritten texts that have varying degrees of loyalty to the scriptural texts that form the basis or source for the newly written texts, scholars continue their debate on the matter.[14] George Brooke is probably more on target here when he recognizes the growing discomfort with the more common categories for describing the literature and textual production at Qumran.[15] H. Gregory Snyder has divided these rewritten texts into three categories: those that lightly rework the Pentateuch (4QReworked Pentateuch or 4QRP), the more profoundly altered works (*Genesis Apocryphon* and *Jubilees*), and finally those books that have a substantial debt to the biblical idiom and are loosely related to the sequence of biblical narrative (*Temple Scroll* and *Hymns* or *Hodayot*).[16]

Daniel Silver draws attention to the remarkable freedom that the scribes at Qumran exercised in altering the order and wording of the Psalms, even to the point of adding the refrain, "Praised be the LORD and praised be his name forever and ever," after each verse of Psalm 145; they also changed the script, spelling, grammar, and content of the two scrolls of Isaiah found in cave 1. When the Qumran scrolls were written, there were no agreed formal methods for the presentation of sacred writings, and so the practice of changing the text was applied to books that were eventually not accepted into the biblical canon but also to the Torah, Prophets, and Writings. The Essenes at Qumran deleted or added sentences and words within the texts and made other changes as well. Matters such as word division, syntax, and spelling appear to have been of little concern to the scribes at Qumran. Silver rightly concludes that in pre-rabbinic times the Law, Prophets, and Psalms carried a large degree of authority in the Qumran community, but they had not yet attained the status given to Scripture by the later rabbinic schools, which copied every letter and word as accurately as possible.[17] This supports the idea that the concept of Scripture as inviolable was not uniformly understood or followed by at least the Essenes in the first century CE.

We have no evidence, however, that the Qumran covenanters handled their sacred texts differently than other Jewish sects, including the Christians in the first century CE. Tov, whose work supports Silver's conclusions, observes that the scribes at Qumran often incorporated their thoughts on the biblical text into the new version of the text that they produced: "In the newly created text scribes and readers inserted sundry changes, which are recognizable because the limitations of the ancient materials and the rigid form of the manuscript did not allow them to hide the intervention."[18] B. Barry Levy adds to this that the notion of establishing the original text of the Hebrew Bible is flawed from the beginning because there was no established text at that time. He claims that "the popular assumption that no changes were ever introduced into copies of the Bible during rabbinic times or under rabbinic auspices simply does not accord with the facts," and adds that during the rabbinic period "no single, authorized, and officially registered Bible text (or Torah text) existed, and therefore it is meaningless to claim that Jews either did or did not alter it."[19] While there is considerable stability in some aspects of the ancient text of the Hebrew Bible, there was still no stable authorized text of the Torah that was in place at that time. The biblical text was hardly more stable before then, even if there are common characteristics in many of the Dead Sea manuscripts that support the later Masoretic Text, which is now commonly called the "proto-Masoretic" text. This challenges what Levy calls the accepted scholarly notion of a fixed consonantal text by the first or second century CE.

Tov adds that notations and changes in the various texts had little to do with whether they were biblical or nonbiblical texts:

Very little distinction, if any, was made between the writing of biblical and non-biblical texts. For example, the scribe who wrote 1QS, 1QSa and 1QSb, as well as the biblical 4QSam[c] and some of the corrections in 1QIsa[a] (e.g. at col. 33:7), employed the same system and notations throughout all five texts (including the use of four dots for the tetragrammaton). In addition, 1QS and 1QIsa[a] also share three unusual marginal signs, which were probably inserted by the same scribe.[20]

Tov goes on to say, however, that in a few cases some scribes did distinguish the biblical texts from the nonbiblical texts by writing on only one side of the parchment for biblical texts and on both sides for nonbiblical texts. Also, he notes that the biblical texts were almost exclusively written on parchment and only a few on papyrus, probably for personal use. Finally, Tov notes that a special arrangement was devised for writing poetical sections in only the biblical books—*and this included Sirach.*[21]

The Jewish Scriptures existed for centuries only in a consonantal text, but later (between 650–750 CE, and perhaps no later than 700 CE) the masoretic scribes, or Masoretes,[22] developed a system of preserving the text of the Hebrew Bible that included the consonantal text of the Scriptures as well as vowel points and accents in the text to ensure correct sounding of the words and to retain as carefully as possible the textual tradition that they had received. Three masoretic systems developed over time, the Palestinian, Babylonian, and Tiberian. By the sixteenth century, the Tiberian system came to be accepted as the most authoritative.[23] While the *Sopherim* (scribes) wrote out the consonantal text of the Hebrew Scriptures, the *Nakdanim* ("pointers") added the vowel points to the text, and the *Masoretes* added the marginal and final notes to the text. Often the same person added the points, marginal notes and endnotes, as in the case of the Leningrad Codex, for which Samuel ben Jacob performed all three functions. The most famous of the Masoretes were Ben Naphtali and Ben Asher. Before the discovery of the Dead Sea Scrolls, modern biblical scholars knew the text of the Hebrew Bible/Old Testament primarily through the Masoretic Text, the Samaritan Pentateuch, and the often-supposed Hebrew *Vorlage*[24] of the Septuagint translation, though the last was generally discounted in terms of its importance.

As a result of new discoveries in the Judean Desert (the Dead Sea Scrolls) and elsewhere, such as at the Cairo Genizah, the textual history of the Hebrew Bible/Old Testament has become much more complex, and discerning the earliest text of the biblical manuscripts much more challenging than before, when the Masoretic Text had little credible competition. Widespread appeal was made to the Masoretic Text of the Hebrew Bible, a text largely based on two major Hebrew manuscripts, the Aleppo and Leningrad codices. As a result of the discovery of the Dead Sea Scrolls especially, but also several important Christian manuscripts of the Old Testament writings, the modern textual critics' understanding of the earliest text of the Jewish Scriptures has shifted considerably. It is much more common now to speak about the three ancient witnesses to the text of the Hebrew Scriptures, the Masoretic Text (MT), the Old Greek (Septuagint/

LXX), and the Samaritan Pentateuch (SP), as well as the Dead Sea Scrolls, to establish the earliest text of the Hebrew Bible. With the discovery of the Dead Sea Scrolls, some scholars have suggested that at times the LXX and the SP may depend upon an earlier form of the Hebrew text than does the MT. This does not suggest in any way that the MT has been abandoned, but only that in some cases the LXX and the SP may be based on an earlier form of the text, a *Vorlage*. Because the LXX and SP are at times considerably different from the MT, the question naturally emerges which text is more reliable and which is the canonical text for the synagogue or the church today. The following discussion is intended only to be a brief introduction to a fairly complex and often debated subject so that the reader will see the broader biblical question: Which form of its text is sacred? When some of the more significant biblical manuscripts disagree at numerous points, the question is not easy to decide. It is also important, as we will explain later, that the synagogue and the church do not have to wait for the scholars to answer those questions before they make use of their sacred Scriptures. The question remains, however, which biblical text is normative for believing communities today. Having already discussed the contents of the various manuscripts in chapter 3, I now will focus more on the text of the sacred Scriptures. How uniform were those texts and did they say the same thing?

The earliest sources or manuscripts that we have for this period are the Dead Sea Scrolls, and so I will begin by focusing on the text of sacred books there.

THE BIBLICAL TEXTS AND THE DISCOVERIES AT QUMRAN

Some of the scrolls discovered at Qumran—not all—have close affinities to the Masoretic Text and are commonly called "proto-Masoretic" manuscripts. According to Harold Scanlin, the Dead Sea Scrolls confirm the stability of the Masoretic Text and thereby advance the antiquity of the Hebrew text by around a thousand years, but these discoveries in the Dead Sea region also confirm that the Septuagint is a significant textual authority for recovering the earliest text of the Hebrew Bible (the Hebrew *Vorlage* of the LXX), and they show that the scrolls are a reliable source for early textual variant readings of the biblical texts.[25] After noting the wide variety of textual variants in the Dead Sea Scrolls, Tov cautions about saying more than can currently be said about them. It is not yet clear what all of the books discovered at Qumran meant to its residents, one small group of the Essene sect. The collection could be called a library if it simply means a collection of religious books, but Tov reminds us that there is no clear statement on their role in that community for over two hundred years, and it is difficult to characterize the collections of manuscripts found in the caves.[26]

In the following sections, I will first focus on the texts of the Hebrew Bible that have survived antiquity and see what conclusions, if any, one can draw from those in the scholarly community who have compared the various textual traditions of the biblical books.

EARLY STAGES OF TEXTUAL STABILIZATION OF THE HEBREW BIBLE/OLD TESTAMENT

Of the thousands of biblical manuscripts that have survived antiquity, no two are exactly alike. While there is early recognition in the rabbinic tradition of this problem, there were no consistent means of controlling the textual variants in the biblical manuscripts. The following examples point to the knowledge of errors or variants in the biblical texts and also the rabbis' concern about them:

> According to *b. Eruvin* 13a: "R[abbi] Meir said: When I came to R. Ishmael [to study Torah], he asked me, 'My son, what is your occupation?' I replied, 'I am a scribe.' He said, 'My son, be careful in your work, for your work is sacred. Should you omit or add a single letter, you will find yourself destroying the entire world, all of it.'"
>
> According to *Genesis Rabbah* 9:5, 20:2, and 94:9: "In the Torah scroll of R. Meir there was found written not 'And behold, it was very (*meod*) good' (Gen. 1:31), but 'And behold, death (*mot*) was good'; not 'And He made for Adam and for his wife garments of skin (*'or*)' (Gen. 3:21), but "Garments of light (*'or*)'; not 'The sons of Dan: Hushim' (Gen 46:23), but 'The son of Dan: Hushim.'"
>
> According to *y. Taanit* 1:1, 64a: "In the scroll of R. Meir they found written, instead of 'The burden of Dumah' (Isa. 21:11), 'The burden of Roma [Rome]'."
>
> Again, according to *b. Ketubbot* 19b, "A scroll of a book of Scripture that has not been corrected, R. Ammi said, may be kept for thirty days. From then on, it is forbidden to keep it, for Scripture says, 'Let not wrong dwell in thy tents.'"
>
> Finally, the care with which the Torah was to be copied can be seen in the following admonition from the post-Talmudic tractate *Soferim* 3: "Books may not be thrown about from one place to another, nor may they be treated disrespectfully. A man is required to have a scroll of Torah written with good ink, a good quill, by competent scribes, on good sheets of parchment made out of the hides of deer. He is then to wrap it in beautiful silks, in keeping with 'This my God, and I will glorify Him' (Exod. 15:2)."[27]

The rabbis clearly knew of the variants in the biblical texts, but there was no consistent focus on textual stabilization for several centuries either earlier among Jews of the Second Temple period or later during the rabbinic period.

When did early attempts at a stabilized text of the consonants in the Jewish Scriptures emerge? So far as scholars are able to determine today, these attempts began to emerge in the rabbinic tradition in the second or third century; but even with special attention focused on the problem, still no two biblical manuscripts were alike (Jewish or Christian) until the invention of the printing press in the fifteenth century. Even after the invention of the printing press textual variants continued in printed Bibles.

Christians did not seriously deal with the problem until the third century, when Origen acknowledged the difficulty of multiple textual traditions in the church's sacred scriptures and prepared his famous Hexapla to address the concern. He prepared an edition of the Bible with six parallel columns, each containing one of the popular textual traditions circulating in the churches and among the Jews. The first column was a Hebrew text of the Jewish scriptures, the second was a transliterated Hebrew text in Greek script, the third was the Greek translation of Aquila, the fourth was Symmachus's Greek translation of the Hebrew text, the fifth was possibly Origen's own translation—or likely one of the various texts of the LXX that was circulating in the area where he lived, which suggests that the Hexapla may have been a document Origen prepared for his own translation as well as to bring some stabilization to the biblical text. The sixth column contained mostly the translation of Theodotion, with the exception of the Psalms and possibly another translation for the Minor Prophets.[28] Origen's Hexapla highlights for us the variety of textual traditions circulating among Jews and Christians in the mid-third century.

THE MASORETIC TRADITION

The Masoretic[29] texts are a group of closely related manuscripts that were finalized in the Middle Ages especially with points in the Hebrew text and notes in the margins, but the consonantal text has roots in the "proto-Masoretic" text dating from the first century CE and possibly earlier, perhaps beginning sometime during the early Maccabean period (ca. 150 BCE). The Masoretes of the Middle Ages added vowels to the consonantal Hebrew text that enabled subsequent generations to sound out the words of the text as well as preserve the text of the Hebrew Bible. The rabbinic sages who were anxious to preserve the consonantal text of the Jewish scriptures provided no written tradition of symbols to indicate the pronunciation of the Hebrew text, and nothing about the later pointing of the text is mentioned in either the Jerusalem (Palestinian) or Babylonian Talmudim. The Yerushalmi or Jerusalem Talmud (*y.*) was completed around 400 CE; the larger Babylonian Talmud (*b.*) was completed at roughly 600 CE. Neither Talmud speaks of the pointing of the Hebrew Bible text. This suggests that the pointing of the Hebrew text originated with the later Masoretes sometime between 650 and 750 CE, perhaps around 700 CE. The text that the Masoretes preserved has many antecedents; the best known today are the "proto-Masoretic" biblical texts that were hidden in caves near Qumran.

Because of the many and often significant differences between the text of the Hebrew Bible and the Greek translation of the Hebrew scriptures, not only in the books that were included or excluded but also in the text of those books, the Septuagint was often marginalized in favor of the Hebrew text. But after years of careful analysis of the Dead Sea Scrolls, some scholars have begun to suggest that the Septuagint might in several instances be dependent upon an earlier form of the Hebrew text than the current Masoretic Text.[30]

The multiple copies of the same books at Qumran demonstrate the textual fluidity of the sacred scriptures of Jews at that time. No two manuscripts are exactly alike, not even the large number that follow a "proto-Masoretic" text. These documents date from the second century BCE to the early second century CE and are invaluable in textual criticism's goal of establishing the earliest and most reliable text of the Hebrew Bible.

Biblical scholars often presume that the Masoretic Text is the original text of the Hebrew Bible/Old Testament, but this has been challenged by Emanuel Tov, who contends that in a number of instances the Masoretic Text "does *not* reflect the 'original text' of the biblical books in many details." He goes on to say that "even if we were to surmise that M [MT] reflects the 'original' form of the Bible, we would still have to decide *which* Masoretic Text reflects this 'original text,' since the Masoretic Text is not a uniform textual unit, but is itself represented by many witnesses."[31] In another context, he acknowledges that the value of the LXX at various places is that it possibly preserves an earlier text of the Hebrew Bible, albeit in Greek. He states unambiguously, "when comparing the LXX evidence with that of the other sources, we found that beyond the MT, the LXX is the single most important source preserving redactionally different material relevant to the literary analysis of the Bible, often earlier than MT."[32] Because of the rather early date of the Greek translation of the Hebrew scriptures (ca. 280–150 BCE), he argues that it is likely that the LXX translators made use of a text of the Hebrew Bible not shared by those who later embraced the MT. He adds that the MT may have its roots in the Maccabean period, but that is difficult to prove and debatable. He concludes that the data in the LXX are an integral part of the transmission of the Bible as a whole, and therefore "in the literary analysis of the biblical books, equal attention should be paid to Hebrew and Greek evidence, as well as to any other ancient source. This analysis thus involves the Qumran biblical texts in Hebrew, and possibly even evidence relating to rewritten biblical compositions dating to the Second Temple period."[33] He cites four instances where the *Vorlage* (or Hebrew antecedent) of the LXX is shorter than the MT and likely earlier in origin. First, the book of Jeremiah is some 15 percent shorter both in the LXX and in 4QJer[b,d] in its number of words, verses, and pericopes, and the material is sometimes arranged differently. Tov calls this likely an earlier edition of Jeremiah. Second, the LXX of Ezekiel is between 4 and 5 percent shorter than the MT, the Syriac Peshitta, the Targumim, and the Latin Vulgate. His third example is the LXX of 1 Samuel 16–18, which is 45 percent shorter than the MT and other editions of the Hebrew Bible. Finally he notes that the list of inhabitants of Jerusalem in LXX 2 Esdras 21 (= Nehemiah 11) is much shorter than that of the MT, Syriac, Targum, and Vulgate in vv. 25–35, and that list is different from the parallel in 1 Chronicles 9. He cites a number of other differences between the LXX and the MT with other versions that are not always shorter, but simply different.[34] He concludes by saying that his intuition tells him "that more often than not the LXX reflects an earlier stage than MT both in the literary shape of the biblical books and in small details."[35] Elsewhere he posits that there was no standardization of the text of the Hebrew Bible in Second Temple Judaism, and the primary reason that the MT triumphed over other texts of the Hebrew Bible current in that time is that it was adopted by the only organized group of Jews who survived the destruction of the Second Temple.[36]

Again, of the more than nine hundred documents discovered at Qumran, most of the biblical books are represented, but also many nonbiblical religious books were discovered. It is difficult to distinguish between the biblical and nonbiblical books since they were placed side by side with no obvious distinguishing marks or comments that set one collection or book (biblical) apart from the others. Indeed, the use of the words "biblical" and "nonbiblical" to identify these writings is anachronistic; that is, they are later terms imposed on these ancient books that cannot be shown in the collections themselves. We do not have anything like a Bible at Qumran since there are no indications that there was a fixed sacred collection or text at that time. Tov reminds us, "The texts from the Judaean Desert show that very little distinction, if any, was made between the writing of biblical and non-biblical texts and more generally, of sacred and non-sacred texts."[37] Similarly, Talmon claims "that the Covenanters [at Qumran] did not consider their assemblage of biblical writings a closed canon of Holy Writ," and he goes on to show the weakness of all such arguments that depend on anachronistic assumptions about the threefold categorization of the Holy Scriptures at that time. He concludes that "Qumran literature evinces not only an 'open-ended biblical canon,' as is argued, but rather gives witness to what I have termed a 'Living Bible,' still in *status nascendi*."[38]

Some scholars have tried to distinguish between the Dead Sea Scrolls books, even suggesting that the noncanonical writings were essentially nothing more than commentary on the biblical writings, but James VanderKam has shown the weakness in that position and asks what biblical book addresses the issue of calendar like Enoch does.[39] How could this be commentary? Scholars are becoming more certain that notions of canon were simply not present before or during the time of Jesus, including at Qumran, even though various collections of sacred books were circulating among the Jews in those times. VanderKam acknowledges this point and disagrees that these were fixed or closed sacred collections. He also affirms the presence of other religious texts that were indistinguishable from the biblical books in early Judaism.[40] Talmon believes that the fall of Judah to the Romans and the destruction of the temple led to the fixation of the scriptures of the Jews, events that had no effect upon the covenanters at Qumran since they ceased to be a community before these events occurred. While some of his argument can be challenged, he is correct that there was no fixed biblical canon at Qumran. His conclusion is significant: "the Qumran biblical scrolls and documents do not offer any decisive new evidence pertaining to the crystallization of a closed canon of Hebrew Scriptures, worded in a fixed or essentially standardized text."[41]

The point here is that the Scriptures of the earliest Christians, and many Second Temple Jews in Israel and in the Diaspora, was the Septuagint or the

Old Greek collection of Scriptures. This collection predates the existence of any *fixed* collection that finally made up the Hebrew Bible, and this Greek translation included many other books besides those that are in the Protestant Old Testament or the rabbinic Hebrew Bible. In the latter case, the Jewish sages in the rabbinic tradition constructed the fixed collection now known as the Hebrew Bible or Tanakh: Torah or (Law), Nebiʾim (Prophets), Ketubim (Writings/ Hagiographa) in the second century CE (possibly in the late first century for some Jews, and later for others). It took several more centuries for the Jews of the Diaspora to accept the scriptural definition constructed by the rabbinic Jews, and many more than that for Christians to do the same. Some church teachers in early Christianity opted for the more narrow parameters of the Hebrew Bible, especially Jerome and Cyril of Jerusalem, both of whom were heavily influenced by the Jews in Judea, but this was not the case for the majority of the Christians. The witness from the surviving Jewish and Christian biblical manuscripts suggests a wider collection of sacred literature before discussions of canonization became a significant issue for both communities of faith.

After the Karaite challenge to the rabbis in the tenth and eleventh centuries CE for accepting more than the Law of Moses as sacred scripture,[42] there appears to be something close to universal acceptance emerging among the Jews of the twenty-four books of the Hebrew Bible and also a widespread acceptance of the Masoretic Text. Until that time, other Jewish books (Sirach especially) were included in the sacred collections of many Jews. It is also true that the books that more heavily influenced the Jews in the time of Jesus, including Jesus and his earliest followers, were for the most part the books of the Hebrew Bible; but also Sirach, the Wisdom of Solomon, and other apocryphal books continued to have considerable influence for centuries among the Jews and Christians.

WITNESSES TO THE HEBREW TEXT
OF THE HEBREW BIBLE/OLD TESTAMENT

Besides the Dead Sea Scrolls, the most important manuscripts that have survived antiquity that were used in producing the *Biblica Hebraica* editions of the Hebrew Bible are the Nash Papyrus and the Ben Asher Aleppo Codex. The manuscripts that deserve special attention now include:

1. The biblical and so-called nonbiblical manuscripts discovered in the Judean Desert at Qumran, Masada, Naḥal Ḥever, and Murabbaʿat in 1947 and following are among the most important finds for establishing the earliest text of the Hebrew Bible. Chief among these manuscripts are the Isaiah Scroll from cave 1 (1QIsᵃ), the *Habakkuk Commentary* from cave 1 (1QpHab), the Psalms Scroll from cave 11 (11QPsᵃ), but these are only a few of the highly significant manuscripts for establishing the earliest text of the Hebrew Bible.

2. The Nash Papyrus is a papyrus sheet that contains a damaged copy of the Decalogue (Exod. 20:2–17) and partly Deuteronomy 5:6–21 with the Shema

from Deuteronomy 6:4–9 appended. It dates probably from the Maccabean period, possibly middle to late second century BCE.

3. The Cairo Genizah manuscripts are some two hundred thousand fragments of sacred texts discovered in a genizah at a synagogue in Cairo, Egypt.[43] The biblical and nonbiblical fragments were written in Hebrew, Aramaic, Greek, Samaritan, and Arabic, and date from the fifth century CE and later. They contain fragments not only of the biblical books but of many others as well, including the Hebrew and Aramaic texts of Tobit and Sirach and the *Damascus Rule* (similar to the *Damascus Document* discovered at Qumran). These fragments were used by the Jews in various ways and were stored in the Ben Ezra Synagogue in Cairo, Egypt, but in the late nineteenth century they began to be stored in various libraries in Europe and the United States, especially in the Bodlian Library at Oxford. We cannot be certain about their canonical status among the Jews then from what is known about them presently. Sadly, many of these fragments have not been studied or published and much about them is not yet known.

4. The Ben Asher manuscripts date from the mid- to late eighth century to the mid-tenth century. The Ben Asher family produced these manuscripts with the vowel pointing and accents following what is now known as the Masoretic Text of the Hebrew Bible. The most important of these are the Aleppo and Leningrad codices. Codex Cairensis (C) contains the Former and Latter Prophets and, according to its colophon,[44] was produced by Moses Ben Asher in 895 CE. It came into the Karaite Jewish community in Cairo. The Aleppo Codex originally contained the complete Old Testament, though as noted above portions of it were destroyed in an anti-Jewish riot in 1947–1948. It is now in Jerusalem.[45] It is presently missing Genesis 1:1–Deuteronomy 28:26 and from Song of Songs 3:12 to the end (it omits Ecclesiastes, Lamentations, Esther, Daniel, Ezra, and Nehemiah). Subsequently, photographs of Deuteronomy 4:38–6:3, Genesis 26:37–27:30, and 2 Chronicles 35:7 have been found in different volumes and in a folio at the Hebrew University Library in Jerusalem. Finally, Codex Leningradensis, or Leningrad Codex (L) is a witness to the oldest surviving Ben Asher text (the Aleppo text) and according to its colophon was copied in 1008 CE from the exemplars of Aaron Ben Moses Ben Asher. This codex is the oldest complete codex of the Hebrew Bible and is a representative of the Masoretic Text containing all the books of the Hebrew Bible and all the textual and marginal notations that enable scholars to reconstruct the history of the textual transmission of the Hebrew Bible. The vowel and accent pointings follow the Tiberian school of Masoretes. In 1998 a beautiful facsimile of this codex was published,[46] and the codex remains one of the most important witnesses to the Masoretic Text.

5. The Petersburg Codex of the Prophets (V^P) dates to 915–916 CE and shows better than any other manuscript the Babylonian pointing system. It contains Isaiah, Jeremiah, Ezekiel, and the Minor Prophets (the Twelve). It used the Eastern (Babylonian) signs, but followed the Western tradition in its consonantal text and pointing.

6. The Erfurt codices were used in the *BHK* edition of the Hebrew Bible and are known as the Erfurtensis (E) 1, 2, and 3. They were housed in the Prussian State Library in Berlin (Ms Orient. 1210/11, 1212, 1213) and are now in the national Library of Prussian Cultural Properties. E1 contains the Hebrew Old Testament, Targumim, and the large and small *Masorah* (Masoretic notes). E2, dating from the thirteenth century CE, contains the Hebrew Old Testament, Targum Onkelos, and the large and small Masorah. E3, the most important of the three, dates before 1100 CE and contains the Hebrew Old Testament, large and small Masorah, and two extracts from *Okhla weOkhla*.[47]

7. Lost Codices. A number of codices have been lost but were referred to in the earlier notes of *BHK*. These include Codex Severi (Sev), Codex Hillel (Hill), Codex Muga (cited in Ms. 4445 and in the Petersburg Codex), Codex Jericho, and Codex Yerushalmi. Nothing aside from the earlier notes in *BHK* is known about these codices.[48]

These textual witnesses to the Masoretic Text frequently differ from the biblical books at Qumran. Tov has aptly commented about them, "There are many differences in reading between the individual Qumran texts, or, phrased differently, these texts reflect many variants vis-à-vis M [MT]."[49] In personal communication with me, following my comments on the some 200,000 to 400,000 variants in the New Testament manuscripts, Tov stated that there were some nine hundred thousand variants in the surviving Hebrew manuscripts! These variants, often spelling errors or omissions, did not go unnoticed by the ancient rabbis, and they set about ways to fix them, even if they were largely unsuccessful. The well-known post-talmudic tractate *Soferim* set a precedent for correcting errant texts of the Scriptures by following the testimony of the majority of manuscripts. The tradition is attributed to a third-century rabbi, but possibly derives from a Second Temple (pre–70 CE) time. The text is as follows:

> Said Rabbi Shimon ben Laqish:
> Three scrolls were located in the Temple court, *Sefer* "*M'wn*," *Sefer* "*Z'twty*," [and] *Sefer* "*Hy'*."
> In one they found written *m'wn 'lhy qdm*, "the dwelling place of the ancient God," and in two they found written *m'wnh lihy qdm* (Deut. 33:27); and they established [the reading in the] two and invalidated [the reading in the] one.
> In one they found written *wyšlh 't z'twty bny yśr'l*, "and he sent the youths of the Israelites," and in two they found written *wyslh 't n'ry bny yśr'l*, (Ex. 24:5); and they established [the reading in the] two and invalidated [the reading in the] one.
> In one they found "she" spelled *hy'* eleven times, and in two they found it spelled *hw'* eleven times; they established [the reading in the] two and invalidated [the reading in the] one (*Soferim* 6:4: *Three Scrolls in the Temple Court*).[50]

Although pious in its focus, the Babylonian Talmudic tractate *Qiddushin* 30a assumes that a letter-perfect text of the Torah had been available to the scribes, namely an exact replica of the original Torah, and rabbis assumed that copies of the Torah were made from a single correct copy, but this is nowhere to be seen in the copies that have survived.[51]

THE GREEK TEXT OF THE OLD TESTAMENT/HEBREW BIBLE

The regular practice of reading the scriptures in Greek by the Diaspora[52] Jews in their synagogues is important here. While it is not clear exactly when or how the translation of the rest of the Jewish scriptures took place, the Greek translations of the Jewish scriptures were eventually united into a whole for the Law and the Prophets, probably by 130 BCE for most of the books, but even later for other sacred books. The Jewish religious books that were translated into Greek are identified by the term "Septuagint," a term that was eventually applied to all the Old Greek translations of the Hebrew scriptures, and were generally well received by Jews in the Diaspora as their sacred scriptures, but also by Christians. Various Greek translations of the Jewish scriptures were used in Jewish worship in the Diaspora, and the implications of this are quite significant since the Greek scriptures contained more books (now called apocryphal and pseudepigraphal writings, as discussed in chapter 3 above) than those that were later included in the Hebrew Bible.[53]

The Greek manuscripts that support the text of the Hebrew Bible/Old Testament are many, but the most important are surely the great codices, Vaticanus (ca. 350–375), Sinaiticus (ca. 375–400), and Alexandrinus (ca. 450–500). The books in these manuscripts were listed in chapter 3, but the text of the books included is also quite significant and provides some of the earliest witnesses to the status of the Greek Old Testament scriptures in the fourth and fifth centuries. These manuscripts are significant because for the first time in the fourth century the technology for producing books or codices was advanced sufficiently to include more than 1,600 pages in one parchment volume. This allowed the church to include both its Old Testament and New Testament scriptures. While there is much that we do not know about these earliest uncial manuscripts (precise date, place of origin, and function in early Christianity), they are still our oldest witnesses to the state of the biblical text at that time; and the books that they contain also inform us about the scope of the earliest Christian Bibles. They contain not only the so-called biblical books, but also some nonbiblical and apocryphal books. It is important to repeat that these volumes served as sacred scripture in the communities that had them. For our purposes; they are also among some of the most important resources for reconstructing the oldest or earliest biblical text for the church.

As in the Hebrew manuscripts, there was also considerable textual fluidity in the early growth and development of the Greek scriptures. As in the Hebrew manuscripts, so also in the Greek manuscripts, no two biblical manuscripts are exactly alike. The textual variants in these manuscripts are considerable and at times overwhelming. The rabbinic teachers sought to stabilize the text of the Hebrew Bible and were largely successful in their attempts, but textual fluidity continued until the invention of the printing press. Before Origen, in the Christian church there was very little concern to stabilize the Greek text of the church's scriptures. As in the case of the Hebrew manuscripts, we have no "original" text that we can appeal to as the earliest or most original text of the Greek Old Testament scriptures, or at least none is recoverable at present. Textual scholars would rejoice if the Hebrew *Vorlage* of the Greek scriptures would one day appear, but that is improbable. The Masoretic Text is the best attempt of the rabbis to stabilize their biblical text, and Origen's Hexapla (early part of third century) is the early church's first attempt at stabilizing the Greek Bible. Another attempt at stabilizing the Latin versions came in the fifth century with Jerome (Hieronymus), who translated his Latin Vulgate from the Hebrew scriptures in the Old Testament and the Greek in the New Testament. Both scholars criticized those who treated their translations carelessly.

For those wanting to have the original text of the Hebrew Bible, that is, the earliest form of the text of the scriptures, the matter is not yet settled and the question still remains, which text of the scriptures is the canon for the churches today? Most biblical scholars continue to appeal to the Masoretic Text as the most stable text of the Hebrew Bible/Old Testament, but that stability was not present in the time of Jesus, as we can see not only at Qumran but also in the Samaritan Pentateuch and Septuagint. As a result of the Dead Sea Scrolls discovery and research there is considerable interest once again in the Septuagint and that has brought about a new translation as well as significant new commentaries on the Greek Old Testament books.[54] The primary text of the Septuagint that is used today is the Rahlfs-Hanhart.[55] This text is based largely on the uncial manuscripts of Vaticanus, Sinaiticus, and Alexandrinus, but also on a few other uncial and minuscule manuscripts from the fifth to the tenth centuries,[56] and ten ancient versions of the Greek text.

Besides these manuscripts and versions, two libraries or collections of books discovered in Egypt are worthy of mention and provide additional information on the texts of several OT books. First, the Chester Beatty papyri contains both Old and New Testament writings, including fragments of Genesis, Numbers, Deuteronomy, Isaiah, Jeremiah, Ezekiel, Daniel, Sirach, *1 Enoch*, and a homily by Melito. These date from the second to the fifth centuries and constitute some of the oldest Christian manuscripts of the Greek Old Testament books along with the apocryphal and pseudepigraphal literature.

The other library or collection of special note is the Bodmer papyri, which contain, along with various New Testament books, also fragmentary copies of Old Testament books in Greek and Coptic. These manuscripts include Genesis (Coptic), Exodus (Coptic), Deuteronomy (Coptic), Joshua (Coptic), Psalms (several manuscripts in Greek), Proverbs (Coptic), Song of Songs (Greek), Isaiah (Coptic), Jeremiah (Coptic), Lamentations (Coptic), Epistle of Jeremiah (Coptic), Baruch (Coptic), Daniel (Coptic), Daniel (Greek), Jonah (Coptic), Susanna

(Greek), Tobit (Coptic), 2 Maccabees (Coptic), and 11th *Ode of Solomon* (Greek). These manuscripts are dated from the fourth to the seventh centuries CE. They were produced by members of the Pachomian monastery and buried in the vicinity of Jebel Abu Mana, near Nag Hammadi, Egypt, in the seventh century during their decline.

These libraries or collections are telling for the books that they contain, but also because they advance our understanding of the text of the Old Testament scriptures as well as several apocryphal and pseudepigraphal texts that informed the faith and life of some early churches. These manuscripts have been assigned identity numbers in the Rahlfs register of Greek Old Testament manuscripts.[57]

In terms of the text of the early translations of the Hebrew Bible, the Jews initially accepted the Old Greek, but not for long. There are strong rabbinic prescriptions against translating the sacred texts. It has long been acknowledged not only by biblical scholars, but also by the peoples of ancient civilizations —including both Jews and Christians—that it is impossible to have an exact equivalent translation from one language to another. As a result, there was considerable hesitation on the part of religious people to translate their sacred texts into another language. Only Christians seem to have had the zeal to translate their sacred texts into other languages, in order to evangelize persons who spoke other languages.

Although Jesus probably spoke mostly Aramaic and Hebrew, the earliest Christian documents were produced in Greek, which eventually were translated into Syriac (we will say more about this in the following chapter). Jesus may also have been able to communicate in Greek in the marketplace, where nonliterary Greek was spoken in several locations in the Land of Israel in his day, such as the Decapolis cities and even in Jerusalem, where we see that one of the earliest conflicts in the church had to do with Greek-speaking widows and Hebrew- or Aramaic-speaking widows (Acts 6:1). A large number of the ossuaries (bone boxes) uncovered in and around Jerusalem that date largely from the first century CE have Greek names on them. Jesus probably spoke in Greek to a centurion (Matt. 8:5–10), the Syrophoenician woman (Mark 7:24–30), and to Pilate after his arrest (Mark 15:2; Matt. 27:11–13; Luke 23:3; John 18:33–38). None of them would likely have been able to speak Aramaic or Hebrew.

STABILITY AND FLUIDITY IN THE HEBREW BIBLE/OLD TESTAMENT

The text of the Jewish scriptures was unstable for several centuries both among Jews and later also Christians. Long after the books themselves were acknowledged as sacred Scripture, the text of those books was still unstable. While attempts at stabilizing the biblical text were made first by Jews and subsequently by Origen and some Christians after him, a completely stable biblical text was not possible until the invention of the printing press and movable type. Until the widespread use of the codex that allowed, by the fourth century, the inclusion of all of the biblical books in one volume, there is little stability in the text or book order in the Hebrew Bible or Old Testament. Nonetheless, there are some indications that a move toward stabilization was taking place in the century or so before the time of Jesus.

More than fifty years ago, M. H. Segal proposed that the origins of the Masoretic Text began in the time following the cleansing and dedication of the temple in the reign of Judas Maccabee (the name likely comes from the Aramaic term for "hammer"), son of Mattathias, founder of the Hasmonean Dynasty (1 Macc. 2:23–41). Segal observes that because of the destruction of the copies of the Jewish Law by the Greek Seleucid Dynasty (1 Macc. 1:56–57) during their persecution of the Jews because they would not sacrifice to the pagan gods nor eat the sacrifices made to them, there was a need for more copies of the Law after the Jews regained control of their temple and could once again practice their sacred traditions. Following in the steps of Nehemiah, who founded a library of sacred books for Jews, Judas gathered copies of the sacred texts of the Jews and made them available to those who would send for them (2 Macc. 2:13–15). This, according to Segal, was logically the time when more copies would be made and the scribes would initiate some consistency in copying the scrolls.[58] He supports his position by showing the differences between two different copies of the Isaiah Scroll discovered at Qumran, 1QIsa^a and 1QIsa^b (he uses the earlier Dead Sea Scrolls identification of DSIa and DSIb). The first of these texts is the older and has several corrections in it, and the more recent one is almost the same as the later Masoretic Text. The corrections to the former text follow the Masoretic Text. From this he deduces that 1QIsa^a is the older text—which was probably rescued by the Jews during the Seleucid Dynasty's destruction of Jewish sacred books—and that the more recent one parallels the Masoretic Text that was later adopted by the rabbis in the second century CE. Segal adds to this that the Greek translations produced in the second century CE (those of Aquila, Theodotion, and Symmachus) all follow the Masoretic Text. Further, he has noted some later talmudic references that reflect the role of correctors of biblical books: "Rabba bar bar Hanah reported in the name of R. Johanan that the correctors of biblical books in Jerusalem received their wages out of the apportionment from the fund of the shekel-chamber in the Temple" (b. Ketubot 106a, trans. Segal).[59] This activity of correcting took place, he claims, before the destruction of the temple, and he believes that it best fits the time immediately after Judas Maccabee's gathering of sacred books for the Jewish people. He also cites another talmudic reference to the numbering of the letters and words of the Torah and Psalms to support his view that before such numbering could take place, the text of the Hebrew scriptures had to be relatively fixed. The additional text reads:

> For this reason were the ancients called sopherim [scribes], because they used to number all the letters of the Torah. For they used to say the waw of nhwn (Lev 11:42) marks the end of half the letters of the Book of the Torah; . . . whtglh (Lev 13:33) marks the end of half the verses of the Torah;

the '*ayin* . . . in *ycr* (Psa 80:14) marks the end of half of the Psalms in respect of the letters; *whw' rhwm* (Psa 78:38) marks its half in verses. (*b. Qiddushin* 30a, trans. Segal)

Segal agrees that no complete stabilization of the text of the Hebrew Bible was recognized by everyone, and concedes: "We have conclusive evidence, both internal and external, that for a long time in the age of the sopherim the text was in a fluid condition, and that scribes were not tied to a standard text."[60] He acknowledges that many changes were made in the text during this time of fluidity, but believes that the stabilizing of the biblical texts that began following Judas Maccabee became more stable in the second century CE and later under the direction of the rabbis. He conjectures, based on a talmudic text, that the official text of the Torah was issued by the official scribes and was laid down in the codex (scroll?) known in early rabbinic literature as "The Book of the Temple Court," which was copied by the king of Israel (*y. Sanhedrin* 2:6).[61] Finally, he notes that during the destruction of the temple in Jerusalem a copy of the official text of the Torah was taken to Rome. It is possible that it was the copy that Alexander Severus returned to the Jews (222–235 CE) along with building a synagogue for them in Rome. In support of this, he also cites an Aramaic *midrash* (interpretation): "This is one of the words which were written in the Torah which came out of Jerusalem in captivity, and went up to Rome and was stored in the synagogue of Severus."[62] As further support that the Roman emperor had such a copy of the Jewish Law, he cites the testimony of Josephus, who claims that when the temple was destroyed, Vespasian and Titus took among their spoils the Law of the Jews. "After these, and last of all the spoils, was carried a copy of the Jewish Law" (*J. W.* 7.150, LCL), and later he states that Vespasian "laid up the vessels of gold from the temple of the Jews, on which he prided himself; but their Law and the purple hangings of the sanctuary he ordered to be deposited and kept in the palace" (*J. W.* 7.161–62, LCL).

The instability of the text of the Hebrew scriptures in the centuries before and after the time of Jesus is also matched by the instability in the sequence of books in the Hebrew Bible. We can see this instability in a comparison of the Masoretic Text sequence of the Twelve with the sequence of books in the Septuagint and 4QXII[a]. In the latter two texts, but not in the Masoretic Text, Jonah is in the last position in that collection. The variation in the sequence of the Twelve in the Masoretic Text and the Septuagint suggests that the collection was not fixed much earlier than the time suggested above, but it also suggests that redactional activity involved in the formation of the collection extended from the time when the earliest documents were gathered into a collection, sometime around 225 BCE.[63] J. K. Elliott observes that the order of the twelve Minor Prophets varies in the Hebrew Bible and Septuagint, that the Latin and English translations generally follow the Hebrew order, that Greek Esther and Hebrew Esther vary considerably in their texts, and that Job is one-sixth shorter in the Septuagint than in the Hebrew. He also notes that there are considerable differences between the Hebrew texts and the Greek texts of Joshua, 1 Samuel, 1 Kings, Proverbs, and Jeremiah.[64]

These and other variations in both manuscripts and lists of sacred Old Testament/Hebrew Bible books speak of the instability of the collection at an early date, before the separation of Christians from Jews, but also later. This instability also accounts for the considerable variation in the order of books in early Christianity. While it is true that the development of the codex allowed for stability only after the fourth century CE, and that various copies of the Old Testament and New Testament scriptures could not be placed in one bound volume before then, it is remarkable that there is still considerable stability in the order of the various codices and lists of sacred Old Testament books through Kings, but after that the order varies considerably in both Jewish and Christian manuscripts.[65] For example, in the interesting and at times strange case of the sequence of the book of Job, in some of the oldest sources we have the following sequences of Job. Most of the evidence is in the Christian traditions, but there are interesting comparisons in the later Jewish manuscripts and also in *b. Baba Bathra* 14b. The following examples of the variables in location are instructive:

1. In the Hebrew Bible: Psalms, Job, Proverbs.
2. In *b. Baba Bathra* 14b: Psalms, Job, Proverbs, with an explanation for putting Job, believed to be written by a person in the days of Moses, after Psalms (one does not begin a section "with a record of suffering").
3. In Codex Leningradensis (L), the sequence of the Writings is Psalms, Proverbs, Job (different from Christian Bibles), which is, of course, the same in the current Hebrew Bible.
4. In the Aleppo Codex the sequence is Psalms, Proverbs, Job (Song of Songs is not in this codex).
5. In the LXX the sequence is Psalms, Psalm 151, *Ode* 12 (or Prayer of Manassah), Proverbs, Ecclesiastes, Son of Songs, Job.
6. The Roman Catholic Bible: Job, Psalms, Proverbs.
7. The Protestant Bible: Job, Psalms, Proverbs.
8. The Eastern Orthodox: Psalms, Job, Proverbs.
9. Codex Vaticanus: Psalms, Proverbs, . . . Job (ellipses indicated one or more books missing)
10. Codex Sinaiticus: Psalms, Proverbs, . . . Job
11. Codex Alexandrinus: Psalms, Proverbs, . . . Job
12. Melito of Sardis: Psalms, Proverbs, . . . Job
13. Origen: Psalms, Proverbs, . . . Job
14. Athanasius: Psalms, Proverbs, . . . Job
15. Cyril of Jerusalem: Job, Psalms, Proverbs.[66]

It is not clear why these sequences vary, but it may have more to do with the fact that the early circulation of most of the books was in single scrolls or, later, codices. With the stabilization of the text also came a greater stability in the order of the books, though that is at a much later time. Christian manuscripts have a different order or sequence of books than the sequence in the Hebrew Bible. Only after the fourth century, when the technology for manuscript production was sufficient to collect all of the sacred books in one volume, is there an increase in the stability of the sequence of books in the Christian Bibles. This stability took longer in Christian churches than in Jewish synagogues, but eventually the sequence became more stable.

In regard to the book of Daniel, its place was no doubt among the Prophets initially, as was true of the Psalms and all sacred writings except the Torah, but this changed in the second century CE when the third part of the Hebrew Bible was separated from the Prophets, and the Writings (Ketubim/Hagiographa) emerged in rabbinic Judaism.

1. Hebrew Bible: Esther, Daniel, Ezra–Nehemiah, 1–2 Chronicles
2. Septuagint: Ezekiel, Epistle of Jeremiah, Susanna, Daniel, Bel and Dragon
3. In *b. Baba Bathra* 14b: Daniel, Esther, Ezra–Nehemiah, and 1–2 Chronicles
4. Orthodox: Epistle of Jeremiah, Ezekiel, Daniel + Prayer of Azariah, Song of Three Young Men, Susanna, Bel and Dragon
5. Roman Catholic: in middle of final part of Old Testament (prophetic collection), sequence = Baruch (includes Epistle of Jeremiah), Ezekiel, Daniel + Prayer of Azariah, Song of Three Young Men, Susanna, Bel and Dragon
6. Protestant: Jeremiah, Lamentations, Ezekiel, Daniel (in middle of prophetic section)
7. Codex Aleppo: Esther, Daniel, Ezra–Nehemiah
8. Codex Leningrad: Dan, Ezra, Nehemiah, 1–2 Chronicles
9. Vaticanus: Jeremiah, Baruch, Lamentations, Epistle of Jeremiah, Ezekiel, Daniel
10. Sinaiticus: missing in fragmented text, probably after Lamentations and somewhere before Joel
11. Alexandrinus: (not at end) Epistle of Jeremiah, Ezekiel, Daniel, Esther
12. Melito: Daniel, Ezekiel, Esdras
13. Origen: Daniel, Ezekiel, Job, Esther
14. Athanasius: Jeremiah/Baruch/Lamentations/Epistle of Jeremiah, Ezekiel, Daniel
15. Cyril: Jeremiah/Baruch/Lamentations/Epistle of Jeremiah, Ezekiel, Daniel

The location varies, but Daniel is often near Ezekiel and the Epistle of Jeremiah. Its variable sequence in the earliest traditions illustrates the lack of stability of the Hebrew scriptures in early Judaism and early Christianity. Again, some of this may be due to Daniel's earlier history of circulating in a single scroll or in a scroll with a smaller number of books, especially Ezekiel, but probably others.

The books, their sequence, and the text of the Clementine Latin Old Testament were fixed as the official Vulgate of the Roman Catholic Church in 1592. Throughout the long history of the canonization of the biblical books, the sequence of books has varied considerably until the invention of the printing press and advances in book technology.

It is likely that a collection of prophetic writings existed much earlier than the fixing of the Book of the Twelve, but nothing suggests that the broader collection of prophetic writings was also fixed at that time. The notion of a fixed collection, apart from the Law (Torah/Pentateuch), is much later in Judaism and certainly after the time of Jesus. Again, it is almost certain that various collections of sacred writings circulated among Jews both before and during the time of Jesus, but had there been any widespread notion of a fixed twenty-two or twenty-four collection of sacred books, it is difficult to understand how the variety of books that were written between 200 BCE and 100 CE gained any currency among Jews or early Christians. The fixed number of sacred books is first mentioned at the end of the first century CE by Josephus (*Ag. Ap.* 1:37–43, twenty-two books) and suggested in *4 Ezra* 14:44–47 (twenty-four books plus seventy others that were inspired by God). One may presume that these fixed numbers preceded both Josephus and the author of *4 Ezra* and likely owe their origin to the format of Homer's *Iliad* and *Odyssey*, which are divided into twenty-four books, each beginning with a letter of the twenty-four-letter Greek alphabet. This sacredness of a text is also seen in the way that Psalm 119 is divided into twenty-two sections, each beginning with a different letter of the twenty-two-letter Hebrew alphabet. See also Psalms 9–10 which are combined to form an acrostic with each verse beginning with a letter *in sequence* of the Hebrew alphabet. This is also true of Psalms 25, 34, 37, 111, 112, 119, 145 and Proverbs 31:10–31.

That a distinct three-part biblical canon emerges for the first *known* time in *b. Baba Bathra* 14b suggests a Babylonian origin of the three-part Hebrew Bible (Law, Prophets, and Writings). Until that time, and well into the rabbinic period, the most common way of referring to the Jewish scriptures was "the Law and the Prophets." Again, there is no doubt that sacred collections existed long before the time of Jesus, but the exact parameters of those collections in the first century CE (that is, whether they were fixed) is not known. Since the early church separated from the Jews before those decisions were made and widely received, there is considerable variation in the Jewish sacred books cited as scripture in early Christianity, and there is no example where the early Christians followed the Jewish model of a three-part Old Testament canon.[67]

The Masoretic Text is the best attempt of the rabbis to stabilize their biblical text, and we can see a number of parallels to it at Qumran among the Dead Sea Scrolls, but with the renewed interest in the text of the Hebrew Bible as a result of comparisons with the Dead Sea texts, it has become more and more difficult to establish a *Vorlage* of the current biblical text. For those wanting to have the earliest text of the Hebrew Bible, the matter is not yet settled and the question still remains, Which text of the scriptures is the final authority for synagogues and churches today? Most biblical scholars continue to appeal to the Masoretic Text as the most stable text of the Hebrew Bible/Old Testament, but that stability was not present in the time of Jesus whether at Qumran, in the Samaritan Pentateuch, or in the Septuagint.

CONCLUSION

The fluidity of the text of the biblical literature should not be weighed too heavily in terms of canonicity, since the stabilization of the text took even longer than the recognition of the biblical writings as sacred Scripture. Stephen Chapman may well have a valid point when he chides those who argue from a fluid text to the conclusion that the canon did not yet exist. He believes that the canon of Moses and the Prophets preceded textual stability. I am not convinced of his whole argument, but he appears to be correct when claiming that "canonicity is not necessarily dependent upon the stabilization of a particular text, although these two processes are clearly joined in some way."[68]

As we have shown, more books than those in the current Jewish and Christian Bibles initially informed the faith and religious life of both Jewish and Christian communities for centuries. The obvious question is whether the same should be true today. This is not a plea for opening the biblical canon and including other books or excluding others, but rather to be informed by them. Christians of all persuasions and many Jews as well have found considerable value in studying these other ancient texts that were left behind in the canonical processes. I should also say that in my opinion there is no major or strategic doctrine of the church or of Judaism that would be lost or placed in jeopardy if these books were included or excluded, but they do add considerably to our understanding of the context and development of the Jewish and Christian traditions.

We will turn now to the scriptures of Jesus and the early church to see what sacred texts informed him and his early followers.

Chapter 7

The Scriptures of Jesus and the Early Church[1]

INTRODUCTION

Some biblical scholars contend that a fixed biblical canon of the Hebrew Scriptures was current among the Jews well before the time of Jesus. A few of these scholars are bold enough to say that Jesus passed on this scripture canon to his disciples and that was the same canon held by the Pharisees and other Jews in the time of Jesus, as well as by the earliest Christians and the later rabbinic Jews. Roger Beckwith, for instance, argues that "the New Testament shows Jesus and his apostles endorsing a canon wider than that of the Samaritans and indistinguishable from that of the Pharisees, which now seems to have been the standard (if not, indeed, the only) Jewish canon."[2] It is strange, however, and even anachronistic to argue that Jesus or his apostles endorsed any biblical canon.[3] Presently, no clear evidence has been produced to substantiate this claim; indeed, the contrary appears to be true. James VanderKam acknowledges that the word "canon" is not used in the later technical sense of a closed or fixed collection of sacred texts by biblical writers or by those contemporary with them and concludes: "since the specialized use of the term [canon] originated among patristic writers, it cannot serve as a useful point of entry into the problem with which we

123

are concerned. There appears to be no single word in Jewish texts of the second-temple age that expresses this specific sense of *canon*."[4]

As members of a Jewish sect, the early Christians would likely acknowledge those sacred texts that were passed on to them by their Jewish siblings before their separation from the mainstream of Judaism in the first and second centuries. We can gather this information from allusions and citations of this literature in the early Christian literature as well as in some of the manuscripts that have survived antiquity. In the former case, there are numerous citations of the Jewish Scriptures in the New Testament and also parallel language, allusions, and some citations of what is often now referred to as apocryphal or pseudepigraphal literature but was not so called initially. As I have shown elsewhere, most of what is cited in the New Testament comes from the books that make up the Hebrew Bible, but all the Hebrew Bible books are not cited in the New Testament and other books are alluded to that did not eventually get included in the Hebrew Bible or some Christian Bibles. The best-known example of this is *1 Enoch*, but there are also several parallels to Wisdom of Solomon, Sirach, and others. Examples of these parallels are listed below.

When Jesus referred to or cited "scripture," we can be certain that he most often referred to texts that eventually were included in Jewish and Christian Bibles, but it appears that he was also familiar with other religious texts that he did not specifically identify. As I will show below, he did not cite all of the books of the current Hebrew Bible, and he was most likely familiar with and even made use of religious texts that were not eventually included in the Hebrew Bible. It is unlikely that Jesus cited all of the literature that he and his followers acknowledged as scripture since most of his teaching was ad hoc in nature and addressed specific concerns that he faced in his ministry. For example, in the temptation stories in Luke 4:1–12 and Matthew 4:1–11, Jesus cited specific texts to address the challenges of the specific temptations. On other occasions he would likely have used only those texts that advanced or supported his teaching. This makes sense, of course, but it does not identify for us what other texts he may have acknowledged as sacred. If we possessed everything that Jesus said, and no one makes this claim (John 20:30–31), what other texts might he have cited as scripture? It is quite possible that Jesus and his disciples accepted as scripture other Jewish writings that were circulating in the land of Israel in the first century, but this is largely an argument from silence. It is unlikely that we will be able to discern all of the writings that Jesus considered sacred scripture since he himself never identified them, but it is possible to show from his teachings which sacred texts most influenced his ministry. The primary sources for this study are, of course, the canonical Gospels. In them we can see which sacred texts influenced Jesus' teaching and which ones he actually cited as scripture. In some instances scholars disagree whether it was Jesus speaking or his later interpreters, but they generally agree that the canonical Gospels are the most fruitful starting place for any investigation into this matter.

Establishing a universally acknowledged database of Jesus' citations of biblical texts and his allusions to or familiarity with other sacred texts, however, is problematic. Many scholars agree that some sayings attributed to Jesus are inauthentic in their current form, for example, Mark 8:34–35 and Matthew 28:19–20, but most agree that the canonical Gospels are the primary sources for our knowledge of the teaching and preaching of Jesus.[5] Several Jesus sayings found outside the canonical Gospels and frequently identified as the *Agrapha* are acknowledged as genuine, but most of them do not have credibility among scholars and those that do make little or no advance in our understanding of Jesus; they simply and generally support the picture of Jesus we find in the canonical Gospels.[6]

It is not likely that we will ever know with certainty all of the literature that Jesus acknowledged as sacred scripture, but we are able to draw some preliminary conclusions about the matter. In pursuit of this goal, I will begin by first describing an appropriate methodological approach and then examine the resulting evidence that permits some qualified questions raised at the beginning of this paper.

THE SEARCH FOR AN APPROPRIATE METHODOLOGY

I will begin with four suggestions that relate to our knowledge of Jesus. First, since Jesus produced no books, the primary sources for our inquiry come from those writings produced by those who were his followers in the first century, the writers of the canonical Gospels and those who composed the rest of the New Testament. Beyond this, it is also important to examine the writings of the early church fathers, the earliest interpreters of the story of Jesus and the New Testament writings. It is also helpful to examine the contemporary writings of early Judaism that focus on beliefs and practices in these matters. Jesus was a Jew; but how similar was he to his contemporaries and how familiar was he with the writings and traditions that informed them? He cited or alluded to a variety of sacred texts in his teaching ministry. How common was this in his time? The canonical Gospels were certainly shaped by the early communities of faith that followed Jesus, and they help us to see what sacred texts most influenced him. Most New Testament scholars agree that Matthew and Luke reshaped the Markan and Q material in view of the needs of their own communities of faith. In some cases they also reshaped or corrected it, as we see in the case of Mark, who states that Isaiah wrote the prophecy that Jesus was proclaiming (Mark 1:2), but this text comes partially from Malachi. Both Luke and Matthew corrected this opening from Mark's Gospel and reshaped it.[7] The historical setting for many of Jesus' teachings in John is similar to the Synoptic Gospels, but not all are the same. Even in those events in Jesus' life that are the same in all four Gospels, the setting and sequence frequently vary. This acknowledgment is not the same, however, as saying that those communities of faith that received the Jesus traditions *invented* those traditions and placed them on his lips or in his life, even if there was some shaping of those traditions to address the needs of the churches that received them. There is an important distinction between "shaping" and "inventing" sacred traditions. The latter suggests that early followers of Jesus were not so much interested in preserving stories about the one they were willing to proclaim and die for as much as they were concerned about inventing stories about him that met their own catechetical and missional needs in subsequent generations.[8]

Second, those who were closest to Jesus and followed him as Lord are more likely to have alluded to or cited the sacred texts that Jesus employed in his proclamation and teaching. Consequently, even if secondary in importance, those texts that the writers of the New Testament and other early Christian sources cited authoritatively are important to examine. If these assumptions are appropriate, we may conclude that the sources that have survived in the early church and Jewish traditions suggest a much larger and more open collection of scriptures in the time of Jesus and following. Indeed, there is no evidence that anyone in the time of Jesus ever discussed the notion of a fixed and more limited biblical canon or its scope.

Third, since early Christianity was initially a Jewish sect, we also have to ask what the surviving Jewish sources from roughly the time of Jesus tell us about the *operative* scriptures of that era. That discussion will involve a study of Philo, the Dead Sea Scrolls, Josephus, early rabbinic texts, as well as the religious litera- ture written in the first centuries BCE and CE that is sometimes called pseude- pigraphal writings or, as James Sanders calls them, "non-Masoretic" texts.[9]

When ancient writers quoted or cited sources, we cannot assume that they regarded them as sacred or inspired literature or that they added them to a fixed collection of writings acknowledged as sacred scripture. For example, according to the author of Acts (17:28), Paul stood before the Areopagus on Mars Hill and cited Epimenides as well as Aratus's opening lines from *Phaenomena*. No one seriously argues today that the author of Acts believed that these writings were part of Paul's *scripture* collection; rather they are evidence of his familiarity with classical writers and his employment of them to attract Athenian residents to his message. On the other hand, it is not always possible to distinguish ancient writers' esteem for a written source from their acknowledgment of its scriptural status. If a source is cited in a scriptural or authoritative manner, normally by using such common designations for scripture as "it is written" or "as the scrip- ture says" or some such designation, then it probably does represent that writer's views about the sacredness of a particular text. This, however, is not always clear from the ancient sources.

Beckwith correctly stresses the difficulty and inappropriateness of drawing conclusions about the scope of the biblical canon in antiquity from simple refer- ences to sources. He lists five major fallacies of method commonly followed by scholars in this regard:

> (i) failure to distinguish evidence that a book was known from evidence that a book was canonical; (ii) failure to distinguish disagreement about the canon between different parties from uncertainty about the canon within those parties; (iii) failure to distinguish between the adding of books to the

canon and the removal of books from it; (iv) failure to distinguish between the canon which the community recognized and used, and the eccentric views of individuals about it; and (v) failure to make use of Jewish evidence about the canon transmitted through Christian hands, whether by denying its Jewish origins, or by ignoring the Christian medium through which it has come.[10]

I agree in principle with each of these points and acknowledge the temptation to judge all quoted or cited texts as scripture or canon. Beckwith assumes, however, that discussions about canon formation had already taken place well before the time of Jesus and claims that the New Testament writers did not quote or cite any of the apocryphal or pseudepigraphal literature as sacred Scripture. He rejects the notion that Jude cited *1 Enoch* 1:9 as sacred Scripture and concludes that all that we can affirm about the New Testament's apparent use of noncanonical writings is that there is "an occasional correspondence of thought which suggests a knowledge of them."[11] Often, however, there is more than an "occasional correspondence of thought" in the New Testament's use of this literature—there are significant verbal parallels, as we will see below. I have argued elsewhere that Jude clearly cited *1 Enoch* (1:9) as prophetic or inspired literature.[12]

I will now focus on the scripture texts attributed to Jesus in the canonical Gospels as well as in the rest of the New Testament, but also on those religious texts circulating among his Jewish contemporaries. I will assume that those closest to Jesus (his early followers) are more likely to reflect his views on scripture and follow his example in their references to sacred texts.

THE SCRIPTURES OF JESUS

What scripture texts did Jesus cite and which ones did he cite most frequently? According to the Synoptic Gospel writers, he appealed to most of the texts now in the Hebrew Bible, but he cited Isaiah, Psalms, Deuteronomy, and Exodus more frequently than all other books. He also showed considerable familiarity with other Jewish scriptures, both those that we now call canonical as well as some that we now call noncanonical (or apocryphal and pseudepigraphal) writings. The Synoptic Gospels indicate that Jesus frequently cited or alluded to four of the books of the Law, but only one time did he refer to Numbers (Num. 28:9–10; cf. Matt. 12:5). In John, Jesus cited the Psalms, Isaiah, Deuteronomy, and Exodus most frequently, but also other Hebrew Bible books to a lesser extent. A collection of these and other texts that have some parallels in verbal and subject matter with the teachings of Jesus is located at the end of this chapter. According to John, Jesus cited all five Torah books but especially Deuteronomy. According to all the evangelists, Jesus was also quite familiar with the Prophets, especially Isaiah. Likewise, in all four Gospels Jesus cited frequently the book of Psalms, for example, Psalm 22:1, and probably all of that psalm (see Mark 15:34),[13] as well as Psalm 69:4–9, cited in reference to Jesus' cleansing of the temple court in John 2:17. While he referred to Daniel and Zechariah on several occasions, he did not cite all the books in the Prophets or many other books in the Hebrew Bible. More specifically, Jesus does not refer to or cite Joshua, Judges, Ruth, 2 Samuel, 1 Chronicles, Ezra, Nehemiah, Esther, Job, Ecclesiastes, Song of Songs, Lamentations, Obadiah, Nahum, Habakkuk, or Haggai. Nothing in the Gospels suggests that Jesus was either aware of them or that he rejected them; they are simply not mentioned, alluded to, or cited in the canonical Gospels. On the other hand, nothing in the canonical Gospels or in early Christianity suggests that Jesus restricted his understanding of scripture to any collection that eventually became fixed in early Judaism and subsequently in early Christianity.

The question here is not so much whether Jesus or his earliest followers, or even the various Jewish sects of the first century CE, recognized the books in the current Hebrew Bible canon as sacred literature, but whether they cited or utilized *all* the books in the Hebrew Bible current in the first century CE. More specifically, did Jesus accept as scripture fewer or more than the books that are now in the Hebrew Bible or Protestant Old Testament? As already noted, there are indications that some later rabbinic Jews questioned the sacredness of several Hebrew Bible books. On the other hand, some rabbis accepted Sirach as scripture (*b. Hagigah* 13a; *y. Hagigah* 77c; *b. Yebamot* 63b; *Gen. Rab.* 8:2b; *b. Baba Qamma* 92b; *y. Berakot* 11b).[14]

While it is clear that Jesus and the early Christians supported their proclamation and mission aims with a variety of Hebrew Bible texts, they apparently were also informed by other religious literature. Clearly the Law (especially Deuteronomy), the Psalms, and Isaiah formed the core of the writings that Jesus and his followers cited as sacred texts; they also made frequent use of Jeremiah, Ezekiel, and Daniel. It is apparent as well that they knew—or were familiar with—Jewish traditions in several other writings now identified as noncanonical writings. Jesus' parallels in language and allusions to the so-called apocryphal and pseudepigraphal literature in the canonical Gospels are often remarkably similar to allusions or citations that appear in other New Testament writings and in other early church writings as well. These allusions, citations, and verbal parallels indicate that Jesus was influenced to some extent and informed by religious literature that was not later included in the Hebrew Bible as well as by a common tradition or expression of wisdom in the Jewish community, though the latter is more difficult to substantiate. While some of the following examples may simply reflect common religious and theological motifs circulating in the Land of Israel in the time of Jesus and later, the multiplicity of these parallels points toward direct influence and dependence.

Besides the lists supplied at the end of this chapter, the following examples are worth noting. Matthew apparently used the language of Wisdom of Solomon in telling the story of Jesus. For example, in Wisdom 2:13 we read: "He professes to have knowledge of God, and calls himself a child of the Lord." There is some coincidence of language in Matthew 27:43: "he trusts in God; let God deliver him now, if he wants to; for he said, 'I am God's Son'" (see also parallels in thought in Wisd. 2:18–20). Likewise, in Wisdom 3:7, the words: "*In the time of their visitation* they will shine forth, and will run like sparks through the stubble," have some parallel with the words in Luke 19:44: "because you did not recognize *the time of your visitation from God.*" In both Wisdom 5:22 ("The water of the sea will rage against them, and rivers will relentlessly overwhelm them") and Luke 21:25 ("distress among nations confused by the roaring of the sea and waves"), the judgment of God comes upon the disobedient through raging waters.

For similar examples, observe the following parallels in word and thought:[15]

1. Compare Tobit 12:15: "I am Raphael, one of the seven *angels who stand ready and enter before the glory of the Lord,*" to Matthew 18:10: "Take care that you do not despise one of these little ones; for, I tell you, *in heaven their angels continually see the face of my Father in heaven,*" and Luke 1:19: The angel replied, "I am Gabriel. *I stand in the presence of God,* and I have been sent to speak to you and to bring you this good news."

2. Compare Sirach 10.14: "*The Lord overthrows the thrones of rulers, and enthrones the lowly in their place,*" to Luke 1:52: "*He has brought down the powerful from their thrones, and lifted up the lowly.*"

3. Compare Sirach 11.19: "when he says, '*I have found rest, and now I shall feast on my goods!*' He does not know how long it will be until he leaves them to others and dies," to Luke 12:19–20: "And I will say to my soul, '*Soul, you have ample goods laid up for many years; relax, eat, drink, be merry.*' But God said to him, "You fool! *This very night your life is being demanded of you. And the things you have prepared, whose will they be?*"

4. Compare Sirach 29:10–11: "Lose your silver for the sake of a brother or a friend, and *do not let it rust under a stone and be lost. Lay up your treasure according to the commandments of the Most High, and it will profit you more than gold,*" to Matthew 6:20: "but *store up for yourselves treasures in heaven, where neither moth nor rust consumes and where thieves do not break in and steal.*"

5. Compare Wisdom 6:18: "and *love of her is the keeping of her laws,* and giving heed to her laws is assurance of immortality," to John 14:15: "*If you love me, you will keep my commandments.*"

6. Compare Wisdom 16:26: "so that your children, whom you loved, O Lord, might learn that *it is not the production of crops that feeds humankind but that your word sustains those who trust in you,*" to Matthew 4:4: "But he answered, '*It is written, 'One does not live by bread alone, but by every word that comes from the mouth of God.'*'"

7. Compare Psalms of Solomon 5:3: "*For no one takes plunder away from a strong man,* so who is going to take (anything) from all that you have done, unless you give (it)?" to Mark 3:27: "But *no one can enter a strong man's house and plunder his property* without first tying up the strong man; then indeed the house can be plundered."

8. Compare *Jubilees* 5:9–11: "*You feed the birds and the fish,* as you send rain to the wilderness that the grass may sprout, to provide pasture in the wilderness for every living thing, and if they are hungry, they will lift up their face to you.

You feed kings and rulers and peoples, O God, and who is the hope of the poor and the needy, if not you, Lord?" to Matthew 6:26: "*Look at the birds of the air; they* neither sow nor reap nor gather into barns, *and yet your heavenly Father feeds them. Are you not of more value than they?*"

9. Compare *1 Enoch* 15:6–7: "Indeed you, formerly you were spiritual, (having) eternal life, and immortal in all the generations of the world. That is why (formerly) *I did not make wives for you, for the dwelling of the spiritual beings of heaven is heaven,*" to Mark 12:25: "For when they rise from the dead, *they neither marry nor are given in marriage, but are like angels in heaven.*" [Note: The similarity here is in the thought that angels do not marry and neither do those who go from this life to the next.]

10. Compare *1 Enoch* 22:9–10: "the spirits of the dead might be separated. And in the manner in which the souls of the righteous are separated [by] this spring of water with light upon it, in like manner, *the sinners are set apart when they die and are buried,*" to Luke 16:26: "Besides all this, *between you and us a great chasm has been fixed, so that those who might want to pass from here to you cannot do so, and no one can cross from there to us.*" The similarity is more in the notion of separation in the afterlife.

11. Compare *1 Enoch* 38:2: "and when the Righteous One shall appear before the face of the righteous, those elect ones, their deeds are hung upon the Lord of the Spirits, he shall reveal light to the righteous and the elect who dwell upon the earth, where will the dwelling of the sinners be, *and where the resting place of those who denied the name of the Lord of the Spirits? It would have been far better for them not to have been born,*" to Matthew 26:24: "The Son of Man goes as it is written of him, but *woe to that one by whom the Son of Man is betrayed! It would have been better for that one not to have been born.*"

12. Compare *1 Enoch* 62:2–3: "*The Lord of the Spirits has sat down on the throne of his glory, and the spirit of righteousness has been poured out upon him.* The word of his mouth will do the sinners in; and all the oppressors shall be eliminated from before his face. On the day of judgment, all the kings, the governors, the high officials, and the landlords shall see and recognize him—*how he sits on the throne of his glory,* and righteousness is judged before him, and that no nonsensical talk shall be uttered in his presence," to Matthew 25:31: "*When the Son of Man comes in his glory, and all the angels with him, then he will sit on the throne of his glory.*"

13. Compare *1 Enoch* 69:27: "Then there came to them a great joy. *And they blessed, glorified, and exalted the Lord on account of the fact that the name of that Son of Man was revealed to them.* He shall never pass away or perish from before the face of the earth," to Matthew 26:64: "*Jesus said to him, "You have said so. But I tell you, from now on you will see the Son of Man seated at the right hand of Power and coming on the clouds of heaven.*" [Note: The parallel is the exaltation of the Son of Man.]

14. Compare *1 Enoch* 94:8: "*Woe unto you, O rich people!* For you have put your trust in your wealth. You shall ooze out of your riches, for you do not

remember the Most High," to Luke 6:24: "*But woe to you who are rich,* for you have received your consolation."

15. Compare *1 Enoch* 97:8–10: "Woe unto you who gain silver and gold by unjust means; *you will then say, "We have grown rich and accumulated goods, we have acquired everything that we have desired. So now let us do whatever we like; for we have gathered silver, we have filled our treasuries (with money) like water.* And many are the laborers in our houses. Your lies flow like water. For your wealth shall not endure but it shall take off from you quickly, for you have acquired it all unjustly, and you shall be given over to a great curse," to Luke 12:19–21: "*And I will say to my soul, 'Soul, you have ample goods laid up for many years; relax, eat, drink, be merry.'* But God said to him, 'You fool! This very night your life is being demanded of you. And the things you have prepared, whose will they be?' So it is with those who store up treasures for themselves but are not rich toward God." [The parallel is in the notion of putting confidence in worldly goods and losing all of one's wealth.]

16. Compare Sirach 24:19–22: "*Come to me, you who desire me, and eat your fill of my fruits.* For the memory of me is sweeter than honey, and the possession of me sweeter than the honeycomb. Those who eat of me will hunger for more, and those who drink of me will thirst for more. *Whoever obeys me will not be put to shame,* and those who work with me will not sin"; also Sirach 51:23, 26: "*Draw near to me, you who are uneducated, and lodge in the house of instruction . . . Put your neck under her yoke, and let your souls receive instruction;* it is to be found close by," with Matthew 11:28–30: "*Come to me, all you that are weary and are carrying heavy burdens, and I will give you rest. Take my yoke upon you, and learn from me;* for I am gentle and humble in heart, and you will find rest for your souls. *For my yoke is easy, and my burden is light.*"[16]

There are also a number of parallels between "the Book of Parables" in *1 Enoch* (chaps. 37–71, ca. first century BCE) and the teaching of Jesus in the canonical Gospels, especially in regard to references to the apocalyptic Son of Man. These are listed at the end of this chapter. It is unlikely that the Book of Parables is a Christian document, as some have argued, because it concludes by identifying Enoch, not Jesus, as the Son of Man (71:5–17). Given that the title "Son of Man" was Jesus' most frequent self-designation, it is unlikely that any Christian group would have created this book and given that title to another hero.[17] It is worth noting that those who deposited the scrolls at Qumran also had a high regard for the Enoch tradition. The recent interest in the books that make up the Enochic collection, probably written over the period between the fourth century BCE to the first century BCE, has resulted in a number of critical works examining the influence of these texts in early Christianity.[18] There are also several significant word parallels between *Joseph and Aseneth* and the canonical Gospels, especially Matthew.[19] It is difficult to date *Joseph and Aseneth* before the beginning of the Christian era, but it is unlikely that Christians wrote it since Christian theological issues are not obvious in the document, even though New Testament writers apparently drew freely from it in several passages.[20]

Some argue that since Jesus cited books from each of the threefold collections of the Hebrew Scriptures (the Law [Torah], Prophets [Nebiim], and Writings [Ketubim]—that is, the Tanakh) that he must have acknowledged all three parts of the Hebrew Bible and that they were complete and fixed by his time.[21] The earliest reference, and the only one in the NT, to three collections of Jewish scriptures is in Luke 24:44, when Jesus speaks of "the law of Moses, the prophets, and psalms" (despite NRSV, the Greek has no definite article before "psalms").[22] Although Beckwith argues that this refers to the later well-defined Law, Prophets, and Writings,[23] nothing in the text suggests that the reference to "psalms" is anything more than psalms that were in circulation in the time of Jesus. Which psalms Jesus refers to is not clear. Similarly, nothing in the New Testament or first-century Jewish literature clearly identifies the books that make up the Prophets. Attempts to identify "psalms" as the complete collection of all of the books that are later called Writings (Ketubim or Hagiographa) in *b. Baba Bathra* 14b or in later rabbinic traditions are only speculation. It is not uncommon in New Testament and early church literature to find Hebrew Bible books called "prophets" in the time of Jesus that were later placed in the Writings identified in Jewish literature, as I will show presently. The notion that "psalms" in Luke 24:44 is a clear reference to the third division of the Hebrew Bible is both anachronistic and flawed.[24]

There are no clear references to the three-part Hebrew Bible that now exists either in the New Testament or elsewhere before the mid-second century CE. The limited twenty-four sacred books of the Hebrew Bible are identified for the first time only in *b. Baba Bathra* 14b, where they are grouped into the three distinct sections identified as Torah, Nebiim, and Ketubim (or Hagiographa). While the Prologue to Sirach, Philo's *De vita contemplativa* 3.25–26, 28, 4QMMT, and Josephus (*Ag. Ap.* 1.37–43) all suggest multiple categories of Jewish scriptures, aside from the Law and the Prophets, those categories and the books that constitute them are not clearly identified for Jews until 140–150 CE, in that one talmudic text that was clearly not representative of all Jews in the Roman Empire. A tripartite biblical canon was probably in its early stages of development in the century before and during the time of Jesus, but there is no tradition that is clear on this matter before the mid-second century CE. There is no evidence that a majority of Jewish rabbis agreed on these matters even centuries later, as I have shown above.

More importantly, when the rabbis of the eastern Diaspora and in the Land of Israel finally agreed on the scope of its sacred literature, there is no evidence that their views had much influence on the Jews in the western Diaspora until the eighth or ninth century CE. They had little contact with the rabbis in the east (from Jerusalem to Babylon) and for centuries continued to make use of the apocryphal and pseudepigraphal writings that were rejected in the east along with most of the books that make up the Hebrew Bible.[25] Further, there is little evidence that *b. Baba Bathra* 14b was even known among the Jews in the Land of Israel in the second century CE, even though Josephus, who was influenced by Hillel from Babylon, does speak of a collection of twenty-two sacred books among the Jews (*Ag. Ap.* 1.37–43). If this tradition had been widely known and broadly accepted in the Jewish community in the Land of Israel, it is strange that it was not included in the Mishnah, which codified the Jewish religious (the Tannaitic) traditions of the first two centuries CE or even later in the Tosefta.

The assumption that since Jesus cited writings from the three collections of books that now make up the Hebrew Bible he must have affirmed all of the books that now make up the whole of the Hebrew Bible is anachronistic and assumes without sufficient evidence a firmly fixed biblical canon well before the time of Jesus. If a threefold Hebrew Bible was in existence during the time of Jesus, it is quite remarkable that the early churches did not divide their Old Testament scriptures into the same three divisions that later became the Tanakh. It appears that both the threefold division of the canon and the books that made it up were established for the Jews only significantly after the time of Jesus and in the east, not the western Jewish communities, who were apparently unaware of these groupings until centuries later.

There is ample evidence in the New Testament, however, that the Law and the Prophets, and some of the books that are later referred to as the Writings, formed the core of the scriptural collections of the earliest Christian churches, even though several Hebrew Bible/Old Testament books apparently played little or no role in the life and ministry of Jesus or the early church. In the New Testament the Jewish scriptures are often referred to as "the law and the prophets" or "Moses and the prophets," as in Matthew 5:17; 7:12; and Romans 3:21, but the "law" is also used in reference to Psalm 82 in John 10:34. Paul likewise speaks of the "law" when he cites a series of references from the Psalms in Romans 3:10–19. It is interesting that John cites Psalm 82:6 as "law" and Paul in 1 Corinthians 14:21 introduces Isaiah 28:11–12 with "in the law it is written." The designation "the law and the prophets" refers several times to all the church's scriptures, as we see in Matthew 22:40; John 1:45; Acts 24:14; and 28:23. In all but one reference in the New Testsament, Luke 24:44 (which includes "psalms"), "the law" or "the law and the prophets" constitute all of the early church's scriptures. According to Acts 13:15, both the Law and the Prophets were apparently read regularly in synagogues: "After reading the law and the prophets, the rulers of the synagogue sent to them [Paul and Barnabas], saying, 'Brethren, if you have any word of exhortation for the people, say it'" (NRSV).[26] The categories of "Law" and "Prophets" do not appear to have been fixed in their current shape in the time of Jesus, or for more than a century later among Jews and Christians.

The numerous other New Testament references to a two-part collection of sacred writings, namely Law and Prophets, with only one New Testament text that refers to a third category (Luke 24:44), suggests that when the Gospel of Luke was written there was no widespread recognition of a three-part biblical canon. Rather, all sacred literature was widely acknowledged as "the law and the prophets." As we will see below, "prophets" could have included what are now called noncanonical writings as well as those books that make up the Writings, or third part of the Hebrew Bible. This does not deny that a three-part biblical canon was *emerging* during the first century BCE and CE, nor that there are signs that more than two divisions of scriptures were emerging in several Jewish traditions, namely, prologue to Sirach (ca. 116–110 BCE), 2 Maccabees 2:13–15 (ca. 105–95 BCE), 4QMMT (or 4Q394–399, C, 6ab–12b; ca. 150 BCE), Philo (*Contempl.* 3.25–26, 28; ca. 20–40 CE), Luke 24:44 (ca. 60–70 CE), and Josephus (*Ag. Ap.* 1.37–43; ca. 90–94 CE). The contents of the emerging categories, however, were not yet settled for most Jews in the Land of Israel. Most Jews in the time of Jesus and most writers of the New Testament knew only the Law and Prophets as their sacred scriptures, even if the latter category appears to be a catchall for all non-Torah scriptures.

Melito (ca. 170–180 CE), the earliest Christian writer to identify a collection of books that made up the Old/First Testament for the church, refers to the whole collection of Old Testament scriptures (except for Esther) including the Hagiographa, but refers to them only as the "Law and the Prophets" and includes the Wisdom of Solomon (Eusebius, *Hist. eccl.* 4.26.13–14). He was apparently unaware of the third category of Writings and simply listed books from that category (Daniel, Ezekiel, Ezra, but also the Wisdom of Solomon) as the "Law and the Prophets." For Christians, as in the case of Melito, differentiating among the Prophets was done much later than it was for the Jews, and the Christians did not adopt the same categories of Scripture that we find in the Hebrew Bible.

THE SCRIPTURES IN THE NEW TESTAMENT

Since Jesus was the acknowledged Lord of the early Christian community, it is likely that the early Christians also accepted and made use of the same sacred texts that he favored in his teaching and mission. What books did the early Christians use as sacred texts? It is remarkable that they cite or allude to the same books and with almost the same frequency as we find in Jesus' teachings in the Gospels, especially the Psalms, Isaiah, Deuteronomy, and some noncanonical writings. Did the rest of the New Testament writers and the early church also acknowledge as scripture some of the books that we now call noncanonical writings? Peter Stuhlmacher lists a number of the parallels and allusions to noncanonical literature in the New Testament writings.[27] See, for example, the following:

1. Mark 10:19 appears to make use of Sirach 4:1 along with Exodus 20:12–16 and Deuteronomy 5:16–20.
2. 2 Timothy 2:19 appears to cite Sirach 17:26 along with Numbers 16:5.
3. It is likely that Paul, in Romans 1:24–32, makes use of Wisdom 14:22–31.

4. In Romans 5:12–21 Paul apparently makes use of the ideas present in Wisdom 2:23–24. Wisdom's canonicity does not appear to concern Paul, but only the theological arguments in it.[28]
5. In 1 Corinthians 2:9 Paul appears to cite as "scripture" either *Ascension of Isaiah* 11:34 or a lost *Elijah Apocalypse* derived from Isaiah 64:3.
6. Jude 14 expressly mentions Enoch who "prophesied" and refers to *1 Enoch* 1:9.
7. The author of 2 Peter 2:4 and 3:6 shows knowledge or awareness of the traditions in *1 Enoch* 10:4 and 83:3–5, respectively.
8. The author of Hebrews 1:3 refers clearly to Wisdom of Solomon 7:25–26.
9. James 4:5 appears to cite an unknown scripture.

The pseudepigraphal *Life of Adam and Eve* (*L.A.E.*) and the *Apocalypse of Moses* (*Apoc. Mos.*) also have several parallels in the writings of the New Testament. For example, see the following:

1. Compare Hebrews 1:6 with *L.A.E.* 13–14, which focuses on angels worshiping the one who is in the image of God.
2. Compare James 1:17 with *L.A.E.* 29:2 and *Apoc. Mos.* 36:3, where the focus is on "the Father of lights"; Revelation 22:2 speaks of a tree of life, and 1 Timothy 2:13–14 has parallels with this text in regard to Eve as the source of sin;
3. Romans 5:12–21; 2 Corinthians 11:3; and 1 Timothy 2:4, like *L.A.E.* 44:1–5; *Apoc. Mos.* 24:1–26:4 speak of death that follows the sin of Adam and Eve;
4. On the understanding of death as the separation of soul and body in 2 Corinthians 5:1–5, and the appearance of Satan in the brightness of an angel in 2 Corinthians 11:14, cf. *L.A.E.* 9:1; *Apoc. Mos.* 17:1.
5. The location of paradise is in the third heaven in 2 Corinthians 12:2; cf. *Apoc. Mos.* 37:5.
6. Paul's reference to *epithymia* ("covetousness") as the root of all sin in Romans 7:7 is similar to *Apoc. Mos.* 19:3.

By themselves these parallels do not necessarily reflect either the New Testament writers' acknowledgment of these noncanonical writings as scripture or a dependence upon them. They may simply reflect a shared knowledge or perspective that was common among Jews of the first century. The cumulative effect of these and other parallels, however, suggests the tenuous boundaries of sacred scripture collections in the first century.[29]

The Law or Torah formed the essential core of sacred scripture for Jesus, as it was for most first-century Jews and the early Christians. Although Jesus regularly cited the Psalms as scriptural support for his teachings, the Torah still formed the backbone of his scriptural collection. There is little question that most of the books of the Hebrew Bible, and several others that were not eventually included in this collection, informed Jesus, the New Testament writers, and the early church. The majority of the references and quotations in Clement of Rome's letter to the Corinthian Christians (*1 Clement*), for example, are from books in the Hebrew Bible/Old Testament writings, with only a few references to some New Testament writings. The apocryphal and pseudepigraphal literature was in many cases marginal in the sense that it was not cited or alluded to in early Christianity as often as the canonical writings, even if some of it appears to have affected often in striking ways both Jesus' teachings and those of his early followers.

THE SCRIPTURES OF THE EARLY CHURCH

The Apostolic Fathers (ca. 90–150 CE), those writings closest in chronology to the New Testament writings, have a number of even more striking parallels, quotations, and allusions to noncanonical literature. Notice, for example, that Clement of Rome (ca. 90–95 CE) cited Sirach 2:11 in *1 Clement* 60.1, Wisdom of Solomon 12:10 in *1 Clement* 7.5, and Wisdom of Solomon 12:12 in *1 Clement* 27.5 (perhaps also alluded to in 3.4 and 7.5). In *1 Clement* 55.4–6 both Judith (8ff.) and Esther (7 and 4:16) are cited authoritatively or scripturally. The author of *2 Clement* (ca. 150 CE) has a number of quotations, allusions, and references from unknown and nonbiblical sources (see 11.2–4, 7, and 13.2) as well as a quote from Tobit 16:4. *Barnabas* (ca. 90–130) employs quotations from Wisdom of Solomon (20.2), *1 Enoch* (16.5), *4 Ezra* (12.1), and from unknown "scripture" as in 7.3, 8, and 10.7. The *Didache* (ca. 70–90 CE) makes use of Wisdom of Solomon in 5.2 and 10.3 as well as an unknown quote in 1.6. Polycarp cites Tobit 4:10 (see also 12:9) in *Martyrdom* 10.2.

James VanderKam notes the widespread use of *1 Enoch* in early Christianity and makes the point that it is highly unlikely that the early Christians, who were significantly influenced by Jewish canonical views, would have such high regard for a book that had no standing within the Jewish community.[30] For example, besides the reference to *1 Enoch* in the *Epistle of Barnabas* (16.5) noted above, acceptance of *1 Enoch* in early Christianity is among such notables as Athenagoras, Irenaeus, Tertullian, Clement of Alexandria, Bardaisan, the author of the *Pseudo-Clementine* literature, Julius Africanus, Origen, Commodian, Zosimus, Cyprian, as well as some earlier Gnostic literature. The book is also found in the Chester Beatty papyri (ca. 200 CE) along with Sirach, and it is not distinguished from other biblical books.[31] Augustine is apparently the first notable church leader who rejected *1 Enoch* as a canonical book. However, that book was translated into Ethiopic (Ge'ez) between the fourth and fifth centuries and continues as a canonical text (as does *Jubilees*) in the Abyssinian Church today.[32]

Tertullian, who wrote at roughly the same time as the production of the Chester Beatty papyri, cites *1 Enoch* as scriptural support in his argument against the worship of idols (*On Idolatry* 4). Knowing that some church fathers rejected *1 Enoch*, Tertullian defended his use of *1 Enoch* with the fact that Jude cited it as scripture (*Apparel of Women* 1.3). Similarly Origen defends a theological position with a reference to scripture as follows: "But some one will perhaps inquire whether we can obtain out of Scripture any grounds for such an understanding of the subject." He then cites as support Psalm 139:16 and follows this with the words: "Enoch also, in his book, speaks as follows," citing *1 Enoch* 17. He follows that text up with the comment: "*For it is written in the same book of Enoch,* 'I beheld the whole matter'" (*First Principles* 4.1.31, translation adapted from ANF, emphasis added). He is obviously citing the book in a scriptural manner. Thus *1 Enoch* clearly influenced the writings of many significant writers and teachers in early Christianity.

Justin Martyr, in *Dialogue with Trypho* 120.5, 14–15 (ca. 160), appears to refer to the report of the death of Isaiah in *Ascension of Isaiah* (5:1–2) in an authoritative (scriptural) manner, and yet contextually seeks to support his arguments on the basis of the scriptural books accepted by the Jews.[33] Like Melito, Justin refers to Genesis, Exodus, Leviticus, "the Kingdoms" (1 and 2 Kings and possibly also 1 and 2 Samuel), Psalms, Proverbs, and he also quotes from Job. He names the prophets Isaiah, Jeremiah, Ezekiel, and Daniel, as well as the twelve Minor Prophets and Esdras (see *Dial.* 72.1). He also quotes, without referring to them by name, Numbers, Deuteronomy, and 2 Chronicles. Again, these references to the biblical literature do not necessarily imply the scope of Justin's scriptures, since he is speaking to specific situations in the *Dialogue*, but it does reflect the commonly accepted scriptural literature among Christians in the mid-second century. Justin is surely on common ground in the former references, but he is silent about Ecclesiastes, Song of Songs, and Esther, a factor that may reflect the doubts that existed about these books in both the rabbinic and Christian communities in the second century.[34] It is likely that later Christians made use of these books only when they allegorized them, because these and other books no longer addressed the immediate concerns of the Christian community.[35] Again, the mere citing of a canonical or noncanonical text does not necessarily mean that it was received as scripture or placed in a fixed biblical canon. Each citation must be considered individually in its context.

There is some debate over how passages from noncanonical books are cited either in the New Testament or in the second-century church fathers—whether there is a specific claim for calling these documents "Scripture"—but Stuhlmacher contends that the above references demonstrate that in the first two centuries there was "no firm decision about the extent of the third part of the Old Testament canon, the so-called Writings."[36] All of this implies that the biblical canon of the early Christian community was still fluid during the time of Jesus' ministry and for some time later, after most of the New Testament writings had already been produced.

The additions to biblical books that appear in the Greek Old Testament (i.e., books that were not accepted by Jews in the second century CE and later) further demonstrate this point. Robert Grant has shown that the Song of the Three Young Men was added to Daniel, that Clement of Alexandria cited Susanna, and that Irenaeus, Tertullian, and Origen accepted Bel and the Dragon as scripture. The Additions to Esther mentioned in Josephus are also referred to by Clement of Rome, Clement of Alexandria, and Origen. The Prayer of Manasseh is found in the Syriac *Didascalia* from the third century CE as well as in the *Apostolic Constitutions* that were produced in the latter half of the fourth century CE in Syria (*Apos. Con.* 2.22.12–14) and it is also in Codex Alexandrinus (fifth century CE).[37] I have argued elsewhere that a careful reading of the Apostolic Fathers shows conclusively that they sometimes appealed to apocryphal and pseudepigraphal literature in much the same way that they appealed to the scriptures of the Hebrew Bible.[38] Grant concludes from this widespread use of noncanonical literature that "we cannot deny, of course, that the Apostolic Fathers did make use of apocryphal documents. Indeed, the only explicit quotation in the *Shepherd of Hermas* comes from the lost *Book of Eldad and Modad* (*Vis.* 2,3,4; cf. Num. 11:26)."[39]

Whatever the traditions behind Josephus (*Ag. Ap.* 1.37–43), *4 Ezra* 14:44–47, and *b. Baba Bathra* 14b, the three text traditions that reflect the notion of a fixed collection of sacred scriptures among Jews from the late first to the mid-second century CE, that interest had no apparent impact on Jesus, the writers of the New Testament, or the early church writers. Stuhlmacher correctly concludes: "nowhere in the New Testament writings can any special interest in the canonical delimitation and fixing of the Holy Scriptures be detected."[40]

Conclusion

There is little agreement among biblical scholars on the closing of the canon of Hebrew Scriptures and the Christian Old Testament or the factors leading to it, and there is conflicting evidence in the surviving traditions. What seems clear is that not all Jews in the time of Jesus held to the same views on the matter. Josephus himself spoke of a continuation of prophecy in the person of Judas of the Essene group (*Ant.* 13.311–13) and that "numerous prophets" were employed to delude the people during the first century (*J.W.* 6.286; see also 300–9). Apparently for him the question was not whether prophets or inspired persons were still functioning, but whether some of them functioned well and whether only prophetic *books* had ceased. E. Earle Ellis observes that the community at Qumran and the early Christian community obviously did not agree that the prophetic manifestation had ceased in Israel.[41] Passages from the Qumran community, the Christian community, and the author of *4 Ezra* 14:19–48 (ca. 100 CE) all suggest that many Jews did not believe that the prophetic Spirit had departed from Israel.

David Aune offers many examples of the various types of prophecy known and practiced within the sects of Judaism in the first centuries BCE and CE that show a widespread belief that prophecy through the presence and activity of the Spirit was still alive in Israel.[42] Was there a difference in the understanding of prophecy in the first century CE that might distinguish the inspiration of an ancient prophet from a more contemporary one? It is difficult to find evidence for this apart from the denial of some writers that the Spirit had departed from Israel, but the view that the Spirit had departed from Israel was not a universally acknowledged belief, and it was clearly not operative in early Christianity (Acts 2:1–21).[43] Early Christians seemed to have found prophetic or inspired texts in a variety of places that supported and advanced their beliefs and mission.

While some have suggested that the inspiration of a text served as its validation within the believing community,[44] there are no clear guidelines from antiquity for assessing the inspiration of a text. It is tempting to say that only books that speak of a revelation from God are to be accepted, but many books that were eventually included in the Hebrew Bible do not make that claim (Ruth, Esther, Ezra–Nehemiah, Samuel, Kings, and Chronicles). Among the writers of the New Testament, only the author of the Apocalypse makes a claim for inspired status (22:18–19), and perhaps also Paul in one of his letters (1 Cor. 7:40). The ancient practice of applying inspiration to sacred writings is widely acknowledged. Ancient books were accepted as scripture and added to the biblical canon because individuals and even religious communities believed that those texts had divine authority in matters of religious beliefs and practices.[45]

Jews who accepted the notion that prophecy had ceased following the time of Ezra had easier decisions to make regarding the scope of their scriptures, but this was not a unanimous view in the time of Jesus *in the Land of Israel*. Notions about prophecy ceasing and the acceptance of certain books as "scripture" were not uniform among Jews in the first century CE or before. Some biblical scholars tend to project back into ancient texts notions that were current only at a later date. Jonathan Smith rightly concludes that canon "is almost always a retrospective category, not a prospective or primary one."[46] Since no Jewish or Christian councils established a canonical list of books before, during, or soon after the time of Jesus, most of the writings that achieved a scriptural status in Jewish or Christian communities achieved something of a "quasi-canonical" status.[47] They acquired this position on the basis of widespread use in various religious communities. Their recognition as sacred literature often emerged as a result of their use by the majority of the respected leaders in those communities of faith. Widespread use in churches was one of the significant criteria some churches used in establishing their religious texts as canon.[48]

At the end of the fourth or in the early fifth century CE, Jerome argued for the acceptance of Jude, *despite* its use of *1 Enoch*: "by age and use it has now earned authority and is reckoned among the Holy Scriptures" (*Vir. ill.* 4). F. F. Bruce concludes similarly: "when the canon was 'closed' in due course by competent authority, this simply meant that official recognition was given to the situation already obtaining in the practice of the worshipping community."[49] I agree in the sense that church councils generally reflected—they did not determine—what books had already obtained acceptance in their geographical locations, even though the operative biblical canons reflected in the ancient codices often tell a different story.[50]

EARLY CHURCH USE OF OTHER CHRISTIAN TEXTS

The early Christians regularly made use of many of the New Testament writings in their worship, apologetics, and catechetical instruction, as I have outlined elsewhere.[51] But they were also informed by other writings that they sometimes acknowledged as scripture, ancient writings that are now identified by some Christians (Protestants) as apocryphal or pseudepigraphal texts. Jesus and his earliest followers, the early church fathers, and some of those later church fathers all made use of those texts in various ways. From the mid-second century CE and later, a number of writings began appearing in the churches reportedly coming from apostolic figures or those from that era closest to Jesus. Some writings that were cited as scripture were not "apocryphal" as such, but were early Christian writings produced under their author's names, such as the letter of Clement of Rome to the Corinthians, the letters of Ignatius to seven churches in Asia Minor, and others. Although anonymous, the *Didache* also functioned as scripture for some early Christian communities. These writings were not eventually included in the Christian biblical canon, but second- and third-century Christians often cited these books as scripture in their churches. The following examples will show considerable use of this literature among the early Christians, at least in the first three centuries, before that use diminishes.

After church councils began in the late fourth century, decisions were made about the sacred status of those and other writings, and Christians began to narrow their use of religious literature to those texts that they believed were produced in the first century and closest to the time of Jesus. From that time (fourth and fifth centuries), fewer citations of the so-called apocryphal Christian texts appear in the church fathers, though they are not completely eliminated for centuries. Today, the vast majority of Christian churches, especially those in the Roman Catholic, Orthodox, and Protestant traditions, have adopted the twenty-seven-book New Testament canon familiar to all. This does not mean that all the books of the New Testament were equally cited or appreciated in churches, or that all noncanonical writings ceased being used in churches. In what follows, we will look at use of this literature in the early churches and see what "Bibles" were left behind in the process.

The Christians began in the first century CE to produce collections of writings that were useful in their catechetical activities in the churches. After persons became Christians, the task of instructing them in the faith was paramount, but initially there were no Christian writings, and Jesus himself did not write anything for the churches. The teaching and preaching ministries of the early churches were supported by the oral traditions circulating in the churches that came to them from reputable eyewitnesses to the primary events.[52] In time, these eyewitnesses were dying or passing away and it was deemed necessary to put these oral traditions in writing to preserve the early witness of the church about Jesus. From the very beginning, these documents circulated as authoritative texts in the lives and ministries of the early Christians.

By no later than the mid-second century, the Gospels were being read alongside the Jewish scriptures in worship in the churches (Justin, *1 Apol.* 64, 67) in a scriptural manner and with commentary in the churches, a sign of their scriptural status even though they were not yet called scripture. Paul's Letters (or some of those letters attributed to Paul, generally without the Pastoral Letters during the second and third centuries) were also circulating in churches, no doubt because of their practical value in the organization and ministry of the churches and the esteem for Paul in the early churches. In time, the Christian collection of scriptures grew to include other writings, some of which were later included in the New Testament canon of scriptures, but some of these ceased their influence in the churches and ceased being circulated among Christians. Some of the noncanonical writings continued to circulate for centuries in the churches because they filled needs in the churches that were not met by those that were considered canonical Scriptures. These writings have continued to influence the church throughout its history and include the *Didache, Shepherd of Hermas, 1–2 Clement,* the *Letters of Ignatius,* and the *Martyrdom of Polycarp.*

Other literature that influenced early Christianity at various times and places has been dubbed "apocryphal" because of its pseudonymous authorship or because its theology was later deemed heretical. Of course, these writings are not all cut from the same cloth, and it is not clear what motivated some of the pseudonymous writers, since what they wrote was well within the proto-orthodox traditions of the churches. Whatever the reasons for their production, this literature supplied a need for many churches, and readers will find much of it very interesting and in keeping with the proto-orthodoxy that emerged in the second century. Some of it, however, was considerably outside what the church considered acceptable boundaries of the Christian faith, such as the writings of the Gnostics and the Montanists, and that literature was eventually dismissed or condemned. It was difficult for the church to establish its canon of sacred texts before it had established its theological underpinnings, and until those decisions were largely finalized during the fourth and fifth centuries, some of the "heretical" writings continued to influence churches throughout the Roman Empire. As the church gradually clarified its understanding of Jesus, his mission, and the church's role in Christian mission, some writings that were once considered sacred and were included in the worship instruction of the early churches ceased their influence in many churches and were eventually dropped or "decanonized."

Sometimes the decanonized writings continued to be cited regularly and were included in some of the uncial biblical manuscripts, but some of them eventually vanished from the churches when they were no longer considered inspired or sacred texts. Far fewer of these ancient documents have survived antiquity, or have arrived only in fragmented form, because, given the considerable time and expense involved in copying and circulating these writings, the churches did not continue making copies of writings that they had rejected as sacred literature. Some of them are known only from comments about them in the Apostolic Fathers or other early church writers. For example, until the recent publication of the *Gospel of Judas* (perhaps written ca. 150–160 CE), the church knew of this writing primarily through the testimony of Irenaeus (*Haer.* 1.31.1), but had little idea of its contents.

The most popular ancient *Christian* books that were not included in the New Testament biblical canon are as follows:

1. *Shepherd of Hermas.* This apocalypse is the most cited noncanonical Christian writing that did not make it into the Christian biblical canon. It is cited more frequently than most of the New Testament writings that were included in the biblical canon, and more copies of it remain from antiquity than most of the New Testament books. It is cited only less frequently than the Psalms and the Gospels of Matthew and John.
2. Apocalypse of Peter
3. Gospel of Peter
4. Didache
5. Acts of Paul and Thecla
6. *1* and *2 Clement*
7. *Letters* of *Ignatius of Antioch*
8. *Epistle of Barnabas*

While some of the so-called noncanonical books were little known and little used in antiquity, others were more popular as one can see from their citations and presence in manuscripts that have survived antiquity. Among the commonly described "apocryphal New Testament writings" are approximately eighty known ancient texts that include several other Gospels, and many more letters and apocalypses (books of revelations) that have been recovered from antiquity but were not canonized by the churches. Because the number of noncanonical texts continues to grow and more ancient sources are likely to be discovered by archaeologists and biblical scholars whether in caves, refuse sites, libraries, or museums, we cannot yet say what their actual number is or even their identity. Little is known of the many Montanist writings except that Hippolytus spoke of "an infinite number of their books" (*Haer.* 8.12), and Eusebius describes the actions of one church leader, Apolinarius, who went among them and refuted their heresies and prophecies (*Hist. eccl.* 5.16.3–4), but that literature has been lost in history.

Likewise, one of the most important doctrinal controversies of the second century would not have been known firsthand, had not some local peasants, looking for a soil mixture called sabach used as a fertilizer, stumbled upon the skeleton of a man who was buried with a large jar containing thirteen codices that are now known as the Nag Hammadi Library. Had it not been for this accidental discovery in Egypt, firsthand knowledge of Gnosticism would have not been possible, and we would have been limited to what was passed on by the early church fathers who argued against it. For the first time, scholars now have access to Gnostic teachings by the Christian Gnostics themselves. Who knows what else is buried somewhere and awaits discovery! The writings in the Nag Hammadi Library of texts are not all Christian texts, as we see in Codex 6, and there is some duplication among the codices as we see in codices 2, 3, and 4. These codices include the following texts:

Codex 1: *Prayer of the Apostle Paul, Apocryphon of James, Gospel of Truth, Treatise on the Resurrection,* and *Tripartite Tractate.*

Codex 2: *Apocryphon of John, Gospel of Thomas, Gospel of Philip, Hypostatis of the Archons, On the Origin of the World, Exegesis of the Soul,* and *Book of Thomas the Contender*

Codex 3: *Apocryphon of John, Gospel of the Egyptians, Eugnostos the Blessed, Sophia of Jesus Christ,* and *Dialogue of the Savior*

Codex 4: *Apocryphon of John* and *Gospel of the Egyptians*

Codex 5: *Eugnostos the Blessed, Apocalypse of Paul, First Apocalypse of James, Second Apocalypse of James,* and *Apocalypse of Adam*

Codex 6: *Acts of Peter and the Twelve Apostles, Thunder: Perfect Mind, Authoritative Teaching, Concept of Our Great Power,* Plato, *Republic* 588B–589B, *Discourse on the Eighth and Ninth, Prayer of Thanksgiving* (and Scribal Note), and *Asclepius 21–29*

Codex 7: *Paraphrase of Shem, Second Treatise of the Great Seth, Apocalypse of Peter, Teachings of Silvanus,* and *Three Stelae of Seth*

Codex 8: *Zostrianos* and *Letter of Peter to Philip*

Codex 9: *Melchizedek, Thought of Norea,* and *Testimony of Truth*

Codex 10: *Marsanes*

Codex 11: *Interpretation of Knowledge,* followed by *A Valentinian Exposition, On the Anointing, On Baptism (A, B), On the Eucharist (A, B), Allogenes,* and *Hypsiphrone*

Codex 12: *Sentences of Sextus, Gospel of Truth,* and *2 Fragments*

Codex 13: *Trimorphic Protennoia* (Primal Thought) and *On the Origin of the World.*[53]

These documents all reflect a Gnostic perspective of sorts and are found in the genres typical of the Christian scriptures, namely, gospels, acts, letters, apocalypses, and prayers. Scholars debate how much authentic material about Jesus or early Christian teaching is found in them, especially whether they reflect authentic sayings of Jesus or what is known about him and the early church. Much of the debate has centered on the *Gospel of Thomas*, which was used by the Gnostic community at Nag Hammadi, but it is no longer clear that the *Gospel of Thomas* itself was a Gnostic document.

No doubt other discoveries of ancient Christian texts will surface one day, and likely by accident as has been true thus far of the discovery of other ancient texts. There are also collections of ancient texts now in the possession of European libraries and museums that are waiting to be published and even catalogued.

The apocryphal New Testament texts include some of those listed above and others, but we can never be sure of a complete list. For our current knowledge, this list includes the following works:

Gospels:[54] *Protoevangelium of James, Infancy Gospel of Thomas, Gospel of Peter, Gospel of the Nicodemus, Gospel of the Nazoreans, Gospel of the Ebionites, Gospel of the Hebrews, Gospel of the Egyptians, Gospel of Thomas, Gospel of Philip, Gospel of Mary.*

Acts[55] (the first five of these are called the "Leucian Acts" and circulated together): *Acts of John, Acts of Peter, Acts of Paul, Acts of Andrew, Acts of Thomas, Acts of Andrew and Matthias, Acts of Philip, Acts of Thaddaeus, Acts of Peter and Paul, Acts of Peter and Andrew, Martyrdom of Matthew, Slavonic Acts of Peter, Acts of Peter and the Twelve Apostles.*

Epistles: *Third Corinthians, Epistle to the Laodiceans, Letters of Paul and Seneca, Letters of Jesus and Abgar, Letter of Lentulus, Epistle of Titus.*[56]

Apocalypses:[57] *Apocalypse of Peter, Coptic Apocalypse of Paul, First Apocalypse of James, Second Apocalypse of James, Apocryphon of John, Sophia of Jesus Christ, Letter of Peter to Philip, Apocalypse of Mary.*

These and other "left behind" books functioned at one time in a sacred and authoritative manner for the religious communities that received and used them in their worship and instruction, but eventually they were left out of Christian collections as the orthodox theological perspective came to play a more dominant role in the ancient churches. Scholars who study these documents often find interesting gems of information that could well be reliable. For instance, the only physical description of the apostle Paul is found in the opening lines of *Acts of Paul and Thecla*. There is little reason to think that the description was made up or invented because nothing in this document hinges on that description and it is altogether plausible. It may simply have circulated among the early Christians and was eventually put in writing in this second-century text.

CONCLUSION

What can we now say about the biblical canon of Jesus or the early churches? The notion of a fixed biblical canon was not discussed in the time of Jesus and, as far as we know, he did not address this matter with his disciples. Since we have no record that Jesus ever produced a list of sacred writings, and since his earliest followers were not bound to the more limited collection of books that now make up the Hebrew Bible or Protestant Old Testament, it is most likely that neither Jesus nor his contemporaries were much concerned with the question of canon formation that perplexes biblical scholars today, and that they were informed and influenced by more than the books of the Hebrew Bible. Likewise, it is not clear that *all* the books of the current Hebrew Bible (or the Protestant OT) had much of an impact on Judaism at the time of Jesus or among the followers of Jesus shortly thereafter. Jesus and his early followers appear to have had a broader collection of writings that at times included some of what we *now* call apocryphal or pseudepigraphal literature.

As far as we can determine today, Jesus, like those who followed him, drew from many wells that few draw from today. Would he have included *all* the books that now make up the Old Testament canon in some sort of scripture canon? Would he have accepted as scripture *1 Enoch* and perhaps other books *not* now included in the Hebrew Bible or Christian Old Testament such as *Jubilees,* Wisdom of Solomon, Sirach, and *2 Baruch*? Again, there is no evidence to suggest that such questions were current in the first century, but it is clear that the earliest followers of Jesus did not hesitate to use and cite these and other books as scripture. Neither Jesus nor his immediate followers cite all of the books that currently constitute the Hebrew Bible/Old Testament, but his teachings have several parallels not only with much of that literature but to a lesser extent also with several of those writings that are later identified as apocryphal or pseudepigraphal books.

That Jesus and his followers did not restrict themselves to the writings of the current Hebrew Bible, nor to a tripartite biblical canon, suggests that he never gave or passed on to his followers a fixed list of scriptural books that his followers later circulated for use in the churches. If Jesus had given a fixed biblical canon to his disciples resembling the current Hebrew Bible with its three divisions, or the Protestant Old Testament, then his disciples clearly lost it since there is no indication in the early church fathers that they were restricted to that canon of scriptures nor did they arrange their Old Testament scriptures in three collections as did the Jews in the second century and later. On the other hand, it would be strange indeed if something as important as a biblical canon would have been lost if Jesus had presented one to his closest followers. It is more likely that such a collection never existed. The arguments that some scholars use to establish Jesus' scripture collection or biblical canon are often couched in anachronisms, that is, they assume that such discussions were part of the lingua franca of the day, but the evidence that canonical thinking was present in New Testament times is very slim.

In regard to the use and impact of some noncanonical writings in early Christianity, one need only consider that homilies, meditations, and liturgical forms were often based on these books, and they also provided inspiration for poets, dramatists, composers, and artists. For example, significant numbers of Renaissance paintings were chosen from themes from the Apocrypha.[58] The Apocrypha had some level of canonical authority among many Christians throughout most of church history.

To answer the question raised at the beginning of this chapter, it is apparent that Jesus did not have a biblical canon in the traditional understanding of canon, at least not exactly like the one that emerged in rabbinic Judaism and ultimately in most Christian churches. While most of his teachings were firmly rooted in the widely accepted books of Moses and several other books of the Old Testament/ Hebrew Bible (especially Isaiah, Deuteronomy, and Psalms), he was also informed by other Jewish religious writings that were later called noncanonical texts, especially *1 Enoch*, Wisdom of Solomon, Sirach, Epistle of Jeremiah, 1, 2, and 4 Maccabees, and probably more. In several instances, he shows more awareness of some of the so-called noncanonical writings than he does of some of the canonical books. Jesus made no known reference to many Hebrew Bible books, and his early followers appear also to have cited authoritatively both what we now call canonical and noncanonical literature. Scholars would do well to consider this additional literature as part of the religious heritage that informed the historical Jesus. The early church was also informed by the many so-called apocryphal New Testament texts, as I have shown elsewhere.[59] If the early churches are in any way models for churches today, these other Christian writings deserve our careful attention. They often provide useful pieces of information on the formative churches and the theological perspectives that formed their identity.

SUPPLEMENT: SCRIPTURE REFERENCES ATTRIBUTED TO JESUS

The following lists are not complete, but do reflect some of the citations of, or allusions to, and parallels in subject and verbal matter with the Old Testament/ Hebrew Bible and the so-called apocryphal writings. The following examples are adapted from Nestle-Aland's *Novum Testamentum Graece*.[60]

Jesus' Citations of Biblical Books in the Synoptic Gospels

Genesis 1:27 (Mark 10:6/Matt. 19:4); 2:24 (Mark 10:7–8/Matt. 19:5); 4:1ff. (Matt. 23:35/Luke 11:51); 4:24 (Matt. 18:22); 6–7 (Matt. 24:37–39/Luke 17:26–27); 19 (Matt. 10:15/11:23–24/Luke 10:12); **Exodus** 3:6 (Mark 12:26/ Matt. 22:32/Luke 20:37); 20:7 (Matt. 5:33); 20:12 (Mark 7:10/Matt. 15:4); 20:7 (Matt. 5:33); 20:12–16 (Mark 10:19/Matt. 19:18–19/Luke 18:20); 20:13 (Matt. 5:21); 20:14 (Matt. 5:27); 21:12 (Matt. 5:21); 21:17 (Mark 7:10/Matt. 15:4); 21:24 (Matt. 5:38); 23:20 (Mark 1:2/Matt. 11:10/Luke 7:27); 24:8 (Mark 14:24; Matt. 26:28); 29:37 (Matt. 23:17, 19); 30:29 (Matt. 23:17, 19); **Leviticus** 13–14 (Luke 17:14); 14:2–32 (Mark 1:44/Matt. 8:4/Luke 5:14); 19:2 (Matt. 5:48/Luke 6:36); 19:12 (Matt. 5:33); 19:18 (Mark 12:31/Matt. 5:43; 19:18; 22:39/Luke 10:27); 24:9 (Mark 2:25–26/Matt. 12:3–4/Luke 6:3–4);

24:17 (Matt. 5:21); 24:20 (Matt. 5:38); **Numbers** 28:9–10 (Matt. 12:5); **Deuteronomy** 5:16–20 (Mark 10:19/Matt. 19:18–19/Luke 18:20); 5:17 (Matt. 5:21); 5:18 (Matt. 5:21); 6:4–5 (Mark 12:29–30/Matt. 22:37/Luke 10:27); 6:13 (Matt. 4:10/Luke 4:8); 6:16 (Matt. 4:7/Luke 4:12); 8:3 (Matt. 4:4/Luke 4:4); 13:2 (Matt. 24:24); 19:15 (Matt. 18:16); 23:22 (Matt. 5:33); 24:1 (Mark 10:5/Matt. 5:31/19:8); 30:4 (Matt. 24:31); **1 Samuel** 21:2–7 (Mark 2:25–26/Matt. 12:4/Luke 6:3–4); **1 Kings** 10:4ff. (Matt. 6:29/Luke 12:27); 10:13 (Matt. 12:42/Luke 11:31); 17:1ff. (Luke 4:25–26); **2 Kings** 5 (Luke 4:27); **2 Chronicles** 24:20–22 (Matt. 23:35/Luke 11:51); **Psalms** 6:9 (Matt. 7:23/Luke 13:27); 8:3 (Matt. 21:16); 22:2 (Mark 15:34/Matt. 27:46); 22:2 (Mark 15:34/Matt. 27:46); 24:4 (Matt. 5:8); 31:6 (Luke 23:46); 37:11 (Matt. 5:5); 48:3 (Matt. 5:35); 50:14 (Matt. 5:33); 110:1 (Mark 12:36; 14:62/Matt. 22:44; 26:64/ Luke 20:42–43; 22:69); 118:22–23 (Mark 12:10–11/Matt. 21:42/Luke 20:17); 118:26 (Matt. 23:39/Luke 13:35); **Isaiah** 5:1–2 (Mark 12:1/Matt. 21:33/Luke 20:9); 6:9–10 (Mark 4:12/Matt. 12:4; 13:14–15/Luke 6:4); 8:14–15 (Matt. 21:44/Luke 20:18); 13:10 (Mark 13:24–25/Matt. 24:39/Luke 21:25–26); 14:13, 15 (Matt. 11:23/Luke 10:15); 23 (Matt. 11:21–22/Luke 10:13–14); 29:13 (Mark 7:6–7/Matt. 15:8–9); 32:15 (Luke 24:49); 34:4 (Mark 13:24–25/ Matt. 24:29/Luke 21:25–26); 35:5–6 (Matt. 11:5/Luke 7:27); 53:10–12 (Mark 10:45/Matt. 20:28); 53:12 (Luke 22:37); 56:7 (Mark 11:17/Matt. 21:13/Luke 19:46); 58:6 (Luke 4:18); 66:1 (Matt. 5:34–35; 11:5/Luke 7:22); 61:1–2 (Luke 4:18–19); **Jeremiah** 6:16 (Matt. 11:29); 7:11 (Mark 11:17); **Ezekiel** 26–28 (Matt. 11:21–22; Luke 10:13–14); **Daniel** 7:13 (Mark 13:26; 14:62/Matt. 24:30; 26:64/Luke 21:27; 22:69); 11:31 (Mark 13:14/Matt. 24:15); 12:11, cf. 9:27 (Mark 13:14/Matt. 24:15); **Joel** 4:13 (Mark 4:29); **Hosea** 6:6 (Matt. 9:13); 10:8 (Matt. 23:30); **Micah** 7:6 (Matt. 10:35–36/Luke 12:53); **Jonah** (Matt. 16:4; cf. 12:39); 2:1 (Mark 8:31); 3:5–9 (Matt. 12:41/Luke 11:32); **Zechariah** 9:9 (Mark 11:1ff./Matt. 21:1ff./Luke 19:29ff.); 13:7 (Mark 14:27/ Matt. 26:31); **Malachi** 3:1 (Matt. 11:10/Luke 7:27); 3:23–24 (Mark 9:12–13; 11:14/Matt. 11:10/Luke 7:27; 17:11–12); 12:12 (Matt. 24:30).[61]

Jesus' Citations of Biblical Books in the Gospel of John

It is commonly recognized today that the Gospel of John, known by that name from the time of Irenaeus (*Haer.* 3.11.1–9), has more archaeological, topographical, and chronological data in it than all three Synoptic Gospels combined.[62] While there is considerable debate about the amount of theology that prevails in this Gospel, scholars are beginning to reassess its value for constructing the life of Jesus. For more than a century its value as a reliable witness to the historical Jesus has been minimized, but recent attention to its historical accuracy has been corroborated through archaeological activity and has led to a new appreciation of its attention to historical detail.[63] This does not mean that John's christological affirmations are any more acceptable to critical scholarship than before, but only that John's Gospel needs to be given more consideration for its historical value in reconstructing the story of Jesus. In terms of the scriptural citations of Jesus, John is similar to the Synoptic Gospels in that he also shows that Jesus cited the Psalms, Deuteronomy, and Isaiah more than the other Hebrew Bible scriptures, although, according to John, he was also acquainted with many other Hebrew Bible/Old Testament books.

Genesis 1:1 (John 1:1); 4:7 (John 8:34); 17:10–12 (John 7:22); 21:17 (John 12:29); 21:19 (John 4:11); 26:19 (John 4:10); 28:12 (John 1:51); 40:55 (John 2:5); 48:22 (John 4:5); **Exodus** 7:1 (John 10:34); 12:10 and 46 (John 19:36); 14:21 (John 14:1); 16:4 and 15 (John 6:32); 22:27 (John 10:34 and 18:22); 28:30 (John 11:51); 33:11 (John 15:15); 34:6 (John 1:17); **Leviticus** 17:10–14 (John 6:53); 20:10 (John 8:5); 23:34 (John 7:2); 23:36 (John 7:37); 23:40 (John 12:13); 24:16 (John 10:33); **Numbers** 5:12 (John 8:3); 9:12 (John 19:36); 12:2 (John 9:29); 12:8 (John 9:29); 14:23 (John 6:49); 16:28 (John 5:30 and 7:17); 21:8 (John 3:14); 27:21 (John 11:51); **Deuteronomy** 1:16 (John 7:51); 1:35 (John 6:49); 2:14 (John 5:5); 4:12 (John 5:37); 11:29 (John 4:20); 12:5 (John 4:20); 17:7 (John 8:7); 18:15 (John 1:21 and 5:46); 19:18 (John 7:51); 21:23 (John 19:31); 22:22–24 (John 8:5); 24:16 (John 8:21); 27:12 (John 4:20); 27:26 (John 7:49); 30:6 (John 3:13); **Joshua** 7:19 (John 9:24); **2 Samuel** 7:12 (John 7:42); 13:25? (John 11:54); **2 Kings** 5:7 (John 5:21); 10:16 (John 1:46); 14:25 (John 7:52); 19:15 (John 5:44); 19:19 (John 5:44); **Nehemiah** 12:39 (John 5:2); **Job** 24:13–17 (John 3:20); 31:8 (John 4:37); 37:5 (John 12:29); **Psalms** 2:2 (John 1:41); 2:7 (John 1:49); 15:2 (John 8:40); 22:19 (John 19:24); 22:23 (John 20:17); 25:5 (John 16:13); 31:10 (John 12:27); 32:2 (John 1:47); 33:6 (John 1:3); 35:19 (John 15:25); 35:23 (John 20:28); 40:11 (John 1:17); 41:10 (John 13:18); 51:7 (John 9:34); 63:2 (John 19:28); 66:18 (John 9:31); 69:5 (John 15:25); 69:10 (John 2:17); 78:24 (John 6:31); 78:71 (John 21:16); 80:2 (John 10:4); 82:6 (John 10:34); 85:11 (John 1:17); 89:4 (John 7:42); 89:27 (John 12:34); 92:16 (John 7:18); 95:7 (John 10:3); 107:30 (John 6:21); 118:20 (John 10:9); 119:142 and 160 (John 17:17); 122:1ff. (John 4:20); 132:16 (John 5:35); 145:19 (John 9:31); **Proverbs** 1:28 (John 7:34); 8:22 (John 1:2); 15:8 (John 9:31); 15:29 (John 9:31); 18:4 (John 7:38); 24:22 (John 17:12); 30:4 (John 3:13); **Ecclesiastes** 11:5 (John 7:38); **Isaiah** 2:3 (John 4:22); 6:1 (John 12:41); 6:10 (John 12:40); 8:6 (John 9:7); 8:23 [9:1] (John 2:11); 9:2 (John 4:36); 11:2 (John 1:32); 12:3 (John 7:37); 26:17 (John 16:21); 35:4 (John 12:15); 37:20 (John 5:44); 40:3 (John 1:23); 40:9 (John 12:15); 42:8 (John 8:12); 43:10 (John 8:28, 58); 43:13 (John 8:58); 43:19 (John 7:38); 45:19 (John 18:20); 46:10 (John 13:19); 52:13 (John 12:38); 53:7 (John 8:32); 54:13 (John 6:45); 55:1 (John 7:37); 57:4 (John 17:12); 58:11 (John 4:14); 60:1 and 3 (John 8:12); 66:14 (John 16:22); **Jeremiah** 1:5 (John 10:36); 2:13 (John 4:10); 11:19 (John 1:29); 13:16 (John 9:4); 17:21 (John 5:10); **Ezekiel** 15:1–8 (John 15:6); 34:11–16 (John 10:11); 34:23 (John 10:11, 16); 36:25–27 (John 3:5); 37:24 (John 10:11, 16); 37:25 (John 12:34); 37:27 (John 1:14); 47:1–12 (John 7:38); **Daniel** 1:2 (John 3:35); **Hosea** 6:2 (John 5:21); 4:18 (John 7:38); **Obadiah** 1:12–14 (John 11:50); **Micah** 5:1 (John 7:42); 6:15 (John 4:37); **Zephaniah** 3:13 (John 1:47); 3:14 (John 12:15); 3:15 (John 1:49); **Haggai** 2:9 (John 14:27);

Zechariah 1:5 (John 8:52); 9:9 (John 12:15); 12:10 (John 19:37); 13:7 (John 16:32); 14:8 (John 4:10 and 7:38); **Malachi** 1:6 (John 8:49); 3:23 (John 1:21).

Allusions to or Verbal and Subject Parallels with Apocryphal and Pseudepigraphal Texts Attributed to Jesus in the Synoptic Gospels

3 Ezra 1:3 (Matt. 6:29); *4 Ezra* 6:25 (Matt. 10:22); 7:14 (Matt. 5:1); 7:36 (Luke 16:26); 7:77 (Matt. 6:20); 7:113 (Matt. 13:39); 8:3 (Matt. 22:14); 8:41 (Matt. 13:3; 22:14); **1 Maccabees** 1:54 (Matt. 24:15); 2:21 (Matt. 16:22); 2:28 (Matt. 24:16); 3:6 (Luke 13:27); 3:60 (Matt. 6:10); 5:15 (Matt. 4:15); 10:29 (Luke 15:12); 12:17 (Matt. 9:38); **2 Maccabees** 3:26 (Luke 24:4); 8:17 (Matt. 24:15); 10:3 (Matt. 12:4); **4 Maccabees** 3:13–19 (Luke 6:12); 7:19 (Matt. 22:32/Luke 20:37); 13:14 (Matt. 10:28); 13:15 (Luke 16:23); 13:17 (Matt. 8:11); 16:25 (Matt. 22:32/Luke 20:37); **Tobit** 2:2 (Luke 14:13); 3:17 (Luke 15:12); 4:3 (Matt. 8:21); 4:15 (Matt. 7:12); 4:17 (Matt. 25:35); 5:15 (Matt. 20:2); 7:10 (Luke 12:19); 7:17 (Matt. 11:25/Luke 10:17); 11:9 (Luke 2:29); 12:15 (Matt. 18:10/Luke 1:19); 14:4 (Matt. 23:38/Luke 21:24); **Judith** 11:19 (Matt. 9:36); 13:18 (Luke 1:42); 16:17 (Matt. 11:22); **Susanna** 46 (Matt. 27:24); **Baruch** 4:1 (Matt. 5:18); 4:37 (Matt. 8:11/Luke 13:29); **Epistle of Jeremiah** 6:24, 28 (Matt. 11:29); 7:14 (Matt. 6:7); 7:32–35 (Matt. 25:36); 9:8 (Matt. 5:28); 10:14 (Luke 1:52); 11:19 (Luke 10:19); 13:17 (Matt. 10:16); 14:10 (Matt. 6:23); 20:30 (Matt. 13:44); 23:14 (Matt. 6:9); 24:19 (Matt. 11:28); 25:7–12 (Matt. 5:2); 27:6 (Matt. 6:12); 28:18 (Luke 21:24); 29:10 (Matt. 6:20); 31:15 (Matt. 7:12); 33:1 (Matt. 6:13); 35:22 (Matt. 16:27/Luke 18:7); 37:2 (Matt. 26:38); 40:15 (Matt. 13:5); 48:5 (Luke 7:22); 48:10 (Matt. 11:14; 17:11/Luke 1:17; 9:8); 48:24 (Matt. 5:4); 50:20 (Luke 24:50); 50:22 (Luke 24:53); 51:1 (Matt. 11:25/Luke 10:21); 51:23 (Matt. 11:28); 51:26 (Matt. 11:29); **Wisdom of Solomon** 2:13 (Matt. 27:43); 2:18–20 (Matt. 27:43); 3:7 (Luke 19:44); 5:22 (Luke 21:25); 7:11 (Matt. 6:33); 15:1 (Luke 6:35); 15:8 (Luke 12:20); 16:13 (Matt. 16:18); 16:26 (Matt. 4:4); 17:2 (Matt. 22:13); *Psalms of Solomon* 1:5 (Matt. 11:23); 5:9 (Matt. 6:26); 16:5 (Luke 22:37); 17:25 (Luke 21:24); 17:26, 29 (Matt. 19:28); 17:30 (Matt. 21:12); 17:32 (Luke 2:11); 18:6 (Matt. 13:6); 18:10 (Luke 2:14); **1 Enoch** 5:7 (Matt. 5:5); 16:1 (Matt. 13:39); 22:9 (Luke 16:26); 38:2 (Matt. 26:24); 39:4 (Luke 16:9); 51:2 (Luke 21:28); 61:8 (Matt. 25:31); 62:2 (Matt. 25:31); 63:10 (Luke 16:9); 69:27 (Matt. 25:31/26:64); 94:8 (Luke 6:24); 97:8–10 (Luke 12:19); 103:4 (Matt. 26:13).[64]

Allusions to or Verbal and Subject Parallels with Apocryphal and Pseudepigraphal Texts Attributed to Jesus in the Gospel of John

4 Ezra 1:37 (John 20:29); 4:8 (John 3:13); **1 Maccabees** 4:59 (John 10:22); 9:39 (John 3:29); 10:7 (John 12:13); **4 Maccabees** 17:20 (John 12:26); **Tobit** 4:6 (John 3:21); **Baruch** 3:29 (John 3:13); *2 Baruch* 18:9 (John 1:9; 3:19;

5:35); 39:7 (John 15:1); **Sirach** 16:21 (John 3:8); **Epistle of Jeremiah** 24:21 (John 6:35); 24:40, 43 (John 7:38); 44:19 (John 8:53); 50:25–26 (John 4:9); **Wisdom of Solomon** 2:16 (John 5:18); 2:24 (John 8:44); 3:9 (John 15:9–10); 5:4 (John 10:20); 6:18 (John 14:15); 8:8 (John 4:48); 9:1 (John 1:3); 9:16 (John 3:12); 15:3 (John 17:3); 15:11 (John 20:22); 18:14–16 (John 3:12); *Psalms of Solomon* 5:3 (John 3:27); 7:1 (John 15:25); 7:6 (John 1:14); 17:21 (John 7:42); *1 Enoch* 69:27 (John 5:22).

PART THREE
THE SECOND
TESTAMENT SCRIPTURES

Chapter 8

Ancient Christian Manuscripts and Their Contents

INTRODUCTION

Was the Bible of the early church through the first three centuries the same as the Bible that Christians use today? The short answer is no, but perhaps it would be better to say not completely, though quite similar. Biblical scholars today know that the early churches (roughly before 400 CE) seldom had complete copies of the books that we now call Scripture, and they often had considerably fewer. They sometimes made use of books that were not included in the Christian biblical canon and often did not use all of the books in the current biblical canon. Most Christians today acknowledge the same twenty-seven-book New Testament[1] canon, but for several centuries several noncanonical writings functioned as sacred literature for some churches, and most Christians through the third and even fourth centuries apparently did not have a complete collection of New Testament writings such as we have today. Nevertheless, they practiced their worship, teaching, and mission activities and developed the major theological positions that are still current in churches, but they did so without the same biblical books or texts that we use today. There are also numerous textual variants in the surviving biblical manuscripts that let us know that the early churches

153

were either incapable in those circumstances of producing a unified text of their Bible or that they were not much interested in preserving an original text of the biblical writings. Several changes in the biblical text no doubt emerged in the second century when the New Testament writings were not yet universally acknowledged as sacred scripture, but a large number of them came after the fifth and sixth centuries when orthodoxy had gained sway in the churches.

By the fourth century, some churches showed considerable interest in preserving lists or catalogues of their sacred books, but that concern is not always seen in manuscripts containing the sacred books. While most of the variants in the biblical texts are inconsequential (spelling errors, accidental omission of a line or accidental repetition of a line, etc.), some of them are more important and affect the theology and ministry practices of the early churches. More specifically, some of the deliberate changes in the biblical text affected such teachings as Trinitarian views, divorce, the role of women in the church, the handling of snakes, and the final words of canonical Gospels, as in the cases of Mark and John. I will share several examples of this below. Most of the non-Greek-speaking Christians did not possess all the New Testament books, and the early translations of the biblical books were generally of poor quality.

For the most part, the early churches of the first three centuries—the important formative years of the church, and even later—did not focus on many of the canonical questions that trouble Bible scholars today. In the early centuries of the church, there was no uniform view on which books were sacred, even after the emergence of various fixed catalogues of New Testament scriptures in the fourth and fifth centuries, as well as the three important council decisions on the scope of the New Testament (Hippo in 393, Carthage in 397, and Chalcedon in 451). This is true whether we are speaking about the selection of books for the ancient manuscripts, the variants in those manuscripts, or the inferior quality of many of those translations of the New Testament books. All surviving biblical and non-canonical manuscripts doubtless functioned canonically or authoritatively in the ancient churches that had them and used them, and this poses a problem for biblical scholars today. There is widespread agreement in the early churches on the value of several of the Christian documents for the church's life and ministry (the Gospels and Pauline Letters), but there was no uniform position in the churches on which books are sacred. This was true even after the fourth- and fifth-century canon activity that eventually led to the emergence of fixed catalogues of New Testament Scriptures. The life, ministry, and theology of the ancient churches were all built on the interpretation and use of their sacred texts, which included the Jewish scriptures that they *began* to identify as "Old Testament" scriptures toward the end of the second century. Likewise, the implications of the sacred texts that they employed for their understanding of God, their identity, and their mission are significant. Remarkably, the differences in the books included in their early canons of scripture, the variable text of those scriptures, or the translations of their sacred books in those formative years do not appear to have inhibited the church's ministry or its ability to conceptualize its theology.

The value of early Christian writings for support in the mission, worship, apologetic, and instruction of the early churches was apparent almost from the beginning of their circulation in the churches. In several cases, the New Testament writers themselves expect that their writings would be circulated among the churches, which emphasizes their importance for the churches (see 1 Cor. 7:40; Gal. 1:2; Col. 4:16; Jas. 1:1; 1 Pet. 1:2; 2 Pet. 3:15–16; Rev. 22:18–19). Because the canonical Gospels tell the story of Jesus, the most significant authority figure in the early church, they had an implied authority attached to them from their initial circulation. If they were believed to be true, which they were, they could not help but become authoritative in the early churches. The first Christian writings that eventually formed the beginning of the New Testament canon for the churches, however, are not generally referred to by name until the mid-second century, and they are not generally called Scripture until the end of the second century. They nevertheless functioned that way (scripturally) from the beginning of their circulation in the churches.[2] It is not difficult to understand why they functioned this way, since they focus on the most authoritative figure in the churches' teaching and preaching, namely Jesus.

The sacredness of the Gospels was perceived in churches well before it was stated, but their *scriptural* status was not clearly or regularly acknowledged much before the end of the second century, even though their use and value in the churches was widely recognized earlier. During the time between their initial use in churches and their recognition as sacred Scripture, there were many changes made to the New Testament texts. I say this on the basis of the large number of variants that we see in the surviving manuscripts of the third century and later. Only a few of the New Testament writings were acknowledged as sacred by the end of the second century and not generally or uniformly by all Christian communities. When churches began to recognize the sacred status of Christian writings, they did not agree on which books would be so recognized.

The processes that led to the listing of New Testament writings in a fixed catalogue of sacred Scriptures began in the first century, but the stabilization or fixing of these catalogues or lists did not come before the mid-fourth century and for some churches even later. It took centuries for most churches to show interest in a *fixed collection* of sacred texts and even longer in a uniform *text* of the New Testament. Those familiar with the significant numbers of textual variants in the New Testament are aware that most of them can be resolved through a careful analysis of the text, but many questions about the biblical text remain. Bruce Metzger and Bart Ehrman offer the sobering conclusion: "Although in very many cases the textual critic is able to ascertain without residual doubt which reading must have stood in the original, there are not a few other cases where only a tentative decision can be reached, based on an equivocal balancing of probabilities." They conclude: "In textual criticism, as in other areas of historical research, one must seek not only to learn what can be known but also to become aware of what, because of conflicting witnesses, cannot be known."[3]

The Gospels, especially Matthew, and most of the letters attributed to Paul gained widespread acceptance in many early churches because of their ability to undergird the theological foundation of the church as well as to clarify its mission and the ethical implications of the gospel. Some Christians began collecting and circulating Paul's writings by at least the end of the first century, first among the seven churches that he addressed, but later also in other churches as well.[4] It took much longer for *all* the New Testament writings to gain widespread acceptance, and even longer for the churches to form them into a fixed collection of sacred Scriptures.

In this chapter I will focus on three important issues that affect the origin and stabilization of the New Testament canon: how the books in the ancient manuscripts point to the *operative* New Testament canons in the churches, how the numerous textual variants in the ancient biblical manuscripts reveal the church's difficulty in establishing an authoritative text for its scriptures, and how the translations of the New Testament writings functioned canonically in the non-Greek-speaking churches. These issues will clarify some of the complexity that surrounds the processes of canon formation and also shed light on the slow development of the New Testament canon itself. The implications of this for our understanding of the emergence of early Christianity are significant. Far too many interpreters of scriptural texts assume anachronistically that the New Testament that we have today is the same as the one that obtained currency in the earliest churches, but that is not the case.

The early church's lack of interest in many of the canonical questions that concern considerable scholarly debate today is evidenced by the fact that the ancient writers left no record of the processes involved in the recognition and canonization of their sacred literature. Today we must piece together many diverse texts to bring some clarity to these matters, but still it is not always clear why some books were recognized or received as sacred literature and others were not. We can discern in some communities of faith that issues of apostolicity, orthodoxy, antiquity, and widespread use were factors for various churches in identifying their sacred literature, but discovering the reasons for the creation of a closed biblical canon and why some books were included and others rejected is not an easy task. For example, some books that were rejected are just as orthodox and as early as some of those that were included (e.g., *Didache, 1 Clement, Shepherd of Hermas*), and they were often cited more frequently in the early churches than some of the literature that was included (Pastorals, 2–3 John, 2 Peter, Jude). What complicates matters further is the scanty information that we possess, a factor that may suggest a general lack of widespread interest in the formation of the biblical canon.

THE DEVELOPMENT OF THE CODEX

Soon after the birth of the early church, and probably in the first century, Christians showed a strong preference, though not an exclusive one (some 70 percent of the biblical manuscripts are in codices), for the codex to transmit their writings. The apostle Paul himself may have initiated this practice, as we will see below, and by the early second century use of the codex was the most common way of transmitting Christian writings.

The Romans are credited with the invention of the codex and were the first to use it for nonliterary documents such as one would find in contracts, bills of sale, personal notebooks, school texts, and other such items. By the end of the first century CE, the use of the codex expanded considerably. The Roman poet Martial (ca. 82–84 CE), for example, encouraged his readers for the sake of convenience to use small codices to transport his epigrams or poems (*Epigrams* 1.2). Later he indicated that other writers' works had also been placed in this format, those of Homer (14.184), Virgil (14.186), Cicero (14.190), Livy (14.190), and Ovid (14.192). At the end of that century, about 20 percent of the Roman writings were circulated in codex form, but the majority of learned writings continued to be published in the roll or scroll format.

The nonliterary style of Paul's letters to churches characterizes the earliest New Testament writings and suggests their reproduction in a codex format. In the initial stages of transmission, abbreviations for special holy words (Jesus, God, Christ, Son) were commonly used in the New Testament texts, and other terms were added to this.[5] The use of these so-called *nomina sacra*,[6] or abbreviations of sacred names, may initially have pointed to the nonliterary style of communication in Christian writings since abbreviations were seldom used in literary texts, but in time they were used in all kinds of Christian texts, including literary and personal correspondence. These abbreviations, which normally included the first and last letter of the Greek word with frequent use of a middle letter and a short line over the top of the abbreviation, are in abundance in ancient Christian biblical manuscripts but also in other Christian texts. Their presence in a manuscript does identify the text in which they were found as Christian, but they do not necessarily mean that the document in which they were found was recognized as scripture. AnneMarie Luijendijk shows clearly that *nomina sacra* were used in nonliterary texts, such as inscriptions and papyrus letters, as well as in the early Christian New Testament texts, and that this phenomenon has not yet received adequate discussion.[7] While scholars still debate over the origin of these abbreviations and why they were used, they all agree that they show that the scribes who used them were Christians. She writes:

> Although the origins of the writing of *nomina sacra* remain under discussion, no one any longer disputes the Christian character of these contractions. As a matter of fact, scholars always interpret the presence of *nomina sacra* in literary manuscripts as an indicator that a Christian scribe has copied the manuscript, and apply this principle both for literary manuscripts and for epigraphical and papyrological sources.[8]

Most of the New Testament and other Christian writings, if not all, with the possible exception of the Gospels, were initially produced for small groups of

Christian communities, and a formal literary style was not required. The use of *nomina sacra* is not compelling evidence that a text was viewed as scripture, but it does show that the text was produced or copied by a Christian.

In the third century CE the codex was used in approximately 50 percent of Roman literary documents. In the fourth century the codex gained parity with the roll or scroll for literary documents, primarily with the use of parchment rather than the traditional papyri sheets.[9] According to Harry Gamble, those who initially produced codex documents for use in Christian churches were generally aware that they were producing second-class books, or handbooks, and not formal literary writings.[10] This suggests that initially the early churches did not receive this literature as sacred scripture, but rather as informal teaching materials for the church. Gamble observes that the "fine bookhand" normally seen in literary documents is only rarely seen in Christian texts before the fourth century. They are more typically produced in the "informal round" type letters often referred to as a "reformed documentary" type of writing.[11]

This predominant use of the codex in the early Christian communities (about 70 percent) may well have its roots in the way that Paul circulated his letters. Early tradition points to Paul's use of the codex for letter writing to churches. For instance, the Latin term *membranai,* transliterated into Greek as *membranas,* is sometimes translated "parchments" as in 2 Timothy 4:13, but the term likely refers to codices.[12] Gamble suggests that the early tradition that Paul wrote to seven churches fits well with the writings attributed to him, namely Romans, Corinthians, Galatians, Thessalonians, Philippians, Ephesians, Colossians—which included Philemon, since his letters were sent to the same places (Colossae and Laodicea), and accounts for ten letters that were attributed to Paul. Circulation of Paul's writings to these seven churches may have inspired a similar pattern of letters to seven churches in the Apocalypse of John (Rev. 2–3) and in the seven letters of Ignatius of Antioch to churches in the early second century. The number itself suggests completeness, and, despite the many items in them that focused on specific matters related to local churches, the letters proved quite useful to many churches.[13]

For our purposes, it is interesting that the ten letters to these seven churches (Romans, 1–2 Corinthians, Galatians, Ephesians, Philippians, Colossians, 1–2 Thessalonians, and Philemon) fit reasonably well on the normal length of a single quire codex of approximately 200–220 pages, but not on a scroll or roll. Gamble notes that these ten letters of Paul would occupy some eighty feet on a roll or scroll manuscript, which is more than double the maximum length of most scrolls in antiquity and three times the average size. On the other hand, the single codex with one quire could accommodate in one volume all the letters of Paul to the seven churches (ten letters). Because the letters were generally placed in order beginning with the largest (Romans) and descending to the smallest (Philemon), a volume with all these letters to the seven churches, in a descending sequence, only made sense if they were placed in one volume rather than in separate rolls or scrolls. The sequence, Gamble claims, would be lost if the letters had circulated in separate rolls, and it is unlikely that the tradition of seven churches used in Revelation 2–3 and the seven letters of Ignatius to churches would have emerged had Paul's letters not circulated together. The length of a single quire codex is also the approximate length of P^{46}, which contains the earliest collection of Paul's writings without the Pastoral Epistles and Philemon, but with the book of Hebrews inserted between Romans and 1 Corinthians (I will discuss this document below).[14]

Before the third century, we know of no papyrus codices that exceed three hundred pages and most were considerably smaller than that. The oldest papyrus codex containing Paul's writings, P^{46} (ca. 200 CE), originally had 208 pages. The last fourteen pages are missing, but the volume comprised fifty-two papyrus sheets folded in the middle with writing on both sides to allow for that number of pages. The rolls or scrolls normally were about thirty to thirty-five feet long. All four Gospels would occupy some eighty feet of scroll space, which is almost three times longer that the average scroll in the first two centuries. On the other hand, all four Gospels could be included in one single quire codex. For example, P^{45} (ca. 250 CE), unlike all other papyri, contains all four canonical Gospels and occupies some two hundred pages. In the fourth century, by contrast, the major scriptural majuscule codices were well over a thousand pages. For example, the fragmentary Codex Sinaiticus (01) has 1,460 pages and the fragmentary Codex Vaticanus (03) originally had approximately 1,600 pages.[15] The technology necessary for including all the books of the current Bible into a single codex was not available before the mid-fourth century. At that time, the codex became a more significant factor in identifying the literature that functioned canonically in the churches. Before the time of Constantine, there is no record of a complete New Testament in one manuscript, let alone a complete Bible with both Old Testament and New Testament.

Before the third century, when churches used codices that were more limited in size, there was often only enough room in these small books for one or more Gospels, or several epistles, or some combination of them, but none of them had the capacity to contain all the New Testament writings. As noted above, only one papyrus manuscript contains all four Gospels plus Acts (P^{45}), and only four papyrus manuscripts have more than one Gospel. These include P^{44} (Matthew and John), P^{64} + P^{67} + P^{4} (Matthew and Luke; all three of these papyri are now commonly believed to be part of the same manuscript),[16] P^{75} (Luke + John), and P^{84} (Mark + John).[17] P^{53} has both the Gospel of Matthew and Acts. Only fourteen papyri manuscripts of the existing 117 have more than one book in them.[18] This raises questions about the significance of the codex for canon studies; perhaps it had no relevance until it could contain all the books of the New Testament. On the other hand, some fifty-two papyrus manuscripts contain apocryphal literature both Jewish and Christian, much of which was discovered near the sites where biblical manuscripts were also discovered. Among this variety of apocryphal religious texts are the following: *Apocalypse of Elijah, Odes of Solomon, Testament of Solomon, Ascension of Isaiah, Apocalypse of Baruch,*

4 Esdras, 1 Enoch (several copies), *Apocryphon of Ezekiel, Sibylline Oracles,* several Gospel fragments, sayings or logia of Jesus, *Gospel of Peter, Protevangelium of James, Acts of Peter, Acts of Andrew, Acts of John, Acts of Paul, Acts of Paul and Thecla,* the Corinthian correspondence with Paul, *Letters from Abgar to Jesus and Letters from Jesus to Abgar, Acts of Andrew and Matthew, Apocalypse of Peter,* and *Apocalypse of Paul.*[19] Given these finds, it is important to know what was in the earlier codices, as much as what was not. The presence or absence of writings in the codex in the second and third centuries does reflect what writings were most important to the communities where this literature was found, even though accounting for what was not in them is a challenge at best during the early centuries when most if not all of the surviving manuscripts are fragmentary.

In the fourth century the codex had developed sufficiently to include all the books of both Testaments, but it was still unusual to find all the books that were listed in the various canonical lists or catalogues in one volume. The earliest manuscripts, as well as those of the fourth century and later, characteristically have a different order or sequence of books than what we are familiar with today. For example, it is fairly common for the book of Acts to be coupled with the General or Catholic Epistles. The Catholic Epistles also generally precede Paul's Letters in the canonical lists and the surviving codices. Various groups or collections of books (e.g., Gospels, Letters of Paul, Catholic Epistles), however, are often found together in manuscripts following the fourth century, but the order of these groups varies. Before the fourth century, there were multiple collections of New Testament books but the sequence often varies. Generally speaking, catalogues or listings of biblical books begin to emerge only in the first half of the fourth century, starting with Eusebius, when it was possible to include all the sacred books in one codex, and at that time some stabilization of sequence of books began to take place.

No manuscripts dating before or during the fourth century contain *all* the books of the New Testament *and only those books.* Indeed, it is rare to find any manuscript with all the New Testament books—*and only those books*—before 1000 CE. Bart Ehrman credits Michael Holmes with the observation that of the thousands of surviving Greek biblical manuscripts, fewer than ten contain the entire Bible and only four of them predate the tenth century, and those manuscripts are missing several pages of text.[20] Daryl Schmidt contends that those manuscripts purporting to be "complete New Testament manuscripts" are in fact not complete if we ask whether they contain only the canonical New Testament books—nothing more or less. He claims that the two earliest "complete New Testament" codices (nothing more or less) date from the ninth to the eleventh centuries (minuscule codices 1424 and 175, respectively).[21]

Most biblical manuscripts that are cited as containing all sections or groups of the entire New Testament seldom contain *all* the New Testament books, and often contain only fragments of the sections or groups of New Testament writings, even if portions of all canonical groups may be present. For example, 1–2 Peter and Jude are the only complete New Testament books represented by the papyrus manuscripts (see P[72]).[22] Frequently, these manuscripts include noncanonical books as well or fewer books than are in our current New Testament or only partial books. Three early majuscule or uncial manuscripts reportedly have the whole New Testament in them (codices Vaticanus, Sinaiticus, and Alexandrinus), and we could add the palimpsest *Ephraemi Rescriptus* (C, 04), but a closer examination of them shows that they are incomplete or fragmented. Of the more than 5,735 (and growing) New Testament manuscripts from antiquity,[23] only about fifty of the sixty (or sixty-one) contain a whole New Testament, and those manuscripts often have important sections missing, variable sequences of books, and occasionally additional noncanonical texts. The number of "complete" books is more determined by their containing the four or five categories of literature commonly known as "e a p r" or "e a p c r." The fold-up inserts or charts of manuscript listings provided in the various editions of the Nestle-Aland *Novum Testamentum Graece* and the United Bible Society *The Greek New Testament* are often misleading. Both texts use the "e a p r" designations to identify the contents of the manuscripts listed. For example, when they list the manuscripts they indicate whether they have the Gospels (e), Acts and the General Epistles (a), Paul's Letters (p), and Revelation (r). Sometimes the letter "c" for Catholic Epistles is separated from "e a p r" to indicate the separation of these letters from Acts. In those cases, the "c" often comes in the sequence "e a p c r." These letters, however, indicate only the *kinds* or *groups* of materials (Gospels, letters, etc.) in the New Testament, not what is actually in them, and nothing is said about the noncanonical writings in them. The letter "p" may refer to a large collection of Paul's writings as in the case of P[46], but it could also refer only to one of Paul's letters, or to a fragment of a letter as in the case of P[92], which has only two small fragments, one fragment of a few verses of Ephesians 1 and another of 2 Thessalonians 1:4–5. Both designations in the fold-up chart have the letter "p."

The unsuspecting viewer of these charts would never guess that P[4] has four pages from the Gospel of Luke when the chart simply reports an "e." Likewise, P[64] consists of one leaf with verses from Matthew 26, but this one also gets an "e" designation. These designations simply do not clarify what is in the manuscripts and what is not. Later we will observe that P[72] contains noncanonical literature along with Jude and 1–2 Peter, but the chart has only a "c" for the whole manuscript. Noncanonical literature in the manuscripts gets no mention in these lists. These fold-up inserts offer much useful information, but they can confuse the students they are designed to help. What this means is that while the groups are all represented, the full contents of each of those sections may not be. Among the most important minuscule manuscripts, according to Kurt and Barbara Aland, only those numbered 61, 69, 209, 241, 242, 522, 1424, 1678, 1704, and 2495 are complete.[24]

The earliest New Testament papyrus manuscripts date from the early or mid-second century to roughly the eighth century and are fragmentary and incomplete. Many have fewer or different books than those in the current New Testament. The papyrus manuscripts are fragmentary and contain only portions of the biblical text. Some of them may not be continuous texts but instead may have been part of a lectionary (a select portion of a sacred text that was read in worship). The earliest known New Testament papyrus manuscripts date from the early to mid-second century, including a fragment of the Rylands Papyrus of John 18:31–33 and 37–38 (P^{52}, ca. 125 CE) and a fragment of John 18:36–19:7 (P^{90}, ca. 140–150 CE) discovered among the Oxyrhynchus papyri. The majority of New Testament papyri date from the end of the second century (or early third century) to the seventh century. The earliest known codex with Paul's Letters, P^{46} (ca. 200 CE, this codex is discussed below), is fragmentary, but contains all of Paul's Letters except 2 Thessalonians, the Pastorals, and Philemon.

There are no manuscripts of any New Testament writings from the first century and almost none from the second century, and those manuscripts that have survived are seriously fragmented. Indeed, with the exception of several collections from Egypt that I will focus on below, we are largely missing significant manuscript evidence until the mid-fourth century. Any conclusions drawn about the status of the Christian scriptures from that period are tenuous, but it does seem reasonable that given the late-second-century recognition of these writings as sacred scripture, the earlier period would more likely be a period in which some of the intentional changes to the text of the New Testament writings were made. This does not mean that there were no changes made after the recognition of the sacredness of the New Testament writings, but that it is reasonable to assume that more changes were made before that recognition than afterward. We know that many intentional changes were made to bring clarity to the text, and I will discuss these changes in the next chapter. There is almost a hundred years, however, with little or no manuscript evidence for the books and texts of the New Testament, and that is important for our understanding of the beginning stages of early Christianity's adoption of its literature as sacred scripture. I will return to this matter in the next chapter.

WHAT BOOKS ARE IN THE EARLY
CHRISTIAN MANUSCRIPTS?

Here it is wise to remember the important factor, along with several others, that Larry Hurtado has noted: only about 1 percent of some five hundred thousand manuscripts from antiquity have been published; whatever conclusions we draw about the ones that have been published should be tempered with that awareness.[25] He also calls upon biblical scholars to investigate not only the biblical but also the other Christian literary texts from antiquity in order to see the biblical texts in their broader context. He has compiled a very useful listing of these manuscripts together with important data on their origin, contents, form (roll, codex, or opisthograph[26]), and identification. These manuscripts date roughly from the second and third centuries, though some of them are from the early part of the fourth century.[27] The majority (approximately 70 percent) of the Christian manuscripts are in codex form, but the roll or scroll was also used. In some cases (some 21 percent) they were written in rolls or scroll volumes, and in a few the opisthograph, or backside of a roll, was used. The codex was by far the most common format used for Christian scriptures, and the roll generally, though not always, for other writings. There is some overlap in the form of the manuscripts for the same book, as in the *Shepherd of Hermas*, which appears in all three forms—codex, roll, and opisthograph.[28]

None of the ancient papyri manuscripts includes all the canonical New Testament books, but noncanonical writings were also found with New Testament writings in several ancient manuscripts (e.g., P[72]) and in the three major forms. Hurtado concludes that the "physical linkage of texts in one manuscript probably reflects a view of them as sharing some common or related subject matter or significance for readers."[29] I agree and would add that this linkage in a number of examples reflects the notion that all the documents in the manuscript are sacred scripture to the community that viewed them bound together.

While most of the early surviving manuscripts were discovered in Egypt (probably because of its dry climate), one must ask how representative Christianity in Egypt was of the rest of the Roman world. Since there were many "translocal" texts in antiquity, that is, texts that made their way to other locations in antiquity such as the writings of Homer, Hesiod, and other classic writers, was this also true in early Christianity, so that many of the texts that were deemed relevant in Egypt did not have their origin in Egypt but elsewhere? For example, Mark was probably written in Rome and Paul's letters in Asia Minor and Greece for the most part, and they made their way to Egypt and to the larger community of Christians throughout the Roman world. The Paschal sermon by Melito from Sardis was also quite popular in many early churches, and while it was crafted in Sardis, it made its way to Egypt. Several studies have shown how quickly literary texts were transferred from one part of the Roman Empire to another, and here these texts were brought to Egypt no doubt by Christian missionaries or church participants.[30] Again, however, since we have access only to a small portion of the manuscripts that existed at that time, there is an element of uncertainty here, but it is clear from the number of surviving manuscripts in the locations where these texts were found, Psalms, Matthew, John, and *Shepherd of Hermas* were among the most popular texts.

When noncanonical texts are included in sacred collections, nothing in them apparently distinguishes the canonical from the noncanonical writings, as in the case of P[72], which I will discuss in the next chapter. Several ancient texts were discovered in Egypt containing in part fragments of a number of Old Testament and New Testament books written over several centuries along with a number of noncanonical writings. These collections have a considerable variety of manuscripts dating from the late second or early third century through the fourth century. Of the surviving New Testament manuscripts, roughly only 8 percent cover *most* of the New Testament and many more contain only small portions of the New Testament, some of which are fragmentary. In 2003 the

Institute for New Testament Textual Research in Münster, Germany, the official registry of biblical manuscripts, listed 5,735 Greek manuscripts of the New
Testament, but more will undoubtedly be added to that number in the near
future. The latest number of New Testament papyrus manuscripts (the oldest
collection of manuscripts dating from the second to the sixth or seventh century)
now stands at 117. The number of majuscule manuscripts or capital-lettered
manuscripts without spaces between the words (the next oldest collection dating
from roughly the fourth to the tenth century) and written on parchment now
stands at 310. There are 2,877 minuscule, or lower-case manuscripts with running letters (roughly from the ninth to the fifteenth century), and some 2,432
Greek lectionaries (selected portions of scriptures that were read in churches),
which are seldom considered in textual evidence of any reading, even though
they may date much earlier than some other manuscripts.[31] According to Eldon
Epp's analysis of the surviving manuscripts, 2,361 contain Gospels, 792 contain
letter(s) of Paul, 662 contain Acts and the Catholic or General Epistles, and 287
contain the book of Revelation.[32]

By way of a brief summary, Hurtado provides the number of Christian manuscripts containing biblical texts in the second and third centuries. Most of these
texts (usually fragments) were found in Egypt. The biblical books and the number of manuscripts found there include the following:

Old Testament: Genesis (8), Exodus (8), Leviticus (3), Numbers (1), Deu-
teronomy (2), Joshua (1), Judges (1), 2 Chronicles (2), Esther (2), Job (1),
Psalms (18), Proverbs (2), Ecclesiastes (2), Wisdom of Solomon (1), Sirach (2),
Isaiah (6), Jeremiah (2), Ezekiel (2), Daniel (2), Bel and Susanna (1), Minor
Prophets (2), Tobit (2), and 2 Maccabees (1).

New Testament: Matthew (12), Mark (1), Luke (7), John (16), Acts (7),
Romans (4), 1 Corinthians (2), 2 Corinthians (1), Galatians (1), Ephesians (3),
Philippians (2), Colossians (1), 1 Thessalonians (3), 2 Thessalonians (2), Phile-
mon (1), Titus (1), Hebrews (4), James (3), 1 Peter (1), 2 Peter (1), 1 John (1? =
P[9] or P.Oxy. 402, possibly fourth or fifth century), Jude (2), and Revelation (5).

Christian apocryphal writings: *Gospel of Thomas* (3), *Protevangelium of
James* (1), *Gospel of Mary* (2), *"Egerton" Gospel* (1), *Gospel of Peter* (2, possibly
P.Oxy. 2949 and P.Oxy. 4009), *"Fayyum" Gospel* (1), *Acts of Paul* (3), *Correspondence of Paul and Corinth* (1), *Apocalypse of Peter* (1), *Apocryphon of Jannes*
(1), and *Apocryphon of Moses* (1).

Other Christian writings, some with an element of doubt about them
(indicated by a question mark): *Shepherd of Hermas* (11); Irenaeus, *Against Heresies* (2); Melito, *Paschal Homily* (1); Melito, *On Prophecy?* (1); Melito, *Paschal
Hymn?* (1); Tatian, *Diatessaron?* (1); *Odes of Solomon* (1); Julius Africanus, *Cesti*
(1); Origen, *Gospel Commentary* (1); Origen, *Homily* (1); Origen, *De Principiis*
(1); *Sibylline Oracles* (1); Theonas, *Against Manichaeans?* (1); some unidentified
theological texts (3); an unidentified eschatological discourse (1); other unidentified homilies and letters (2); a Jewish and Christian dialogue (1); prayer texts
(3); Hymn to the Trinity (1), and exorcistic/apotropaic[33] texts.[34]

Several ancient collections of Christian manuscripts found in Egypt allow us to see that there was no complete agreement on the scope of the Christian scriptures at that time. These include the Chester Beatty papyri, the Bodmer papyri, and the Oxyrhynchus papyri. While they are sometimes called "libraries,"[35] it is probably safer to call them collections, since the largest number of them were found in a refuse site and we simply cannot know their relationships for the Christian communities that discarded them in the same vicinity. A fourth important collection discovered in the same approximate area in Egypt, the Nag Hammadi papyri, contain no biblical books, but rather a number of Gnostic religious texts that have a number of apostolic names attached to them. These collections are arbitrarily put together, as best we can tell from available evidence, and we do not know the original structures in which these books were placed.[36] We can probably say that Christians in the locations where these writings were found did make some use of them, but it is often not clear what that specific use was. For instance, the form of these texts, whether produced in a codex, or a roll, an opisthograph (see Rev. 5:1), may indicate the way that they were viewed in a community. If a text was written in a codex format, is it more likely that it functioned as scripture in the community that produced it? If it was produced in a used roll or in an opisthograph, did it not receive recognition as sacred? Approximately one-third of the earliest Christian manuscripts of what we now call "extracanonical" or "noncanonical" texts were written on rolls (scrolls). It is difficult to say what this all means. Did the use of the roll *always* suggest that the writing was not yet viewed as scripture?[37] Probably not, but that may often have been the case.

The first of the collections is the Chester Beatty papyri (early third–fourth century), discovered in the Nile Valley in Egypt in the early 1930s. It included a large number of papyri containing both Old Testament and New Testament writings as well as some other writings.[38] The New Testament part of that collection has the Gospels and Acts (P[45]), the earliest collection of Paul's Letters (without the Pastorals and Philemon, P[46]), and Revelation (P[47]). While it is an argument from silence and based only on the texts that survived decomposition and decay, it is a wonder that more New Testament books were not found there. Since P[46] is a fragmented codex, it is likely that other books were part of that collection, but it is not clear which one or ones, as we will explain below. It is clear, however, that there was inadequate room to include the Pastoral Letters.

The Bodmer papyri (third–sixth century) were discovered in Upper Egypt in the early 1950s and, besides a large collection of classical texts and correspondence, contain both Old Testament and New Testament books dating from the third to the seventh century, but also a number of noncanonical religious texts.[39] The New Testament collection (P[66], P[72], P[73], P[74], P[75]) is missing Mark, all of Paul's writings except Romans and 2 Corinthians, as well as Hebrews and Revelation. On the other hand, the collection includes the *Protevangelium Jacobi, 3 Corinthians, Acts of Paul, Apology of Phileas, Vision of Dorotheos, Shepherd of Hermas,* an apocryphon, other liturgical hymns, and three of Melito's homilies.

What can we make of this find of Christian religious manuscripts? What is missing from the collection is as much a puzzle as what it contains.

An important example of a Bodmer papyrus manuscript that has more in it than New Testament writings is P[72] (third to fourth century), which is generally identified as the oldest surviving manuscript of Jude and 1–2 Peter (that order). What is often ignored is that P[72] includes several other writings besides the above-noted New Testament writings in the following order: the *Nativity of Mary*, correspondence of Paul with the Corinthians and *3 Corinthians*,[40] an apocryphal letter from the *Ode of Solomon 11*, then Jude, followed by Melito's *Homily on the Passover*, a hymn fragment, *Apology of Phileas*, Psalms 33 and 34, and finally 1–2 Peter. This manuscript is not uniform, that is, by the same hand, and the writings in it are not from the same time.

Finally, the Oxyrhynchus papyri collection (from ca. late third to fourth to late sixth or early seventh century and designated or identified by P.Oxy. followed by a number), includes many New Testament writings besides other noncanonical writings. Since they were found in a refuse site, it is difficult to make a strong case about distinguishing between canonical and noncanonical texts. Were they all sacred texts that Christians simply discarded after they wore out? We are uncertain. They are only arbitrarily put together because they were found in the same refuse site, but we cannot be sure that they formed some kind of library, though we can say that the discovery of all of these Christian texts in the same vicinity suggests that they were significant texts for the community that at one time held them. There are no clear marks or notations to distinguish these texts, aside from the form in which they were produced (roll, codex, or opisthograph). This collection has the largest number of New Testament papyri found in any one location and warrants a closer look. It includes Matthew, Luke, John, Acts, Romans, 1 Corinthians, Galatians, Philippians, 1–2 Thessalonians, Hebrews, James, 1 John, Jude, and Revelation. Missing from the earlier Oxyrhynchus papyri are Mark, 2 Corinthians, Ephesians, Colossians, 1–2 Timothy, Titus, Philemon, 1–2 Peter, and 2–3 John. Mark and 1 Peter were included in the later Oxyrhynchus papyri.[41] This raises canonical questions about why some New Testament books were not found there and why some noncanonical books were found among the canonical texts. What did this mean to the community that preserved these writings in the late third and fourth centuries?

The presence of more than one copy of a manuscript in an ancient collection likely indicates the special status the document had in the community that preserved it. With that in mind, note the multiple and the single copies of noncanonical books at Oxyrhynchus: *Shepherd of Hermas* (7), *Gospel of Thomas* (3), *Gospel of Mary* (2), *Acts of Peter* (1), *Acts of John* (1), *Acts of Paul* (1), *Didache* (1), *Sophia Jesus Christi* (1), *Gospel of Peter* (2), *Apocalypse of Peter* (1?), three unknown Gospels or sayings of Jesus, and *Acts of Paul and Thecla* (1).

Eldon Epp notes that all these books, except perhaps the *Letter of Abgar* (not listed above), were second-century writings and suggests that they all may have been candidates for inclusion in the New Testament. More importantly, and for our purposes, he observes that nothing found at Oxyrhynchus distinguishes the New Testament books from the noncanonical Christian books also found there.[42] Because there are no obvious distinguishing marks in these texts, the community that produced, copied, and received these religious manuscripts most likely received them as sacred literature. It is not clear if enough is known about them at this point to say that all the texts that were in a roll or codex format were considered sacred scripture on the basis of their format. Even opisthographs containing a biblical or noncanonical text may have been viewed as scripture to the communities that had them. Because of the scarcity of writing materials and the relative expense to produce them, opisthographs may have been used to copy Christian sacred texts by the community of Christians in the region where the Oxyrhynchus papyri were found. There are too many variables here to make a dogmatic statement about their format and how they were viewed in that region. It is still likely, however, that the community that produced, copied, and received these religious manuscripts received all of them as sacred literature that informed their faith and religious conduct.

Other examples include P[42] (ca. seventh or eighth century) that contains portions of Luke 1 and 2 in Greek and Coptic, but also an extensive collection of odes or hymns taken from the Jewish Bible and apocryphal literature; and P[apr] (or P$_2$, a palimpsest) includes Acts, the Catholic Epistles, and Revelation, but also fragments of 4 Maccabees. I should pause to observe that generally the literature that is later described as noncanonical literature, with the exception of the *Shepherd of Hermas* and a few others, are in the minority of manuscripts in most of the places where collections of sacred Christian texts were found.[43] This is to be expected since once a community decides that some books are no longer considered useful or sacred, there is little motivation in that community to continue producing manuscripts with those texts in them.

In his study of Paul, David Trobisch claims that less than 8 percent of all known manuscripts with collections of Paul's writings contain the whole New Testament.[44] The oldest manuscript containing the Letters of Paul is the fragmentary P[46], which breaks off at 1 Thessalonians 5:28; it originally had fourteen more pages. That, however, is not sufficient space to include the rest of the writings attributed to Paul (2 Thessalonians, 1 and 2 Timothy, Titus, and Philemon), which would take between twenty and twenty-three more pages. It is likely that the copier included 2 Thessalonians since in all other manuscripts where 1 Thessalonians is included so also is 2 Thessalonians, but including 2 Thessalonians does not account for the rest of the space in the codex. There is simply not enough room in the codex to include the rest of the Pauline corpus and it is difficult to find any books of appropriate size by Paul or others to fit into that limited space.[45] Scholars debate whether other letters were known to the scribe, whether the scribe planned poorly and did not have room for the rest, and whether the scribe knew the rest but did not include them and chose something else (one or more smaller letters?) in their place. Since P[32] contains Titus and P[87] contains Philemon, and both of these manuscripts were produced in the same general area at roughly the same time as P[46] (ca. 200–220 CE), it may be that the scribe of P[46] knew of more writings attributed to Paul. It is more likely that the *complete* collection of writings later attributed to Paul was not known earlier and that the notion of a *fixed* Pauline collection was not widespread at the end of the second century, even if several collections of many of his writings or those attributed to him were circulating earlier. Some New Testament scholars claim that P[46] is a *complete* collection of Paul's writings, including the Pastorals and Philemon, but no other such collection or parallel exists for at least another hundred years. Only eight of the manuscripts dating before the sixth century contain all or most of the letters attributed to Paul in the New Testament. It is unlikely, therefore, that the rest of P[46] contained the Pastoral Epistles.

The famous Nag Hammadi collection of sacred texts was also found in Egypt, but there are no biblical books in that collection of Gnostic texts, only numerous other religious texts that were clearly part of the sacred collection belonging to Christians in the Nag Hammadi region. Many of those documents, such as *Gospel of Thomas, Apocryphon of John, Gospel of Philip*, and *Acts of Peter and the Twelve Apostles* have the names of apostles in their titles. Apostolic names attached to ancient texts suggested apostolic authority, which emerges as a very influential factor in recognizing Christian literature as scripture in the last half of the second century CE. This suggests that this religious literature was also received and treated as sacred and inspired literature by those Gnostic Christian communities that received and transmitted it.[46]

Except for the Nag Hammadi Library, the above examples have both canonical and noncanonical books in the papyri codices, and no collection has the complete Old Testament or New Testament books in them. The Bodmer and Oxyrhynchus papyri have not only New Testament writings but also noncanonical literature. The Chester Beatty papyri include noncanonical writings (*1 Enoch* and a homily by Melito) in the Old Testament manuscript collection. None of the so-called libraries has a complete collection of the New Testament writings, but it is likely that most of these religious texts functioned in some sacred and authoritative manner in the churches of that region. This is not a big stretch in the world of possibilities, but it is likely given the time and effort to copy and circulate these texts in antiquity. It is difficult to explain their preservation if that were not the case.

On the basis of the surviving fourth- and fifth-century canonical lists or catalogues, it is easy to assume that the New Testament canon was closed no later than the fourth century, but Daryl Schmidt brings to our attention two twelfth-century manuscripts containing noncanonical writings. He mentions minuscule 339 (now missing), which was reported by F. J. A. Hort to contain not only the four Gospels but also the *Epistle of Pilate and Reply, On the Genealogy of the Virgin*, Revelation, *Synaxarion*, Acts, the Catholic Epistles, the Letters of Paul, *Lives of the Apostles*, and a Psalter. Additional material is also found in minuscule 180 from the twelfth century.[47] There is little doubt that many churches had accepted the canonical Gospels, Acts, and the Letters of Paul as

Christian scripture by the end of the second century, but the collections in sub-sequent codices suggest that other literature was also used in churches long after the fourth and fifth centuries. Likewise, in the late minuscule manuscript 1505 not only the Psalms but *Odes* were also included. It is not certain if the latter is *Odes of Solomon,* and it is not certain which psalms were included.

In the mid-fourth-century Codex Vaticanus (B 03) lacks 1 and 2 Timothy, Titus, and Philemon.[48] What to make of this is difficult to tell, since the codex is fragmented at the beginning (omitting the first forty-five chapters of Genesis) and end (breaking off in the middle of Hebrews 9), but some scholars continue to argue that the missing books (the pastorals and Philemon) were originally a part of this fragmented manuscript since they are in the major codices (Sinaiticus and Alexandrinus), but the evidence is simply not yet there to draw such con-clusions about the contents.[49] Later, the palimpsest codex Ephraemi Rescriptus (C 04, ca. fifth century) reportedly included all the New Testament books, but it is not certain that 2 John and 2 Thessalonians were included.[50] Codex Sinaiticus (ℵ, ca. fourth century) contains all the New Testament books, but also *Epistle of Barnabas* and *Shepherd of Hermas.* Codex Alexandrinus (A, fifth century), includes all the New Testament as well as *1–2 Clement* and *Psalms of Solomon.* Codex Bezae (D, fifth century) contains the Gospels and Acts. Codex Clara-montanus (D[P], sixth century) includes most of Paul's Letters but also *Epistle of Barnabas, Shepherd of Hermas, Acts of Paul,* and *Apocalypse of Peter;* however, it lacks Philippians, 1–2 Thessalonians, and Hebrews.

Interestingly, the only evidence before the fourth century that 2 and 3 John were seriously considered authoritative by anyone in the church are a few brief and vague allusions to these letters in the second and third centuries.[51] The witness to them is such that there is no clear evidence that they were accepted as part of a sacred collection of the church until the fourth century, and even then these letters continued to be rejected by the Syrian church.[52] The difficulty that some churches had in accepting these letters probably had to do with their brevity as well as their lack of significant theological content. The same can be said of Jude, but in that case the difficulty may have been a result of its citing *1 Enoch* (v. 14) in a scriptural (authoritative) manner ("Enoch . . . prophesied"). The absence of the Pastoral Epistles from many early papyri manuscripts is diffi-cult to explain, unless perhaps they were written after Paul and were not initially acknowledged as Pauline literature. It is also possible that because they were sent to individuals and not to churches they were not included, but the evidence to support these conclusions is lacking (cf. Philemon and 3 John).

LISTS AND CATALOGUES OF BOOKS

The production of catalogues or lists of sacred books began in the fourth and fifth centuries, but one encounters considerable difficulty finding biblical manu-scripts that reflect the books and only those books in these lists.[53] While there may have been some agreement in principle on what was in the biblical canon, there was less agreement in practice. I have shown elsewhere that the various lists or catalogues of sacred books from the fourth to the sixth centuries do not reflect a uniform view of what books make up the church's New Testament canon in the fourth and fifth centuries.[54] Not only are there variations in the surviving lists, there is also considerable variance in those lists from what has survived in the biblical manuscripts themselves.

Eusebius (ca. 320–330) offers the first datable catalogue of sacred New Testament writings that belong to what he called the "Recognized [Greek *homolegoumenois*] Books."[55] His list includes the four canonical Gospels, Acts, the Letters of Paul (13), 1 John, 1 Peter, and possibly Revelation (that order). Among the doubted or disputed books (Greek *antilegomenon*) in the churches, he lists James, Jude, 2 Peter, 2 and 3 John, and Revelation (*Hist. eccl.* 3.25.1–3). He himself seems conflicted about the widespread acceptance of Revelation.[56] His analysis of what books were widely acknowledged as sacred or "encovenanted" (Greek *endiathēkēs* or *endiathēous*) in his generation reflects one of the earliest moves toward a fixed New Testament canon. After him, other catalogues and lists of sacred books appear, and a comparison of these lists shows that although a widely accepted core of New Testament writings was circulating in the churches of that time, there was also considerable flexibility on the fringes of the New Testament canon.

Some books that were initially included in the sacred collections of churches were later removed, especially *Shepherd of Hermas, Epistle of Barnabas*, and *1–2 Clement*. A few churches continued to accept and read other literature in worship for many centuries, as we see from both the surviving manuscripts and the lists or catalogues of sacred books. The implications of this for an understanding of canonical formation are considerable. Athanasius of Alexandria (367 CE) produced a list of Old Testament and New Testament books, with the latter containing the first list of the twenty-seven New Testament books familiar to the Christian community today. The multiple lists and catalogues of New Testament writings after Athanasius demonstrate that he was *not* speaking for all churches of his own generation, nor for many churches for centuries after that, even though he probably reflected the most popular views of churches in his general vicinity (Alexandria), though not necessarily in regions south of him as the collections of manuscripts from Egypt described above suggest.

The current interest in establishing the time, causes, and boundaries of a fixed Christian biblical canon was of little concern in the early centuries of the church, though by the fourth century such interest began to emerge. To gain an appreciation of that interest, it is important to examine the fourth-century social context when this canon formation began its final stages. Because of the persecutions of the church, accompanied by the burning of its sacred literature, as well as the conversion of Constantine and his subsequent call for religious unity in his new Constantinian Roman Empire, there was a need to determine what literature was viewed as sacred and what literature was not. This process of stabilizing the books that formed the Christian biblical canon was largely settled for most churches by the late fourth and early fifth centuries.[57]

Historically churches have never fully agreed which books should be included in the Bible, and those that do agree sometimes ignore the books of the Bible that do not address their own specific needs. Most Christian churches agree on the books of the New Testament, though not completely. Although he included Hebrews, James, Jude, and Revelation, Martin Luther famously was not pleased with them. In practice, the ancient churches, like many today, tended to have a canon within the canon, and often in practice a canon different from what church councils accepted. The ancient manuscripts regularly reflect diversity in the churches in terms of the books they acknowledged as scripture and the text of those books. Those manuscripts also reflect the fluidity of the biblical canon in the times in which they were produced and used in the variety of churches that welcomed them. In the next chapter I will focus more on the text and translations of the early Christian scriptures and on the fluidity of that text and the variety of those translations.

Chapter 9

Texts and Translations
of Scripture

With one exception, namely the book of Revelation (Rev. 22:18–19; cf. Deut. 4:2), we have no evidence that the writers of the New Testament books were aware that they were producing sacred or inspired literature. The same is true of those who made some of the earliest copies of those texts—they showed little awareness that they were preserving *sacred* texts. Many changes were made during the copying of the New Testament texts, and those changes were transmitted and multiplied through the production of copies from altered or flawed copies. Within a generation the autographs or original manuscripts were lost, destroyed, or even worn out, and new copies of the manuscripts were made from existing copies. Those who copied the New Testament manuscripts not only reproduced unintentional errors in transmission, but also introduced intentional changes to their New Testament texts. I will focus on these changes below.

CHANGES IN THE BIBLICAL TEXTS

All of the manuscripts within each of the primary text families, namely the Alexandrian, Western, and Byzantine text families, as well as the so-called Caesarean text,[1] differ slightly from one another. No two manuscripts are exactly alike, and many changes both accidental and intentional were made in them. Bart Ehrman observes that "the texts of these books were by no means inviolable; to the contrary, they were altered with relative ease and alarming frequency. Most of the changes were accidental, the result of scribal ineptitude, carelessness, or fatigue. Others were intentional, and reflect the controversial milieu within which they were produced."[2]

Craig Evans illustrates three well-known textual variants, noting that many errors were made in the transmission of Christianity's sacred literature. The first is the long ending of Mark's Gospel (Mark 16:9–20), which grammarians, textual critics, and commentators have agreed was not a part of the original Gospel.[3] It could well be that the original ending (following 16:8) was lost as the result of damage to the manuscript or for some other reason, but most agree that 16:9–20 was an intentional insertion into the text of Mark. Evans also discusses John 7:53–8:11, another insertion into a biblical text. He adds that if this text was not an original part of John's Gospel, nothing of great significance would be lost. Likewise, Luke 22:43–44 (cf. with Matt. 26:36–46; Mark 14:32–42; Luke 22:39–46) focuses on the prayer of Jesus with an insertion into the text of an angel appearing from heaven and Jesus sweating, as it were, drops of blood. These verses are not in the oldest manuscripts, but it seems clear that the scribes wanted to insert them early on to enhance the drama and experience of Jesus.[4]

Changes in the biblical texts continued until the invention of movable type and the printing press when copies of biblical texts could finally be reproduced exactly alike. Helmut Koester claims that the most significant corruptions of the New Testament Gospel texts came during the first and second centuries.[5] Although the evidence for this is not compelling to some textual critics, and it is mostly inferential and largely based on the lack of fixed Christian scriptures throughout most of the second century, the variety of variants in the third- and fourth-century manuscripts suggest that Koester may be right. This coincides with the fact that while several New Testament writings were read and cited in the second-century churches, often more frequently than many Old Testament texts, they were generally not yet called "scripture" before the end of that century. Changes to these texts would not likely have caused much concern if they had not yet received scriptural recognition. One should note, however, that there is little evidence from this period that can inform such conclusions, and it is better to make more cautionary observations about changes to the biblical text as well as the literary quality of the texts that survive. Some of those texts were completed in a responsible and careful manner (P^{66}, late second century, and P^{75}, early to mid-third century), as I will note below.

Many, if not most, of the intentional textual changes were made in good conscience with the aim of clarifying or improving the meaning of the biblical text, and no doubt all such changes have not been identified, thereby leaving many questions about the authenticity of the New Testament texts unanswered.

We have examples of well-copied manuscripts, such as P[75] and many of the manuscripts in the Alexandrian family, but some text traditions often show little correlation between the recognition of the sacredness of the New Testament writings and the carefulness of their transcription. While some Christians were initially not as careful in transmitting their sacred scriptures as their Jewish cousins, especially in the Western texts but in others as well, some were much more careful and quite skillful.[6]

Accidental errors are frequent even among the best manuscripts, and well-intentioned and well-trained scribes were always susceptible to a careless moment. The ancient biblical manuscripts differ from one another in quality of transmission to greater or lesser degrees, and the variations in the biblical texts, patristic citations, and lectionaries are considerable. Some copiers display skillful attention to the details of the text. Michael Holmes says about one copier: "the scribe of P[75] is one of the best workmen ever to copy a biblical text," and adds that unlike this copier the later "scribe of Beza—quite apart from the character of the text he was copying—is not a careful workman."[7]

The number of variants in the New Testament manuscripts appears to be greater than the words in the New Testament,[8] but again, most of them are obvious copying errors. Intentional changes were fewer and often had the aim of promoting a particular bias, such as bringing the biblical texts in line with the orthodox beliefs and practices of the communities that received and used these texts. Reuben Swanson addresses the many intentional changes in the biblical texts, even after their scriptural status had been determined, and claims that these changes demonstrated the "freedom scribes exercised in the transcription of the text. Evidently there were scribes who did not have a concept of the inviolable nature of the text of scripture. They exercised their freedom to innovate and to express in their own language what a passage of scripture meant to them." He adds: "the living character of the tradition is perhaps the most possible explanation to account for the marked changes that took place in the sources over the centuries."[9]

These variants in the ancient manuscripts make the work of text-critical scholars highly complex, and in some cases their conclusions about the original text are at best educated guesses. All ancient biblical manuscripts were copied by hand from earlier copies, and the changes in the manuscripts multiplied in transmission over many centuries. The trained eye readily identifies most of the accidental and deliberate changes, but what accounts for some changes is not clear. Textual scholars know that alterations of the biblical texts were incorporated into the New Testament manuscripts, and they were received as sacred literature in the early churches. They also know that the task of recovering the earliest New Testament texts is daunting. Swanson also makes this point repeatedly with many examples and reminds us that each manuscript, regardless of the textual changes made by the copiers, was scripture in an early Christian community.[10]

ANCIENT ACKNOWLEDGMENT OF TEXTUAL CHANGES

Until the fourth century, when Christianity received official sanction from the emperor Constantine and the churches began to prosper, those who copied the Christian scriptures were often less trained than the skilled, handbook-quality scribes who were employed to copy formal literature. This was true especially in the Western text-type manuscripts that originated in the middle to late second century. The rapid spread of the Christian churches in the first few centuries led to the need for many more copies of the church's scriptures, and those who made those copies sometimes made them in haste. Paleographers have identified four basic types of handwriting that produced the ancient manuscripts: the *professional* hand, with careful attention to detail and excellent craftsmanship (P[46], P[75]); the *documentary* hand, who was an experienced literate copier (ca. 200–225); the *reformed documentary* hand, used in copying literary documents and called a "book hand" or "literary hand"; and finally the *common* hand, who was semi-literate and untrained in making documents and is characterized by an inelegant cursive script. Biblical manuscripts reflect all of these hands, including at times the last.[11] Because literate and sometimes lesser skilled scribes who produced the earliest copies of the New Testament writings did not generally have the handbook quality skills, it is not surprising to find many errors in the copies they produced.[12] Bruce Metzger and Bart Ehrman explain why New Testament manuscripts of the first two centuries are considerably more prone to error:

> The earliest copyists would not have been trained professionals who made copies for a living but simply literate members of a congregation who had the time and ability to do the job. Since most, if not all, of them would have been amateurs in the art of copying, a relatively large number of mistakes no doubt crept into their texts as they reproduced them. It is possible that after the original was placed in circulation it soon became lost or was destroyed, so all surviving copies conceivably have derived from one single, error-prone copy made in the early stages of the book's circulation.[13]

A qualification of this comes from Larry Hurtado, who claims that while some copiers of early biblical literature may have been "amateurs," it may be better to say that some of the earliest Christian production of biblical manuscripts "seem largely to be by skilled scribes, but apparently not of formal bookhand quality," which, he says, is "likely a reflection of the socio-economic level of most Christians: able to afford a skilled copyist, but not able to afford the luxury trade."[14]

Perhaps we are on surer ground by suggesting that a large number of the early translations of the biblical literature were made by those with good intentions but amateur skills. Metzger and Ehrman cite Augustine, who wistfully reflects on the frequent mistakes in translating the biblical manuscripts: "anyone who happened to gain possession of a Greek manuscript and who imagined that he had some facility in both Latin and Greek, however slight that might be, dared to make a translation" (*Doctr. chr.* 2.11.16).[15]

Several ancient writers speak of the diversity and errors in the texts of the New Testament writings that were circulating in the churches, but overall little was done to correct the problem. Irenaeus (ca. 170), when discussing the number 666 in Revelation 13:18, acknowledged the problem of errors among existing copies of manuscripts as well as the lack of original texts to correct them. He concluded that the evidence supports the number 666, but then adds: "I do not know how it is that some have erred following the ordinary mode of speech, and have vitiated the middle number [6] in the name. . . . I am inclined to think that this occurred through the fault of copyists, *as is wont to happen,* since numbers are also expressed by letters; so that the Greek letter which expresses the number of sixty was easily expanded into the letter Iota of the Greeks."

After explaining how changes may have happened, Irenaeus goes on to warn those who deliberately change the sacred texts adding that, "there shall be no light punishment [inflicted] upon him who either adds or subtracts anything from the Scripture" (Irenaeus, *Haer.* 5.30.1, ANF; emphasis added). Eusebius observes that Irenaeus also warns those who would later copy his own work to take extra care in their work. Irenaeus wrote the following colophon at the end of *On the Ogdoad*: "I adjure thee, who shalt copy out this book, by our Lord Jesus Christ, by his glorious advent when he comes to judge the living and the dead, that thou compare what thou shalt transcribe and correct it with this copy whence thou art transcribing, with all care, and thou shalt likewise transcribe this oath and put it in the copy" (Eusebius, *Hist. eccl.* 5.20.2, LCL).

Origen also expressed his concern about eliminating the errors in biblical transmission and establishing an authoritative and accurate biblical text when he produced his Hexapla (or six-columned Bible) in the third century. He included critical marks in his text to say what he thought should be omitted and what he thought should be included in the translation, which was his attempt to revise the Septuagint (LXX) from the Hebrew text.[16] Jerome was also aware of the deliberate and accidental changes in the biblical texts and was commissioned by Pope Damasus in 384 to produce a Latin text that eliminated these errors. His Latin Vulgate was eventually received with wide acclaim in the church, but Jerome's concern about errors in the manuscripts was not widely shared and only rarely did the early church take steps to deal with those errors. The above notwithstanding, until the time of Erasmus in the sixteenth century little attention was given to stabilizing the New Testament texts and dealing with the many errors present in them.[17]

Textual scholars generally divide the New Testament text types into three primary families. The Alexandrian text family began in Egypt probably in the early to mid-second century and is generally known for its faithful preservation of the original text and more careful and accurate transmission of the biblical text. In a few instances the Western text appears to preserve a more reliable reading than the Alexandrian text,[18] but that is unusual and text-critical scholars generally prefer readings from the Alexandrian text family.

The Western text emerged at roughly the middle to late second century but was not as carefully produced as the Alexandrian texts. According to Metzger, "the chief characteristic of Western readings is fondness of paraphrase. Words, clauses, and even whole sentences are freely changed, omitted, or inserted. Sometimes the motive appears to have been harmonization, while at other times it was the enrichment of the narrative by inclusion of traditional or apocryphal material."[19]

The later Byzantine (Syrian or Koine) text type, on which the KJV is based, is characterized by inferior and secondary readings and is no longer the preferred text of most New Testament scholars.[20]

The Alexandrian texts were more carefully prepared than the Western texts, but no biblical text is completely consistent. The chief witnesses to the Alexandrian text include the well-known P^{66}, P^{77}, Codex Vaticanus (B), and Codex Sinaiticus (א).[21] Codex Vaticanus, a mid-fourth-century uncial manuscript produced mostly in three columns per page, probably originated in Alexandria, Egypt, as its text type suggests, and it is often acknowledged as the oldest codex manuscript containing both the Old Testament and New Testament books. Its beginning is fragmentary, with more than forty chapters of Genesis missing, and the New Testament part of the volume breaks off in Hebrews 9:14 in the middle of a word (*kathariei*), and the rest of Hebrews and Revelation are supplied by a later hand in a minuscule script. Vaticanus is one of the most important and reliable ancient NT texts, but it is also an edited text that is both fragmentary and defective in places. It does not contain all of the letters attributed to Paul, though it may also have included writings of the Apostolic Fathers, as did some other uncial or majuscule manuscripts of the fourth and fifth centuries, but that is uncertain. Its Old Testament portion includes without differentiation several books from the apocryphal collection; that is, they are mixed with the canonical books and not included at the end of the Old Testament portion of the manuscript as we see in Protestant Bibles that include them.

Because of the significant expense involved in securing the services of professional scribes, the early Christians did not generally prepare careful literary copies of the New Testament books. Professional scribes in the ancient world were paid well, namely some 750 denarii per year plus the scribes' regular maintenance (home, etc.). That amount was more than double what the average workman received. The early churches were not regularly able to employ the best scribes with the technical skills to produce careful copies of its sacred scriptures, and the use of amateur copiers is reflected in many of the earliest manuscripts of the New Testament. No doubt as a result of this circumstance, many of the errors and changes in the New Testament writings that emerged early were passed on in subsequent copies, and later still other changes were introduced.[22]

The care in copying New Testament manuscripts generally improved in the fourth century, when it became more common for churches, for a time, to use professional scribes to produce copies of their scriptures. The cost of producing both the Old Testament and New Testament by professional scribes in the fourth century was approximately 30,000 denarii, or roughly four years salary for a legionary some 100 years earlier.

Kurt and Barbara Aland have noted that by the fourth century those manuscripts prepared on parchment or animal skins (mostly sheep or goats) replaced most of the papyri manuscripts. One sheep or goat normally provided two double folios, only four folios of a finished manuscript. Copying the whole of the New Testament required between 200 and 250 folios. This means that at least fifty to sixty sheep were needed to produce a volume or codex containing *all* and *only* the New Testament books. They conclude that only the upper classes could afford such an expensive undertaking.[23]

The commercial centers for literary productions were called *scriptoria*, and great care was taken in the scriptoria to produce copies of the Christian Scriptures. In the Byzantine era, however, the task of producing copies of the Scriptures was often given to monks in monasteries who produced copies in their private cells and often with less precision than copies produced in the professional scriptoria.

Accidental and even intentional changes continued to appear in biblical manuscripts, until the invention of movable type and the printing press in the mid-fifteenth century, though with less frequency than was true in the earlier centuries. Difficulties in transcription were compounded by the weariness of posture necessary to make such copies in less than comfortable places. With the use of an ink pen, such copying required a fresh dip in the inkwell after every four to six letters. One can imagine the difficulty in producing such manuscripts and the sheer effort in maintaining attention to the details of a manuscript while at the same time sitting in cramped positions that strained many of the muscles of the body. As the body wearied and tired, many unintentional errors crept into the copies, whether those prepared in the scriptorium or in the cell of a monastery.[24] There is a greater stabilization in the biblical text after around 850 CE, and the variants decline but are not completely eliminated until the invention of the printing press.[25]

Readers generally understand accidental changes to the biblical text because of the difficulties involved in making copies by hand and often in difficult circumstances, but intentional changes, which are also common in Christian biblical texts, present a greater challenge. Many changes were simple corrections of what the scribes believed were errors in the texts they were copying, or there were attempts to harmonize apparently contradictory passages. Intentional changes were often introduced to bring clarity to a contemporary theological issue facing the church and to support various orthodox positions of the church. Ehrman cites a number of these deliberate changes in the second to the fourth centuries that reveal the orthodox tendencies to deal with various heresies. The best-known corruption of the biblical text for christological purposes is the *Comma Johanneum* (or the "Johannine Comma"), where the Trinitarian addition to 1 John 5:7–8 was introduced. This change is not found in any known Greek manuscript, but Erasmus likely translated it from the Latin Sistine

Clementine edition of the Latin Vulgate and inserted it under pressure from his contemporaries into the second edition of his Greek New Testament. The Johannine Comma includes the words: "For there are three who bear witness in heaven, the Father, the Word, and the Holy Spirit, and these three are one. And there are three who bear witness on earth, the spirit and the water and the blood, and these three are one." This addition was intended to support the church's understanding of the Trinity, but it has no Greek textual support. Cyprian in the third century may have known of this addition, which may have originated in North Africa, but that is all uncertain.[26]

Likewise, several additions to the end of Mark's Gospel following 16:8 indicate the widespread belief that the original Gospel did not end with the words "for they were afraid" (Greek *ephobounto gar*). A later scribe added 16:9–20, which is partially a summary of the conclusions of the other three canonical Gospels. It is likely that a well-intentioned scribe added what was believed to be a more appropriate conclusion to a Gospel, which is, after all, about good news (see Mark 1:1), instead of ending it on a note of fear. How Mark concluded his Gospel continues to bother many scholars today.[27] Interestingly, Codex Vaticanus ends the Gospel in 16:8 in the middle column with scribal marks in the margins suggesting some question about the text, but uncharacteristically it also leaves a blank column (the third column, or right-hand column, on the page) following the ending of that Gospel. The copier may have known or believed that something else was needed to complete the Gospel, but was unsure what it was and simply left room for a later hand to complete it.

There are also some twenty variations in the texts on marriage and divorce in the Synoptic Gospels. The early churches had considerable stake in this issue, and a number of additions or changes were introduced into the New Testament texts to bring clarity to the matter. It is not always easy to identify the original text of the New Testament, and yet the variants in the surviving manuscripts were welcomed as canonical in the communities that received these texts.[28] Similarly, the role of women in the church was clearly an issue of contention for some churches, as we see in the variants in the texts that mention Priscilla or Prisca, who is sometimes diminished in stature in the ancient texts. The reference to Junia as an apostle in Romans 16:7 is also challenged in several late Greek texts, even though the early church fathers all agreed that she occupied that role. One can also see in the problematic texts of 1 Corinthians 14:33b–36 and 1 Timothy 2:8–15 that some early churches were anxious to marginalize the role of women in the church's ministries.[29]

Many intentional changes were likely introduced throughout the second century before the scriptural status of the New Testament writings was recognized, but later changes also occurred and are more difficult to explain.[30] While all the various biblical manuscripts functioned authoritatively or canonically in the churches that possessed and read these texts, the New Testament texts were still fluid and at times varied considerably. Epp aptly concludes: "our multiplicities of texts may all have been canonical (that is, authoritative) at some time and place."[31] The second century has been called the period of most intense changes to the biblical texts,[32] perhaps because at that time their sacred status had not yet been established. That factor may have contributed to many changes during the formative period.[33]

A STABILIZED GREEK TEXT

In 1516 Erasmus of Rotterdam produced the first modern published Greek text of the New Testament, which was based primarily on two twelfth-century minuscule manuscripts that he found in the university at Basel, Switzerland. In subsequent editions, he included five or six additional Greek manuscripts, but none of them dated before the tenth century. His Greek text also included a correction of several Latin translations in Jerome's Vulgate, as well as texts from a late edition of the Vulgate that he translated into Greek when he found the Greek text lacking; this was the case especially in the final six verses of Revelation but also in the Johannine Comma (1 John 5:7–8) that was discussed above.

Erasmus's first edition of the Greek text was revised four more times, in 1519, 1522, 1527, and 1535. The first edition contained hundreds of typographical errors that reveal the haste in which the text was prepared. Finally, Theodore Beza revised it again and produced his own Greek text relying heavily on Erasmus's text. This became the textual basis for the New Testament in the KJV.[34] Beza's Greek text was eventually called the *textus receptus* or "received text" because for generations biblical scholars based their translations and exegesis on it.[35] While there is little substantial theology lost in the KJV translation, and little of significance changed by it, it is nonetheless an inferior translation in that it does not generally reflect the earliest and most reliable New Testament Greek text tradition. It includes numerous additions to the biblical text, for example, in John 3:13; 7:53–8:11; Mark 16:9–20; and 1 John 5:7–8. The more equivocal texts, such as 1 Corinthians 14:33b–36, are more readily seen in the earlier manuscripts, such as Codex Vaticanus, with dots in the margin of the text suggesting that passage's questionable status in that context, but these dots are absent from the textus receptus.

All translators and interpreters of a New Testament text know the importance of discerning the most reliable biblical text. They are especially concerned with the evidence that supports authenticity, and they generally rely heavily on the most recent editions of the Greek New Testament, the Nestle-Aland 27th edition of *Novum Testamentum Graece* and the United Bible Society's 4th edition of *The Greek New Testament*. They also know that many factors are involved in establishing a reliable Greek text, including discerning not only the earliest text but also the competence of the transcribers of that text. It is quite possible to produce a very good translation of an inferior early Greek text as well as a poor translation of a very reliable text.

The diversity in the ancient New Testament *texts* is evidence that for centuries the church's primary focus in canon formation was on *books* of the Bible and not on the integrity of the biblical text itself. Kent Clarke recognizes this and observes that there is little ancient concern about a single canonical text of the Bible, and the diversity of biblical texts shows that there is no single ecclesiastical form of text.[36] Given the large number of variants and modifications in the ancient New Testament texts, is there a way to bring these texts into a manageable and reliable biblical text? Undoubtedly the church's orthodoxy influenced, and to some extent limited, the scope of the intentional changes in these ancient texts. The church's canon of faith, or *regula fidei*, was clearly operative during the transmission of these texts, and Bart Ehrman is no doubt correct when he observes that loyalty to orthodoxy often affected their transmission. The early church's vigorous defense against what it called heresy in the second through the fourth century and even later testifies to the limits of diversity that were acceptable in the ancient churches. This tendency toward orthodoxy in the textual changes is attested in the surviving New Testament manuscripts. Ehrman also observes that some ancient Christian scribes often "altered the words of the text by putting them 'in other words.' To this extent, they were textual interpreters. At the same time, by *physically* altering the words, they did something quite different from other exegetes, and this difference is by no means to be minimized." He concludes that only from a distance, namely ours, can we evaluate the causes and recognize the effects of these kinds of scribal modifications, and so designate them "the orthodox corruptions of Scripture."[37]

Which text of the New Testament is authoritative for the church today? This question has not gone unnoticed by biblical scholars. Only two New Testament manuscripts can reliably be dated in the second century; the vast majority are from the third century and later. What text preceded these manuscripts for more than a hundred years? We can only make an educated guess, but in most instances it may have been something similar to the eclectic text in the recent editions of the Greek New Testament. On the other hand, the period of the most intense changes to the biblical texts probably happened during the time when their sacred status had not yet been recognized or established, namely in the second century CE.[38] We do know that many intentional changes were introduced after these texts were received as sacred scripture and one can only imagine what the situation was *before* that reception.

It is worth noting that throughout the church's history it has carried on its ministries and established its doctrines without the use of the *original* manuscripts of the New Testament or even the eclectic text of modern construct. No ancient or modern translation is based on those original texts, and their absence has not hindered the church from using the only biblical texts that it possesses in its worship, instruction, and mission. Despite the many variants in them, all the New Testament manuscripts from the end of the second century at the latest functioned canonically in the communities of faith that received, transmitted, and used them. In other words, the biblical texts that informed the early Christians contained many transcriptional and intentional alterations.

Uniform original manuscripts at no known time informed the majority of the earliest churches' theology, worship, and mission. Since normal manuscript life with regular use was about twenty to thirty years, the loss of the original texts of the biblical literature occurred rather early in the first Christian gatherings. Subsequent copies were produced, but thereafter all manuscripts were made from copies of copies, and what we see in those that have survived antiquity is that no two copies are exactly like, even though some copies are better and more faithful to the earlier circulated text than others.

THE "ORIGINAL" TEXT

Which text of the New Testament is the "original" text? Perhaps we should ask rather which text is the canonical text, that is, the one that should be read, studied, and followed in the churches? Can such a text be established, and how important is the pursuit of it today? Metzger and Ehrman doubt the possibility of ever recovering the original New Testament text, and they cite the case of Paul as evidence against the likelihood. Since Paul often used an amanuensis, it is unlikely that we will ever be able to get back to the very words that he dictated orally to his writers.[39] They ask even more pointedly, "what does it mean to establish an 'original' text?"[40] For example, it is likely that 2 Corinthians initially existed in two or three and possibly even more pieces of correspondence. While it is highly likely that Paul wrote 2 Corinthians 10–13, it was probably not at the same time or occasion that he wrote 2 Corinthians 1–9. Did any changes take place in the original texts that allowed these two writings (or more) to be included in the same letter? The subject matter and tonal change in the letter between these two sections makes it likely that they were composed on different occasions. Similarly, 2 Corinthians 6:14–7:1 is probably an interpolation, *even if Paul wrote it.* The passage reads more smoothly and coherently if after 6:13 one goes directly to 7:2. The place of 6:14–7:1 in the text is certainly awkward and probably a later addition. Does Philippians 3:2 begin another letter that Paul had written later or earlier? There appears to be a break in the flow and tone of the letter between 3:1 and 3:2. Were there two letters written by Paul to the Philippians and did someone later bring them together? If so, what did the "originals" look like?

In regard to the Gospels, Koester argues that Matthew and Luke probably used an earlier form of Mark's Gospel (the so-called Ur-Mark) than the one in our current New Testament manuscripts.[41] Is the text of John 4–7 original or was it added piecemeal to the Gospel? The changes in location between Galilee and Jerusalem are choppy at best, and it is unlikely that the stories in these chapters occurred in the sequence they are presented. It is problematic to say that their sequence was an *original* part of the text of the Gospel. Did John's Gospel end with chapter 20 or 21? There is a conclusion added in John 20:30–31, but the beginning of chapter 21 seems to ignore the earlier meeting of the risen Christ with the disciples; there is a problem of recognition; and after they were commissioned in chapter 20, they are back fishing in chapter 21, and at least 21:24–25 is clearly not from the writer of the Gospel. The purpose of chapter 21 appears to be to restore Peter back into the good graces of Jesus following his threefold denial of Jesus, but may also be to explain the death of John that had likely recently occurred when this addition was penned. Further, was the doxology in Romans 14, 15, or 16 the original ending of that letter? Changes were doubtless made at an earlier stage of the transmission of these writings, and it is nearly impossible to consider establishing an original text.

The traditional goal of textual criticism has been to establish the "original" or earliest possible biblical text, but the overwhelming number of textual variants and the overlapping of several textual traditions make that goal a significant if not impossible challenge. Some scholars continue the hope of recovering the originals and eliminating all the ambiguities in the present texts, but they appear to be in a minority.[42] Most text-critical scholars contend that unless some new manuscripts are discovered, we are about as close to the original biblical texts now as we will get.[43]

The methodologies employed by textual critics to establish the earliest New Testament text have limitations, and those who investigate the ancient manuscripts are well aware that they are involved in both science and art. Doubts about the methodologies used to establish the earliest texts of Scripture linger among scholars, and few believe that they will ever be able establish the original text through such techniques. Some scholars are openly skeptical of those who believe that the establishment of an original text is still possible.[44] Epp, for instance, insists that we must now speak differently about an original text: "It is therefore indisputable, in my view, that the often simplistically understood term *original text* has been fragmented by the realities of how our New Testament writings were formed and transmitted, and *original* henceforth must be understood as a term designating several layers, levels, or meanings, though I prefer to call them *dimensions* of originality."[45] Having himself abandoned the quest for original texts, Epp sees a significant change in the direction of his discipline that includes the "diminution or even the abandonment of the traditional search for the original text in favor of seeing in the living text and its multiplicity of variants the vibrant interactions in the early Christian community," and he concludes that the term "original" has "exploded into a complex and highly unmanageable multivalent entity."[46]

Because of the complexity of tracking textual variants in the New Testament manuscripts, many text-critical scholars no longer depend upon a single family of texts to establish the earliest text of the New Testament and have instead opted for an eclectic approach to the ancient manuscripts, that is, they appeal to selective multiple textual traditions to determine the earliest and most reliable New Testament texts, hence a so-called eclectic text of the Scriptures. According to Gordon Fee, an eclectic methodology of dealing with the biblical manuscripts means that the "original" or earliest text of the biblical manuscripts is selected "variant by variant, using all the principles of critical judgment without regarding one MS or text-type as necessarily preserving that 'original.'"[47] Some textual scholars follow what is called a "reasoned eclectic method" that seeks to employ both the documentary evidence that examines internal criteria as well as the external manuscript traditions in seeking to recover the most reliable biblical text. Epp says this recognizes that "no single criterion or invariable combination of criteria will resolve all cases of textual variation, and it attempts, therefore, to apply evenly and without prejudice any and all criteria—external and internal—appropriate to a given case, arriving at an answer based on the relative probabilities among those applicable criteria."[48] These scholars call for a greater understanding of the differences between the surviving manuscripts and the social contexts that account for them.[49]

Textual scholars are not yet ready to ascribe originality to any current text of the Greek New Testament, and the eclectic text that is represented in both the Nestle-Aland *Novum Testamentum Graece* (27th ed.) and the United Bible Societies' *Greek New Testament* (4th ed.),[50] so far as can be determined, never functioned canonically in any identifiable ancient church nor did it serve to advance any known church's worship, instruction, and theology, or mission. It is a modern construct and it fills a useful role today, but it may not do so in the future if further discoveries are made in the places where early Christians lived. In other words, it is still theoretically possible that scholars will be able to get even closer to the elusive original manuscripts, but considerable uncertainty is attached to the pursuit.

Through either "reasoned eclecticism" (Michael Holmes) or "thoroughgoing eclecticism" (J. K. Elliott, Bart Ehrman), many contemporary New Testament textual critics now seek to establish the most reliable New Testament text and make more informed decisions about it.[51] Ehrman, like Epp, is skeptical about any significant changes in what we know about the original text and concludes that the practice of textual criticism today "amounts to little more than tinkering" with the text rather than significantly altering it. He suggests instead that the most important task of textual scholars today is to write a history of the development of the biblical text that clarifies how the various social influences affected its transmission.[52]

The problem we face today is that we cannot point to any ancient biblical manuscripts that are the same as the standard eclectic Greek New Testament text constructed for scholarly use today. All ancient texts have some variance with the Greek biblical texts that we use today, including our earliest and most reliable manuscripts (the Alexandrian text family). Textual critics have solved many of the textual problems for the church today, but still many remain. The most significant issue here has to do with the fact that the selectivity of which manuscripts to cite and use in the textual apparatus for the New Testament books cannot be settled with finality at present. Thomas Kraus believes that the New Testament critical editions are "on principle reliable" and they reflect a careful analysis of the manuscript tradition, but none of the critical editions considers all of the manuscript evidence, and indeed, cannot do so in any reasonable format. Kraus is certainly correct in drawing attention to the fact that in constructing the best biblical text, many pieces of information are left out of the reconstruction.[53] Following J. K. Elliott's citing manuscript evidence from noncanonical sources in the Nestle-Aland 26th edition of the Greek New Testament (the *Fayyum Gospel*) and in the Nestle-Aland 27th edition (*P.Egerton* 2) in support of Mark 14:28 and John 5:39, respectively, Kraus acknowledges the difficulty of a stabilized collection of resources for establishing the text of the New Testament. He cites these examples to show that there is no objective selectivity going on, but rather demonstrates "the partially random selection of witnesses for establishing an eclectic text and its critical apparatus."[54] Should text-critical scholars make use of apocryphal Christian writings in establishing the most reliable text of the New Testament? And what about the lectionaries which are often overlooked in favor of the continuous text manuscripts? It is infrequent when such evaluation of these texts take place, but it does highlight the randomness of the selectivity of resources in establishing the eclectic text of the New Testament. I agree with Kraus that overall there is considerable responsible activity taking place here and that the text-critical scholars are doing a commendable job in establishing the earliest and most reliable Greek text, but there is still some subjective selectivity involved in that process.[55]

TRANSLATIONS OF THE BIBLE

By the year 2000, there were some 6,809 known living languages and dialects in the world, and the whole Bible has been translated into 371 of them. Portions of the Bible have been translated into 1,862 other languages and dialects.[56] To our current knowledge, by the early seventh century, the Scriptures of the church existed in Greek, Old Latin, Gothic, Syriac, Coptic, Armenian, Georgian, Ethiopic, and Sogdian. Generally speaking, the early translations were of poor quality and some of them included other so-called noncanonical books. When movable type and the Gutenberg printing press were invented in 1456, the Bible had been translated into only thirty-three languages, and several of those translations contained only portions of the Bible.

The use of translations has been part of the church almost from its beginning. When Jesus spoke, it is generally agreed that he spoke in Aramaic and probably Hebrew, even if he had some facility in Greek, as some scholars argue. All four of the canonical Gospels were written in Greek, however, so whatever words Jesus originally said were first translated into Greek before they were included in the canonical Gospels. One of the oldest traditions about Matthew, according to Papias of Hierapolis (60–130 CE), is that he collected "oracles" of Jesus in the Hebrew language, and "each teacher interpreted [or translated] them as best he could" (Eusebius, *Hist. eccl.* 3.39.16). The Gospel of Matthew as we now have it was written in Greek, and it is difficult to say what was gained or lost in this initial translation of Jesus' sayings, but the early Christians took their Gospel about Jesus to various places *in Greek* and there is no indication that they thought they were taking something with them that was second rate because it was a translation. The following discussion focuses on the use and significance of translations in the early church.

Early Translations of the Bible

The first translation of the Hebrew Scriptures (the First or Old Testament) was a translation of the Law or Pentateuch into the Greek language in the early part of the third century BCE (281 BCE) at the instigation of Ptolemy II of Alexandria.[57] Demetrius of Phalerum, his chief librarian, compiled the largest library in the ancient world with estimates of up to half a million volumes. While most scholars acknowledge the legendary and apologetic nature of the *Letter of Aristeas*, some elements in the letter have a higher probability of authenticity. For instance, the author of that letter claims that Demetrius requested that the king include in his library a copy of the Jewish scriptures, but noted that they would need to be translated by competent persons before being placed in the "Museum" (or royal library) in Alexandria. While it is unlikely that the Jews initiated this translation,[58] they subsequently made considerable use of it in their synagogues in the Mediterranean world. The initial translation of the Jewish scriptures was only of the Law or Pentateuch, but in time was expanded to include other sacred writings of the Jews, some of which (apocryphal and pseudepigraphal books) did not eventually make it into the final corpus that made up the Hebrew Bible and the Protestant Old Testament. The initial translation is generally known as the "Septuagint" (abbreviated "LXX").[59] This designation has subsequently been applied to all the literature in the Old Greek Bible. There is much that we can say about this translation, but the point here is that the precedent of a translation of the scriptures was already established well before the time of Jesus.

Approximately nine thousand manuscripts of versions or translations of the New Testament texts have survived antiquity, but as yet they have received little or no attention from biblical scholars. They have an important lesson, however, for those interested in the formation of the New Testament. While some early translations have been lost, the ones that survive are an important source for letting us know what literature the translators believed was sacred and they also help textual critics piece together the earliest possible text of the New Testament. The early Christians freely translated their scriptures into several languages including Syriac, especially the Syriac Peshitta, Old Latin, and the Armenian translations.

Given the complexity of producing a translation, when a translation of Christian writings began, we may assume that those who translated them and those who made use of them recognized their value for worship, instruction, and mission. We may also assume that their recognition as sacred or inspired writings was well on its way, if it had not already taken place. The following early translations have considerable significance for understanding the development of the Christian biblical canon.[60]

1. The *Old Syriac* version. Although only the four canonical Gospels are preserved in two fragmented manuscripts of this translation that date from the fourth or fifth century, the translation probably dates originally from the end of the second or beginning of the third century, and the Eastern church fathers who used this translation often refer to Acts and the Letters of Paul.

2. The *Peshitta* (or Syriac Vulgate, designated Syr^P) likely comes from the beginning of the fifth century and contains twenty-two New Testament books (it omits 2 Peter, 2 and 3 John, Jude, and Revelation).

3. The *Philoxenian* version, perhaps produced in the early sixth century; also known as the *Harclean* version because of a later revision by Thomas of Harkel in the early seventh century. For the first time in this translation the Catholic Epistles and Revelation were added to the Syrian churches' collection of scriptures.

4. The *Palestinian Syriac* version (ca. fifth century). Only a few fragments of this translation exist and they include the Gospels, Acts, and several (not all) of the letters of Paul.

5. The *Old Latin* versions (perhaps late second to early third century). A number of Old Latin manuscripts that were produced during the third century and later fall generally into two categories: African and European versions. In the surviving fragments, portions of the four canonical Gospels, Acts, and portions of Paul's Letters survive, along with a few fragments of Revelation. It may be that Tatian (ca. 170) used an Old Latin version for his *Diatessaron*, but he may also have used a Greek text that was translated into Syriac.

6. The *Latin Vulgate* version produced by Jerome in the late fourth century in Judea (Bethlehem). A good number of surviving copies of this version contain the whole Bible, but two codices (Codex Dublinensis, ca. eighth century and Codex Fuldensis, ca. sixth century) also contain the apocryphal letter of Paul to the *Laodiceans*.

7. The *Coptic* versions (ca. beginning of the third century). Those versions in the Sahidic and Bohairic dialects are the most important among the various manuscripts that have survived, and the contents of these versions include the four Gospels, Acts, and the Pauline Letters.

8. The *Gothic* version (ca. middle to end of fourth century). The earliest manuscripts of this version include the four Gospels and some Pauline letters along with a portion of Nehemiah 5–7.

9. The *Armenian* versions (late fourth and early fifth centuries). None of the fourth- or fifth-century manuscripts have survived but the fifteen hundred or more copies that have survived date from the eighth century and later and some have all of the New Testament writings, but others are missing various New Testament books. It is interesting that *3 Corinthians* is also in this version of the New Testament writings.

10. The *Georgian* version. It is possible that the origin of this version goes back to the fourth or fifth century, but the oldest surviving manuscripts of it

date from the ninth century. It contains the four Gospels, Acts, and the Catholic Epistles. Near the end of the tenth century, the book of Revelation was translated and added to the collection.

11. The Ethiopic version (as early as the fourth or as late as the seventh century). Most of the surviving manuscripts of this version date after the thirteenth century, and currently it is not possible to know how much of the New Testament was translated into this language at the earliest stages of the translation since only partial manuscripts have been discovered. This version is the largest known Bible, however, containing more than eighty books, and its New Testament included the twenty-seven books of our New Testament, but also *Sinodos*, *1 Clement*, *Book of the Covenant*, and *Didascalia*.

Other later and less important translations for our purposes include the Arabic versions from the eighth century to the nineteenth century, the Sogdian (or Middle Iranian) version, which dates from the ninth to the eleventh century, and the Old Church Slavonic version from the ninth century, which was important especially for the Bulgarians, Serbians, Croats, and eastern Slavs. In the late third to early fourth century, some churches were planted in Nubia, but when the Arabs to the north essentially cut them off from the rest of Christendom, they declined numerically and eventually disappeared. There was considerable growth in the church there during the sixth century, and it is likely that a vernacular Nubian version was produced between the third to the sixth century, but it is not clear exactly when it was translated or what was included in it.[61]

The obvious point here is that these translations do not contain the same books, though they overlap considerably in terms of the Gospels and Paul, and they often omit portions of the larger New Testament canon. Only one of them contains all the New Testament books, but it contains more besides. With the exception of Jerome's Latin Vulgate, none of the translations appears to have been well prepared, and Jerome did not improve on the apocryphal texts that he included in his translation, nor did he think highly of several of the New Testament writings and this showed in his translation of them. Some of the difficulties with these early translations had to do with translating the many nuances of the Greek into other languages. Metzger and Ehrman explain that not only were incompetent translators involved in preparing many of these translations, but also features of Greek syntax and vocabulary are not easily transferred to another language. They explain that: "Latin [unlike Greek] has no definite article; Syriac cannot distinguish between the Greek aorist and perfect tenses; Coptic lacks the passive voice and must use a circumlocution. In some cases, therefore, the testimony of these versions is ambiguous."[62]

These various ancient translations tell us which books were received as authoritative scriptures at various times and places as well as something about the churches that used and transmitted them. None of the translations before the fourth century includes all the New Testament books and very few after that do. There is much that we do not know about the contents of these translations, since some exist only in fragments and only a few of them have been studied adequately, but the point is still valid that most of the early versions contain only *some* of the New Testament books, not all of them or only those books. In time, some of these versions expanded to include more of the canonical books, but the earliest versions omit several New Testament books. The same can be said of some of the earliest Greek New Testament manuscripts. Codex Sinaiticus, for example, contains a complete collection of the New Testament books, but it also contains some noncanonical books (*Epistle of Barnabas* and a fragment of *Shepherd of Hermas*). The various churches that received the early translations generally did not have the whole of the New Testament and *only* the New Testament books for use in their worship and instruction.

Implications

The greater church in antiquity never claimed that God inspired only one translation of the Scriptures (Greek) and that all others were uninspired. The Syriac Peshitta was surely Scripture to Syrian-speaking Christians who welcomed and used it in their churches. They did not conclude that their Bible was less inspired than the one used by Greek-speaking Christians. The Ethiopian and Coptic Christians also had their own translations of the New Testament and they also accepted them as divinely inspired as Scripture. The Latin Vulgate as a translation came close to a sacred status in the Western church but not completely, and no early church father made such a claim for any translations, even if some church fathers (Augustine and Jerome) noted the poor quality of some translations. The vast majority of Christians today still cannot read their Bibles in the biblical languages of Hebrew, Aramaic, and Greek, but they nonetheless receive what they have in their native tongues as inspired sacred texts. This situation is not unlike what occurred in antiquity.

Is there an authoritative translation for the church today? That question seems strange given the variety of languages spoken in our world. Although some theological schools continue to teach seminary students to anchor their faith and teaching in the Hebrew, Aramaic, and Greek texts of their Scriptures, there are still no universally established *texts* in those languages or perfect translations of them available to readers. No one producing translations today suggests that any one translation of the Bible is perfect or solely authoritative for all churches, even though translators appropriately seek to produce translations that they hope will garner widespread approval in many churches, such as the NIV and the NRSV.

Can there be any translation of the Bible that has final authority in the church today?[63] The differences in most of the recent translations of the New Testament are not generally considered all that important, and most of them reliably tell the story of Jesus and clearly present the biblical call to an obedience of faith. Remarkably, the authority of the Bible has not been significantly affected in most churches despite fluidity in the ancient New Testament texts and the many problems associated with translating it.

CONCLUSION

The New Testament of the earliest Christian churches differs in a number of respects from the one that most Christians use today, both in terms of the books contained in it, the texts of those books, and the translations of those texts. Some early Christian communities produced copies and translations of the New Testament texts from weaker textual traditions circulating among their churches, and initially they either did not know or they did not use all the books that currently make up our New Testament canon. Some Christians may have adopted something like a canon within a canon by teaching and preaching only those books that had more relevance for their communities of faith, but it is more likely that many early churches simply did not have access to all the books in the current biblical canon. In other cases, some early churches also accepted for centuries other books that are now considered noncanonical writings. Eventually those books, especially *Shepherd of Hermas, Epistle of Barnabas, 1* and *2 Clement,* and *Didache,* were excluded from various sacred collections and later did not attain canonical status. This suggests something akin to decanonization in the early church. Both inclusion and rejection of some early noncanonical Christian writings was present in various ancient churches.

The churches that had their scriptures in translation generally had fewer books available to them than those who had Greek Bibles. In all cases, however, there is no ancient view of inspiration that distinguished the translations from the original languages. Those who received their scriptures in translation also believed that God had inspired their scriptures. Remarkably, the church's oldest theological beliefs were developed often without the aid of complete or carefully translated New Testament manuscripts.

The early churches that had translated scriptures made use of them in their worship, instruction, and mission, even though the translations were not uniform in the books they used or the biblical text they preserved. They also did not use the same books, and the quality of their translations was sometimes poor. Nevertheless, those churches accepted these translations as inspired by God and established their doctrine, worship, and mission on the basis of these translations. How significant is it that they and the Greek-speaking churches did not have the same New Testament books or text that churches have today? If they had owned and used a complete set of the New Testament books *and no others,* and if their New Testament books all had the same or a similar biblical text, what difference would that have made in their worship, mission, and theology? On another note, what might be gained if Christians today were informed by the same texts that informed the faith of many ancient Christians, though some of those texts are not included in the current Greek New Testaments? Swanson has raised this question and offers in a highly readable format the various readings of the New Testament books and indicates that ancient manuscripts with those texts were all read as scripture in the communities that had those manuscripts. What differences in our understanding of the theology of the New Testament books would some of those readings that text-critical scholars rejected make? Swanson makes this point in the introduction of his work, and it might well be interesting to pursue that inquiry by comparing the various texts that he cites in his work and the theological implications that the intentional changes to the biblical text make.[64] In terms of the theme of this book, what if the Scriptures left behind at least informed the faith and understanding of Christians today?

Chapter 10

Conclusion

The Scriptures that informed the faith of early Judaism (200 BCE to 200 CE), and early Christianity (first–third centuries CE) are not exactly the same as the Scriptures that inform the faith of Jews and Christians today. There is evidence that from the beginning of Second Temple Judaism (ca. 586 BCE) there was a resurgence of commitment by the Jews to live in accord with the Law of Moses, but in time, many Jews were also informed by other sacred texts that came to be called the Prophets. Along with the Prophets, which may or may not be equivalent to the collection now known as the Prophets recognized by the Jews, the early Christians, including Jesus himself, cited, alluded to, or were informed by other sacred texts. We have observed that the collection of the Twelve (the Minor Prophets), probably Jeremiah, Job, and Ezekiel, and likely other books known as prophets were circulating among the Jews by around 200–180 BCE (Sir. 49:7–10). The literature that now makes up the Hebrew Bible and Protestant Old Testament canon was certainly among the core of the most influential books for Jews and early Christians, if not *the* core, of the sacred books that informed their faith. The Dead Sea Scrolls discovered at Qumran and elsewhere in the vicinity of the Judean Desert include almost all the Old Testament books, but also many of the so-called noncanonical or apocryphal and pseudepigraphal books. It is clear that many of these additional texts informed the faith of those at Qumran, and many of them informed the faith of early Christians.

The relationship between the early churches with their sacred writings and the formation of the biblical canon is both complex and challenging. We have also seen that there is little correlation between a fixed text of Scripture and a fixed biblical canon. The books were welcomed and recognized sooner than most attempts to stabilize their text. Textual fluidity in the surviving manuscripts of both the Old Testament/Hebrew Bible and the New Testament shows that after the inspiration and authority of the sacred texts were recognized, the texts continued to be fluid for centuries to come, indeed, until the invention of movable type and the printing press in the fifteenth century. Nevertheless, the individual manuscripts that have survived—which are only about 1 percent of those that existed—served as sacred scripture to the churches that possessed these ancient texts. While some of the texts survived in rolls, most survived in codices and a few in opisthographs, but it is likely that they were all welcomed as sacred texts in the communities that had them and read them. They were the early church's sacred scripture, regardless of the condition of their construction, which was sometimes rather poor.

I agree with Margalit Finkelberg and Guy Stroumsa that we have as yet no reasonable *comparative* study of canon formation, that is, comparing it with literature in the ancient world as well as the notions of canon that were present in and around the time of Jesus. It is remarkable thus far that there has been little focus on the parallels between the literary (Greco-Roman) or religious (Judeo-Christian) canons.[1] The parallels between the canonization of the books of Homer and those of the Bible are very interesting and until recently have not received much attention. It is also true that both the Mishnah and the New Testament writings were in parallel development at roughly the same time. Why did both the Jews and the Christians see the need for additional sacred literature at roughly the same time when both claimed the Old Testament/Hebrew Bible as their sacred scriptures? The interpretive steps taken by the Amoraim almost immediately after the codification of the Mishnah show that this literature was received in a canonical fashion by the rabbinic sages and they began interpreting it and adding clarifications to it almost as soon as it was adopted (early third century). The myth of the "Oral Torah" tradition perpetuated by the rabbis, namely that there was a written law given to Moses at Sinai and also an oral law that was handed down (passed on) by the Jews, was welcomed by the majority of Jews in the East and eventually in the West. While the Mishnah was not called scripture as the New Testament writings eventually were, it nonetheless functioned that way among the Jews.

We have seen that a considerable variety of sacred books in early Judaism and in the early church functioned as scripture for both Jews and Christians. Some of this literature was the Old Testament writings themselves, but other books also had this function. The discovery of the Dead Sea Scrolls has challenged previous notions of what texts were sacred and which ones were not. Through the second century CE, as both the scrolls and the New Testament writings themselves, as well as the early church fathers, show, early Christians as well as Jews of the Second Temple period were informed by a much larger collection of writings than those that eventually formed the Bibles of both the synagogues and the churches.

Not only the books, but also the text of the sacred scriptures was not uniform in ancient Israel or in the churches. The stabilization of the biblical text occurred earlier for the Jews, especially in the second century CE and following, but for the church it began with Origen (third century) and later with Jerome (fourth century), but stabilization was not possible for the text of either Testament before the invention of the printing press. For those whose faith rests upon the ever elusive inerrant biblical manuscripts, the above survey shows that this is very unstable ground since no two manuscripts are alike exactly and the number of variants in the manuscripts in both Testaments is staggering. Which text is the authoritative text of the Bible for today? Is it the eclectic texts of either or both Testaments? Does faith ultimately depend upon a fixed and stable text of the church's scriptures? If so, then faith has again a very unstable foundation. For Christians, the final and firm foundation of faith is in the risen Lord who comes to us through the proclamation of the church's gospel. As has been true since the time of the first disciples, Jesus himself is the final authority for the church, and Scripture is always a derived authority that points us toward him (Matt. 28:19–20).

The earliest translations of the Christian sacred scriptures are not uniform in terms of the books they contain and the quality of the translations, and they pose important questions for the church today. Since they most often do not have the same books in them as are in the fixed biblical canons of the church today, what can we say about them? How much of the gospel is lost in translation? Also, how many books can vary and there still be a church of Christ? The *core* of the books cited and found in the surviving manuscripts and translations are generally the same. Most have the major books of the Old Testament and most have one or more of the Gospels and the Letters of Paul. They vary on what other books they contain. They have considerable overlap in text, translations that are used, and the books contained in them, but few of the ancient manuscripts have all the books of the New Testament and only the books of the New Testament until near the year 1000. Similarly, the Old Testament manuscripts also vary in the books they contain, the text they present, and the quality and content of the various translations. As we have seen, some books in the biblical canons of the church generally contain the core books that are cited in the earliest teachings of the church and in the Christian literature that survives.

So what are the implications of all this? Should we change the biblical canons that have survived antiquity? If so, what should we include or exclude? Since the core of texts that informed both early Judaism and early Christianity are not in dispute, perhaps we can infer from that there is *sufficient* witness both from the Old Testament/Hebrew Bible and the New Testament to build and promote the faith familiar to Christians.

As a biblical scholar committed to teaching and preaching the message of the Bible, I often need to advise Christians who tend to be more dogmatic about certain teachings than the Scriptures are. When there is sufficient obscurity in the Scriptures on a particular matter, there should be freedom for a variety of positions taken. Should the church be clearer than the Bible is on such matters? Wherever there is vagueness in the biblical text, we should have a fair amount of grace and patience in our dealings with those with whom we disagree. I do not believe that we would gain any more clarity in the church by changing the current biblical canons, because such activity would bring more division in an already too divided family of Christ, but I do think that Christians of all persuasions can learn from those books and texts that were left behind. In many instances, they can enhance our understanding of the biblical literature. Some books were left behind for good reason, and in other cases we are unsure why such decisions were made. As new discoveries of ancient literature have been made over the last century and more, we can glean from such texts that were decanonized or removed from sacred collections a lot of valuable information on the social context of the early Christians and what issues faced them that were enabled by the literature that they selected.

This volume is partly in response to continuing arguments that Jesus had inherited a fixed biblical canon and that his disciples and the early church received it. The primary reason that I do not hold this position is that it simply no longer has any historical credibility. First, there is clear evidence that Jews of the first century welcomed more books as sacred literature than simply the books of the Hebrew Bible or (arranged in a different order) the Protestant Old Testament. Second, if the disciples of Jesus received such a biblical canon from Jesus, it is remarkable that the early churches of the second and later centuries acknowledged as scripture more writings than are in the current Old Testament biblical canon. They frequently call "scripture" what we now term noncanonical writings and include them in a number of early Christian biblical manuscripts as well as some earlier Jewish manuscripts at Qumran. If the disciples had such a fixed collection that came from Jesus and that looked exactly like the current Protestant Old Testament canon, then we have to say that the disciples or their disciples simply lost that collection—which I find to be incredible. Finally, if Jesus gave such a fixed collection to his disciples, it is remarkable that he does not cite all the current Old Testament books in his teaching recorded in the Gospels and that he shows familiarity with some books that were not finally included in the Hebrew Bible or the Protestant Old Testament canon.

The evidence that the Old Testament biblical canon was still developing in the first century comes both from Qumran and the New Testament. In the former instance, there was still considerable freedom among the Essenes at Qumran to rewrite several of those scriptures and also to include a number of others. There is no evidence that Esther was ever part of their sacred collection. Also, it is difficult to imagine that the Old Testament or Hebrew Bible would have been closed at the same time that a number of other books were being produced that were receiving popular recognition among the Jews at Qumran but also among the early Christians. If the canon were closed, how is it possible that additional writings were welcomed as sacred literature and even called scripture?

Some of my dear colleagues in the more conservative side of theological education have been concerned that I have gone too far in this journey and that I could no longer affirm earlier statements of faith that once defined my particular beliefs. I should say, however, that in all of the essentials of the Christian faith, I do not believe that any of my research has adversely affected my commitment to the core teachings of the church. In areas not as essential, however, I agree that I have moved away from earlier positions because I can no longer affirm them. In a class that I was invited to teach at Princeton Theological Seminary during my sabbatical in 2007–2008, I had a useful discussion with some of the students about the so-called slippery slope among conservative evangelicals. That is, if one gets away from an inerrant Bible, then one has to make a decision subjectively about which text is the Word of God and which is not. Often that means if one does not affirm an inerrant Bible, then the interpreter has to make subjective judgments about what is truth and what is not. While I agree that it is much easier to affirm an inerrant Bible and avoid the appearance of the slippery slope, I see no way around it, and I also think all of us make subjective calls when it comes to interpreting the Bible. Which text do we use? Is it the eclectic Greek text of the current editions of the Greek New Testament that has so many variants? We are probably about as close as we can get to the original text unless some more ancient manuscripts come to light to change the current situation. However, we are not there yet, and it is unlikely that we ever will be able to recover the original text of the New Testament writings.

And what about that status of those biblical texts about which the text-critical scholars themselves cannot agree? Both the Hebrew and the Greek texts of the Bible that we have are not absolute, and those who produced the various editions of the Hebrew or Greek Scriptures will be the first to agree. Many will also affirm that we are about as close as we can get to the original text, but we are not there yet. We have relatively little evidence for the New Testament text from the time of their writing to roughly 350 CE. There are still challenging biblical texts that puzzle even the biblical scholars. Which text, which books, which translations, and which interpretation of the Bible should we follow? There is no consensus on those questions in biblical scholarship today among either conservatives or liberals.

I have also been accused by some scholars (fewer) on the left of the theological perspective of "punting" when I got to the end of my work on the biblical canon. What I think they meant by this was that I did not carry through and state what they thought were the logical implications of my research, but I have to challenge that. I have tried to state the actual historical development of the Bible to the extent that one can discern it today, and I do not believe that awareness will largely or significantly impact the essence of Christianity. By and large, the church made the right decisions regarding the shape of its faith and the contours of its biblical canon. It was, however, informed and influenced by that literature that was closest to the time of Jesus, and that literature included many of the books that we now label as apocryphal and/or pseudepigraphal writings. Did the early church get it right at the very core of sacred writings? Yes, I believe that they did. Are there some sloppy edges here and there in terms of what went into the biblical canon and what was eventually excluded? Of course! Can we live with seeing now through the "dim glass" until we know even as we are known? In the words of Paul, we have been in many aspects of this discussion shut up to faith, and that is not a bad thing. While we could at various places wish that the early church had left us with a bit more clarity on what they did and why they did it, we do not yet have that possibility and so we must often draw inferences from a sketchy collection of ancient texts. What we do see from the manuscripts that have been left behind, however, is what I have been calling the operative biblical canons of early Christianity, namely those writings that are in the surviving manuscripts. At times the manuscripts do not reflect what the early church councils concluded about the books that should be part of our biblical canons, but they were the texts that informed the faith of the Christians that had them and they functioned as Scripture.

Several years ago I was invited to be one of two plenary speakers at the Jesus Seminar group that was meeting in Santa Rosa, California. I gave some lectures on Wednesday for six hours and had also prepared a paper for the seminar members to discuss on Friday afternoon. At that meeting, following some comments that I had made, eight hands went up to ask a question about my comments. At that time Robert Funk, the founder of the Jesus Seminar, said: "We only have time for three more questions because we have to vote [on the proposal I had made to them] by 3:15 p.m." I quickly responded that "since you do not like the biblical canon that took over a thousand years to construct, what makes you think that you will be able to come up with a better one that is more acceptable by 3:15 p.m.?" Schubert Ogden, the other plenary speaker, was sitting beside me and agreed that the challenge could not be met in short notice.

Should the church be open to revising its biblical canon? My first thought is, "at its own peril," but there is nothing wrong with the church evaluating its Scriptures and determining their message and relevance for our day. Historically the church has had the freedom to do that for most of its two-thousand-year history. All of us are aware of the challenges that Luther made to the viability of the books of James, Hebrews, Jude, and Revelation. It is not inappropriate for Christians to ask tough questions of the early churches and evaluate the evidence that they left behind. Nor is it inappropriate for the church today to be informed by the same religious texts that informed the earliest Christians, especially those Christians who lived prior to the fourth century before the Bible began to take on more stability. It took centuries for the Catholic Church to welcome the Latin Vulgate, and it came after many significant disagreements from leaders and laity in the churches. What we have all learned over the years is that the church does not readily welcome change, especially in its theology or the scope of its Bible.

The biblical canons as we have them today sufficiently inform our faith, but should we also be open to learning more about the early church and what decisions they made and why? I think so. Does being informed by the same sacred texts of antiquity that informed the earliest followers of Jesus violate something sacred in the church today? I think not. Even those biblical scholars of a more conservative bent, who would reject any attempts to broaden the current Protestant biblical canon today, regularly investigate these ancient texts and discover a great deal of value in them.[2] This can only be a threat if somehow the notion that investigating them makes one obligated to change his or her basic Christian faith or even the books that make up the Bible. If that issue is settled, can there be any serious challenge to reading these texts? Thus far, I know of no major teaching in the extracanonical literature that adversely affects or undermines the core teachings of the Christian faith today. While some teachings in them are sometimes strange to Protestants (e.g., the notion of purgatory supported by 2 Macc. 12:39–45), generally speaking these additional books do not challenge the basic tenets of the Christian faith. Also, if they informed the faith of many of the earliest Christians, it might be a useful exercise to read this literature to understand something of the development of their faith and journey. By looking at the ancient documents that were *not* canonized, we frequently gain a better understanding of why they were rejected by some or ceased to function as Scripture altogether. We also have a much clearer understanding of the context of the biblical writings. As we look at those writings that the early church later called heretical or deemed to be of less importance than those that it canonized, we can at the least have a better grasp of the faith that has been passed on to us and often at great cost over the last two thousand years.

Chapter 11

Postscript: The Search for a Perfect Bible

INTRODUCTION

Many Christians come from conservative churches where they are taught to accept biblical inerrancy as an essential doctrine of their faith. The authority and inspiration of the Scriptures have been linked to a belief that the original manuscripts of the Bible were inerrant, even though all acknowledge that the manuscripts that have survived antiquity were corrupted over the centuries through transmission. These Christians nevertheless affirm that the Scriptures were inerrant in the autographs, the original manuscripts prepared by their authors. Such persons are often frustrated when they engage a critical inquiry of the Bible or participate in a Bible class taught from a different perspective. They have generally been taught that there are no errors of any kind in the Bible and that any person who claims that such errors exist is either uninformed, denying biblical authority, needs to be challenged, or should be avoided.

Well-intentioned pastors regularly teach the doctrine of biblical inerrancy and often argue that there can be little or no fellowship with persons who do not affirm that teaching. Some colleges, universities, and seminaries regularly employ professors only if they are willing to sign statements affirming inerrancy.

Sadly, all too often professors are willing to sign such statements in order to obtain a teaching position even when they do not and cannot in good conscience subscribe to this doctrine. I have heard professors say that they would sign anything in order to obtain or to keep a teaching post. In time some of them are discovered and they lose their positions, but sometimes they are not discovered and regularly affirm such statements to keep their positions.

Leaders of these institutions, and pastors also who trained in such places, often contend that those who deny biblical inerrancy as it is taught in their institutions or places of worship are headed toward the slippery slope of *subjectively* trying to decide what is truth and what is error in the biblical text. They do not seem to acknowledge that everyone makes a subjective decision about which text of Scripture is original, and they trust that text-critical scholars have established the original text. Interestingly, some scholars and church leaders have made such affirmations following the publication of the various editions of the Nestle-Aland or United Bible Society editions of the text of the Greek New Testament. Similarly, earlier Old Testament/Hebrew Bible textual critics used almost exclusively the Masoretic Text in establishing the text of the Jewish Scriptures. However, current textual critics are beginning to reconsider this stance since many are already acknowledging that the Dead Sea Scrolls, the Samaritan Pentateuch, and the *Vorlage* (or model text) of those Scriptures used by the translators of the Septuagint (Greek version) often reflect an earlier stage of the text of the Hebrew Bible and may be more accurate ("original") than the text produced by the Masoretes in the ninth and tenth centuries.

While admittedly it is easier to acknowledge the complete inerrancy of the Bible than to decide what is in error and what is not, this does not settle the matter. Most biblical scholars today recognize that there is considerable subjective analysis in making determinations about the meaning of biblical texts. Those who hold to biblical inerrancy are not immune to subjective analysis when they approach the biblical text. Since all translations of the Bible are a significant step removed from the original languages in which the biblical books were crafted, who decides which translation is free and without error? I recently attended a church where the pew Bible was the New King James Version, but the pastor used the New International Version for his sermon, and several church members had other translations. None of these translations is the same; why is one chosen over the other? The usual comment is that "we want to get as close to the original biblical text as possible," but even here we are no closer than the third and fourth centuries to the original documents. We have only two small manuscript fragments that come from the second century and both are small portions of the Gospel of John (P^{52} and P^{90}).

THE ORIGINAL MANUSCRIPTS (AUTOGRAPHS)

Many assume that if we just had those "originals" that they would be perfect and without any error, but there is no way to demonstrate that view. Unless there is some significant new find of manuscripts similar to the Dead Sea Scrolls discovery, we are not likely to get any closer than we are today. Most of the text of the New Testament is rooted in manuscripts that date largely from the mid-fourth century and later. Affirmation of biblical inerrancy is in itself a step of faith since it has to do only with the original manuscripts. As no one has seen them or has them, and the copies of the biblical books that we do have are all copies of copies and have hundreds of thousands of variants in them, our Bibles are completely based on manuscripts that have both accidental and intentional deletions or additions and many errors. Text-critical scholars know that there are no perfect biblical texts in existence, and translators know that no perfect translation exists. If it did, there would be no reason to continue to revise them, but all the major translations of the Bible have been revised periodically. Should the churches wait until a final revision has been made? Of course not, and no biblical translators that I know believe that they have finally produced a perfect translation of the Bible.

So why is there such interest in manuscripts that we do not have and so little focus on the ones that we do have? Christian scholars who advocate an inerrant biblical text regularly make use of the eclectic Greek or Hebrew texts of the Bible, and ignore the fact that we do not have the original texts and that all translations are based on the only ancient texts that we do have, namely those with many copyists' errors in them. As Craig Allert has argued, many Christians who hold to a fairly rigid view of biblical inerrancy have not adequately considered the implications of the formation of the Bible for their doctrine of inspiration.[1] I am encouraged that a number of evangelical scholars are beginning to acknowledge the difficulty of maintaining traditional notions of inspiration that emphasize inerrancy of the autographs but ignore the status of the manuscripts that we have today.[2] John Brogan has concluded that the church has never had an inerrant manuscript, but has not been devoid of an authoritative Word of God. The church, he claims, "must affirm that the people of God have never had access to the 'inerrant autograph,' but that they have always had access to the authoritative Word of God."[3] Similarly, and in the same volume, J. Daniel Hays acknowledges that textual critics who have to deal with the data, or *realia*, that remain seldom communicate well with the systematic theologians who formulate the doctrine of inerrancy, and the latter seem oblivious to the finds of the text-critical scholars.[4]

I am disappointed that many of those who advocate biblical inerrancy regularly ignore the status of the only Bibles in use in churches today. Are they inspired or not? Do they faithfully set forth the identity and mission of God or do they not? All acknowledge that we do not have an inerrant biblical text, so what does that mean? Is what we have inspired of God even if it is not inerrant? The only biblical texts that we regularly use in churches and the classrooms today are a composite of what text-critical scholars selectively consider the most original text. They also regularly disagree with one another about the authenticity of a number of texts. We have precious little information about the text of the New Testament books before 200 CE. Similarly, the earliest Hebrew manuscripts that we have of the Old Testament books were discovered at Qumran and nearby sites, and those manuscripts have considerable textual fluidity. While the Masoretic text is well represented there, so are several other textual traditions.

If we are to teach and preach in our churches only the original inspired and infallible[5] text of Scripture from texts in the original languages (Hebrew, Aramaic, and Greek) that scholars have given to us—who themselves do not believe that they have established the original text—how do non-specialists get around simply taking their word for what is in the Bible? They cannot. The church has regularly affirmed the importance of translating its Scriptures into the language of the people, and the message of the Bible seems to come through adequately in most translations. We can only depend on the biblical manuscripts that have survived antiquity, and all biblical scholars acknowledge that no two of them are exactly alike. The question therefore remains regarding the inspired status of the only texts that we do have, all of which functioned in antiquity as scripture to those who received, made use of, and transmitted them. Most Christians read their Bible in translation and assume the inspired status of their Bibles, but no credible scholar, to my knowledge, affirms that the Bibles we have in translation are inerrant. Most Christians regularly read their Bibles and teach or preach the messages of the Bible from a translation. The church's credibility is on the line when scholars confuse some pastors and laity by continuing to affirm what should not be affirmed about the inerrancy of the Bible. In an age when Christians are taught to read critically in university training, they will invariably bring a number of critical questions to Bible studies in their churches and will not be convinced by flimsy arguments about inerrancy that ignore the data of Scripture itself. The church's theological statements must be rooted in the biblical texts and what we know about those texts.

As one who served for eight years as the chief examiner at ordination councils for those entering Christian ministry in Eastern Canada, I regularly heard candidates express their views about Scripture. While many of the candidates expressed their views carefully, some affirmed the authority of an inerrant Bible rooted in the inspired and inerrant "original manuscripts." I often asked them whether the Bible they brought with them, almost always a translation (generally the NIV, the New American Standard Version, or the NRSV), was inspired? Invariably they would say yes, but then I reminded them that their translations were in English and not the original languages and in any case their translations were not based on the original manuscripts. My goal was to get them to think about the status of the only Bibles they had. That is the important question today.

There appears to be no way to avoid the subjectivity of making one's own decision about wherein lies the truth or error in the biblical text. Most Christians are willing to defer this decision to those who establish the biblical texts and to those who translate those texts, but they also regularly make subjective decisions based on their best understanding of the context of the biblical books and their experience in translating and teaching them. If we affirm everything that we see in the text, we must still acknowledge that at present we do not have the original text of the Bible, and so the question of the inspiration of the text arises once again. I regularly affirm almost all the modern translations and paraphrases of the biblical text used in churches today, even the older KJV with all its problems. I assure members in churches that the traditional affirmations about Jesus and the Christian faith are not in serious question in most of the translations used today. I have reservations about a few translations, but generally speaking they all affirm the most important teachings of the church. The traditional *regula fidei*, or confession of faith, handed down through the churches remains unblemished, but not in an inerrant form. The message of the Bible is clear, even if there are a few rough edges here and there, whether in the books incorporated into the Bible or in the text of the Bible.

A few years ago I worked briefly on a translation of the New Testament and experienced the impasse that some very fine Greek scholars had when translating challenging texts from the Bible. On one occasion, the chair of the translation committee was quite heated in his view of what the translation had to be, but another on the committee, who is also an expert in the Greek language and with credentials from Harvard University, advocated keeping the traditional translation of the text—here it was "Son of Man"—saying, "why should we exchange a bad translation for a worse one?" No final decision was made that day, since the atmosphere was not conducive to it. There is considerable subjectivity in determining the original text of the biblical books and considerable subjectivity in translating it. Even more so, there is subjectivity in accepting which books go into the Bible and even greater subjectivity in interpreting them!

It is easier and sounds much more pious and Christ honoring to say that we simply trust the Bible and that there are no errors in it. Such affirmations are calming to members of churches. If one could find errors in the Bible, so the argument goes, it would lose its authority; since God is without error and cannot err in his activities, God could not inspire an errant Bible. If God inspired the Bible (the given presupposition), then the Bible has to be without error. In instances where the reader decides what is truth and error in the Bible, it is claimed, the final authority is no longer the Bible but the interpreter of the Bible. Persons in churches are often taught as justification for this belief the rather familiar syllogism assumed in the argument above. The syllogism, of course, states that God is perfect, what God does is perfect, God inspired the Bible, and therefore the Bible is perfect. If one accepts the first three premises, then the last is a logical conclusion about the Bible. If anyone has a problem affirming the inerrancy of the Bible, so the argument goes, the problem lies with those who are unable to resolve the apparent difficulties, but not with the Bible. The problem cannot be with the Bible, the argument continues, since it is the Word of God. These protections of the Bible are quite popular in churches today, and eventually Christians trust by faith what the Bible says is true, even if what they see with their eyes seems to be at odds with this affirmation from time to time. As we have seen above, however, what books the early churches affirmed and what text they finally accepted as Scripture is not as clear as some Christians today would hope.

If one begins with what appears to be a reasonable inference about the nature and activity of God (God is perfect), then it follows that if God inspired the Bible it too must also be without error of any kind. The odd thing about this affirmation is that the Bibles we have do have errors in them, either in the many variants in the text they rely on or in the translation they present. Since thus far no one has come up with a perfect translation of the Bible and the church has existed for almost two thousand years without either an inerrant Bible or an inerrant translation of it, and an inerrant interpretation of it, one wonders about the value of that elusive inerrant original for the church today. If we have never had such a text among us, how can we be so adamant about affirming that it exists or that it is essential to the church today? None of us will say that ministers are perfect; even biblical personalities were sometimes wrong and had feet of clay, but remarkably God accomplished ministry through them and continues to accomplish the ministry of Christ through fallible human beings today. God seems to continue to delight in using the weak and foolish to confound the mighty and the wise among us (1 Cor. 1:27). The problem that occurs when we deal with the Bible in syllogistic ways is that the matter is decided prior to an examination of the biblical data.

I propose that any responsible position on the nature of Scripture must begin first with the data (or *realia*) of Scripture. If the data of Scripture (what it teaches or claims and what we actually find in the surviving manuscripts of the Bible—the phenomena of Scripture) do not support the church's statements about Scripture, then it is important to find a statement that does fit the church's investigation of its Bible and its experience of investigating it. It is no longer possible for the defenders of inerrancy to retreat to the safer ground of "original manuscripts."

In the case of those in the churches who depend on the decisions of biblical scholars for their view of Scripture, there is no escape from subjectivity. The question of inerrancy is impossible to prove and must ultimately be a statement of faith that denies what we see with our eyes, namely a biblical text that shows the humanity and failure of its greatest heroes and a text that manifests everywhere the limitations of those who wrote the biblical text. Wherein lies the burden of proof? I believe that the basic message of the Bible comes through with clarity, but a lot of questions remain about particular readings and why some books were excluded from or included in the Bible. Christian faith continues to acknowledge Jesus Christ as Lord and affirm the mission of Christ in making disciples and showing God's love in practical ways in our world, but we move to unstable ground when we affirm what we can show neither intrinsically nor extrinsically from the Bible.[6]

Those who hold to inerrancy explain the obvious corruptions in the biblical manuscripts generally as the result of copyists' errors; they did not exist in the autographs. But on what basis can we say that they occurred only when the books were copied, not when they were written? Since no two biblical manuscripts are the same, we have to ask which one (or ones) is inspired and what criteria do we use to distinguish between them? We often forget that all the manuscripts, regardless of their textual integrity, functioned as scripture in the churches that received and used them. Which text of Scripture is without error and consequently inspired and which is not? If the original manuscripts, or autographs, were available for scrutiny today, would they have errors of any kind? On whom is the burden of proof placed? The inability to produce the elusive original manuscripts to justify the inerrancy position does not appear to be a problem for many who advocate that position. And although ultimately they must admit that this teaching is a matter of faith incapable of proof from the biblical data, this does not dissuade proponents from making this belief a mandatory affirmation for fellowship, for graduation from certain schools, for serving in leadership roles in some churches, and for teaching in various evangelical schools.

THE RELIABILITY OF SCRIPTURE

The question we should focus on more is the reliability of the Scriptures in what they affirm in this area. Affirmation of biblical inerrancy says nothing about the inspired status of the only Bibles that we have. What is the status of the translations that we do have that are based on manuscripts that clearly have scribal errors in them? While some of the ancient biblical manuscripts were better copied than others and contain fewer errors than others, there are still many variants in all of them, and again, no two biblical manuscripts and no two translations are exactly alike. It is essential that a more coherent perspective on biblical inspiration emerge in the church if we are to have credibility among those who examine the Scriptures carefully.

Recently I had the opportunity to talk with a highly skilled and engaging Wycliffe Bible translator who told me of the difficulty that she and her colleagues had in translating biblical ideas and notions that have no parallel in the language and experience of tribespeople in many third-world countries. She indicated that they do their best to have as close an equivalent as possible and that they expand considerably what many would call a literal translation since otherwise no one could understand their translation. I asked her if the tribespeople for whom she translated the Scriptures also became followers of Jesus Christ, and if she believed her translations were also inspired of God? She quickly answered yes, without equivocation! She acknowledged that she and her colleagues had produced the best *equivalent* of the text of the New Testament. (She was using the United Bible Society's 4th edition of *The Greek New Testament*.)[7] My point in this is that if the translation brought people to faith in Christ and encouraged them in their journey of faith, then clearly God was at work in her translation, and I agree with her that it is also inspired by God—certainly for the tribespeople who received it.

A similar situation was current in early Christianity when the Christian message moved into areas where Greek was not the common language spoken.

As a result, translations were made from the Greek scriptures. Many of those early translations are now generally considered to be of poor quality, but they nevertheless met an important need in the communities that received them. Less than highly skilled copiers prepared most of the early copies of the biblical manuscripts, and the translations of those texts into other languages were sometimes made by those ill prepared for the task. Many of these early translators were prone to error in the work they did. Given the limited resources of the early churches, they had little choice but to use persons with limited ability to translate if they wished to have a copy of the sacred texts to inform their faith. A number of the early churches were born and nurtured with faulty copies of the scriptures and weak translations. While we have much better and more sophisticated translations today than were available in early Christianity, it is highly unlikely that any translators today would claim that they have produced an infallible[8] translation of the Bible. Nevertheless, the work that the ancients produced and that of the moderns continue to give us access to a proclamation that transforms lives again and again.

We might say for the sake of argument that even if we had the original documents from the Old Testament prophets and the New Testament apostles, and even if we found them to be inerrant as many Christians claim, this does us very little good if we do not have an inerrant translation or an inerrant interpretation of them available to us. Thus far, no one has argued convincingly that we have either, though some preachers seem to be convinced that they have found both! Essentially, they have considerable confidence in those who establish the biblical text for churches and those who translate it in their language.

Some of the so-called errors or glitches in the biblical manuscripts are easy to identify and correct, while others are not as apparent at first glance. I will illustrate that with several examples in the next section. Those who make inerrancy inseparable from their understanding of the inspiration of the Bible often have difficulty discussing the nature of the only Bibles that we do have, namely, those in translation, which are based on manuscripts that have many transmission errors, harmonization problems, and scribal insertions.

If the inspiration and authority of Scripture are vested only in what we do not have, namely, original inerrant autographs, one can wonder what must be said to the layperson who has only a copy of the Scriptures in translation, whether English, Spanish, German, or another language. If inerrancy is essential for the inspiration of the biblical text, how can the early and even later translations possibly be the basis for life-changing experiences with God and for a careful understanding of the Christian faith?

The most important question for the church in these matters is what is the status and reliability of the Bibles and translations that we currently have and use in our churches. Those Bibles regularly nourish the churches strengthening their understanding of the will of God. If God uses only infallible means to accomplish his mission in the world, as the presumption goes, one wonders about the errant preachers and teachers in churches who regularly make mistakes not only in giving incorrect interpretations of the Scriptures, but also in frequently misquoting the very Scriptures they are proclaiming. They often get their statistics and supporting arguments confused or just plain wrong. God apparently does not suspend the ability, weakness, or human characteristics of ministers, teachers, and scholars in the church. Remarkably God regularly accomplishes the church's mission in the world with ministers and leaders in the church who are not perfect, so why do we have to plead for an inerrant biblical text without inerrant interpretations and delivery systems in place? Do not our own experience and the Bible as well inform us that God uses human beings who are weak and prone to sin, who make mistakes and err in their judgments from time to time? On what basis do we say that God suspended human frailty when he inspired the Bible, but not the frailties and weaknesses of ministers and teachers who occasionally mishandle the biblical message that they present to their churches? Roman Catholics have seen this problem of interpretation for centuries and have appealed to the church's authority in matters of biblical interpretation through its bishops. The evangelical Protestant tradition does not have such a fallback position.

Not long ago, my wife and I were visiting a church in New Jersey and the pastor gave a very stirring and eloquent message. He made two mistakes in handling the Greek text in his sermon, but his point was well founded biblically even if it was not based on the text that he had selected for his sermon. I noticed that many people were moved by his message, as I was, despite his errors in exegesis of the biblical text. I have heard Billy Graham make similar mistakes, but have always been moved by the simplicity and power of his preaching and the remarkable response to his message. He sometimes makes a historical or exegetical error, but his ministry has drawn thousands into a right relationship with God. Both of these examples support the case that God regularly uses fallible human instruments to accomplish ministry in this world. This seems to be true for every generation of the church, and it is difficult to argue that God suspended the human frailty only of the writers of the Bible, but not of the interpreters and proclaimers of its message.

INSPIRATION

In the first four centuries of the church, Christians did not distinguish clearly between the inspiration of the Scriptures and the inspiration of the preachers. Indeed, some early writers even preferred the oral preaching and teaching in the church over the written traditions, as we see in the case of Papias, bishop of Hierapolis, around 140 CE (Eusebius, *Hist. eccl.* 3.39.4). Early Christian preachers, teachers, and writers were all believed to be inspired by God, and essentially all were cut from the same cloth, that is, they were believed to be inspired by the same God and without clear distinction in the quality or nature of inspiration. Clement of Rome and Ignatius of Antioch believed that they, like Paul, were inspired by God (see *2 Clem.* 11.2 citing *1 Clem.* 23.3–4 and Ignatius, *Phld.*

7.1b–2, LCL). In the first five centuries of the church, essentially whatever was believed to be true about the Christian faith was also believed by Christians to be inspired by God.

"Inspire," "inspired," and "inspiration" were not at first reserved for books of Scripture alone, but for everything that was moved by the Spirit of God, whether preachers proclaiming good news or the writings produced by those who told the story of Jesus and the Spirit's work in the churches in the decades following the time of Jesus. The term "inspiration" itself is from a Latin word used in the Vulgate to translate the Greek term *theopneustos*, which occurs only in 2 Timothy 3:16 in the New Testament.[9] The notion of inspiration is also found in Numbers 24:2 (cf. Hos. 9:7). The New Revised Standard Version and the New Jerusalem Bible translate the term in context as "All scripture is inspired by God." The New International Version translates the term in context as "All scripture is God-breathed." *Theopneustos* is perhaps best translated as "God-breathed" and suggests that the Scriptures have a divine origin. In 2 Timothy 3:16 inspiration of the Scriptures means that Scriptures originate with God and have a function in developing individuals to do the will of God and be the people of God. The most important focus of the passage is on the purpose of the Scriptures, that is, their usefulness in enabling human beings to accomplish the will of God and be what God intends.[10] This is not unlike *theodidaktos* ("God-taught") in 1 Thessalonians 4:9 that qualifies the believer.[11] In other words, Scriptures have their origin with God. This agrees with 2 Peter 1:21, which indicates that "no prophecy ever came by the impulse of human beings, but persons moved by the Holy Spirit spoke from God." Therefore, when we are speaking about the inspiration of the Bible, we are not speaking of some writings that come from human beings, but that the Scriptures have their source in God, who led the writers to write what they wrote.

Some Christians contend that in the process of the actual writing of the Scriptures God preserved or superintended the writers from all error in everything that they wrote. The problem with this view is that it robs the writers of their individuality, reducing them to stenographers. That view leads to a dictation or mechanical theory of inspiration in which God dictates the very words of Scripture to the writers. That this is the logical result of the doctrine of inerrancy is regularly challenged, and it is maintained rather that when God inspired and moved the writers of Scripture to write, he suspended the operation of their human sinfulness without destroying the humanity of the persons involved.[12] The reasoning is that freedom is essential to the nature of humanity, but sin is not. Therefore, God suspended the operation of human sinfulness in the writing of Scripture, but did not remove human freedom. This freedom is exhibited in the varying vocabularies, abilities, and styles of the individual authors of Scripture. The assumption is, however, that to write divine revelation God had to preserve the writers from all sin. But it is difficult to see how God could allow for the individual freedom of expression of each author but at the same time not also allow for the author's limitations. Some writers of the New Testament have a rather poor grammar (Mark and sometimes Paul, as in Galatians), while others are exceptionally well versed in the principles (rules?) of good grammar in their day (Luke, Hebrews, James, 1 Peter). While the biblical perspective is that the Scriptures had their origin in God alone (inspiration) and demonstrate the power of God in their use, they have come to us in human language and through human authors with all of the limitations that that involves. God nevertheless and remarkably continues to speak through the Bible and makes the divine will known through it to humankind.

James Barr expresses the basic thrust of the traditional view of inspiration and the canon of Scriptures when he says: "If we take a really strict old-fashioned view of inspiration, all books within the canon are fully inspired by the Holy Spirit, and no books outside it, however good in other respects, are inspired."[13] As he later stressed, one of the difficulties in the whole idea of the canon in the early church was the difficulty the church had in distinguishing inspired from non-inspired writings.[14] The problem that the early church had in deciding what literature was or was not inspired demonstrates a lack of agreement on the meaning of inspiration,[15] and this is illustrated by the differences in which sacred authoritative books of antiquity are cited.[16]

The church has difficulty presenting a consistent definition of inspiration, and it has been unable to articulate clearly the distinction between the inspiration of a biblical text and the inspiration resident in the ongoing life of the church or in the act of preaching. The continuing prophetic ministry of the Spirit of the first century that called individuals through the proclamation of the good news to faith in Christ was clearly believed by the church of the second and following centuries to be resident in *their* community of faith and in *their* ministry as well. The Christian community believed that God continued to inspire individuals in their proclamation *just as God did* the writers of the New Testament literature. The early Christians believed that the Spirit was the gift of God to the whole church and not simply the possession of its writers of sacred literature (Acts 2:17–18). Does this pose an affront to the uniqueness, inspiration, and authority of biblical literature? Everett Kalin says that would be true if the only unique factor of that literature were its inspiration.[17] Inspiration was not the distinguishing factor that separated either the apostles from subsequent Christians or the Christian Scriptures from all other Christian literature. Krister Stendahl rightly claims that "inspiration, to be sure, is the divine presupposition for the New Testament, but the twenty-seven books were never chosen because they, and only they, were recognized as inspired. Strange as it may sound, inspiration was not enough. Other standards had to be applied."[18]

Along with the difficulty of identifying and understanding inspiration in antiquity, we also have difficulty comprehending the human dimension of Scripture. The extent to which the Word of God is equal to the words of human agents is precisely the question I am raising here. On a more challenging note, consider when Samuel judged Saul for not killing the men, women, infants, as well as "suckling, ox and sheep, camel and ass," when the Israelites conquered cities (1 Sam. 15:1–3). Saul's failure to do this killing (15:9) was condemned by Samuel through the word of the Lord (15:9–11). There is no question that the prophet Samuel believed that such violence was the will of God, but was this in fact the word of the Lord or what Samuel believed was the will of God based on his conscience that was informed by the limited revelation of God available to that generation? In Old Testament times there is a frequent call to destroy one's enemies and even hate them (see Psalm 109), while in the New Testament Jesus asks his followers to love their enemies and even to pray for them (see Matt. 5:43–48; 18:21–35).

ALLEGED ERRORS

As surprising as it might seem, no one definition of "error" in the Bible has gained widespread approval, though it is probably best not to use the term "error" at all since it indicates to some a general distrust of the Bible. Following B. B. Warfield's criteria, it would indeed be difficult to prove that an error exists at all in the biblical text. He argues that one cannot finally say that an error has been established unless the following can be shown: (1) The error existed in the original manuscripts (which no one has). (2) No question concerning the grammar, style, or wording of a text touches upon the issue of errors. (3) No objection touches the question that is obtained by pressing the primary sense of phrases or idioms.[19] (4) No question against the biblical text is valid when it overlooks the prime question of the intentions and professions of the writer. Inspiration secures what the writer says he will do, not what he does not intend to do. Unless the writer says he is quoting word for word from the Old Testament, then no question can be raised against verbal inspiration from the fact that the writer does not give the exact words.[20] (5) Finally, it is not enough to point to passages in the Bible that are difficult to harmonize; one must show that they are impossible to harmonize. He adds that an error cannot be admitted unless two statements are clearly contradictory and "without any possibility of being harmonized." Warfield safely concludes that after running a supposed error in Scripture through this gauntlet of qualifications, "Not a single case of disharmony can be proved."[21] Indeed! It is clear from these criteria that Warfield decides the issue well before he starts his inquiry, but the data of Scripture will not support these arbitrarily imposed criteria. For Warfield, the most natural explanation of a biblical text gives way or is secondary to his assumptions about the text.

Are there examples or instances where contradictions in Scripture seem likely? Besides the thousands of textual variants in the surviving manuscripts, there are a number of apparent contradictions in the most likely established text of the Bible. I will now focus on a few examples of the phenomena of Scripture that challenge the traditional notions of biblical inerrancy; these are not intended to be a complete list.[22]

THE PHENOMENA OF SCRIPTURE

The following collection of examples from the Scriptures show apparent difficulties, contradictions, or inconsistencies in the biblical text that challenge the traditional notion of biblical inerrancy. Some apparent errors or difficulties in the biblical text may be due to the inability of the interpreter to know all the relevant facts surrounding the biblical passages, but some of them are very difficult if not impossible to harmonize. As noted above, the matter of biblical inerrancy is often defended syllogistically or philosophically, using many carefully constructed rational arguments, but the biblical data are often ignored.

Hebrews 2:6–8. Warfield stipulated that no New Testament writer can be questioned when quoting the Old Testament unless one can prove that the New Testament writer quotes the Old Testament in a different sense from that in which it was written, that is, the use of the quotation turns on this change of sense of the original Old Testament text.[23] Numerous times the New Testament author cites a text that is clearly used in a different sense from that intended in the Old Testament text. See, for example, the citation in Matthew 2:15 of Hosea 11:1. See also how Ephesians 4:8–11 cites Psalm 68:18. The original intent of the text is clearly changed. Observe also how in Hebrews 2:6–9 we find a quote from the Greek translation (LXX) of Psalm 8:4–6, but with a different focus than is found in the Hebrew text. In Psalm 8 it is "humankind" that is made lower than God (with no time element) and given dominion over the earth by God. The author of Hebrews picks up on the words "son of man," the most frequent title Jesus used of himself, and makes the passage refer to Jesus rather than to humanity. He also indicates that Jesus was made lower than the angels "for a little while" (a temporal possibility of the Greek *brachy ti*) so that he may experience death for everyone. The author of Hebrews also quotes from the Septuagint (LXX), not from the original Hebrew, and there are important differences between them. While this form of textual citation is typical of Jewish *pesher*[24] exegesis, it is clearly not the original sense of the passage in Psalm 8.

Ephesians 4:8. In this passage Paul quotes Psalm 68:18 to support his argument that Christ *gave* gifts to his church, but the Hebrew and Greek forms of the passage in the Psalms indicate that gifts were *received*, not *given*. The original context of the Old Testament is obscured when the writer used a normal and typical Jewish interpretive tool, often called *pesher* exegesis, that was perfectly acceptable in the writer's day but is no longer considered so today.

In both of these cases, the interpreter makes changes to the original sense of the text and in keeping with normal Jewish practices of that day. The interpretation is clearly contrary to the original sense of the passage, but it is not out of step with what took place in antiquity. It is remarkable how some modern interpreters of these passages have done exegetical handstands to make these and other New Testament passages harmonize with the original intent of the cited passage.

The two animals in Matthew's triumphal entry story (Matt. 21:5–7). In Matthew's telling of the story of Jesus' entry into Jerusalem, he, like the other evangelists, quotes a passage from Zechariah 9:9, but apparently interprets that passage to indicate that there are two animals brought to Jesus and he rode on both of them. Mark, Luke, and John all have but one animal involved. It would appear that Matthew understood the Hebrew letter *waw* in Zechariah 9:9 to be a connective rather than an explicative ("and" instead of "even" or "especially"), which the context in Zechariah demands and the other Gospels recognize. Matthew is probably using the Greek text of Zechariah in this instance, since the Greek *kai* ("and" or "even") can be understood as an explicative (even) or a connective (and). While it is possible to say, as some have, that Jesus was riding on the mother of a foal and that the foal went alongside its mother, this is not what Matthew says. It is an interesting and challenging text for any interpreter. Mark does not cite Zechariah 9:9 but rather Psalm 118:25–26, yet still has one animal, not two (Mark 11:1–10). Luke follows Mark in this (19:29–40) and does not cite the passage in Zechariah, but like Mark has Jesus riding on one animal only. John, on the other hand, cites the Zechariah passage in his triumphal entry story (John 12:12–15), but has only one animal for Jesus to ride. He clearly takes the Greek *kai* to be an explicative "even" rather than a connective "and." This passage has often led to some very creative commentary.

Jude 14. This passage quotes the apocryphal, or more specifically pseudepigraphal, book of *1 Enoch* (1:9) and states that Enoch, the seventh from Adam, "prophesied" and then he *cites 1 Enoch* 1:9. *First Enoch* is a compilation of some five books that have differing origins and dates, the earliest of which was written around 300 BCE (possibly earlier) and the latest around 40 BCE. Virtually no biblical scholar today argues for an earlier dating of *1 Enoch*, during the time of the biblical Enoch (Gen. 5:18–24); it is a pseudepigraphal book and no one can identify its author. The collection of all five books of the Enochic corpus probably dates sometime after the invasion of the Parthians into Palestine ca. 40 BCE. The work itself was of particular interest to the Jews at Qumran and later to the Ethiopian Christians, who continue to have it in their Bible. It was cited as scripture regularly in the early church, and it is clear that Jude cites this work as originating with the Enoch of the Old Testament. Is this an error of judgment on Jude's part?

David's numbering of the people. Both accounts in 2 Samuel 24:1–2 and 1 Chronicles 21:1–2 agree that the census was an evil act, but 2 Samuel says that David counted the people because *the Lord* incited him to do it. The 1 Chronicles passage, however, says that David did it because *Satan* induced him to do so. Notice also the actual numbers that are mentioned in counting the troops. In 2 Samuel 24:9 there were 800,000 warriors in Israel and 500,000 in Judah. The parallel passage in 1 Chronicles 21:5 mentions 1,100,000 warriors in Israel and 470,000 in Judah. Which of these reports is correct? Perhaps we should ask whether it matters. It is easy to say that the 2 Samuel passage simply rounded off the 470,000 to an even 500,000, but in the case of the warriors from Israel, the solution is not so simple—there is a difference of some 300,000 troops. Which of these two traditions is correct? Can they both be correct?

The mustard seed. According to Matthew 13:31–32, Jesus said that the mustard seed was the smallest of all seeds. According to botanists, there are orchid seeds and others that are smaller than the mustard seed. Did Jesus not know this, did Matthew report incorrectly the words of Jesus, did Jesus not intend to say that the mustard seed was the smallest seed, or was Jesus simply accommodating himself to the understanding of the people of the day? Any response must clearly acknowledge that the mustard seed is not the smallest of all seeds. Since this expression was, however, commonly used in antiquity, it should probably not be pressed too far.[25] But does this remove questions related to scientific inquiry from the table? Are all questions related to the sciences off limits?

Matthew's quotation of Jeremiah, in Matthew 27:9–10. Matthew states that the activity surrounding the betrayal of Jesus for thirty pieces of silver is a fulfillment of what Jeremiah the prophet said, and he goes on to cite specifically Zechariah 11:12–13. Although Jeremiah 18:1–3 speaks about a potter's house and the potter making a vessel, and Jeremiah 32:6–9 mentions the price of 17 shekels for a field, the quote in Matthew comes directly from Zechariah 11:11–13. See also the price of a slave in Exodus 21:32. Did Matthew misquote the passage or attribute wrongly the Zechariah passage to Jeremiah? Matthew's quote attributed to Jeremiah is not found in its entirety anywhere in the Old Testament. There is no complete text quite like the one found in Matthew.

The accompanying "staff." Just before Jesus sent his disciples out on a preaching mission he charged them to take nothing with them "*except a staff*" (Mark 6:8), but in Matthew's parallel account the disciples are prohibited from taking anything: "take no gold, nor silver, nor copper in your belts . . . *nor a staff*" (Matt. 10:9–11). Luke's account also says, "Take nothing for your journey, *no staff*, nor bag" (Luke 9:3). Why did Matthew and Luke change Mark's report and forbid the taking of a staff?

The numbers in Stephen's speech and the Hebrew Bible. Acts 7:2–53 presents several difficulties. One of these has to do with when Abraham left his father, Terah. In Genesis 11:26 Terah was 70 years old when Abraham was born and he died at age 205 (Gen. 11:32), that is, when Abraham was 135 years old. However, Genesis 12:4 states that Abraham was 75 years old when he left for Canaan. This would be 60 years *before* the death of Terah. If Abraham was 135 years old when his father died and had been in Palestine some 60 years already, why does Acts 7:4 place his leaving Haran for Canaan *after* the death of Terah, which would have been at the age of 135? How do we account for the gap of some 60 years?

The Law came 430 years after the promise to Abraham. In Galatians 3:16–17 Paul refers to God giving the Law to Moses 430 years after the promise given to Abraham. The problem is that Paul is referring to the Septuagint (Greek) text of the Old Testament (Exod. 12:40) that is at odds with the Hebrew text. The Septuagint text states: "Now the residence of the sons of Israel during which they dwelt in the land, Egypt, and in the land of Chanaan was four hundred and thirty years and all the host of the Lord went out from the land of Egypt during the night." The Masoretic Text states: "The time that the Israelites had lived in Egypt was four hundred thirty years. At the end of four hundred and thirty years, on that very day, all the companies of the LORD went out from the land of Egypt" (Exod. 12:40–41 NRSV). Paul is citing the LXX text here and dates the promise to Abraham 430 years before the giving of the Law. The problem has to do with the amount of time between the promise and the giving of the Law. Was it 430 years or 645 years? How long were the children of Israel in the land of Egypt? The problem may be seen more clearly if, following the Hebrew text, we diagram it as follows:

According to the Hebrew text:	a. Abraham was 75 years old when he went to Canaan and received the promise (Gen. 2:4).
25 years	b. Abraham was 100 when Isaac was born (Gen. 21:5).
60 years	c. Isaac was 60 when Jacob was born (Gen. 5:26).
130 years	d. Jacob was 130 when he went to Egypt (Gen. 47:9).
430 years	e. The Jews were in Egypt 430 years (MT of Exod. 12:40), then Law given.
645 years	Total time from promise to receiving of the Law. Difference: 215 years.

The Genealogy of Jesus and the father of Joseph. The Gospels offer two significantly different genealogies of Jesus. Within these the father of Joseph is called Jacob in Matthew's genealogy (1:16) and Heli in Luke's genealogy (3:23). Traditionally this conflict, as well as the significant difference in the other names in the genealogies, has been resolved by saying that Matthew presents the genealogy of Joseph and Luke the genealogy of Mary, but neither text mentions Mary in the genealogy. This tradition came to the church for the first time in 1490 CE by Annius of Viterbo. If these two genealogies are to be taken literally, then one is obviously wrong. It is better to see that Matthew used the genealogy as a means to say that Jesus is the legitimate heir to the throne of David, since David's name is listed three times (Matt. 1:1–17), and the genealogy has three divisions of fourteen generations (the numerical equivalent of David's name in Hebrew is fourteen). Matthew emphasizes Jesus' rightful claim as heir to the throne of David (see also Rom. 1:3). His role as Israel's king is present in several passages, especially in the birth story with the subsequent arrival of the magi bringing gifts worthy of a king and Herod's feeling threatened by the birth of Jesus (Matt. 2:1–12). Also Matthew has forty-two generations for the same time frame that Luke has fifty-five. Since Matthew's list is so neat (three times fourteen generations), because it has fewer generations than Luke has for the same time, and because it serves his presentation of Jesus as the son of David, it is likely that Luke is closer to presenting the actual genealogy than is Matthew, but it could be that neither is authentic and both have a particular interest that they are preparing. Since Luke presents his genealogy at the beginning of Jesus' ministry after his baptism (Luke 3:23–38), this may suggest that Luke wants to present Jesus as the new Moses (whose genealogy begins after he begins his ministry, Exod. 6:14–25). Luke may also be seeking to connect Jesus (and his salvation) to the whole of humanity by reversing the order of his genealogy and going back not only to Abraham but also to Adam. Whatever the explanation given, the fact remains that the genealogies are quite distinct, but both claim to be the genealogy of Jesus through Joseph.

The resurrection narratives. There are numerous problems of harmonization in the resurrection narratives. The following are only a few of the more significant examples:

Who buried Jesus? All four evangelists are clear that Joseph of Arimathea (a disciple [Matt. 27:57–60; John 19:38–42], or a good man [Mark 15:43–46; Luke 23:50–53]) buried Jesus, but in Acts 13:29 it would appear that the enemies of Jesus buried him. Could it be that when Joseph of Arimathea buried Jesus he was not a disciple of Jesus but simply wanted to carry out the requirements of Jewish law (see Deut. 21:22–23)?[26] Was Joseph of Arimathea a disciple before or after the death of Jesus? Was his aim in burying Jesus only to fulfill the custom of Jewish burial practices by burying a corpse on the day of death? This is not clear, and Acts and the Gospels appear to be out of harmony on this matter.

The time of the discovery of the empty tomb. Mark 16:2 indicates that the women came to the tomb early "when the sun had risen," whereas John 20:1 indicates that Mary came "while it was still dark." Attempts to harmonize this discrepancy are based on an argument from silence that John intended to separate Mary's visit from the visit of the other women.

The opening of the tomb. Was it opened in the presence of the women (Matthew), or was it already opened before they arrived (Mark, Luke, John)?

The number of angels at the empty tomb. Matthew and Mark have one angel attending while Luke and John have two. Matthew's angel is "an angel of the Lord" (see Matt. 28:2).

The location and message of the angels. Was it one or two angels who stood (or sat) at the tomb of Jesus? Matthew and Mark have one, and Luke and John have two (cf. Matt. 28:2 and Mark 16:5–6 with Luke 24:4 and John 20:12–13). Were they inside or outside the tomb, standing or sitting? What did they say? There are different numbers, positions, and comments in all four Gospels.

The response of the women to the message of the angels. Compare Matthew 28:5–10; Mark 16:8; Luke 24:8–10; John 20:11–18. Were the women to tell the disciples to stay in Jerusalem or to go to Galilee? Compare Matthew and Mark with Luke and John.

The location of the appearances. Were the appearances in Galilee (Matthew, Mark, and John 21) or in Jerusalem (Luke and John 20)?

To whom did Jesus first appear? Was it to the women (Matthew) or to Mary (John)? Luke holds out the tradition that Jesus has already appeared to Peter (Luke 24:34), but this comes after the appearance to the two men on the road to Emmaus, and no appearance to the women or a woman (Mary) is described. Mark concludes with a promise of an appearance to the disciples in Galilee, but the women only have a revelation from the angel (or man) at the tomb. Paul says that the first appearance was to Peter, and he does not mention women (1 Cor. 15:5).

The touching of Jesus after his resurrection. See John 20:17 and Matthew 28:9. Both stories speak of the women or Mary grasping or attempting to grasp Jesus after his resurrection. John uses the occasion to speak of the ascension, and Jesus advises Mary not to touch him before his ascension (20:18–19), but Matthew says nothing of the ascension, and the women grasp his feet. Later, Jesus invites Thomas to touch him (John 20:27).

The earthquakes. Matthew is the only Gospel to mention the earthquake at the death of Jesus (Matt. 27:51–52) and another at the opening of the tomb of Jesus (28:2). A hint on the significance of the earthquakes may be seen in 24:7, when earthquakes precede the end of time. Has Matthew tried to speak of the end of the ages in the death and resurrection of Jesus? How literally should this be taken? Clearly the evangelists' stories differ at strategic points about phenomena accompanying Jesus' death and resurrection.

The ascension story in John and Luke. John has an ascension of Jesus between his first and second appearances (see John 20:17–19), with no final appearance noted. Luke has the ascension of Jesus after his final appearance. Interestingly, both accounts of the ascension have the giving of the Holy Spirit after the ascension, although with a longer delay in the sending of the Holy Spirit in Luke and Acts (Luke 24:50–52 and Acts 1:6–9). Matthew omits the story of an ascension altogether, but has the promise of Jesus' presence with his disciples always (Matt. 28:20).

Matthew and Luke correcting Mark. An interesting problem for the inerrancy discussion is the tendency by both Matthew and Luke to correct Mark, as in the case of Mark attributing to Isaiah a quote that combines Isaiah 40:3 and Malachi 3:1 to Isaiah alone (cf. Mark 1:2 with Matt. 3:3 and Luke 3:4). Since it is clear that Isaiah did not say all that Mark attributes to him, both Luke and Matthew took the liberty to change what they felt was incorrect, and both dropped the quote from Malachi.

The many other apparent contradictions or problems of harmony in the Bible narratives, especially in the Gospels, suggest that traditional notions of biblical inerrancy and inspiration should be reconsidered. One's confidence in the written Word should not thereby be shaken, however, if we understand that in the mystery of God the good news of hope, forgiveness, and love was offered to fallible human beings through divinely inspired but still fallible human instruments.

FINAL NOTE

We may ask in closing whether God ever intends for Christian disciples to deny in their hearts what they see clearly with their eyes, namely, that there are some apparent contradictions in the Scriptures that are difficult if not impossible to reconcile. When one starts from an already preconceived notion of what God could or could not have done or said in regard to the Bible, then one is compelled to either dismiss what appears obvious in the biblical text or to ignore what is manifestly obvious even to casual observers of the Old Testament or New Testament. To say that God could have nothing to do with the origin of the Scriptures if they show the flawed side of their human writers and transmitters is to deny our own experience with God and that of Christians in every generation. No one would say today that the apostle Peter was flawless in his conduct. Indeed, one of the most encouraging examples to Christians who have failed in their conduct is the story of Peter and how he was reconciled and restored following his failure and denial of Jesus. His failure did not cease after Jesus' resurrection, as we see in Peter's inconsistency at Antioch that Paul exposes openly (Gal. 2:11–14). On what basis do we say that the imperfections of Peter (whether his denial of Jesus, his impetuousness, or his inconsistency at Antioch) were somehow suspended when he taught, wrote, or preached? The book of Acts makes clear that Paul was not as forgiving as Barnabas was in regard to the actions of Mark when they began their second missionary journey (Acts 15:36–41), but by the end of his career Mark was apparently forgiven by Paul and did quite well in his ministry after that if church history serves us well (2 Tim. 4:11). When we have failed in areas of life, most of us would probably prefer to deal with Barnabas rather than Paul, but we are grateful that Paul evidently gave Mark another chance in ministry.

Is it really true that a Bible that reflects human frailty and was produced by imperfect servants of God cannot be the Word of God? Peter Enns raises this question and, I believe, answers correctly. He asks whether the "fact of diversity" in the biblical text is "fundamentally contrary to the Bible being the word of God." He answers no.[27] He also claims that there is no superficial unity in the Bible and that portions of the Bible are "in tension with each other." He concludes that if we "take seriously both the historical dimension of Israel's story and God's making himself a part of that story, one would expect this complex historical matrix to be reflected in the pages of the Old Testament, which is precisely what we find."[28] I agree.

The above examples are intended to serve as a basis for dialogue on this highly complex and yet extremely important issue. They are not intended to exhaust the subject, but rather to initiate further discussion. I believe that many of the problems surrounding the inerrancy question may be resolved or clarified through careful investigation of the Scriptures, but not all. All the problems of harmony and the many examples of different perspectives taught in the Bible cannot be resolved until a greater understanding of the biblical notion of truth has been explored. The inspiration and the authority of the Bible are not fully understood when truth is simply perceived in terms of facts and figures, that is, in terms of empirical data (historical, cognitive, and scientific information). Another dimension is more important in the Bible. The truthfulness of the Bible will best be grasped when the truth of *being* and *doing* are better understood. Truth in the biblical sense is not at variance with cognitive truth, and yet it is never equal to it, nor fully comprehended on that level of understanding. For example, Jesus said, "I am the truth" (John 14:6; see also 4:24; 8:32). It is not the truth of "the jot and the tittle" that saves or transforms, but the life-changing presence of the Son of God of the church's confession who himself is the truth that we seek in the Bible. Knowing Christ cannot be reduced to knowing what the Bible says about him; rather it means becoming his disciple. We can see the relevance of this in Matthew 7:21–23, which is a frightful warning to those who reduce Christian faith to knowing skills and performing activities but not knowing Christ. Knowing in the Bible is more complex than simply knowing data about God. It is amazing to see in 1 Samuel that Samuel was born to a godly mother through divine intervention (1:19–20), was raised in the house of God (1:25–28; 2:18–3:21), sat at the feet of Israel's spiritual leader and grew up in the presence of the Lord (2:21), even "ministered unto the LORD" (2:11, 18; 3:1), and still did not yet "know the LORD" (3:7). God's transforming and life-changing truth will not be perceived through discussions of inerrancy or historical (or scientific) inquiry, but rather through faith in Jesus Christ alone.

We should also think of a fresh way of speaking about the "Word of God," which has become such a focal point of controversy. Is every word of Scripture equal to the "Word of God," or does the Word of God come to us through the words of human beings even though they may not be perfect in every way? Bible scholars and clergy are sharply divided over these matters, but however one answers them, the responses and positions taken about the Scriptures should be rooted in an inquiry of the Scriptures rather than in some sophisticated syllogistic argument.

In terms of the biblical canon, we must ask whether inspiration and divine guidance (perhaps the same) extended also to the early Christians living in the fourth to the sixth centuries since they had much to do with the scope of the biblical canons that are recognized in churches today around the world. Few discussions of inerrancy or the inspiration of the Bible focus on this very important matter. The popular assumption among persons in the church is that everything about the Bible was pretty well settled by the end of the first century CE, but the matter was not settled at that time. It is also common to say that the matter was in the providence of God, and the church, led by the Spirit of God, recognized the authoritative scriptures for the church. While this view is naive, it may be more accurate than much of what we have said to this point, namely God was involved in the process of recognition of the church's Scriptures even if the church has never fully agreed on the scope of its contents. The core of the Scriptures proclaim appropriately the Word and will of God, but this does not diminish the human dimension involved in the writing, transmission, preaching, and teaching of those sacred texts.

The main focus in the doctrine of biblical inerrancy is on the *writers* of the biblical literature, but what about the preservation and interpretation of the Scriptures? Was the writing accomplished without error, but everything that followed prone to error? Also, what is the value of inerrancy related only to original autographs if no infallible interpretation is available or even an infallible transmission of the text of the Scriptures? Discussions of inspiration and inerrancy are almost exclusively carried on in terms of the production of Scripture, but not in its preservation, transmission, and interpretation. If inerrancy does not extend to the full phase of the history of the transmission and preservation of the Scriptures as well, then the infallibility of the former, the inerrant original manuscripts, seems irrelevant.

Notes

Chapter One

1. See Bart D. Ehrman, *The Orthodox Corruption of Scripture: The Effect of Early Christological Controversies on the Text of the New Testament* (Oxford: Oxford University Press, 1993). He makes a substantial point about the fluidity of the text of the Christian Scriptures well into the third century and beyond. His *Lost Christianities: The Battles for Scripture and the Faiths We Never Knew* (Oxford: Oxford University Press, 2003), appears to offer political reasons for the triumph of orthodoxy and concludes with a chiding of the victors for not being patient with what they called "heretical" movements in the churches. His more recent *Misquoting Jesus: The Story Behind Who Changed the Bible and Why* (San Francisco: HarperSanFrancisco, 2005), reflects more of his own personal journey from faith to unbelief or agnosticism than it adequately reflects the actual story of the triumph of orthodoxy in the church. This volume seems to have an axe to grind and is not as helpful as the first volume. Ehrman is a careful scholar who has contributed considerably to our understanding of the context of early Christianity and the text of the NT, and he should not be unilaterally dismissed but understood in light of his own theological journey and the careful contributions he has made to biblical inquiry—which are considerable.
2. See William W. Klein, Craig L. Blomberg, and Robert L. Hubbard, *Introduction to Biblical Interpretation*, rev. ed. (Dallas: Word, 2004), 53.
3. The term "Hebrew Bible" is a modern construct by biblical scholars; a more common term for the sacred Scriptures of the Jews is *Miqra*, which means that which is recited, namely the Jewish Scriptures. Because some passages in the Jewish Scriptures are written in Aramaic, the term "Hebrew Bible" is not precise; but perhaps because the writing of the Jewish Scriptures in the Hebrew language was very significant in the rabbinic tradition, the term continues. In this volume I will regularly use "Hebrew Bible" (or HB) for the collection of sacred Jewish writings that are the same collection that makes up the Protestant OT and forms the largest part of the Roman Catholic and Eastern Orthodox OT Scriptures, though the sequence and divisions in the Hebrew Bible differs considerably from that in the Christian Bibles.
4. Lee Martin McDonald, *The Biblical Canon: Its Origin, Transmission, and Authority* (Peabody, MA: Hendrickson, 2006), 190–223.

5. See Daryl D. Schmidt, "The Greek New Testament as a Codex," in *The Canon Debate*, ed. L. M. McDonald and J. A. Sanders (Peabody, MA: Hendrickson, 2002), 469–84.

Chapter Two

1. Much of this chapter was presented at the Society of Biblical Literature in San Diego in November of 2007.
2. Bart Erhman, ed., *Lost Scriptures: Books that Did Not Make It into the New Testament* (Oxford: Oxford University Press, 2003), 4.
3. I have addressed this issue earlier, but probably without adequate clarity for some scholars. See the criticism of my earlier attempts in Eugene Ulrich, "The Notion and Definition of Canon," in *The Canon Debate*, ed. L. M. McDonald and J. A. Sanders (Peabody, MA: Hendrickson, 2002), 21–35; and more recently in Stephen B. Chapman, "How the Biblical Canon Began: Working Models and Open Questions," in *Homer, the Bible, and Beyond: Literary and Religious Canons in the Ancient World*, ed. Margarit Finkelberg and Guy G. Stroumsa (Leiden: Brill, 2003), 35 n. 20. In the former instance, Ulrich is correct in citing the inconsistency in my use of terms to describe the phenomena of canon formation; and in the latter case, Chapman may be right by focusing on the confusion in my statements. The problem in both instances lies with the acknowledgment of sacred books as authoritative in some communities, though the book has not yet been added to a fixed canonical list. In some instances, we are talking about some books that were initially cited as sacred Scripture, but in time they no longer were. "Decanonization" fails to appreciate this phenomenon since it seems to say that there was a fixed canon before such matters were discussed in the churches. The problem here again is that the language we use fails to communicate adequately the point we want to make. I do not disagree with either author on their assessment of my earlier attempts at clarification, but I hope to be more clear here.
4. Alexander Souter, *The Text and Canon of the New Testament*, Studies in Theology (London: Duckworth, 1913; rev. C. S. C. Williams, 1954), 186.
5. See, for example, the opening sentence of the preface (p. v) and the opening paragraph in the introduction (p. 1) and in chapter 1 (p. 11) in Bruce M. Metzger, *The Canon of the New Testament: Its Origin, Development, and Significance* (Oxford: Clarendon, 1987).
6. Besides the books of the HB, the Eastern Orthodox include in their OT 1 Esdras, Judith, Tobit, Wisdom of Solomon, Ecclesiasticus (Sirach), Baruch, as well as the additions to Daniel and Esther, 1–3 Maccabees, and Psalm 151 (or forty-nine books, plus the additions to Daniel and Esther). The books not in the HB are called deuterocanonical books. Their NT has the same twenty-seven books that are common to the Roman Catholic and Protestant Bibles.
7. Their OT canon is similar to the Orthodox (they have forty-six books) along with the additions to Daniel and Esther, but they do not have 3 Maccabees or Psalm 151. Roman Catholics call their sacred books that are not in the HB the "deuterocanonical" books, and Christian doctrine is not generally based on them. Their NT contains the same books as the Orthodox and the Protestant Bibles.
8. The Protestants accept only the books in the HB, but in a different order, and the twenty-seven books of the NT.
9. The church in Ethiopia adopted as its OT the books adopted by the Eastern Orthodox, but also *Jubilees*, Ethiopic *Enoch*, *IV Esdras*, and *The Rest of the Words of Baruch*. Their NT consists not only of the twenty-seven books of the NT but also four other lesser known books: *Sinodos*, *Book of Clement* (not *1* or *2 Clement*), *Book of the Covenant*, and *Didascalia*.

10. *Orthodoxy and Heresy in Earliest Christianity*, ed. and trans. R. Kraft and G. Krodel (Philadelphia: Fortress, 1972).

11. Bart D. Ehrman, *The Orthodox Corruption of Scripture: The Effect of Early Christological Controversies on the Text of the New Testament* (Oxford: Oxford University Press, 1993), 7. There was certainly considerable diversity in the churches during those two centuries and even later, and it appears that an orthodox majority began to emerge at the end of the second century, even though that did not mean that there was unanimity in theological thought at that time. The continuing debates among various strands of early Christianity suggest this, but that does not deny the emerging orthodoxy a prominent role. It is not clear that orthodoxy won out only because of the Roman church's power, wealth, and influence in the fourth century. That has not been adequately demonstrated. The first-century documents to which it appealed, especially the Gospels, surely weighed heavily in favor of orthodoxy.

12. This does not take away from Ehrman's point in *Orthodox Corruption of Scripture* that Christian orthodoxy variously and significantly influenced the transmission of the biblical text. That appears incontrovertible.

13. See especially the impressive three-volume series of essays in James H. Charlesworth, ed., *The Bible and the Dead Sea Scrolls: The Second Princeton Symposium on Judaism and Christian Origins* (Waco: Baylor University Press, 2006), but also Philip R. Davies, *Scribes and Schools: The Canonization of the Hebrew Scriptures* (Louisville, KY: Westminster John Knox Press, 1998), 152–69; Alan J. Avery-Peck, Jacob Neusner, and Bruce D. Chilton, eds., *Judaism in Late Antiquity*, part 5: *The Judaism of Qumran: A Systemic Reading of the Dead Sea Scrolls*, vol. 1: *Theory of Israel*, Handbook of Oriental Studies 1/56 (Leiden: Brill, 2001); plus vol. 2 in the same series, *World View, Comparing Judaisms*, Handbook of Oriental Studies 1/57 (Leiden: Brill, 2002); and the useful introductory chapter of James C. VanderKam, *From Revelation to Canon: Studies in the Hebrew Bible and Second Temple Literature* (Boston: Brill, 2002). These significant works represent only a small amount of the literature published in this field in recent years, and much more is on the way.

14. The case for this diversity between the Jews in the east and those to the west of Judea is reasonably argued by Arye Edrei and Doron Mendels, "A Split Jewish Diaspora: Its Dramatic Consequences," in *JSP* 16, no. 2 (2007): 91–137.

15. Abraham Wasserstein and David J. Wasserstein, *The Legend of the Septuagint: From Classical Antiquity to Today* (Cambridge: Cambridge University Press, 2006), 217–37, describe the differences between the Karaites, Samaritans, and Rabbanite Jews over their sacred scriptures.

16. For a listing of several examples of the use of *kanōn* for a standard or measurement in antiquity, see Lee Martin McDonald, *The Biblical Canon: Its Origin, Transmission, and Authority* (Peabody, MA: Hendrickson, 2007), 38–48.

17. Ibid.

18. Tertullian writes: "Of the apostles, therefore, John and Matthew first instill faith into us; whilst of apostolic men, Luke and Mark renew it afterwards" (*Marc.* 4.2.2 ANF trans). Later in the same treatise he chides the Marcionites for adopting Luke as their Gospel instead of Matthew and John: "Luke, however, was not an apostle, but only an apostolic man; not a master, but a disciple, and so inferior to a master" (*Marc.* 4.2.5 ANF trans.).

19. The criteria that were used broadly to establish this standard of scripture (canon) in the fourth century included widespread use in the churches, orthodoxy, apostolicity, and antiquity (proximity to the apostolic era). These criteria are discussed in Lee Martin McDonald, "Identifying Scripture and Canon in the Early Church: The Criteria Question," in *The Canon Debate*, ed. Lee

Martin McDonald and James A. Sanders (Peabody, MA: Hendrickson, 2002), 416–39. I should note, however, that they are not all found in one ancient text explaining the canonizing process, but rather they are cited separately in various places as important in the selection process.

20. A Jewish source in the Middle Ages, *Shalshelet ha-Qabbala* (a document written in Hebrew), claims that the *Letter of Aristeas* was part of the Christian "canon" of scriptures. This is noted in Joseph Dan, "Gedaliah Ibn Yahya," *EncJud* 8:1208–9, and cited by the Wassersteins, *Legend of the Septuagint*, 230. The actual quote is as follows: "And the Christians have recorded this entire deed [translation of Hebrew Torah into Greek] in a book all to itself and have included it in the canon (Heb. *Minyan*) of their Bible (Heb. *Biblia*), and they call it/him (Heb. them) Aristeo, and I have chosen to present it before you very briefly so that you can see the high rank of the Torah of Moses."

21. Rudolf Pfeiffer, *History of Classical Scholarship: From the Beginnings to the End of the Hellenistic Age* (Oxford: Clarendon, 1968), 207.

22. G. A. Robbins, "Eusebius' Lexicon of 'Canonicity,'" *Studia Patristica* 25 (1993): 134–41.

23. For a similar definition see Bruce M. Metzger, "The Context and Development of the Christian Canon," in *Living Traditions of the Bible: Scripture in Jewish, Christian, and Muslim Practice*, ed. James E. Bowley (St. Louis: Chalice, 1999), 85.

24. The term "apocrypha" (Greek *apokryphos*, "hidden"), like "canon," is also a late designation for Jewish literature composed roughly between 300 BCE and 100 CE, originated in Judea, and was included in the Greek manuscripts of the LXX and the Christian OT, but was not included in the rabbinic Hebrew Bible that was established in second century CE and later. Early church synods recognized what Protestants call the apocryphal writings as canonical scripture from the time of the Third Council of Carthage (397). They are received by the Orthodox churches (both Eastern and Russian) as scripture, and, since the bishops at the Council of Trent declared these writings to be canonical on April 8, 1546, they are also in the Roman Catholic Bible, though they were widely read and received as canonical scriptures by them before that time. The Protestant designation of these writings as "apocryphal" is obscure but may depend on *4 Ezra* 14:45–47, which states that some seventy "secret writings" were divinely transcribed by Ezra and his scribes and they are reserved for the wise (see *4 Ezra* 14:6, 26, 46–47). The designation of thirteen books as "Apocrypha" (there is a debate over how many books are included here) seems to go back to Carlstadt in Germany (ca. 1480–1541), but that designation for those writings did not mean then that they should not be read. For a useful summary of this literature, see Hermann Lichtenberger, "Apocrypha," *The Encyclopedia of Early Christianity*, ed. Erwin Fahlbusch et al.; trans. Geoffrey W. Bromiley (Grand Rapids: Eerdmans, 1999), 1:97–102; and James H. Charlesworth, "Apocrypha," *ABD* 1:292–94. On the NT Apocrypha see the discussion by Stephen J. Patterson, "New Testament Apocrypha," *ABD* 1:294–97. See also A. Oepke and R. Meyer, "*kryptō*," *TDNT* 3:976–1000, for the background and influence of the so-called NT Apocrypha. For careful discussions and introductions to this literature, see J. K. Elliott, ed., *The Apocryphal New Testament* (Oxford: Clarendon, 1993); and Wilhelm Schneemelcher, *New Testament Apocrypha*, trans. and ed. R. McL. Wilson, 2nd ed., 2 vols. (Louisville, KY: Westminster/John Knox, 1991).

25. For a helpful discussion of this literature, see James H. Charlesworth, "Introduction for the General Reader," *OTP* 1:xxi–xxxv; and his more extensive discussion in his *Old Testament Pseudepigrapha and the New Testament*, Society

for New Testament Studies Monograph Series 54 (Cambridge: Cambridge University Press, 1985).

26. The books normally included in the OT Apocrypha include: Tobit; Judith; Esther, with the six extensive Greek additions to it; Wisdom of Solomon; Sirach; Baruch; Letter of Jeremiah; Additions to the Book of Daniel (= The Prayer of Azariah, Song of the Three Jews, Susanna, and Bel and the Dragon), 1 Maccabees, 2 Maccabees, 1 Esdras, the Prayer of Manasseh, Psalm 151, 3 Maccabees, 2 Esdras, 4 Maccabees. Although many still view *4 Ezra* (= 2 Esdras) and the *Prayer of Manasseh* as part of the OT Apocrypha, these writings are generally now placed among the OT Pseudepigrapha. Some of these books are also what we now call pseudonymous literature, for example, Wisdom of Solomon, 2 Esdras, and 4 Maccabees, and there is often little clear distinction between the Apocrypha and Pseudepigrapha.

27. Sirach, for instance, is cited as scripture in *b. Hagigah* 13a; *y. Hagigah* 77c; *b. Yebamot* 63b; *Gen. Rab.* 8:2b; *b. Baba Qamma* 92b. Interestingly, M. H. Segal in *Sefer Ben-Sirah ha-Shalem* (Jerusalem: Bialik, 1953) cites eighty-five quotations of Sirach in rabbinic literature through the tenth century CE. It was obviously a popular book among Jews in the east for a long time, even if it was officially rejected as part of the HB. It is also interesting that the following books were excluded by the rabbis from public reading: Song of Songs (see *m. Yadayim* 3.5; *b. Megillah* 7a), Ecclesiastes (*m. Yadayim* 3:5; *b. Shabbat* 100a; see Jerome on Eccl. 12:14), Ruth (*b. Megillah* 7a), Esther (*b. Sanhedrin* 100a; *b. Megillah* 7a), Proverbs (*b. Shabbat* 30b), and Ezekiel (*b. Shabbat* 13b; *Hagigah* 13a; *Menahot* 45a).

28. See Joseph van Haelst, *Catalogue des papyrus littéraires juifs et chrétiens* (Paris: Sorbonne, 1976), 199–220.

29. Jean Daniélou, *A History of Early Christian Doctrine Before the Council of Nicaea*, vol. 3: *The Origins of Latin Christianity*, trans. David Smith and John A. Baker (Philadelphia: Westminster Press, 1977), 154.

30. Ibid., 3:155–57, he also offers several other examples of Latin Christianity citing apocryphal texts as scripture.

31. Ibid., 3:157 and 161–76. Daniélou also has an important discussion of the use of Jewish or OT Pseudepigrapha and the NT Apocrypha in early Christianity in *A History of Early Christian Doctrine Before the Council of Nicaea*, vol. 1: *The Theology of Jewish Christianity*, trans. and ed. J. A. Baker (Philadelphia: Westminster Press, 1964), 1:11–54; see also his *Origins of Latin Christianity*, 140–89.

32. For a more complete discussion of the significant role that *1 Enoch* had in the early churches, see James C. VanderKam, "1 Enoch, Enochic Motifs, and Enoch in Early Christian Literature," in *The Jewish Apocalyptic Heritage in Early Christianity*, ed. James C. VanderKam and William Adler, CRINT 3/4 (Minneapolis: Fortress, 1996), 33–101.

33. "Tearing Down Walls of Separation," *Henoch* 28, no. 2 (2006): 3–4.

34. Ibid., 3–6.

35. Robert A. Kraft, "Para-mania: Beside, Before and Beyond Bible Studies," *JBL* 126, no. 1 (2007): 5–27, here 17.

36. See Theodor Zahn, *Geschichte des neutestamentlichen Kanons*, vol. 1: *Das Neue Testament vor Origenes*, 2 vols. (Erlanger/Driden/Leipzig, 1888–89), 2. *Urkunden und Belege zum ersten und dritten Band* (Erlangen and Leipzig: Deichert, 1888–92); Zahn's views on canon formation are presented in his subsequent work, *Grundriss der Geschichte des neutestamentlichen Kanons* (Leipzig: Deichert, 1901; 2nd ed., 1904). Bruce Metzger refers to his work as "an indispensable mine of information," *Canon of the New Testament*, 23–24.

37. Adolf von Harnack, *Das Neue Testament um das Jahr 200* (Freiburg 1.B, 1899); his *History of Dogma*, trans. Neil Buchanan et al., 7 vols. (London: Williams & Norgate, 1900), 38–61; and especially his *New Testament Studies*, vol. 6: *The Origin of the New Testament and the Most Important Consequences of the New Creation*, trans. J. R. Wilkinson (London: Williams & Norgate, 1925).

38. See John Barton, "Marcion Revisited," in *Canon Debate*, ed. McDonald and Sanders, 341–42.

39. Hans Freiherr von Campenhausen, *The Formation of the Christian Bible*, trans. J. A. Baker (Philadelphia: Fortress, 1972), 147–233.

40. *Canon of the New Testament: Its Origin, Development, and Significance.*

41. Albert C. Sundberg Jr., *The Old Testament of the Early Church* (Cambridge: Harvard University Press, 1964). See also his more recent, "The Septuagint: The Bible of Hellenistic Judaism," in *Canon Debate*, ed. McDonald and Sanders, 68–90.

42. Sundberg, "Canon Muratori: A Fourth-Century List," *HTR* 66 (1973): 1–41. Everett Ferguson, "Canon Muratori: Date and Provenance," in *Studia Patristica* 17, no. 2 (1982): 677–83, responded carefully and critically to Sundberg's dating of the MF, and many scholars thought that this was the end of the matter. For example, Metzger, *Canon of the New Testament*, 191–93, dismissed Sundberg in a footnote and claimed that Ferguson had demolished his arguments. Sundberg's work, however, spurred a more substantial examination of the MF by Geoffrey Mark Hahneman in *The Muratorian Fragment and the Development of the Canon*, Oxford Theological Monographs (Oxford: Clarendon, 1992). His work has led many scholars to reexamine their earlier positions on NT canon formation. While his and Sundberg's examination of this ancient fragment have drawn more supporters for a fourth-century dating of the MF, many others are still not convinced. For a recent example defending the second-century dating of the MF, see J. Verheyden, "The Canon Muratori: A Matter of Dispute," in *The Biblical Canons*, ed. J.-M. Auwers and H. J. de Jonge, BETL 163 (Leuven: Leuven University Press, 2003), 487–556. I have argued earlier that if the MF is a second-century document that it has no second-century parallels until the fourth century, and if it made no discernible impact on any churches in the second century, then it fits in well in the fourth century, when scripture catalogues and lists begin to appear in various parts of the Roman Empire. Also, a fourth-century dating makes better sense since the MF treats the four Gospels as though they were already well established and there is no need to defend their status as Irenaeus does earlier (ca. 170–180 CE). The MF's reference to the Gospels is similar to Eusebius, who, after calling them the "holy tetrad," offers no argument for their inclusion in a collection of recognized books in the church (*Hist. eccl.* 3.25.1). No one else in the second century speaks of four canonical Gospels or defends them like Irenaeus (*Haer.* 3.11.8–9; cf. 3.1.1). Also 2 *or* 3 John along with Jude are accepted, but they are disputed in Eusebius's collection in the fourth century. Why would they be widely accepted in the second century and disputed in the first part of the fourth, and then reappear as accepted at the end of the fourth century as in the case of Athanasius (367) and the councils of Hippo (393) and Carthage (397)? Further, the addition of the Wisdom of Solomon in an *NT* list is found elsewhere only in the fourth-century writings of Eusebius (*Hist. eccl.* 5.8.1–8) and Epiphanius (*Pan.* 76.5). I have summarized the arguments for and against the fourth-century dating of the MF with an eastern provenance in *Biblical Canon*, 369–81. Much in the fragment does not make much sense and more study of it is needed, but again, it has closer parallels in the fourth century than in the second.

43. For a brief but careful discussion of the contributions of Zahn, Harnack, and Sundberg, see John Barton, *Holy Writings, Sacred Text: The Canon in Early Christianity* (Louisville, KY: Westminster John Knox Press, 1997), 1–7; for von Compenhausen see 7–8, 30–31, *et passim*.

44. George Aichele, *The Control of Biblical Meaning: Canon as Semiotic Mechanism* (Harrisburg: Trinity Press International, 2001), 15.

45. Ibid., 20–21.

46. Barton, *Holy Writings*, 2. He also has a very helpful summary of these three positions on canon formation in 1–34.

47. I have discussed this activity in *Biblical Canon*, 310–14.

48. James A. Sanders, *From Sacred Story to Sacred Text* (Philadelphia: Fortress, 1987), 22–30. He writes: "At the heart of canonical criticism are the questions of the nature of authority and the hermeneutics by which that authority was marshaled in the situation where needed" (23), and after observing that adaptability and stability are at the heart of canon, he explains that "each generation reads its authoritative tradition in the light of its own place in life, its own questions, its own necessary hermeneutics" (30).

49. I first saw this term in James D. G. Dunn, *The Living Word* (Philadelphia: Fortress, 1987), 156. He used it to describe how the Law in the church's OT ceased being canon for Christians in the same way that it did for the Jews.

50. Souter, *Text and Canon*, 163–66. He also notes on p. 166 that Epiphanius (ca. 380) indicated that Pseudo-Clement's *De Virginitate* was also read in church services in his day (see Epiphanius, *Haer.* 30.5).

51. Metzger discusses this phenomenon in his *Canon of the New Testament*, 165–89. See A. van der Kooij and K. van der Toorn, eds., *Canonization and Decanonization*, Studies in the History of Religion 82 (Leiden: Brill, 1998). Van der Kooij and van der Toorn and several of their contributors show awareness of the problem that temporal canonicity poses for canon studies.

52. Carolyn Osiek, *The Shepherd of Hermas: A Commentary*, Hermeneia (Minneapolis: Fortress, 1999), 1–6, has a useful summary of the life of this book in early Christianity. She notes: "No other noncanonical writing was as popular before the fourth century as the *Shepherd of Hermas*" (1).

53. G. T. Sheppard, "Canon," in *The Encyclopedia of Religion*, ed. M. Eliade (New York: Macmillan, 1987), 3:62–69; cf. also McDonald, *Biblical Canon*, 55–58.

54. James A. Sanders, *Torah and Canon* (Philadelphia: Fortress, 1972), 91: and his later article, "Canon: Hebrew Bible," *ABD* 1:847, where he names and explains these terms. See also his more recent explanation of them in "The Impact of the Judean Desert Scrolls on Issues of Text and Canon of the Hebrew Bible," in *The Bible and the Dead Sea Scrolls: The Princeton Symposium on Judaism and Christian Origins*, vol. 1: *Scripture and the Scrolls*, ed. James H. Charlesworth (Waco: Baylor University Press, 2006), 28–29. These terms are used by both Lutherans and some Roman Catholics in the sense that Scripture is *norma normans non normata* (scripture is the norm that norms, but is not normed) and *norma normata* (tradition is the norm that is normed by Scripture). See the explanation in Joseph A. Fitzmyer, "Scripture in the Catholic Tradition," in *Living Traditions of the Bible: Scripture in Jewish, Christian, and Muslim Practice*, ed. James E. Bowley (St. Louis, MO: Chalice, 1999), 159.

55. For a helpful corrective to the use of "canon" see Eugene Ulrich, "The Notion and Definition of Canon," in *Canon Debate*, ed. McDonald and Sanders, 33–34; and his *Dead Sea Scrolls and the Origins of the Bible*, Studies in the Dead Sea Scrolls and Related Literature (Grand Rapids: Eerdmans, 1999).

56. Dunn, *Living Word*, 145–53, suggests that there were at least four levels of canonical formation: the *tradition-history level* (the stages of a text's prehistory, both oral and written), the *final author or final composition level* (discerning the meaning of the author of the document), the *canonical level* (the primary context of a document is in its relation to the larger group of documents), and the *ecclesiastical level* (the continuing meaning of the text). Those levels are not contrary to what we have already said, but rather add to our understanding of the complexity of canon formation in antiquity and today.

57. This information is noted in Hahneman, *Muratorian Fragment*, 90–93; and a good discussion of Marcion's contributions to the formation of the NT canon can be found in Barton, *Holy Writings*, 36–62. He and Hahneman stress that Marcion was especially hostile to the OT writings, but there is no clear evidence that the Marcionite churches restricted their sacred texts to Luke and Paul alone. Indeed, as I have shown elsewhere, there is evidence to the contrary; see *Biblical Canon*, 330–31.

58. Hahneman, *Muratorian Fragment*, 91–93. He also notes that some of the Armenian Marcionites made use of Tatian's *Diatessaron*, which combines the four Gospels into one. The evidence that Marcion's collection of books was closed is not substantial, and, according to a tenth-century source, Marcion and his followers may also have produced their own books for use in their churches (cf. the *Fihrist al-Ulum* of al-Nadim [d. 995]). See also R. Casey, "The Armenian Marcionites and the Diatessaron," *JBL* 57 (1938): 185–94. Daniel Theron, *Evidence of Tradition* (Grand Rapids: Baker, 1957), 51–55, lists the anti-Marcionite Gospel prologues that circulated in early Christianity as a response to Marcion.

59. See these listed in Theron, *Evidence of Tradition*, 78–83. If these prologues were genuine, it would dispel notions of a fixed biblical canon in the time of Marcion since they also include prologues to the Pastoral Epistles, which Marcion did not initially include in his list of books. Also see Barton's conclusions about these prologues in "Marcion Revisited," in *Canon Debate*, ed. McDonald and Sanders, 353–54.

60. For a credible defense of this view, see Everett Kalin, "Re-examining New Testament Canon History, 1: The Canon of Origen," *Currents in Theology and Mission* 17 (1990): 274–82.

61. See also *m. Yadayim* 4:5, which indicates that only scripture written in Hebrew "in the Assyrian character and on leather, and in ink" could defile the hands, that is, are sacred texts.

62. Barton, *Holy Writings*, 112.

63. See McDonald, *Biblical Canon*, 20–37, for more discussion of the origins and meaning of the term "scripture" in Judaism and early Christianity.

64. Ibid., 285–322.

65. Sanders, *From Sacred Story to Sacred Text*, 175–92.

66. Martin Hengel, *The Septuagint as Christian Scripture: Its Prehistory and the Problem of Its Canon*, trans. Mark Biddle, Old Testament Studies (Edinburgh: T & T Clark, 2002), 46, who has brought to our attention that the Cairo Genizah contained five Hebrew manuscripts of Sirach and fragments of Tobit in Hebrew and four Aramaic manuscripts. This is remarkable since the manuscripts in the Cairo Genizah are approximately a thousand years after the manuscripts that were discovered at Qumran and after the HB had presumably become a settled issue for most Jews in the east. Evidently the dictum of Rabbi Aqiba that those who "read in the excluded books possess no portion in the coming world" (*m. Sanhedrin* 10:1) simply did not carry much weight among the Jews who were already using this literature both when Aqiba spoke and later.

67. Gamble has a careful discussion of the origin of the codex and early Christian preference for it in *Books and Readers in the Early Church: A History of Early Christian Texts* (New Haven: Yale University Press, 1995), 49–81.

68. Ehrman, *Orthodox Corruption of Scripture*, 9–10 and 36 n. 30, lists several scholars who have pursued this aspect of Gnostic life in detail. They include Klaus Koschorke, *Die Polemik der Gnostiker gegen des kirchliche Christendum*, NHS 12 (Leiden: Brill, 1978); Birger Pearson, "Anti-Heretical Warnings in Codex IX from Nag Hammadi," in *Essays on the Nag Hammadi Texts in Honor of Pahor Labib*, ed. M. Krause, NHS 6 (Leiden: Brill, 1975), 145–54.

69. Robert M. Grant, "The New Testament Canon," in *The Cambridge History of the Bible*, vol. 1: *From the Beginnings to Jerome*, ed. P. R. Ackroyd (Cambridge: Cambridge University Press, 1970), 284.

70. *Lost Christianities*, 7.

71. Kraft, "Para-mania," 10.

72. Ibid., 21.

73. J. D. G. Dunn, "How the New Testament Canon Began," in *From Biblical Criticism to Biblical Faith: Essays in Honor of Lee Martin McDonald*, ed. Wm. Brackney and C. A. Evans (Macon, GA: Mercer University Press, 2007), 122–37.

74. I agree with Richard Bauckham, "For Whom Were Gospels Written," in *The Gospels for All Christians*, ed. R. Bauckham (Grand Rapids: Eerdmans, 1998), 9–48, who claims that the Gospels were intended for wider audiences than what contemporary scholars sometimes recognize, and their intention was to tell the story of Jesus in a compelling way first for the Christian community at large, but with applicability for the non-Christian as well. Since Jesus was the Lord of the earliest Christians, any text that cited his teachings and ministry would surely have been welcomed in an authoritative manner in the churches. I also appreciate Bauckham's recent volume, *Jesus and the Eyewitnesses: The Gospels as Eyewitness Testimony* (Grand Rapids: Eerdmans, 2006), which stresses the importance of eyewitness testimony in the creation of the Gospels; such testimony underscored their reliability and authority in early Christianity. Moody Smith also made this point in his presidential address to the Society of Biblical Literature in which he focused on the authoritative stature of the Gospels almost immediately after they were written. See his "When Did the Gospels Become Scripture?" *JBL* 119 (2000): 3–20. See also Birger Gerhardsson, *Tradition and Memory in Early Christianity*, rev. ed., Biblical Resource Series (Grand Rapids: Eerdmans, 1998), 40–47. More recently, Dunn makes this point in "How the New Testament Canon Began."

75. For a useful listing and discussion of the citations of the Enoch tradition in early Christianity, see James C. VanderKam, "1 Enoch, Enochic Motifs," in *Jewish Apocalyptic Heritage*, ed. VanderKam and Adler, 33–101. He lists numerous references to the Enoch tradition in early Christianity, including both citations of the books of *Enoch* and references to this OT person.

76. Barbara and Kurt Aland, *The Text of the New Testament*, trans. Erroll F. Rhodes, rev. ed. (Grand Rapids: Eerdmans; Leiden: Brill, 1989), 78–79, list 2,361 ancient biblical manuscripts containing the Gospels (or portions of them), 792 manuscripts containing the Letters of Paul (or portions of them), 662 manuscripts of Acts and the Catholic Epistles (or portions of them), and 287 manuscripts of the book of Revelation (or portions of it). Many of the manuscripts are fragmentary, but one can glean from them that the Gospels (Matthew, Mark, Luke, and John) were among the most favored texts in early Christianity.

77. This information is conveniently located in van Haelst, *Catalogue des Papyrus*, 199–220; and Cornelia Römer's supplement online, http://www.ucl.ac.uk/

GrandLat/research/christianpapyri.htm. Professor Larry Hurtado at New College in Edinburgh, Scotland, pointed these helpful references out to me.

Chapter Three

1. Shemaryahu Talmon, "The Crystallization of the 'Canon of Hebrew Scriptures,'" in *The Bible as Book: The Hebrew Bible and the Judaean Desert Discoveries*, ed. Edward D. Herbert and Emanuel Tov (London: British Library, 2002), 5–20, and here 9–11. Talmon also lists names of works mentioned at Qumran that have been lost (10–11).
2. See McDonald, *Biblical Canon*, 73–189, for a more complete description of this process.
3. *Sirach* is the Greek spelling of Hebrew *Sîrā'* for the same book, which is also called *Ecclesiasticus* in the Old Latin Bible—a term that identifies it as "a book belonging to the church" or "the church's book."
4. This data is cited in Hengel, *Septuagint as Christian Scripture*, 78–79. His primary source is H. Leisegang, "Index locorum Veteris Testamentis," in L. Cohn and P. Wendland, eds., *Philo von Alexandrien*, Opera quae supersunt 7/1 (Berlin: Reimer, 1926), 29–43.
5. For a summary of these, see McDonald, *Biblical Canon*, 87–90.
6. This translation is from Florentino García Martínez, *The Dead Sea Scrolls Translated*, trans. Wilfrid G. E. Watson, 2nd ed. (Grand Rapids: Eerdmans, 1996), 84.
7. The "memoirs of the apostles" in Justin is a reference to the Gospels. In *1 Apology* 66 Justin writes: "For the apostles, in the memoirs composed by them, which are called Gospels, have thus delivered unto us what was enjoined upon them; that Jesus took bread, and when he had given thanks, said, "this do in remembrance of me, this is My body. . . ."
8. See D. W. Suter, "Apocrypha, Old Testament," *Harper's Bible Dictionary*, ed. P. J. Achtemeier (San Francisco: Harper & Row, 1985), 36–38; Bruce M. Metzger, *An Introduction to the Apocrypha* (New York: Oxford University Press, 1957); and Kee, *Cambridge Annotated Study Apocrypha*.
9. W. Adler, "The Pseudepigrapha in the Early Church," in *Canon Debate*, ed. McDonald and Sanders, 211–28, has a useful discussion of the mixed reception of this literature in early Christianity.
10. An important and careful study on the early use and final rejection of Sirach in rabbinic Judaism is Giuseppe Veltri, *Libraries, Translations, and 'Canonic' Texts: The Septuagint, Aquila and Ben Sira in the Jewish and Christian Traditions*, JSJSup 109 (New York: Brill, 2006), especially 191–222.
11. Veltri lists numerous places where the book was received as Scripture, read only in private, and finally rejected as a spurious book. He shows in the rabbinic tradition how Sirach was once viewed as sacred scripture among the Jews but was first marginalized and eventually later decanonized by them. See his careful discussion of this in ibid., 190–230.
12. The word is the plural form of the Aramaic word *'amora'* ("speaker" or "interpreter"), which is the name given to a rabbinic teacher in both Judea and Babylon during the talmudic period (ca. 220 CE to 600 CE). The Amoraim regarded the Mishnah and other Tannaitic (Hebrew *tanna'*, "one who studies, teaches, or repeats traditions") sources from roughly the first and second centuries CE to be the authoritative basis for their rulings on Jewish behavior and beliefs. The most frequently cited *tannaim* lived after 70 CE, the time of the destruction of Jerusalem.
13. Sarna, "Canon, Text, and Editions," *EncJud* 4.826. He adds that a third-generation *Amora* cited Sirach and placed it in the Writings (see *b. Baba Qamma* 92b).

14. James H. Charlesworth, "Pseudepigrapha," *Harper's Bible Dictionary*, ed. P. Achtemeier (San Francisco: Harper & Row, 1996), 894–99.

15. These categories are an abbreviation of a longer list in H. J. Rix and P. J. Parsons, "Pseudepigraphic Literature," *Oxford Classical Dictionary*, ed. S. Hornblower and A. Spawforth, 3rd ed. (Oxford: Oxford University Press, 1996), 1270. For a discussion of pseudonymous literature in early Christianity, see also David Meade, *Pseudonymity and Canon: An Investigation into the Relationship of Authorship and Authority in Jewish and Earliest Christian Tradition* (Grand Rapids: Eerdmans, 1986), especially 1–16 and 194–218. The following list is from James H. Charlesworth, *OTP*, vols. 1–2.

16. A *khirbet* (Arabic term from *khirbeh*, equivalent to Hebrew *ḥorbat*, "ruin") refers to a ruin that normally was visible above the ground. Khirbet Qumran is actually a reference to a "ruin of the grayish spot" and is the common designation of the location where a community of Essenes lived near the Dead Sea in the first two centuries BCE and the first century CE. For useful summaries of the Qumran inhabitants, see J. Magness, *The Archaeology of Qumran and the Dead Sea Scrolls* (Grand Rapids: Eerdmans, 2002), 32–46; Vermes, *Dead Sea Scrolls*, 87–136; E. P. Sanders, "The Dead Sea Sect and Other Jews," in *The Dead Sea Scrolls in Their Historical Context*, ed. T. Lim (Edinburgh: T & T Clark, 2000), 7–44; and C. M. Patte, *Communities of the Last Days* (Downers Grove, IL: InterVarsity Press, 2000), 53–84.

17. Because Josephus's account is as detailed as it is, some scholars have postulated that he may have been involved in that community earlier in his life, or at the least was in close contact with someone else who was connected with it.

18. This practice of largely ignoring the textual testimony from Qumran in favor of the MT has been observed by Harold P. Scanlin, "Text, Truth and Tradition," in *Bible as Book: Hebrew Bible*, ed. Herbert and Tov, 293–97.

19. This summary of Essene characteristics comes from F. H. Colson, "Appendices," in *Philo* 9 (Cambridge: Harvard University Press, 1960), 514–15. For Philo's other description of the Essenes, see his *Good Person*, 75–87; and also *Hypothetica* 11.

20. Recent works on the relevance of the Qumran literature for understanding Judaism in the time of Jesus and the biblical canon at that time include M. G. Abegg, P. Flint, and E. Ulrich, *The Dead Sea Scrolls Bible* (San Francisco: Harper, 1999); J. A. Fitzmyer, *The Dead Sea Scrolls and Christian Origins* SDSSRL (Grand Rapids: Eerdmans, 2000); P. Flint and J. C. VanderKam, *The Dead Sea Scrolls after Fifty Years*, 2 vols. (Leiden: Brill, 1998–1999); García Martínez, *Dead Sea Scrolls Translated*; L. H. Schiffman, *Reclaiming the Dead Sea Scrolls* (Philadelphia: JPS, 1994); J. C. Trebolle Barrera, *The Jewish Bible and the Christian Bible*, trans. W. G. E. Watson (Grand Rapids: Eerdmans, 1998); E. Ulrich, *The Dead Sea Scrolls and the Origins of the Bible*, SDSSRL (Grand Rapids: Eerdmans, 1999); and J. C. VanderKam, *The Dead Sea Scrolls Today* (Grand Rapids: Eerdmans, 1994).

21. For examples of Qumran texts that clarify the meaning of NT passages, see C. A. Evans, "Jesus and the Dead Sea Scrolls," 573–98; J. A. Fitzmyer, "Paul and the Dead Sea Scrolls," 599–621; and D. Aune, "Qumran and the Book of Revelation," 622–48, all in *Dead Sea Scrolls after Fifty Years*, ed. Flint and VanderKam, vol. 2.

22. Although the majority of the so-called Dead Sea Scrolls were found in the caves at Qumran, several others were found in the general vicinity of Qumran and also at Masada, Wadi Murabba'at, and Naḥal Ḥever. For a helpful summary of the scrolls, see F. M. Cross, *The Ancient Library at Qumran*, 3rd ed. (Minneapolis: Fortress, 1995), 19–53; and Abegg, Flint, and Ulrich, *Dead Sea Scrolls Bible*, xiv–xv.

23. These figures are taken from Emanuel Tov, "The Biblical Text from the Judaean Desert—An Overview and Analysis of the Published Texts," in *Bible as Book: Hebrew Bible*, ed. Herbert and Tov, 139–66, here 140–43. Tefillin are small leather cases containing passages from Exod. 13:1, 11; and Deut. 6:4–9; 11:13–21. They are written on parchment and worn on the left arm and forehead by adult males in a morning service of the synagogue. Mezuzot (pl. of mezuzah) are the first two paragraphs of the Shema (Deut. 6:4–9; 11:13–21; Num. 15:37–41) that are rolled tightly and attached to the doorpost of an observant Jewish person's home.

24. Ibid., 141–45. Tov shows the differences in writing of biblical texts by the rabbinic sages/scribes that are far more particular in scribal detail. He notes especially the rules outlined in the *Massekhet Soferim* for the writing of sacred texts (see *Sof.* 1:15; 2:3, 20; 3:9, 10).

25. Ibid., 154–55.

26. *Genizah* ("to hide, store up") is an Aramaic loanword for a storeroom in a synagogue. Such places emerged from a need to retire old sacred manuscripts. The most famous genizah is the one discovered in an old synagogue at Fustat in Cairo, Egypt, and is commonly known as the Cairo Genizah, containing an amazing collection of ancient texts with thousands of manuscripts and fragments of manuscripts that have yielded significant resources for both textual and canonical research. Genizahs are quite valuable since they can tell us what books functioned as Scripture in various Jewish synagogues or communities. See an early discussion of genizahs in *m. Shabbat* 16:1.

27. For example, 11Q13 or 11QMelch is the *Melchizedek Scroll* from Qumran cave 11. One of the common difficulties that beginning students have when investigating the now translated Dead Sea Scrolls is that they are not consistently identified by the scholars who examine and refer to them. Perhaps in the future, scholars will find a more consistent set of identification tags to facilitate easier access to these important texts.

28. The data are listed in Emanuel Tov, "A Categorized List of All the 'Biblical Texts' Found in the Judaean Desert," *DSD* 8 (2001): xxiii; and in his *Textual Criticism of the Hebrew Bible*, 2nd ed. (Minneapolis: Augsburg Fortress, 2001), 104–5. See also C. D. Elledge, *The Bible and the Dead Sea Scrolls*, Resources for Biblical Studies 14 (Leiden: Brill, 2005), 87, for a slightly different set of numbers. These numbers are only approximate due to the fragmentary nature of the scrolls.

29. The terms "biblical" and "nonbiblical" are modern terms that are included here only to clarify our discussion. To some extent, the Essenes valued everything found in the caves at Qumran. Whether it was valued in the same sense that sacred Scripture is understood today is not always clear, but that the literature discovered there—biblical and nonbiblical texts alike—was not only copied but also stored in the caves without distinguishing features regarding its canonicity indicates the value that the community attached to it. While much of this literature was probably considered sacred scripture, it is difficult to makes such claims about all the Qumran literature, including some of the so-called *biblical* literature.

30. These figures come from Martin G. Abegg Jr., "The Hebrew of the Dead Sea Scrolls"; and Leonard J. Greenspoon, "The Dead Sea Scrolls and the Greek Bible," in *Dead Sea Scrolls after Fifty Years*, ed. Flint and VanderKam, 325–58, 101–27, respectively. For a more complete list of the Qumran writings, see García Martínez, *Dead Sea Scrolls Translated*, 466–519; Vermes, *Complete Dead Sea Scrolls in English*, 602–18; Stephen A. Reed et al., *The Dead Sea Scrolls Catalogue*, SBLRBS 32 (Atlanta: Scholars Press, 1994); and Emanuel Tov and Stephen J. Pfann, *Companion Volume to the Dead Sea Scrolls Microfiche Edition* (New York: Brill, 1993).

31. Geza Vermes coined the widely used term "rewritten Bible" in "Bible Interpretation at Qumran," *ErIsr* 20 (1989): 184–91; but the term has come under considerable challenge in recent years. The problem with it is that it presumes a biblical canon before such matters were ever discussed or considered in ancient Israel. Deuteronomy and 1–2 Chronicles are biblical examples of this practice, as well as Josephus's *Antiquities*, but so are a number of other texts, including *Jubilees* and the *Temple Scroll*. For a careful discussion of the use of rewritten or reworked biblical texts, see Sidnie White Crawford, *Rewriting Scripture in Second Temple Times*, SDSSRL (Grand Rapids: Eerdmans, 2008). She largely follows the careful considerations of Moshe Bernstein, "'Rewritten Bible': A Generic Category which Has Outlived Its Usefulness?" *Textus* 22 (2005): 169–96; and also George J. Brooke, "Rewritten Bible," in *EDSS* 2:777–81; see also his "The Rewritten Law, Prophets, and Psalms: Issues for Understanding the Text of the Bible," in *Bible as Book: Hebrew Bible*, ed. Herbert and Tov, 31–40. The focus now is more properly on "rewritten Scriptures" than on a rewritten *Bible*.

32. See Abegg, Flint, and Ulrich, *Dead Sea Scrolls Bible*, xv.

33. This list of the main Qumran documents is based in part on Milik's earlier *Ten Years of Discovery in the Wilderness of Judea*, Studies in Biblical Theology 1/26 (London: SCM, 1963), chap. 2, supplemented from later sources. For a discussion of recently released documents, see García Martínez, *Dead Sea Scrolls Translated* xxxii–lvii.

34. Several biblical scholars argue that Esther was not found at Qumran and was omitted because of calendar conflicts. While no part of the biblical book of Esther has been found to date at Qumran, several fragments of a loosely parallel work called Proto-Esther were discovered and should cause some hesitation in concluding that the Qumran community did not know Esther: 4Q550^{a-f}, and perhaps 4Q550^e (see Florentino García Martínez and Eibert J. C. Tigchelaar, *The Dead Sea Scrolls Study Edition*, 2 vols. [Grand Rapids: Eerdmans, 1997–1998], 2:1096–1103; and Wise, Abegg, and Cook, *Dead Sea Scrolls*, 437–39). In these texts Bagasraw (or Bagasro) seems to play the role of Haman. Mordecai and Esther are not mentioned, but the story, as best as can be discerned from the fragments, seems to resemble the story of the book of Esther (C. A. Evans, personal correspondence). It is difficult to know what to make of such discoveries, but one cannot leap from these texts to say that Esther was part of a biblical canon at Qumran.

    The argument to include Nehemiah among the books found at Qumran stems from a later development in Judaism when Ezra and Nehemiah were often coupled together in one scroll; since, therefore, Ezra was found at Qumran, Nehemiah must have been at Qumran as well. This argument is anachronistic and not well supported. See arguments against the presence of Nehemiah at Qumran in Philip R. Davies, *Scribes and Schools: The Canonization of the Hebrew Scripture* (Louisville, KY: Westminster John Knox, 1998), 154, 197; and James C. VanderKam, "Ezra-Nehemiah or Ezra and Nehemiah?" in *From Revelation to Canon*, JSJSup 62 (Leiden: Brill, 2000), 60–80.

35. Most English translations of the OT Scriptures are based mostly, though not completely, on the Leningrad Codex, which was copied in 1008–9 and is the oldest and most complete manuscript of the MT of the HB. An earlier manuscript, the Aleppo Codex, was produced in 925 CE, but it is not complete and must be augmented by the Leningrad Codex. The Masoretic scribes produced many biblical manuscripts that exist now largely in fragmentary condition, but the Bible they produced is essentially the same as what is available today, though the books are not always in the same order. This rabbinic Bible is based

on a meticulous amount of painstaking work to maintain textual consistency in the biblical text. The group of scribes known as the Masoretes carried out the final stages of this process and added vowel points to the consonantal text to ensure that it could be properly pronounced and carefully interpreted. The standardized form of the text that resulted is found in both the Leningrad and Aleppo texts. See Abegg, Flint, and Ulrich, *Dead Sea Scrolls Bible*, x–xi.

36. I owe this observation to Crawford, *Rewriting Scripture*, 9.

37. For a discussion of whether 7Q5 is a fragment of Mark 6:52–53, see Graham Stanton, *Gospel Truth? New Light on Jesus and the Gospels* (Valley Forge, PA: Trinity Press International, 1995), 20–32, who concludes that it is not.

38. For a discussion of the similarities and differences, a convenient summary of their relationships and a chart reflecting the order and parallels with the canonical Psalms, see Abegg, Flint, and Ulrich, *Dead Sea Scrolls Bible*, 505–11.

39. Ibid., 509.

40. Lee Martin McDonald, *The Biblical Canon: Its Origin, Transmission, and Authority* (Peabody, MA: Hendrickson, 2006), 90–93.

41. I have discussed this earlier in ibid., 93–96.

42. The Greek term *diaspora* (dispersion, scattered abroad) was first used as a reference to Jews living in exile in Babylon (Jer. 28:6; 2 Chr. 36:20), but eventually was used in reference to all Jews living outside the land of Israel. Among the rabbis, the Hebrew term *galut* (exile) was used often with theological implications and also in a negative sense of those exiles living in captivity outside of the land of Israel, but more generally, it was simply a reference to Jews living outside Israel.

43. Emil Schürer, *The History of the Jewish People in the Age of Jesus Christ (175 B.C.–A.D. 135)*, ed. Geza Vermes, Fergus Millar, and Martin Goodman (Edinburgh: T & T Clark, 1986), 3.1:478–79.

44. See the discussion and examples of this in McDonald, *Biblical Canon*, 98–100.

45. These matters are carefully discussed in Schürer, *History of the Jewish People*, 3.1:138–49.

46. Ibid., 142.

47. Ibid. Edrei and Mendels, "Split Jewish Diaspora," 102, also support this.

48. See his *Jewish Law from Jesus to the Mishnah* (London: SCM, 1990), 256.

49. This is described by Edrei and Mendals, "Split Jewish Diaspora," 99.

50. Ibid., 91–137.

51. This is discussed at length by Isaiah M. Gafni, *Land, Center and Diaspora: Jewish Constructs in Late Antiquity*, JSPSup 21 (Sheffield: Sheffield Academic Press, 1997), 19–27. He cites not only OT texts (Deut. 28:63–64; Jer. 5:19; 9:15, but also see *Ep. Arist.* 249; *T. Levi* 10.3–4; *T. Asher* 7.2–7; Tob. 3:4; Jdth. 5:18; *2 Bar.* 1.2–4; *Sib. Or.* 3:267–76; *Mid. Ps.* 71:4. These texts all reflect a well-known view that exile was a judgment from God, and it is difficult not to think that this also affected the views of the Jews in Israel toward Diaspora Jews in the west who did not speak their language. See also Edrei and Mendels, "Split Jewish Diaspora," 102–14, for further reasons for this divide among the Jews in the east and west and how pervasive it was.

52. For further discussion of the notion of dispersion as punishment of the Jews, see Gafni, *Land, Center and Diaspora*, 21–27. Gafni also lists references to rabbinic judgment of the Diaspora Jews (see *b. Nedarin* 32a; *b. Ta'anit* 29a; *Lev. R.* 29.2) and concludes that lack of faith regarding the inheritance of the Land of Israel as cause for banishment and dispersion. Dispersion was viewed as the result of sins.

53. Edrei and Mendes, "Split Jewish Diaspora," 114.

54. I owe this observation to Elledge, *Bible and Dead Sea Scrolls*, 72.
55. I owe much of this summary information to J. K. Elliott, "Manuscripts, the Codex, and the Canon," in *JSNT* 63 (1996): 113–23. For a careful description of the Judean Desert finds, see Emanuel Tov, "The Biblical Texts from the Judaean Desert—An Overview and Analysis of the Published Texts," in *Bible as Book: Hebrew Bible*, ed. Herbert and Tov, 139–66.
56. "OTs" is plural here to account for the different OTs in Christian churches today. Four OT canons are used in Christian churches today.
57. See David Chapman's review of Lee Martin McDonald, *The Biblical Canon: Its Origin, Transmission, and Authority* (Peabody, MA: Hendrickson, 2007), in *Review of Biblical Literature*, August 2007.
58. See David L. Paulsen, "Are Christians Mormon? Reassessing Joseph Smith's Theology in His Bicentennial," *BYU Studies* 45, no. 1 (2006): 35–128; see especially 45–55.

Chapter Four

1. C. A. Evans, "The Scriptures of Jesus and His Earliest Followers," in *The Canon Debate*, ed. L. M. McDonald and J. A. Sanders (Peabody, MA: Hendrickson, 2002), 186.
2. For a helpful summary of the contents of these scrolls, see Frank Moore Cross, *The Ancient Library at Qumran*, 3rd ed. (Minneapolis: Fortress, 1995), 19–53; also Martin Abegg Jr., Peter Flint, and Eugene Ulrich, The *Dead Sea Scrolls Bible: The Oldest Known Bible Translated for the First Time into English* (San Francisco: HarperSanFrancisco, 1999), xiv–xv. While the title of this volume is misleading, implying something of a fixed biblical canon among the Jews at Qumran, the volume itself contains important and useful information about this collection of ancient books.
3. Evans, "Scriptures of Jesus," 195.
4. These include Tobit, Judith, the six additions to Esther, 1–2 Maccabees (Orthodox include 3 Maccabees and Ps. 151), Wisdom of Solomon, Sirach (Ecclesiasticus), the Prayer of Azariah, Song of the Three Young Men, Susanna, Bel and the Dragon, Baruch, plus the Epistle of Jeremiah. The Eastern Orthodox Christians made the final decision about the scope of their biblical canon at the Council of Jerusalem in 1672. It is slightly longer than that of the Roman Catholics. They earlier had accepted essentially the books of the Roman Catholic OT, but added the books mentioned above. For a brief summary of the development of the Greek version, see S. A. Nigosian, *From Ancient Writings to Sacred Texts: The Old Testament and Apocrypha* (Baltimore: Johns Hopkins University Press, 2004), 19–23. See also his lists of Jewish and Christian Scriptures (28–29).
5. See Joseph van Haelst, *Catalogue des papyrus littéraires huifs et chrétiens* (Paris: Sorbonne, 1976), especially 96–119 and 199–205. The Web site with updates to this from Cornelia Römer is at http://www.ucl.ac.uk/GrandLat/research/christianpapyri.htm.
6. Stichometry is an ancient method of calculating the number of lines in a manuscript that were used as a basis for payment to the scribe or copier. The term comes from the Greek *stichos* (pl. *stichoi*), referring to a line in a manuscript that normally had 16 syllables or some 36 letters. The following lists come from the dated but still useful description of these ancient texts in Montague Rhodes James, *The Lost Apocrypha of the Old Testament: Their Titles and Fragments* (London: SPCK, 1920), xii–xiv.

7. This list is found in some of the manuscripts of the *Quaestiones* (or *Questions and Answers*) of Anastasius, abbot of the monastery of St. Catherine at Mount Sinai (d. ca. 700 CE).

8. This is similar to the list in the *Sixty Books* above, but *Sibyl* is substituted for *Lamech*, *Testament of Moses* is omitted, and the last four items are replaced by the *Seventh Vision of Daniel.*

9. These and a number of unnamed apocryphal or pseudepigraphal writings are discussed in James, *Lost Apocrypha*, 87–95. He carefully lists many of the ancient texts where these writings are either cited or quoted.

10. Tov, *Textual Criticism of the Hebrew Bible*, 195.

11. Cross, *From Epic to Canon*, 225. Cross adds, "an additional worm, and Chronicles, too, would have been missing."

12. F. F. Bruce, *The Canon of Scripture* (Downers Grove, IL: InterVarsity Press, 1988), 40.

13. Roger Beckwith, *The Old Testament Canon of the New Testament Church* (Grand Rapids: Eerdmans, 1985), 291–94, 312–13, and especially 358–66.

14. For example, *Jubilees* is found in 14 or 15 manuscripts, and *1 Enoch* in 12; by contrast, if the biblical books were considered more valuable at Qumran, why do Genesis and Exodus have only 15 manuscripts each, with similar counts for Deuteronomy (25), Isaiah (19), and Psalms (30)? Also, why do some nonbiblical books have more copies than some biblical books? For further discussion, see VanderKam, *From Revelation to Canon*, 25–28; Davies, *Scribes and Schools*, 154–57.

15. *Jub.* 6:29–31; *OTP* 2:68. See Beckwith, *Old Testament Canon*, 362; cf. 359–60. See also Davies, *Scribes and Schools*, 163–65.

16. VanderKam, *From Revelation to Canon*, 27–28.

17. Ibid., 27.

18. When I questioned one of the authors of this volume about its title, he admitted that it was unfortunate and that it was the publisher's choice because it was believed that "Bible" in the title would make the volume more marketable! The title nevertheless confuses readers. Interestingly, Harold Scanlin, "Text, Truth and Tradition: The Public's View of the Bible in the Light of the Dead Sea Scrolls," in *The Bible as Book: The Hebrew Bible and the Judaean Desert Discoveries*, ed. E. D. Herbert and E. Tov (London: British Library, 2002), 289–99, here 291, also agrees with this assessment. He notes that the title "is likely to leave general readers with the impression that there was a 'Bible,' a fixed collection of canonical books bound in black leather and so designated, at least *de facto*, by the Covenanters at Qumran," and adds, "The additional jacket blurb, 'Over 1000 years older than any previously discovered manuscripts' is plainly wrong"!

19. I should note that Abegg, Flint, and Ulrich acknowledge that the term "Bible" is historically anachronistic and used uncritically to represent the works found at Qumran and that "there is little evidence that people were seriously asking the question yet about the extent or the limits of the collection—the crucial question for a 'Bible' or 'canon'—which books are *in* and which books are *outside* this most sacred collection. Thus, *The Dead Sea Scrolls Scriptures* may be a more historically accurate title for this volume. At any rate, it presents the remains of the books for which there is good evidence that Jews at that time viewed them as Sacred Scripture" (vii). I accept this explanation if they drop the definite article "The," which also obscures the actual finds at Qumran, but still it does not address the question of what is omitted from their book. Titling their work *Dead Sea Scrolls Scriptures* would be more accurate than the current title and better reflect the status of canon formation in the first centuries BCE and CE.

20. Ulrich, "Qumran Biblical Scrolls," 69–70.

21. The term *Hodayot* is given to a number of thanksgiving hymns discovered at Qumran. The title takes its name from the opening verb to the various hymns, "I thank you [O Lord]," usually with gratitude for knowledge or that the righteous will eventually overcome the trials facing them, and so on.

22. Jacob Neusner, *The Talmud: A Close Encounter* (Minneapolis: Fortress, 1991), 174.

23. De Jonge, "Old Testament in the Pseudepigrapha," 478.

24. M. Broshi argues this point in "What Jesus Learned from the Essenes: The Blessing of Poverty and the Bane of Divorce," *Biblical Archaeology Review* 30, no. 2 (2004): 32–37, 64. He makes a very good case and also acknowledges that this influence likely comes directly from John the Baptist, who may have grown up in such a community.

25. So argues Armin Lange, "The Status of the Biblical Texts in the Qumran Corpus and the Canonical Process," in *Bible as Book: Hebrew Bible*, ed. Herbert and Tov, 23. See also James VanderKam, *Dead Sea Scrolls Today* (Grand Rapids: Eerdmans, 1994), 154–55.

26. I owe these observations to Lange, "Status of the Biblical Texts," 23.

27. So Tov, "Biblical Texts from the Judaean Desert," 159.

28. Lange, "Status of the Biblical Texts," 23–24.

29. Bastiaan Van Elderen, "Early Christian Libraries," in *The Bible as Book: The Manuscript Tradition*, ed. John L. Sharpe III and Kimberly Van Kampen (London: British Library, 1998), 45–59, here 46–47.

30. Ibid., 47.

31. Ibid., 51–56. I will survey the NT collection in chapter 8 below.

32. The numbers attached to these manuscripts do not suggest their date, but rather the order of their discovery or what was perceived as their significance. Most of the 310 uncial manuscripts are fragmentary, containing only one or more books. These first three manuscripts are considered the most important biblical manuscripts from the fourth and fifth centuries because all were produced to include all the received sacred texts at that time.

33. Observe the order or sequence of these books in these three major manuscripts. The variety of sequence shows that at this time (fourth and fifth centuries CE) the order of the biblical books had not yet been fixed in the churches. I will say more about this below.

34. Sanders, *From Sacred Story*, 127–47, 175–90, explains that it was not the cultus or the monarchy or anything other than a story of Israel's life and heritage, wrapped up in the call of Yahweh, that gave Israel its identity and the incentive to continue its existence in the face of overwhelming odds.

35. The dating of these events and the conflict that ensued is summarized in Cross, *From Epic to Canon*, 188–89.

36. Ulrich, "Qumran Biblical Scrolls," 75–76.

37. R. Anderson, "Samaritans," *ABD* 5:946.

38. James D. Purvis, "The Samaritans and Judaism," in *Early Judaism and Its Modern Interpreters*, ed. R. A. Kraft and G. W. E. Nickelsburg (Atlanta: Scholars Press, 1986), 90–92. See also idem, *The Samaritan Pentateuch and the Origin of the Samaritan Sect*, Harvard Semitic Monographs 2 (Cambridge: Harvard University Press, 1968).

39. Cited by R. Anderson, "Samaritan Literature," *Dictionary of New Testament Background*, ed. C. A. Evans and S. E. Porter (Downers Grove, IL: InterVarsity Press, 2000), 1053.

40. B. K. Waltke, "Samaritan Pentateuch," *ABD* 5:938–39.

41. Emanuel Tov, "The Nature of the Large-Scale Differences between the LXX and MT, S, T, V, Compared with Similar Evidence in Other Sources," in

The Earliest Text of the Hebrew Bible: The Relationship between the Masoretic Text and the Hebrew Base of the Septuagint Reconsidered, ed. Adrian Schenker, SBLSCS 52 (Atlanta: Society of Biblical Literature, 2003), 121–43, here 133–34. He illustrates this with the change in the Samaritan Pentateuch when its producers rewrote the Decalogue in Exod. 20 and Deut. 5 by producing a sectarian tenth commandment that refers to the sanctity of Mount Gerizim.

42. I discuss the significance of this number and its relation to the Hebrew alphabet in McDonald, *Biblical Canon*, 150–69.

43. Louis Feldman, Daniel Silver, Sid Leiman, and F. M. Cross. See McDonald, *Biblical Canon*, 151–58, for a discussion of their interpretation of Josephus. Louis H. Feldman, *Studies in Josephus' Rewritten Bible*. Supplements to Journal for the Study of Judaism (Leiden: Brill, 1998). Sid Leiman, "Josephus and the Canon of the Bible," *Josephus, The Bible, and History*, ed. L. H. Feldman and G. Hata (Detroit: Wayne State University Press, 1989), 50–58. Daniel J. Silver, *The Story of Scripture: From Oral Tradition to the Written Word* (New York: Basic, 1990). F. M. Cross, *From Epic to Canon: History and Literature in the Ancient World* (Baltimore: Johns Hopkins University Press, 1995).

44. See 1 Macc. 4:46; 9:27; and 14:41; Josephus, *Ag. Ap.* 1.37–41; *2 Bar.* 85.3; *Seder Olam Rabbah* 30; and especially *t. Sotah* 13:2. We see a similar view in later rabbinic texts such as *b. Yoma* 9b, *Sotah* 48b and 11a–b.

45. Schürer, *History of the Jewish People*, 3.1:478–79.

46. Ibid.

47. The translation of this text comes from Sid Z. Leiman, The *Canonization of Hebrew Scripture: The Talmudic and Midrashic Evidence* (Hamden, CT: Archon, 1976), 52–53.

48. Cross, *From Epic to Canon*, 217–22, makes this suggestion. He also cites *b. Sukkah* 20a: "When the Torah was forgotten in Israel, Ezra came up from Babylon and established it [*wysdh*]; and when it was once again forgotten, Hillel the Babylonian came up and reestablished it [*wysdh*]" (trans. by Cross, ibid., 217).

49. A useful collection of these examples is in appendix 4, Loci citati vel allegati, in Barbara Aland et al., 770–806, especially 800–806. I have also collated them in an NT canonical order in McDonald, *Biblical Canon*, 452–64.

50. Howard Clark Kee offers a useful summary of the apocryphal books in early Christianity in *Cambridge Annotated Study Apocrypha* (Cambridge: Cambridge University Press, 1994), xiii–xvi. There are also helpful introductions to each of the apocryphal books (xvii–xxxii). There is a significant error on p. xiii, where Kee states that the LXX as reported in the *Letter of Aristeas* included all the books of the Hebrew canon plus the books of the Apocrypha. That translation originally included only the Pentateuch. Kee also mentions that the HB canon was closed at the Council of Yavneh (Jamnia) ca. 100 CE (p. xiii), but canon scholars now regularly reject it as the date for the closing of the HB canon. In general, however, the summary is very useful and clearly presented. Also, there is continuing value for reading about the Jewish apocryphal and pseudepigraphal books in the dated but still relevant volume by Henry B. Swete, *An Introduction to the Old Testament in Greek*, rev. R. R. Ottley (Cambridge: Cambridge University Press, 1914), especially 265–88.

51. Bruce M. Metzger, "Introduction to the Apocryphal/Deuterocanonical Books," in *The New Oxford Annotated Bible with the Apocryphal/Deuterocanonical Books*, New Revised Standard Version, ed. Bruce M. Metzger and Roland E. Murphy (New York: Oxford University Press, 1991), viii–xi.

52. This designation is technically reserved for the Pentateuch alone, but in time the Greek translation of the Pentateuch broadened to include the rest of the books of the HB as well as other books accredited in the Roman Catholic and Eastern Orthodox traditions.

Chapter Five

1. John F. A. Sawyer, *Sacred Languages and Sacred Texts* (London: Routledge, 1999), 76–80, discusses this practice among ancient religious people.

2. Ibid., 82–85. Sawyer has several explanations of this besides the desire to evangelize, namely to overcome a prejudice against the Aramaic dialect of Jesus' followers and the need to distinguish themselves from their Jewish siblings.

3. Lee Martin McDonald, *The Biblical Canon: Its Origin, Transmission, and Authority* (Peabody, MA: Hendrickson, 2006), 119–21.

4. The traditional name given to the Greek translation of the Jewish sacred scriptures is the Septuagint (LXX), which should technically be applied only to the Pentateuch, though it is commonly used as a reference to the whole Greek Bible. The term supposedly derives from the tradition in the *Letter of Aristeas* that seventy-two translators worked on the translation. Edward Lohse, *The New Testament Environment*, trans. John E. Steely (Nashville: Abingdon, 1976), 129, suggests that the number seventy-two was simply rounded off to seventy, but it is also quite possible that the number derives from the tradition of the seventy elders who accompanied Moses to Mount Sinai when he received the law from Yahweh on tablets of stone (Exod. 24:1, 9); see Helmut Koester, *Introduction to the New Testament*, 2nd ed., 2 vols. (New York: de Gruyter, 1995–2000), 1:252; J. W. Wevers, "Septuagint," *Interpreter's Dictionary of the Bible*, ed. G. A. Buttrick, 4 vols. (New York: Abingdon, 1962), 4:273; and A. R. C. Leaney, *The Jewish and Christian World, 200 B.C. to A.D. 200*, Cambridge Commentaries 7 (Cambridge: Cambridge University Press, 1984), 153. If this is the case, then the use of the term "Septuagint" could well be an acknowledgment of the early belief in the divinely inspired status of the translation, that is, it authentically and faithfully conveyed the full intent of the law given to Moses. The number seventy-two is elusive, however, and could be a reference to the seventy elders of Israel plus Moses and Joshua who went up to the mountain to receive the law (Exod. 24:13). This is speculative, but a parallel is mentioned in the legend of the preservation of the works of Homer by the seventy-two grammarians under the direction of Peisistratus ca. 550–525 BCE. It is not certain which tradition came first, Aristeas or Peisistratus's recension of Homer. See discussion of this below.

5. The author of the *Letter of Aristeas* may allude to previous translations of the Law into Greek. He infers that earlier attempts were inadequate versions of the Law (*Let. Aris.* 314). It is also possible that v. 30 speaks of an earlier and inferior translation of the Jewish Law into Greek, but scholars debate this. The text there reads: "Scrolls of the Law of the Jews, together with a few others, are missing (from the library), for these (works) are written in Hebrew characters and language. But they have been *transcribed* [the Greek here, *sesēmantai*, is uncertain and possibly means "interpreted" or "translated"] somewhat carelessly and not as they should be, according to the report of the experts, because they have not received royal patronage" (*OTP* 2:14–15, italics supplied). This interpretation of *Aristeas* is highly debated, and may not be correct, but it does seem to fit the context of the letter.

6. Natalio Fernández Marcos, *The Septuagint in Context: Introduction to the Greek Versions of the Bible*, trans. W. G. E. Watson (Leiden: Brill, 2000), 40–41, suggests that this document best fits between those two dates, but the latest possible times are ca. 35 CE, when Philo refers to the Aristeas tradition (*Mos.* 2:32–40).

7. See *Commentarius Melampolis seu Dimomedis*, Cod. C, ed. Hilgard, pp. 29–30, = *Scholia Marciana* (VN), ed. Hilgard p. 316. Josephus also refers to the circulation of Homer by memory and in song (*Ag. Ap.* 1.13).

8. See Gregory Nagy, *Pindar's Homer: The Lyric Possession of an Epic Past* (Baltimore: Johns Hopkins University Press, 1990); and also his earlier work, *The Best of the Achaeans: Concepts of the Hero in Archaic Greek Poetry* (Baltimore: Johns Hopkins University Press, 1979). See also his *Homeric Questions* (Austin: University of Texas Press, 1996) and his more recent *Homer's Text and Language*, Traditions (Urbana: University of Illinois Press, 2004). This discussion is also researched at length in Jed Wyrick, *The Ascension of Authorship: Attribution and Canon Formation in Jewish, Hellenistic, and Christian Traditions* (Cambridge: Harvard University Press, 2004), 138–280.

9. Ernst Würthwein, *The Text of the Old Testament*, trans. E. F. Rhodes, 2nd ed. (Grand Rapids: Eerdmans, 1995), 52–78, especially 53–54, supports this view and suggests that the rest of the LXX is something of a Greek targum of the Hebrew Scriptures. It is often very loose in the translation, though parts are rather precise.

10. Ibid., 53–54.

11. *Scholia* (plural of Greek *scholion*, "note") refers to any critical notes, from one word to a commentary, on a text that were often written around the text in the margins in smaller and less formal script. The term used in this way is first found in Cicero (*Att.* 16.7.3). The Scholia to Dionysius Thrax currently dates to the sixth or seventh century CE, but the legend in it likely dates to the third to the fifth century CE, and some elements may have their origin in historical facts from the second century BCE or earlier.

   Aristarchus of Samothrace (ca. 216–144 BCE) became head librarian at Alexandria, teacher of Ptolemy VII, son of Ptolemy Philometor, and he produced a critical text and treatises on Homer's *Iliad* and *Odyssey*.

12. See Giuseppe Veltri, *Libraries, Translations, and 'Canonic' Texts: The Septuagint, Aquila and Ben Sira in the Jewish and Christian Traditions*, JSJSup 109 (Leiden: Brill, 2006), 79–89, for an interesting discussion of these parallels, including the later additions to the story that include the editing by the seventy-two grammarians. The legends about the LXX and Peisistratus's recension are strangely fused in Isidore of Seville's "On Libraries" and "On Translators" in his *Etymologies* 6.3.3–4).

13. Nina L. Collins presents the historical features of the legendary *Letter of Aristeas* in *The Library in Alexandria and the Bible in Greek* (Leiden: Brill, 2000).

14. This treatise was falsely attributed to Justin Martyr, so it is now called "Pseudo-Justin," but the author is unknown; he expands the tradition of *Aristeas* in his work.

15. Martin Hengel, *The Septuagint as Christian Scripture: Its Prehistory and the Problem of Its Canon*, Old Testament Studies (Edinburgh: T & T Clark, 2002), 41.

16. What follows here is largely dependent on the work of Bruce M. Metzger, *The Bible in Translation: Ancient and English Versions* (Grand Rapids: Baker Academic, 2001), 25–51, especially in the Syriac, Latin, Coptic, Gothic, Armenian, and Arabic versions.

17. Translation by R. J. H. Shutt, *OTP* 2:14–15. The notes on this text in *OTP* do not agree with my conclusions here, but the context seems to demand it especially in light of v. 314 that refers to "previously translated passages from the Law" (*OTP* 2:33). I should also note that this translation includes the first time that the term "Bible" was applied to the OT scriptures; see v. 316, which refers to Theodectus, the tragic poet, who was about to include a passage from "what is written in the *Bible*" (see *OTP* 2:34).

18. Craig A. Evans, *Ancient Texts for New Testament Studies: A Guide to the Background Literature* (Peabody, MA: Hendrickson, 2005), 185–215, has a useful

and careful summary of the various targumim and the recent debates about their relevance for NT studies.

19. See Jacob Neusner, "Targums in the New Testament," *Dictionary of Judaism in the Biblical Period: 450 B.C.E. to 600 C.E.*, ed. Jacob Neusner, 2 vols. (New York: Macmillan, 1996), 2:616.

20. Daniel Sperber, "Targum," *Oxford Dictionary of the Jewish Religion*, ed. R. J. Zwi Werblowsky and Geoffrey Wigoder (New York: Oxford University Press, 1997), 675–76.

21. The Syriac word *peshitta* ("simple" or "common") is the term given to the collection of Jewish and Christian scriptures. By the end of the second century CE, Christian writings were added to this collection and Christians largely oversaw the continuing transmission and preservation of these scriptures.

22. This view is advocated by M. P. Weitzman, *The Syriac Version of the Old Testament: An Introduction* (Cambridge: Cambridge University Press, 1999), 1. Metzger also makes this observation in *The Bible in Translation*, 26–29.

23. Metzger, *Bible in Translation*, 26.

24. Ibid., 28.

25. Ibid., 25–29.

26. Ibid., 30.

27. Augustine, *On Christian Doctrine* 2.16, cited by Metzger, ibid., 31.

28. Some of the most important manuscript finds in Egypt, such as the Chester Beatty collection now in Dublin and the Martin Bodmer collection now in Cologny-Geneva, are in the Sahidic Coptic dialect.

29. Metzger, *Bible in Translation*, 42.

30. The data come from R. W. Cowley, "The Biblical Canon of the Ethiopian Church Today," *Ostkirchliche Studien* 23 (1974): 318–23.

31. Besides these versions, Metzger, *Bible in Translation*, 38–51, goes on to discuss the Gothic version, which rejected Samuel and Kings, the Georgian version, the Arabic versions, the Old Slavonic version, and the Nubian version, but for our purposes, the ones described above more than make our point about the various books that were included in the ancient translations.

Chapter Six

1. The value and content of these texts and translations are described in Ernst Würthwein, *The Text of the Old Testament*, trans. E. F. Rhodes, 2nd ed. (Grand Rapids: Eerdmans, 1995), 10–106.

2. It is well to remember that the various antecedents, or Vorlage, of the Greek translations are also important in establishing the earliest text of the Hebrew scriptures. In the middle of the third century CE, Origen included in his Hexapla a *Greek* text that is known as the *Quinta* and *Sexta* (5th and 6th columns). The Quinta reflects *probably* the so-called Kaige-Theodotian revision, and is an important source for establishing the Hebrew text. See E. Tov, *Textual Criticism of the Hebrew Bible*, 145–47.

3. The work thus far has been published as *The Hebrew University Bible: The Book of Isaiah*, ed. Moshe H. Goshen-Gottstein (Jerusalem: Magnes, 1995); and *The Hebrew University Bible: The Book of Jeremiah*, ed. C. Rabin, S. Talmon, and E. Tov (Jerusalem: Magnes, 1997).

4. The text and the history of this manuscript and its description are now available online at www.aleppocodex.org.

5. For a brief history of this famous text, see Yosef Ofer, "The Shattered Crown: The Aleppo Codex 60 Years After the Riots," *BAR* 34, no. 5 (2008): 39–49; and the summarizing description in Würthwein, *Text of the Old Testament*, 36.

6. Ulrich, "The Qumran Biblical Scrolls—The Scriptures of Late Second Temple Judaism," in *The Dead Sea Scrolls in Their Historical Context*, ed. Timothy Lim (Edinburgh: T & T Clark, 2000), 67–87, here 69–70.

7. As noted in chap. 3, Geza Vermes coined the widely used term "Rewritten Bible" in "Bible Interpretation at Qumran," *ErIsr* 20 (1989): 184–91, but the term has come under considerable challenge in more recent years. For a careful discussion of the use of rewritten or reworked biblical texts, see Sidnie White Crawford, *Rewriting Scripture in Second Temple Times*, SDSSRL (Grand Rapids: Eerdmans, 2008); and also George J. Brooke, "Rewritten Bible," in *EDSS* 2:777–81; idem, "The Rewritten Law, Prophets and Psalms: Issues for Understanding the Text of the Bible," in *The Bible as Book: The Hebrew Bible and the Judaean Desert Discoveries*, ed. Edward D. Herbert and Emanuel Tov (London: British Library, 2002), 31–40.

8. See Esther G. Chazon, Devorah Dimant, and Ruth A. Clements, eds., *Reworking the Bible: Apocryphal and Related Texts at Qumran*, Studies on the Texts of the Desert of Judah 58 (Leiden: Brill, 2005); Daniel K. Falk, *The Parabiblical Texts: Strategies for Extending the Scriptures among the Dead Sea Scrolls*, Library of Second Temple Studies 63 (London: T & T Clark International, 2007). See my review of this volume in *RBL* 07/2008.

9. See his *Rewriting the Sacred Text: What the Old Greek Texts Tell Us about the Literary Growth of the Bible*, Text-Critical Studies 4 (Atlanta: Society of Biblical Literature, 2003).

10. Yigael Yadin, "The Temple Scroll—The Longest and Most Recently Discovered Dead Sea Scroll," in *Archaeology and the Bible: The Best of BAR*, vol. 2: *Archaeology in the World of Herod, Jesus and Paul*, ed. Hershel Shanks and Dan P. Cole (Washington, DC: Biblical Archaeology Society, 1990), 161–77. See also his most extensive work, and still the standard resource on the book, *The Temple Scroll*, 3 vols. (Jerusalem: Israel Exploration Society, 1977–1983).

11. Yadin, "Temple Scroll," 168.

12. Ibid., 172.

13. Falk, *Parabiblical Texts*, 152–53.

14. Again, see Falk's useful discussion of these categories in the introduction to his work in ibid., 1–25.

15. Brooke, "Rewritten Law, Prophets and Psalms," in *Bible as Book: Hebrew Bible*, ed. Herbert and Tov, 31–40. See also his more recent "Between Authority and Canon: The Significance of Reworking the Bible for Understanding the Canonical Process," in *Reworking the Bible: Apocryphal and Related Texts at Qumran*, ed. Esther G. Chazon, Devorah Dimant, and Ruth A. Clements (Leiden/Boston: Brill, 2005), 85–104.

16. H. Gregory Snyder, *Teachers and Texts in the Ancient World: Philosophers, Jews, and Christians*, Religion in the First Christian Centuries (London: Routledge, 2000), 151; see also his discussion on 151–89.

17. Daniel J. Silver, *The Story of Scripture* (New York: Basic Books, 1990), 136–41.

18. Tov, "Scribal Practices Reflected in the Texts from the Judean Desert," in *The Dead Sea Scrolls after Fifty Years: A Comprehensive Assessment*, ed. P. W. Flint and J. C. VanderKam (Leiden: Brill, 1998), 424.

19. B. Barry Levy, *Fixing God's Torah: The Accuracy of the Hebrew Bible Text in Jewish Law* (Oxford: Oxford University Press, 2001), 4.

20. "Scribal Practices," 425.

21. Ibid., 426. See also idem, "Scribal Practices Reflected in the Paleo-Hebrew Texts from the Judean Desert," *Scripta Classica Israelica* 15 (1996): 268–73.

22. The terms come from the Hebrew verb *masar*, "hand down" and here it is probably a reference to "those who hand down." In the technical sense, the

Masorah refers to the apparatus for the writing and reading of the biblical text. The MT is based on the biblical text that was "handed down" over the centuries by the various schools of the Masoretes. There appears to be no consensus on the full meaning of "Masorah." Some have suggested that the term, which is used in *m. Abot* 3.14, comes from the famous Rabbi Aqiba, "The tradition is a fence around the Law" (H. Danby, *The Mishnah* [Oxford: Oxford University Press, 1933], 452). The text in some witnesses is: *masoret seyag la-tora*, meaning, "masoret is a fence around the Torah." For this explanation, see Levy, *Fixing God's Torah*, 14.

23. See "Masorah," *Dictionary of Judaism in the Biblical Period: 450 B.C.E. to 600 C.E.*, ed. Jacob Neusner, 2 vols. (New York: Macmillan, 1996), 2:415.

24. *Vorlage* is a German term meaning an antecedent, model, or prototype. Here and throughout this chapter *Vorlage* is a technical term that refers to the earlier Hebrew text that the translators of the LXX used to produce their translation of the Torah/Pentateuch.

25. Harold P. Scanlin, "Text, Truth and Tradition: The Public's View of the Bible in the Light of the Dead Sea Scrolls," in *Bible as Book: Hebrew Bible*, ed. Herbert and Tov, 295–96.

26. Tov, *Textual Criticism*, 101.

27. These examples are taken from the translations of H. N. Bialik and Y. H. Ravnitzky, eds. *The Book of Legends: Sefer Ha-Aggadah: Legends from the Talmud and Midrash*, trans. William G. Brande (New York: Schocken, 1992), 448.

28. Emil Schürer, *The History of the Jewish People in the Age of Jesus Christ (175 B.C.–A.D. 135)*, ed. Geza Vermes, Fergus Millar, and Martin Goodman (Edinburgh: T & T Clark, 1986), 3.1:480–81.

29. A group of Jewish scholars known as the Masorah or Masoretes (Hebrew *masoret*, "that which is handed down" or "tradition") possibly ca. 500–950 CE, but more likely around 700–800 CE, developed various signs and notes to enable them to preserve a careful transmission and preservation of the text of the Hebrew Scriptures. Of the three Masoretic communities—the Palestinian, the Babylonian, and the Tiberian—the last had the greatest impact on the preservation of the text of the Hebrew Bible. The pointing of the Hebrew Bible does not date much before 650–750 CE, since nothing is said about pointing the Hebrew text of scripture in the Babylonian Talmud (completed ca. 600 CE). The Masoretes preserved the consonantal text for the rabbinic Jews that likely dated perhaps from the first century BCE and also the vowels and accents in the text. The primary texts that have survived from their work are the Aleppo (900–950 CE) and the Leningrad (1008 CE) codices—which are still vitally important in establishing the earliest text of the Hebrew Bible. For a careful description of the Masoretes and the manuscripts they produced, see Ernst Würthwein, *The Text of the Old Testament*, trans. E. F. Rhodes, 2nd ed. (Grand Rapids: Eerdmans, 1995), 28–38.

30. This is discussed convincingly by Emanuel Tov in "The Status of the Masoretic Text Editions of the Hebrew Bible: The Relevance of Canon," in *The Canon Debate*, ed. L. M. McDonald and J. A. Sanders (Peabody, MA: Hendrickson, 2000), 234–51.

31. Tov, *Textual Criticism*, 11. His argument is based on the mistakes, changes, and corrections in the various textual witnesses to the MT (see 8–12).

32. E. Tov, "The Nature of the Large-Scale Differences between the LXX and MT S T V, Compared with Similar Evidence in Other Sources," in *The Earliest Text of the Hebrew Bible: The Relationship between the Masoretic Text and the Hebrew Base of the Septuagint Reconsidered*, ed. Adrian Schenker, SBLSCS 52 (Atlanta: Society of Biblical Literature, 2003), 121.

33. Ibid., 121–22, 142.
34. Ibid. 127–39. Tov makes clear that those who produced the LXX used none of the MT manuscripts, and he shows how at times the Dead Sea Scrolls manuscripts are closer to the text of the LXX than to the MT.
35. Ibid., 143 n. 64. Not everyone agrees completely with Tov on these points, but Natalio Fernández Marcos agrees substantially with him on the variations in the texts of the Hebrew Bible present in Second Temple times. He states that many of the LXX variants from the MT may go back to the Hebrew *Vorlage* of the LXX that Marcos claims "is earlier than the standardization of the consonantal text" that began in the second century with the rabbis. See the useful discussions in *The Septuagint in Context: Introduction to the Greek Versions of the Bible* (Leiden: Brill, 2000), 76; and also his discussion of the transmission and textual history of the LXX on 191–236.
36. Tov, *Textual Criticism*, 195. See also his helpful collection of comparisons between the LXX and the MT in "A Computerized Database for Septuagint Research," in *The Greek and Hebrew Bible: Collected Essays on the Septuagint*, VTSup 72 (Leiden: Brill, 1999), 31–40; also his discussion on "The Contribution of the Qumran Scrolls to the Understanding of the Septuagint," 285–300. He observes that less than 5 percent of the biblical texts discovered at Qumran reflect the *Vorlage* of the LXX and that the Hebrew scrolls from which the LXX was translated in Egypt have not been found at Qumran, despite some of the similarities here and there in a few manuscripts. He adds, "Since many, if not most, of the biblical texts of the third and second centuries BCE were unique, they should be sought only in Egypt itself, even though they were originally imported to Egypt from Palestine" (300).
37. Tov, "The Biblical Texts from the Judean Desert," in *Bible as Book: Hebrew Bible*, ed. Herbert and Tov, 143.
38. Shemaryahu Talmon, "The Crystallization of the 'Canon of Hebrew Scriptures,'" in *Bible as Book: Hebrew Bible*, ed. Herbert and Tov, 5–20, here 11.
39. See, e.g., Beckwith, *Old Testament Canon*, 274–77. James VanderKam offers a careful critique of Beckwith, as well as of Sid Leiman, *Canonization of Hebrew Scripture*, 120–24, in *From Revelation to Canon: Studies in the Hebrew Bible and Second Temple Literature*, JSJSup 62 (Boston: Brill, 2002), 11–30.
40. VanderKam, *From Revelation to Canon*, 17.
41. Talmon, "Crystallization," 10–12, and 15.
42. The Karaite Jews (scripturalists) were a religious sect of Judaism in Babylonia founded by Anan ben David in the mid-to-late eighth century CE who claimed to establish the original form of Judaism. They are nontalmudic, that is, they do not follow the prescriptions of the rabbinic sages who taught the Mishnah and its implications for living. This sect of Jews still exists today, but their time of greatest influence was in the late ninth to eleventh centuries.
43. *Genizah* is a Hebrew and Aramaic term meaning "to store" or "to hide" and is used for a special storage place in synagogues for old sacred manuscripts that contained the sacred name of God. The oldest text to speak of the *genizah* is found in *m. Shabbat* 16:1: "In no matter what language they [the Holy Scriptures] are written [if they become unfit for use] they require to be hidden away [*genizah*]. . . . Whither should they be taken for safety? To an alley-way that is no thoroughfare" (Danby trans.).
44. A colophon (Greek *kolophon*, "finish" or "end") is usually a note at the end of a book indicating the date or location of the production, and sometimes authorship or other details of the scribe thought important to communicate. Many ancient manuscripts have them.
45. Yosef Ofer, "Shattered Crown," 42–44.

46. *The Leningrad Codex: A Facsimile Edition*, ed. D. N. Freedman (Grand Rapids: Eerdmans, 1998).

47. In the famous Rabbinic Bible of 1524/1525 CE published by Rabbi Jacob ben Chayyim, the rabbi used a medieval collection of notes called *Okhla weOkhla* that begins with an alphabetical list of words occurring only one time in the Scriptures. It derives its name from the Hebrew letters in 1 Sam. 1:9 and Gen. 27:19.

48. I have largely followed here the texts described by Würthwein, *Text of the Old Testament*, 30–38; but also Tov, *Textual Criticism*, 21–154.

49. Tov, *Textual Criticism*, 111.

50. This translation is from Levy, *Fixing God's Torah*, 7. Of notable interest is his quote on p. 97 of Rabbi Joel Sirkes (1561–1640), who says of this procedure, "In regard to an error in the word *ha-hi'* that is written with a *yod* in place of the *waw* [i.e., which should be spelled *hhw'* but is spelled *hhy'* and modifies a feminine noun], not one person in the world who has a brain in his head would agree to take out another [scroll] because of an error of this sort"!

51. Ibid., 8.

52. The term *diaspora* (Greek = "dispersion" or "scattered abroad") was first used as a reference to Jews living in exile in Babylon (Jer. 28:6; 2 Chr. 36:20), but eventually was used in reference to Jews who lived outside of the Land of Israel. Among the rabbis, the Hebrew term *galut* (exiles) was used often with theological implications and also in a negative sense of those exiles living in captivity outside of Israel, but more generally, it was simply a reference to Jews living outside of the Land of Israel.

53. Schürer, *History of the Jewish People*, 3.1:478–79.

54. See *A New English Translation of the Septuagint*, ed. Albert Pietersma and Benjamin G. Wright (New York: Oxford University Press, 2007). A group of Greek scholars led by Stanley E. Porter have begun preparing a commentary on the Old Testament that focuses on the LXX Greek text.

55. Alfred Rahfls and Robert Hanhart, eds., *Septuaginta*, rev. ed. (Stuttgart: Deutsche Bibelgesellschaft, 2006). Robert Hanhart revised slightly the 1935 edition prepared by Alfred Rahlfs that was initially published by the Privilegierte Württembergische Bibelanstalt in Stuttgart, Germany.

56. The uncial manuscripts include the Ephraemi Rescriptus (C), Cottonianus (D), Ambrosianus (F), Colberto-Sarravianus (G), Purpureus Vindobonensis (L), Coislinianus (M), Marchalianus, Vat. Gr. 2125 (Q), Veronensis (R), Turicensis (T), Venetus (V), Freer Mss (W). The minuscule manuscripts most frequently appealed to include 393, 911, 1098, and 2013.

57. Bastiaan Van Elderen has provided a useful summary of this collection of manuscripts in "Early Christian Libraries," in *The Bible as Book: The Manuscript Tradition*, ed. John L. Sharpe III and Kimberly Van Kampen (London: British Library, 1998), 45–59.

58. M. H. Segal, "The Promulgation of the Authoritative Text of the Hebrew Bible," *JBL* 72 (1953): 35–47.

59. Ibid., 38.

60. Ibid., 39.

61. Ibid., 43–44.

62. Ibid., 45–46.

63. Various views on the formation of the twelve books of the Minor Prophets are discussed in Barry Alan Jones, *The Formation of the Book of the Twelve: A Study in Text and Canon*, SBLDS 149 (Atlanta: Scholars Press, 1995), 1–42.

64. J. K. Elliott, "Manuscripts, the Codex, and the Canon," *JSNT* 63 (1996): 117–19.

65. See H. B. Swete, *An Introduction to the Old Testament in Greek* (Cambridge: Cambridge University Press, 1902), 200–214. See also H. P. Rüger, "The Extent of the Old Testament Canon," *Bible Translator* 40 (1989): 301–8, for lists of OT books. See also H. St. J. Thackeray, *The Septuagint and Jewish Worship*, 2nd ed. (London: Oxford University Press, 1923).

66. See the various locations of Job in the collections or catalogues in McDonald, *Biblical Canon*, 439–44.

67. Stephen B. Chapman, "How the Biblical Canon Began: Working Models and Open Questions," in *Homer, the Bible, and Beyond: Literary and Religious Canons in the Ancient World*, ed. Margalit Finkelberg and Guy G. Stroumsa (Leiden: Brill, 2003), 29–52, argues against the traditional threefold development of the HB. He also seems to be saying that the biblical texts were acknowledged as canonical—which seems to mean as religiously authoritative—before they were placed into their various divisions.

68. See Chapman, "How the Biblical Canon Began," 48–49. While I agree with his conclusion, I am not certain that he has clarified the picture a great deal, since he leaves the relationship between canon and text rather open, acknowledging that they are related "in some way" (49). He acknowledges—correctly—that at Qumran there does not appear to have been either a fixed text or a fixed list of canonical books (ibid.).

Chapter Seven

1. This chapter is in several parts a revision of a chapter in the forthcoming volume, James H. Charlesworth and Gerbern S. Oegema, eds., *The Pseudepigrapha and Christian Origins: Essays from the Studiorum Novi Testamenti Societas* (Edinburgh: T & T Clark, 2009).

2. R. T. Beckwith, "Canon of the Hebrew Bible and the Old Testament," in *The Oxford Companion to the Bible*, ed. Bruce M. Metzger and Michael D. Coogan (New York: Oxford University Press, 1993), 100–102, here 102.

3. In what follows, I will use the terms "canonical" and "noncanonical" to identify literature that did or did not find a place in the current HB or Protestant OT, but those terms are admittedly anachronistic and imposed *back* on writings that had no such designation in the time of Jesus. See chapter 2 for a discussion of such terms. I will use those terms in what follows for the sake of identifying the literature that makes up the Bible and the literature that was not accepted *later* as canonical literature in the churches, but again, they are understood here as anachronistic terms and foreign to the context of early Christianity or early Judaism.

4. *From Revelation to Canon: Studies in the Hebrew Bible and Second Temple Literature* (Boston: Brill, 2002), 2. We should also note that there is a distinction between "canon" and "scripture." While the former presumes the existence of the latter, the reverse is not true. Many ancient writings were acknowledged as sacred texts (scripture) well before they were placed in an unchangeable biblical canon.

5. Richard Bauckham's new volume, *Jesus and the Eyewitnesses: The Gospels as Eyewitness Testimony* (Grand Rapids: Eerdmans, 2006), makes a very strong case for this point.

6. These extracanonical sayings are identified and discussed in Joachim Jeremias, *Unknown Sayings of Jesus*, trans. Reginald H. Fuller (London: SPCK, 1964); W. D. Stroker, *Extracanonical Sayings of Jesus*, SBLRBS 18 (Atlanta: Scholars Press, 1989); as well as Otfried Hofius, "Unknown Sayings of Jesus," in *New Testament Apocrypha*, ed. Wilhelm Schneemelcher, rev. ed., 2 vols. (Louisville, KY: Westminster/John Knox, 1991–1992), 1:88–91; and idem, "Isolated

Sayings of Jesus," in *The Gospel and the Gospels*, ed. P. Stuhlmacher (Grand Rapids: Eerdmans, 1991), 336–60; and J. H. Charlesworth and C. A. Evans, "Jesus in the Agrapha and Apocryphal Gospels," in *Studying the Historical Jesus: Evaluations of the State of Current Research*, ed. B. Chilton and C. Evans (Leiden: Brill, 1994), 479–533.

7. Compare Mark 1:2 with Matt. 3:3 and Luke 3:4. In other places they chose to smooth out, change, or even soften Mark's story (cf. Mark 1:10 with Matt. 3:16 and Luke 3:22; cf. Mark 8:29 with Matt. 16:16 and Luke 9:20). See also Mark's description of Herod Antipas (cf. Mark 1:10 with Matt. 14:1; etc.) and Jesus' family concerns about his stability and his seeming disrespect for his family (cf. Mark 3:21 and 33–34 with Matt. 12:49 and Luke 8:21). Mark refers to Jesus as "teacher" (Mark 4:38), while Matthew calls him "Lord" (Matt. 8:25) and Luke calls him "master" (Luke 8:24).

8. I reject the radical application of the so-called criterion of dissimilarity. It is often used not only to isolate the unique aspects of Jesus' teachings, but more frequently, by some in the Jesus Seminar and others, to reject elements of Jesus' teachings that are similar to Jewish and early Christian teaching. That criterion wrongly assumes in practice that those closest to Jesus had little interest in preserving his teachings. No doubt there were many modifications and expansions of the Jesus tradition in early Christianity, but assuming that there was little interest in his story, as the radical application of this criterion suggests, invites deserved criticism. Likewise, one may reasonably assume that since Jesus was a Jew, his teachings and practices would overlap with some sect or sects of Judaism in the first century CE. What some members of the Jesus Seminar discovered through the application of this criterion is a *unique* Jesus, but certainly not the *typical* Jesus, who was both Jewish and revered and remembered by his followers. An excellent discussion of this subject is in Birger Gerhardsson, *Memory and Manuscript: Oral Tradition and Written Transmission in Rabbinic Judaism and Early Christianity* with *Tradition and Transmission in Early Christianity*, Biblical Resource Series (Grand Rapids: Eerdmans, 1998). See also Bauckham, *Jesus and the Eyewitnesses*, 264–89.

9. See J. A. Sanders, J. H. Charlesworth, and H. Rietz, "Non-Masoretic Psalms," in *Pseudepigraphic and Non-Masoretic Psalms and Prayers*, ed. Charlesworth with Henry W. Rietz, Princeton Theological Seminary Dead Sea Scrolls Project 4A (Louisville, KY: Westminster John Knox, 1997), 1:25–36, here 32.

10. Roger Beckwith, *The Old Testament Canon of the New Testament Church* (Grand Rapids: Eerdmans, 1985), 7–8.

11. Ibid., 387.

12. See Lee Martin McDonald, *The Biblical Canon: Its Origin, Transmission, and Authority* (Peabody, MA: Hendrickson, 2006), 191–94. For further evidence that *1 Enoch* was recognized as scripture both in Jude and also in early Christianity, see VanderKam, *From Revelation to Canon*, 16–27.

13. No one seriously doubts that Jesus made use of this psalm at his crucifixion. It is not the kind of text the early church would have placed in the mouth of Jesus without some historical basis, since it appears to report Jesus' loss of faith. For an old but still interesting interpretation of the meaning of the passage, however, see Martin Dibelius, *From Tradition to Gospel*, trans. Bertram Lee Woolf (repr. Cambridge: James Clarke, 1982), 193–94, who claims that the reference to the first verse of this psalm was in fact a reference to the whole of it.

14. M. H. Segal, *Sefer Ben-Sirah ha-Shalem* (Jerusalem: Bialik, 1953), cites eighty-five citations of Sirach in rabbinic literature through the tenth century CE. See also Solomon Schechter, "The Quotations from Ecclesiasticus in Rabbinic Literature," *Jewish Quarterly Review* 3 (1890–91), 682–706.

15. The following translations are taken from the NRSV (apocryphal books) and the OTP (pseudepigraphal books). The NT translations are from the NRSV.

16. Added to this list are some parallels mentioned in Peter Stuhlmacher, "The Significance of the Old Testament Apocrypha and Pseudepigrapha for the Understanding of Jesus and Christology," in *The Apocrypha in Ecumenical Perspective*, ed. Siegfried Meurer, trans. Paul Ellingworth, UBS Monograph Series 6 (New York: United Bible Societies, 1991), 8–10. Stuhlmacher also notes the close parallels in Matt. 11:25–28 and the apocryphal Psalm 154 (11QPs^a 18.3–6).

17. See James H. Charlesworth, "The Books of Enoch or 1 Enoch Matters: New Paradigms for Understanding Pre–70 Judaism," in *Enoch and Qumran Origins: New Light on a Forgotten Connection*, ed. Gabrielle Boccaccini, ed. (Grand Rapids: Eerdmans, 2005), 436–54.

18. For a helpful discussion of the Enoch tradition at Qumran and the current status of the research on this subject, see the introduction and later summary of this discussion by Gabriele Boccaccini (1–14 and 417–25) and the summary chapter by James H. Charlesworth (436–54) in *Enoch and Qumran Origins*, ed. Boccaccini. See also James C. VanderKam, "1 Enoch, Enochic Motifs, and Enoch in Early Christian Literature," in *The Jewish Apocalyptic Heritage in Early Christianity*, ed. James C. VanderKam and William Adler, CRINT 3/4 (Minneapolis: Fortress, 1996), 33–101. See also VanderKam, *From Revelation to Canon*, 19–27, for several examples of the influence of the Enoch tradition both at Qumran and in early Christianity.

19. There are some 24 parallels in Matthew (e.g., 1:18–21 cf. *Jos. Asen.* 21:1; Matt. 5:13 cf. *Jos. Asen.* 11:4; Matt. 5:43–48 cf. *Jos. Asen.* 29:5; Matt. 6:19–21, cf. *Jos. Asen.* 12:15; Matt. 6:23 cf. *Jos. Asen.* 6:6); 23 in Mark (e.g., 1:10 cf. *Jos. Asen.* 14:2; Mark 1:17 cf. *Jos. Asen.* 21:21; Mark 6:3 cf. *Jos. Asen.* 4:10; Mark 10:21 cf. *Jos. Asen.* 10:11), 54 in Luke (e.g., 1:5 cf. *Jos. Asen.* 1:1; Luke 1:48 cf. *Jos. Asen.* 11:12; Luke 2:52 cf. *Jos. Asen.* 4:7; Luke 7:44 cf. *Jos. Asen.* 7:1; Luke 11:7 cf. *Jos. Asen.* 10:2; Luke 15:18 cf. *Jos. Asen.* 7:4), and 28 in John (e.g., 1:4 *Jos. Asen.* 12:2; John 1:10 cf. *Jos. Asen.* 12:2; John 1:27 cf. *Jos. Asen.* 12:5; John 3:5 cf. *Jos. Asen.* 8:9; John 13:23 cf. *Jos. Asen.* 10:4; John 20:22 cf. *Jos. Asen.* 19:11; John 20:28 cf. *Jos. Asen.* 22:3). See Steve Delamarter, *A Scripture Index to Charlesworth's The Old Testament Pseudepigrapha* (Sheffield: Sheffield Academic Press, 2002), 90–93, for the additional texts. He lists even more parallels throughout the rest of the NT.

20. For a discussion of the date of this document, see Ross Shepherd Kraemer, *When Aseneth Met Joseph: A Late Antique Tale of the Biblical Patriarch and His Egyptian Wife, Reconsidered* (New York: Oxford University Press, 1998), 5 and 225ff. He challenges the consensus on the date for Aseneth, namely 100 BCE–135 CE, saying there is no support for it and it is based on assumptions rather than fact. On the other hand, Gideon Bohak reviewed Kraemer's book in the *Review of Biblical Literature* [http://www.bookreviews.org] (2000) and concluded that Kraemer's arguments have not overturned the consensus. Bohak's book, *Joseph and Aseneth and the Jewish Temple in Heliopolis*, Society of Biblical Literature Early Judaism and Its Literature 10 (Atlanta: Scholars Press, 1996), presents the consensus position.

21. E. E. Ellis argues this way in *The Old Testament in Early Christianity: Canon and Interpretation in the Light of Modern Research* (Grand Rapids: Baker, 1991), 37–46 and 125–30; see also Beckwith, *Old Testament Canon*, 111–15 and 221–22.

22. The Greek does not include a definite article ("the") before "psalms," unlike before "law" and "prophets." While the law and the prophets may well have

had clear definition for some Jews in the first century CE, it does not appear to be so for the "psalms." The larger collection of psalms at Qumran in the first century BCE and CE suggests this.

23. Beckwith, *Old Testament Canon*, 111–15. For a related topic see also his discussion of "fifths" on 438–47.

24. See Lee Martin McDonald, *The Biblical Canon: Its Origin, Transmission, and Authority* (Peabody, MA: Hendrickson, 2006), 103–13.

25. For a careful discussion of the influence of rabbinic tradition on the Jews in the western Diaspora, see the significant contribution to this topic by Arye Edrei and Doron Mendels, "A Split Jewish Diaspora: Its Dramatic Consequences," *JSP* 16, no. 2 (2007): 91–137. They argue that the limits on the scope of the Jewish sacred literature in the rabbinic tradition did not reach western Jews for centuries afterward, and they continued to make use of the apocryphal and pseudepigraphal writings as well as the books of the HB. They also bring to our attention that there are only a handful of references in the Talmud to the Jews in the western Diaspora, and since those in the west spoke only Greek or Latin, they would not have had access to the Mishnah and the Talmudim, which were produced in Hebrew and not translated into Greek.

26. Sid Z. Leiman, *The Canonization of Hebrew Scripture: The Talmudic and Midrashic Evidence* (Hamden, CT: Archon, 1976), 40.

27. Peter Stuhlmacher, "Significance," 2–12, cites a number of references in the NT that depend on or have verbal and subject parallels with noncanonical writings. Some of these will be explored below. Daniel J. Harrington, "The Old Testament Apocrypha in the Early Church and Today," in *The Canon Debate*, ed. L. M. McDonald and J. A. Sanders (Peabody, MA: Hendrickson, 2002), 196–210, challenges the view that there was a lot of dependency on this literature in early Christianity. He acknowledges the use of Tobit, 2 Maccabees, and Sirach, but adds caution regarding how inclusive the early Christians were in this regard. He is certainly correct in recognizing that there were two clear tendencies at the end of the first century CE: in Judaism a tendency toward a three-part scripture canon, and in Christianity a growing acceptance of a wider and more inclusive OT canon.

28. J. Barton, *People of the Book?* 25, 34, makes this observation.

29. Stuhlmacher, "Significance," 1–12, argues convincingly that several NT themes have their roots in the apocryphal and pseudepigraphal literature and cites the above examples as evidence.

30. See James VanderKam, *From Revelation to Canon*, 23–28, for a summary of the significance of this literature at Qumran and in early Christianity. See also J. T. Milik, *The Books of Enoch: Aramaic Fragments of Qumran Cave 4* (Oxford: Clarendon, 1976); and Boccaccini, ed., *Enoch and Qumran Origins*.

31. For examples of the Enochic texts cited by these individuals, see VanderKam's useful summary in "1 Enoch, Enochic Motifs," 33–101.

32. For a full discussion of *1 Enoch* in the Ethiopian church tradition, see R. W. Cowley, "The Biblical Canon of the Ethiopian Orthodox Church Today," *Ostkirchliche Studien* 23 (1974): 318–23.

33. The *Ascension (Martyrdom) of Isaiah* was also cited in the rabbinic literature to tell the story of Isaiah's death at the command of Manasseh (*b. Yebamot* 496; *y. Sanh.* 10).

34. Robert Grant, *The Formation of the New Testament* (New York: Harper & Row, 1965), 38–41, offers this suggestion.

35. Ibid., 41.

36. Stuhlmacher, "Significance," 3.

37. Grant, *Formation*, 44, makes this observation.

38. McDonald, *Biblical Canon*, 194–214.

39. Grant, *Formation*, 46.

40. Stuhlmacher, "Significance," 2.

41. Ellis, *Old Testament in Early Christianity*, 50.

42. David E. Aune, *Prophecy in Early Christianity and the Ancient Mediterranean World* (Grand Rapids: Eerdmans, 1983), 106–52.

43. I discuss this in *Biblical Canon*, chapter 6.

44. R. Laird Harris, *Inspiration and Canonicity of the Bible* (Grand Rapids: Zondervan, 1957), 219–35 and 274–82, makes this argument; and according to Craig D. Allert, *A High View of Scripture? The Authority of the Bible and the Formation of the New Testament Canon* (Grand Rapids: Baker Academic, 2007), 147–48, it is still frequently argued in some evangelical seminaries today.

45. For a capable discussion of the notion of inspiration in early Christianity, which is at odds with my own perspective on the matter, see Carl R. Holladay, *A Critical Introduction to the New Testament* (Nashville: Abingdon, 2005), 586, and his expanded CD-ROM version that has a more in-depth discussion and argument of this topic. Holladay's argument is considerable, but I still contend that inspiration is more of a corollary than a criterion. Writings believed to be true were considered inspired; those that were not considered true were not deemed inspired.

46. Jonathan Z. Smith, "Canons, Catalogues, and Classics," in *Canonization and Decanonization*, ed. Arie van der Kooij and Karel van der Toorn, Studies in the History of Religion 82 (Leiden: Brill, 1998), 298.

47. I have explained earlier that many documents in antiquity often served in a canonical or authoritative manner long before they were placed in a fixed collection of sacred scriptures. It is difficult to find an adequate term that identifies this phenomenon. Following Alan Sheppard, I call this practice of using ancient texts in an authoritative manner before they were placed into fixed collections "canon 1" as distinguished from those writings called scripture and placed into a fixed collection of sacred writings ("canon 2"). See McDonald, *Biblical Canon*, 55–58.

48. See Lee Martin McDonald, "Identifying Scripture and Canon in the Early Church: The Criteria Question," in *Canon Debate*, ed. McDonald and Sanders, 416–39.

49. F. F. Bruce, *The Canon of Scripture* (Downers Grove, IL: InterVarsity Press, 1988), 42.

50. I discuss this in "Wherein Lies Authority? A Discussion of Books, Texts, and Translations," in *Exploring the Origins of the Bible*, ed. Craig A. Evans and Emanuel Tov (Grand Rapids: Baker Academic, 2008), 203–39, esp. 204–9 and 221–29. For a helpful discussion of this topic, see Daryl Schmidt, "The Greek New Testament as a Codex," in *Canon Debate*, ed. McDonald and Sanders, 469–84.

51. *The Biblical Canon*, 384–400.

52. On this matter, see Richard Bauckham, *Jesus and the Eyewitnesses: The Gospels as Eyewitness Testimony* (Grand Rapids: Eerdmans, 2006), 1–38 and 240–63.

53. These documents are translated in James M. Robinson, ed., *The Nag Hammadi Library in English*, rev. ed. (San Francisco: HarperSanFrancisco, 1990), and summarized and listed in Van Elderen, "Early Christian Libraries," 47–50.

54. For an excellent discussion of the apocryphal Gospels, see Koester, *Ancient Christian Gospels*, as well as Schneemelcher, *New Testament Apocrypha*, vol. 1. Other ancient Gospels are discussed in this volume.

55. For a useful source on the apocryphal Acts, see François Bovon, Ann Graham Brock, and Christopher R. Matthews, ed., *The Apocryphal Acts of the Apostles*, Harvard Divinity School Studies (Cambridge: Harvard University Press, 1999).

56. Some would add here the canonical Pastoral Epistles and 2 Peter.

57. The term "apocalypse" is a transliteration of Greek *apokalypsis*, meaning "revelation" or "disclosure." Aune, *Prophecy*, 108, defines this literary genre as a form of revelatory literature in which the author narrates both the visions he has purportedly experienced and their meaning, usually elicited through a dialogue between the seer and an interpreting angel. The substance of these revelatory visions is the imminent intervention of God into human affairs to bring the present evil world system to an end and to replace it with an ideal one. This transformation is accompanied by the punishment of the wicked and the reward of the righteous.

58. Bruce M. Metzger, "Introduction to Apocryphal/Deuterocanonical Books," in *The New Oxford Annotated Bible with the Apocryphal/Deuterocanonical Books*, New Revised Standard Edition, ed. B. M. Metzger and R. E. Murphy (New York: Oxford University Press, 1991), viii–xi.

59. *Biblical Canon*, 200–214, 323–49.

60. See 770–86, especially 800–806. A more detailed collection of references can be found in Steve Delamarter, *A Scripture Index to Charlesworth's The Old Testament Pseudepigrapha* (Sheffield: Sheffield Academic Press, 2002). The most complete current listing of these references can be found in Kevin P. Edgecombe's collection. Edgecombe has expanded the Nestle-Aland[27] list of allusions considerably and added comparisons in translation. See his Web site, http://bombaxo.com/allusions.html as well as his lengthy index of comparisons with the pseudepigraphal writings at http://www.bombaxo.com.

61. What we see from this survey is that the evangelists attribute to Jesus the use of the Pentateuch, especially Deuteronomy, Psalms, and Isaiah.

62. This claim is made by Paul N. Anderson, "Aspects of Historicity in the Gospel of John," in *Jesus and Archaeology*, ed. James H. Charlesworth (Grand Rapids: Eerdmans, 2006), 596, and supported by Urban C. von Wahlde, "Archaeology and John's Gospel," in *Jesus and Archaeology*, 523–86.

63. Several studies of John's Gospel highlight this emerging change in reassessing the historical features of John's Gospel: James H. Charlesworth, *Jesus within Judaism: New Light from Exciting Archaeological Discoveries* (New York: Doubleday, 1988), 103–30, especially 118–27, followed by his *Beloved Disciple: Whose Witness Validates the Gospel of John?* (Valley Forge, PA: Trinity Press International, 1995); von Wahlde, "Archaeology and John's Gospel," 523–86; Anderson, "Aspects of Historicity in the Gospel of John," in *Jesus and Archaeology*, ed. Charlesworth, 587–618; idem, "John and Mark—the Bi-Optic Gospels," in *Jesus in Johannine Tradition*, ed. Robert T. Fortna and Tom Thatcher (Louisville, KY: Westminster John Knox, 2001), 175–88; A. J. B. Higgins, *The Historicity of the Fourth Gospel* (London: Lutterworth, 1960); Franz Müssner, *The Historical Jesus in the Gospel of John*, trans. W. J. O'Harah (New York: Herder & Herder, 1966); and J. A. T. Robinson, *The Priority of John*, ed. J. F. Coakley (London: SCM, 1985).

64. Stuhlmacher adds some other parallels to this list in "Significance," 8–10. As noted above, Stuhlmacher also notes the parallels between Matt 11:25–28 and the apocryphal psalm 11QPs 154 (11Q5 XVIII, 3–6).

Chapter Eight

1. The term "New Testament" is a later designation for the Christian writings. There is no record of its use as a designation for Christian writings before 170 CE by Irenaeus (*Haer.* 4.28.1–2; 4.15.2), Melito (Eusebius, *Hist. eccl.* 4.26.13–14), Clement of Alexandria (*Strom.* 15.5.85), and later, Origen (*Prin.* 4.11). Since there is considerable distance between these writers, it is likely that the term originated before any of them, but this is difficult to establish. There is no reference to either testament being closed, however, before the fourth century.

2. D. Moody Smith argues this point convincingly in "When Did the Gospels Become Scripture?" *JBL* 119 (2000): 3–20. See also Lee M. McDonald, "The Gospels in Early Christianity: Their Origin, Use, and Authority," in *Reading the Gospels Today*, ed. S. E. Porter. McMaster New Testament Studies (Grand Rapids: Eerdmans, 2004), 150–78; and Richard Bauckham, *Jesus and the Eyewitnesses: The Gospels as Eyewitness Testimony* (Grand Rapids: Eerdmans, 2006).

3. Bruce M. Metzger and Bart D. Ehrman, *The Text of the New Testament: Its Transmission, Corruption, and Restoration.* 4th ed. (Oxford: Oxford University Press, 2005), 343.

4. David Trobisch's view that Paul himself collected, edited, and circulated his writings in the churches is novel but unsupportable. There is virtually no evidence for this supposition and scholars who cite his work as evidence for this often fail to examine carefully Trobisch's arguments. What *could* have happened is not evidence that it *did* happen. See my review of David Trobisch, *Paul's Letter Collection: Tracing the Origins* (Minneapolis: Fortress, 1995) in *Critical Review of Books in Religion* 8 (1995): 311–14. For a more detailed analysis of Trobisch's arguments and their weakness see S. E. Porter, "When and How Was the Pauline Canon Compiled?" in *The Pauline Canon*, ed. S. E. Porter, Pauline Studies (Leiden: Brill, 2004), 113–27.

5. Hurtado in his very helpful *Earliest Christian Artifacts: Manuscripts and Christian Origins* (Grand Rapids: Eerdmans, 2006), 134, has conveniently listed the most frequently used abbreviations or *nomina sacra*. After the most common names—Jesus, God, Lord, and Christ—the other terms include spirit, man, son, father, David, cross, mother, savior, Israel, Jerusalem, and heaven. He also lists the Greek words and their abbreviations in this collection.

6. AnneMarie Luijendijk, *"Greetings in the Lord": Early Christians and the Oxyrhynchus Papyri*, Harvard Theological Studies 69 (Cambridge: Harvard University Press, 2009). See chapter 3, "What's in a Nomen?" in which Luijendijk observes that the relatively modern term for this ancient practice, *nomina sacra*, comes from Ludwig Traube, who coined it in his 1907 book, *Nomina sacra. Versuch einer Geschichte der christlichen Kürzung*, Quellenund Untersuchungen zur lateinischen Philologie des Mittelalters 2 (Munich: Beck, 1907). She continues: "Since then, these Christian contractions have constituted a topic among textual critics and students of Christian literary manuscripts that competes in popularity only with the development of the codex. Scholars have debated their origins (whether Jewish or Christian) and studied their forms (regular and derivate) and their theological implications. All scholars who have written about this practice agree that the reverence of the name of God is Jewish, but the debate persists about whether that has any explanatory significance."

7. Ibid.

8. Ibid.

9. Pliny the Elder gives a description of manufacture of papyrus sheets (*Natural History* 13.74–82), which replaced the wood and wax used in the earlier manufacture of the codex.

10. Harry Y. Gamble, *Books and Readers in the Early Church: A History of Early Christian Texts* (New Haven: Yale University Press, 1995), 70, cites E. G. Turner in this regard saying that "scribes who copied on a codex of papyrus in a single column were aware that they were writing a second-class book." Gamble also has an excellent discussion of the origins of the codex and its widespread use in the early churches, including arguments that suggest Paul's use of them as the background for the church's acceptance and continuation of their early use. See pp. 49–61.

11. Gamble, ibid., 66–71, discusses the early Christian preference for the informal codices over scrolls.

12. Ibid., 50–55. Hurtado discusses this possibility in *Earliest Christian Artifacts*, 76–79, and while generally sympathetic to Gamble, nevertheless is not convinced that Paul either carried with him a collection of books (codices) or whether early church history supports this interpretation; but he agrees that it is "perfectly possible" that someone in the mid-first century could have used codices or books.

13. Gamble, *Books and Readers*, 59–63.

14. Ibid., 58–66.

15. Eldon Jay Epp, "Issues in the Interrelation of New Testament Textual Criticism and Canon," in *The Canon Debate*, ed. L. M. McDonald and J. A. Sanders (Peabody, MA: Hendrickson, 2002), 499 and 510–12, describes these documents and others.

16. Metzger and Ehrman, *Text of the New Testament*, 53.

17. The most recent update of the Aland lists and categories of Greek NT papyri are by Wieland Willker, online at http://www-uner.uni-bremen.de/~wie/texte/Papyri-list.html.

18. These include P[30] (1, 2 Thessalonians; 3rd century), P[34] (1 Corinthians, 2 Corinthians; 7th century), P[44] (Matt, John; 6th–7th century), P[45] (Matt, Mk, Lk, Jn; 3rd century), P[46] (Romans, 1 Corinthians, 2 Corinthians, Galatians, Ephesians, Philippians, Colossians, 1 Thessalonians, Hebrews; ca. 200), P[53] (Matt, Acts; ca. 3rd century), P[61] (Romans, 1 Corinthians, Philippians, Colossians, 1 Thessalonians, Titus, Philemon; ca. 700), P[4] + P[64] + P[67] (Matt, Lk; ca. 200; recent scholarly opinion concludes that these three manuscripts belong together), P[72] (1 Peter, 2 Peter, Jude [+ *Nativity of Mary*, correspondence of Paul, *3 Corinthians*, letter from *Ode of Solomon* 11, Melito's *Homily on Passover*, hymn fragment, *Apology of Phileas*, Pss. 33 and 34]; 3rd–4th century), P[74] (Acts, James, 1 Peter, 2 Peter, 1 Jn, 2 Jn, 3 Jn, Jude; 7th century), P[84] (Mk, Jn; 6th century), P[92] (Ephesians, 2 Thessalonians; 3rd–4th century).

19. These are listed with particular information on their date and provenance in Joseph van Haelst, *Catalogue des papyrus littéraires juifs et chrétiens* (Paris: Sorbonne, 1976), 199–220.

20. Bart D. Ehrman, *Misquoting Jesus: The Story Behind Who Changed the Bible and Why* (San Francisco: HarperSanFrancisco, 2005), 222–23, n. 13. See also Daryl D. Schmidt, "The Greek New Testament as a Codex," in *The Canon Debate*, ed. McDonald and Sanders, 469–84, who makes a similar observation.

21. Schmidt, "Greek New Testament," 470–75.

22. This observation comes from Stanley E. Porter, "Why So Many Holes in the Papyrological Evidence for the Greek New Testament?" in *The Bible as Book: The Transmission of the Greek Text*, ed. Scot McKendrick and Orlaith O'Sullivan (London: British Library, 2003), 173.

23. Almost yearly new finds are reported, and so the number of ancient biblical manuscripts climbs. Porter, "Why So Many Holes," 178–79, reports that he

has seen nine large file boxes of Byzantine papyri that have never been studied, edited, or even added to the number of available manuscripts for study. Bruce Metzger, "The Future of New Testament Textual Studies," in *The Bible as Book: Transmission of the Greek Text*, ed. McKendrick and O'Sullivan, 203, also speaks of known manuscripts that await availability, study, and classification.

24. *The Text of the New Testament: An Introduction to the Critical Editions and to Theory and Practice of Modern Textual Criticism*, trans. Erroll F. Rhodes, 2nd ed. (Grand Rapids: Eerdmans, 1989), 138–40. See also Daryl Schmidt, "Greek New Testament as a Codex," 470–71, who points out the exceptions to this list.

25. Hurtado, *Earliest Christian Artifacts*, 24–25.

26. An *opisthograph* (Greek for "writings from behind") is a roll with writing on the front and back. This practice was unusual; the backside of a roll was often used to insert a text for personal use. In a number of cases, the text of the biblical literature was written on the backside of a roll that had other literary texts on the opposite or "recto" (horizontal) side of a papyrus or parchment sheet or roll. See Rev. 5:1, which mentions a scroll written on both sides.

27. Hurtado, *Earliest Christian Artifacts*, 209–29.

28. *Hermas* exists in two rolls (P.Oxy. 4706 and BKT 6.2.1), in seven third-century codices (P.Oxy. 4706, P.Iand. 1.4/LDAB 1094; P.Oxy. 3528/LDAB 1095; P.Oxy. 1828/LDAB 1099; P.Mich. 129/LDAB 1097; P.Oxy. 3527; LDAB 1098; and P.Oxy. 404/LDAB 1101), and in two opisthographs (P.Oxy. 4705; P.Mich. 130/LDAB 1096). These are in noted in Hurtado's list, *Earliest Christian Artifacts*. He has a complete collection of these second- and third- (and early-fourth) century Christian artifacts, pp. 209–29.

29. Ibid., 35.

30. Ibid., 25–27. Hurtado contends that the Christian texts discovered in Egypt are "translocal" and are representative of the wider Christian community. He cites for support Lionel Casson, *Travel in the Ancient World* (London: Allen & Unwin, 1974); and Richard Bauckham, "For Whom Were the Gospels Written?" in *The Gospels for All Christians: Rethinking the Gospel Audiences*, ed. Richard Bauckham (Grand Rapids: Eerdmans, 1998), 9–48, especially 32.

31. These numbers are listed in the most recent edition of Metzger and Ehrman, *Text of the New Testament*, 50. The figures change almost annually as more manuscripts are found and placed in the public domain. By the time this book is published, the number of biblical papyri manuscripts may climb even higher.

32. "Issues in the Interrelation of New Testament Textual Criticism and Canon," 505.

33. Apotropaic (Greek *apotropaios*, "turning away") refers to exorcisms or turning away from evil. One who is apotropaic has the power to turn away from evil or misfortune.

34. Hurtado, *Earliest Christian Artifacts*, 19–24. Hurtado lists these texts with notes on each one.

35. Three of these four collections, Bodmer, Chester Beatty, and Nag Hammadi manuscripts, are called "libraries" by Bastiaan Van Elderen, "Early Christian Libraries," in *The Bible as Book: The Manuscript Tradition*, ed. John L. Sharpe III and Kimberly van Kampen (London: British Library, 1998), 45–60.

36. See also Hurtado, *Earliest Christian Artifacts*, 24–26.

37. Hurtado, ibid., 44–89, has an extended and carefully crafted discussion of this.

38. The OT portion of that collection included Genesis, Numbers, and Deuteronomy, but strangely omitted Exodus and Leviticus, all the Former Prophets,

the Psalms, and all Wisdom literature. Among the Latter Prophets only Isaiah, Jeremiah, Ezekiel, and Daniel are included, but the collection also includes Sirach and *1 Enoch* as well as a homily by Melito. The fragmentary nature of this collection should give one pause before drawing too many conclusions about the Bibles of early Christianity, but again, the presence of these books in one location—or the absence of some books that were popular later among the Christians and added to the biblical canon—should raise some questions about the scope of the sacred collections of Christian scriptures at that time (late second to late third century CE).

39. The OT lacks Leviticus, Judges, Ruth, Samuel, and Kings, Ezra, Nehemiah, Esther, Ecclesiastes, Ezekiel, and the Minor Prophets, but it contains Susanna, Tobit, 2 Maccabees, and *Ode of Solomon* 11.

40. This literature was accepted as scripture in the Syrian as well as Armenian churches from the fourth century and for several centuries later. *Third Corinthians* continued to be included in some Latin sacred manuscripts (some Vulgate manuscripts) for almost a thousand years. As recently as 1728, William Whiston of Cambridge accepted *3 Corinthians* as an authentic Pauline correspondence (see his *Collection of Authentick Records Belonging to the Old and New Testament*, part II [London: 1728], 585–638, cited in Bruce M. Metzger, *The Canon of the New Testament* [Oxford: Clarendon, 1987], 15). It was included in the biblical canon of the Armenian and Syrian Bibles for several centuries. It was rejected by the Syrians probably by the end of the fifth century at the latest, but continued on in the Armenian churches. *Third Corinthians* still stands at the end of the NT in Zoharb's 1805 edition of the Armenian Bible (see Metzger, *Canon of the New Testament*, 223). It continues in Armenian Bibles in an appendix following the NT today. Both Aphraat (ca. 340 CE) and Ephraem Syrus (ca. 360 CE) commented on it as if it were an authentic correspondence of Paul, and Aphraat (and probably Ephraem Syrus as well) clearly treats it as scripture. A Greek version of it survives in the Bodmer collection of ancient manuscripts (P. Bodmer X/ P[72], 3rd century CE). The five Latin manuscripts that contain *3 Corinthians* are Cod. Ambrose. E53 inf. (10th century, Milan); Codex Laon 45 (13th century, L); Codex Paris. Lat. 5288 (10/11th century, P); Codex Zürich Car.C 14 (10th century, Z); Codex Berlin Ham. 84 (13th century, B). For a discussion of this literature, see Eldon Jay Epp, "Issues in the Interrelation of New Testament Textual Criticism and Canon," in *Canon Debate*, ed. McDonald and Sanders, 491–92; repr. in *Perspectives on New Testament Textual Criticism: Collected Essays 1962–2004* (Leiden: Brill), 603–4.

41. The later Oxyrhynchus source for Mark is 069 and for 1 Peter is 0206.

42. Eldon Jay Epp, "The Oxyrhynchus New Testament Papyri: 'Not without Honor Except in Their Hometown'?" *JBL* 123, no. 1 (2004): 5–55, especially 10–30.

43. After the Psalms, Matthew, and John, the *Shepherd of Hermas* was the most widely circulating religious text in the early centuries of the church—at least, more manuscript copies of that book have survived than any other Christian writings or OT writings save the ones just mentioned.

44. See Trobisch, Web site: http://www.bts.edu/faculty/trobisch.htm. According to him, only 59 of 779 manuscripts that contain the Letters of Paul also contain the whole NT. But this means portions of the whole NT, since most of the manuscripts are fragmentary. Trobisch also discusses here Codex Alexandrinus, Codex Ephraemi Rescriptus, Codex Sinaiticus, Codex Vaticanus, Codex Boernerianus, Codex Augiensis, and P[46].

45. Epp, "Issues in Interrelation," 495–502, discusses this papyrus codex at length, and concludes we cannot be certain about its contents.

46. For a description of this collection, see van Elderen, "Early Christian Libraries," in *Bible as Book: Manuscript Tradition*, ed. Sharpe and van Kampen, 45–60.
47. Schmidt, "The Greek New Testament as a Codex," in *Canon Debate*, ed. McDonald and Sanders, 474, took this reference from F. H. A. Scrivener, *A Plain Introduction to the Criticism of the New Testament for the Use of Biblical Students*, ed. Edward Miller, 4th ed., 2 vols. (London: George Bell, 1894), 200.
48. Epp, "Issues in Interrelation," 503, has noted that these same books are missing from the earlier P[46].
49. James Charlesworth has shared with me that he has seen the missing pages of this codex at St. Catherine's Monastery in the Sinai Peninsula, but is not yet able to publish them due to restrictions from the monastery. See his earlier "St. Catherine's Monastery," *BA* 42 (1979)" 174–79; "The Manuscript of St. Catherine's Monastery," 43 (1980): 26–34. Awareness of these missing pages has been around for a number of years, e.g., Raymond E. Brown took note of this unpublished discovery in *Recent Discoveries and the Biblical World* (Wilmington, DE: Michael Glazier, 1983), 47–48.
50. The oldest and most complete NT manuscripts (Codex Vaticanus, Codex Sinaiticus, Codex Ephraemi Rescriptus, and Codex Alexandrinus) have Acts combined with the General Epistles and not with the Letters of Paul, and the General Epistles come before the Letters of Paul, except in the case of Sinaiticus.
51. For example, there are some possible parallels in language in the Apostolic Fathers, but they are not conclusive. The earliest and clearest references to 2 and 3 John are in Clement of Alexandria (*Strom.* 2.15.66) and in Irenaeus, who quotes 2 John 11 and 7 (*Haer.* 3.17.8). Neither Irenaeus, nor Tertullian refers to 3 John, and none of these early references calls 2 and 3 John scripture. See McDonald, *Biblical Canon*, 372.
52. I owe this observation to Rudolf Schackenburg, *The Johannine Epistles: A Commentary*, trans. Reginald and Isle Fuller (New York: Crossroad, 1992), 42–47.
53. I am aware of the recent defense of a mid- to late-third-century dating of the Muratorian Fragment by Jonathan J. Armstrong, "Victorinus of Pettau as the Author of the Canon Muratori," *Vigiliae Christianae* 62 (2008): 1–34. The arguments need to be studied in more detail and do show some promise of challenging both the usual second-century dating of the Muratorian Fragment and also the more recent arguments that it was a fourth-century document. If Victorinus of Pettau was the author of that document, then he is much closer to Eusebius in the fourth century than to Bishop Pius in the second century. Again, Armstrong's careful work needs further study, and he may provide several missing links in this ongoing debate among canon scholars.
54. These collections are listed in McDonald, *Biblical Canon*, 439–51.
55. I reject a second-century dating of the Muratorian Fragment since its closest parallels are in the mid-fourth century and later and it does not reflect the sacred collection of any known writer in the second century. Again, the work of Armstrong noted above needs more careful scrutiny and may alter positions on this document, but Armstrong's views are much closer to those at the time when these matters of fixed canons were in view in the churches. For further discussion see McDonald, *Biblical Canon*, 369–78; but for a different perspective carefully argued see J. Verheyden, "The Canon Muratori: A Matter of Dispute," in *The Biblical Canons*, ed. J.-M. Auwers and H. J. de Jonge, BETL 163 (Leuven: Leuven University Press, 2003), 487–556.

56. He writes: "In addition to these should be put, if it seem desirable, the Revelation of John" (*Hist. eccl.* 3.25.2), and later adds that Revelation may be among the "not genuine" books (*en tois nothois*), "if this view prevails," and continues, "some reject it, but others count it among the recognized books" (3.25.4).

57. I discuss this in McDonald, *Biblical Canon*, 285–322.

Chapter Nine

1. These text families are described in Bruce M. Metzger, *A Textual Commentary on the Greek New Testament*, 2nd ed. (Stuttgart: Deutsche Bibelgesellschaft/United Bible Societies, 1994), 4*–7*; and in Metzger and Ehrman, *Text of the New Testament*, 276–80, 306–13.

2. Ehrman, *Orthodox Corruption of Scripture*, 275, also claims that many of the debates over Christology affected the accuracy of the transcription of the NT manuscripts. For a helpful discussion of the kinds of errors or mistakes and changes made in the transmission of the ancient manuscripts, see Metzger and Ehrman, *Text of the New Testament*, 250–71.

3. Craig A. Evans, "Textual Criticism and Textual Confidence: How Reliable Is Scripture?" in *Textual Reliability of the New Testament*, ed. R. Stewart (Minneapolis: Fortress, forthcoming).

4. Ibid. He also cites Raymond E. Brown, "The Lucan Authorship of Luke 22:43–44," in *Society of Biblical Literature 1992 Seminar Papers*, ed. Eugene H. Lovering Jr. (Atlanta: Scholars Press, 1992), 154–64; and Bart D. Ehrman and M. A. Plunkett, "The Angel and the Agony: The Textual Problem of Luke 22:43–44," *CBQ* 45 (1983): 401–16.

5. Helmut Koester, "The Text of the Synoptic Gospels in the Second Century," in *Gospel Traditions in the Second Century: Origins, Recensions, Text, and Transmission*, ed. W. L. Petersen, Christianity and Judaism in Antiquity 3 (Notre Dame, IN: University of Notre Dame Press, 1989), 37.

6. Metzger and Ehrman, *Text of the New Testament*, 24, observe that in the early Christian manuscripts, "the speed of production sometimes outran the accuracy of execution." On 276–77 they describe the characteristics of the Western text family that was used by Marcion, Irenaeus, and Tertullian. The chief witnesses of the Western text include P^{48}, P^{38}, as well as Codex Bezae (D) and Old Latin versions. For a useful discussion of the variants in these and other NT manuscripts, see Aland and Aland, *Text of the New Testament*, 282–316; and Metzger and Ehrman, *Text of the New Testament*, 186–206. Some of these changes are also summarized with illustrations in Paul D. Wegner, *The Journey from Texts to Translations* (Grand Rapids: Baker, 1999), 225–26; and in Arthur G. Patzia, *The Making of the New Testament: Origin, Collection, Text & Canon* (Downers Grove, IL: InterVarsity Press, 1995), 138–41. Patzia also gives a number of examples of intentional changes on pp. 141–46.

7. Michael Holmes in personal correspondence, August 16, 2006.

8. Ehrman, *Misquoting Jesus*, 89–90, claims that there are between 200,000 and 400,000 known variants in the more than 5,700 known Greek manuscripts of the NT! He earlier notes that in 1550, John Mill, fellow of Queens College, Oxford, surveyed some one hundred NT manuscripts, as well as patristic citations and versions of the NT, and made the disturbing discovery of some 30,000 variants in them (83–88). Eckhard J. Schnabel, "Textual Criticism: Recent Developments," in *The Face of New Testament Studies: A Survey of Recent Research*, ed. Scot McKnight and Grant R. Osborne (Grand Rapids:

Baker Academic, 2004), 59, claims that of the more than 5,700 Greek NT manuscripts known at the time of his writing, and the approximately 9,000 versional manuscripts, there are some 300,000 variant readings!

9. Reuben J. Swanson, ed., *New Testament Greek Manuscripts: Variant Readings Arranged in Horizontal Lines Against Codex Vaticanus: Romans* (Wheaton, IL: Tyndale House Publications, 2001), xxv.

10. Ibid., xxv–xxxi.

11. Philip W. Comfort and David P. Barrett, eds., *The Text of the Earliest New Testament Manuscripts,* rev. ed. (Chicago: Tyndale, 2001), 15.

12. Metzger and Ehrman, *Text of the New Testament,* 24–25.

13. Ibid., 275. Again, the life expectancy of a biblical manuscript that was regularly used seldom exceeded thirty years.

14. These welcomed comments come from personal correspondence with Professor Hurtado on September 29, 2006.

15. Metzger and Ehrman, *Text of the New Testament,* 24–25.

16. See Bruce M. Metzger, "Explicit References in the Works of Origen to Variant Readings in New Testament Manuscripts," in *Biblical and Patristic Studies in Memory of Robert Pierce Casey,* ed. J. N. Birdsell and R. W. Thomson (Freiberg: Herder, 1963), 78–95, repr. in Bruce M. Metzger, *Historical and Literary Studies: Pagan, Jewish, and Christian,* New Testament Tools and Studies 8 (Grand Rapids: Eerdmans, 1968), 88–103. I learned of these works in personal correspondence with Michael Holmes and in his "Textual Criticism," in D. A. Black and D. S. Dockery, eds., *New Testament Criticism & Interpretation* (Grand Rapids: Zondervan, 1991), 101–34.

17. For a discussion of this concern, see Bruce M. Metzger, "St Jerome's Explicit References to Variant Readings in Manuscripts of the New Testament," in *Text and Interpretation: Studies in the New Testament Presented to Matthew Black,* ed. Ernest Best and R. McL. Wilson (Cambridge: Cambridge University Press, 1979), 179–90.

18. Westcott and Hort earlier dubbed these few instances as "Western non-interpolations," but they preferred to speak of a "Neutral Text" of the NT manuscripts characterized by the Alexandrian text family. These so-called Western non-interpolations include Matt. 27:49; Luke 22:19–20; 24:3, 6, 12, 36, 40, 51, and 52. Other passages may be in this category, but those in Luke and the one in Matthew are the ones most often listed.

19. Metzger, *Textual Commentary,* 6*.

20. Metzger and Ehrman, *Text of the New Testament,* 218–22.

21. Sinaiticus and Vaticanus occasionally disagree, as in the case of the ending of Mark 1:1 (the last two Greek words). Following an earlier study by Gordon Fee, John J. Brogan observes that Sinaiticus sometimes displays Western text family characteristics in John 1–8. See Brogan, "Another Look at Codex Sinaiticus," in *The Bible as Book: The Transmission of the Greek Text,* ed. S. McKendrick and O. O'Sullivan (London: British Library, 2003), 18–19. Gordon Fee has concluded that "Codex Sinaiticus is a leading Greek representative of the Western textual tradition in John i.1–viii.38," in "Codex Sinaiticus in the Gospel of John: A Contribution to Methodology in Establishing Textual Relationships," *NTS* 15 (1968/69): 23–44.

22. Metzger and Ehrman, *Text of the New Testament,* 15.

23. Kurt and Barbara Aland, *The Text of the New Testament,* trans. Erroll F. Rhodes, rev. ed. (Grand Rapids: Eerdmans, 1989), 76–77.

24. Metzger and Ehrman, *Text of the New Testament,* 25–27, provide a useful summary of the processes employed in copying Scripture in antiquity.

25. Ibid., 275. By that time there appears to be a more consistent attempt to produce error-free manuscripts. The manuscripts generally are more consistent and with fewer errors than before. What factors led to this is unclear.

26. Ehrman, *Orthodox Corruption of Scripture*, 91–99, describes the history of this passage in the Christian Bible. For a brief discussion see Rudolf Schnackenburg, *The Johannine Epistles: A Commentary*, trans. Reginald and Ilse Fuller (New York: Crossroad, 1992), 44–46. Erasmus added the *Comma* to the second edition of his Greek text.

27. For a careful discussion of the conclusion of Mark's Gospel and the various theories and texts that relate to it, see N. Clayton Croy, *The Mutilation of Mark's Gospel* (Nashville: Abingdon, 2003). Now a majority of NT scholars, unlike earlier, do not believe that 16:8 is the original ending of the Gospel.

28. Epp, "Issues in the Interrelation," 514–15, discusses this point and cites the work of David C. Parker, *The Living Text of the Gospels* (Cambridge: Cambridge University Press, 1997), 78–93.

29. In the case of Priscilla, see Dominika A. Kurek-Chomycz, "Is There an 'Anti-Pricscan' Tendency in the Manuscripts? Some Textual Problems with Prisca and Aquila," *JBL* 125, no. 1 (2006): 107–28. In the latter cases, see E. J. Epp, *Junia: The First Woman Apostle* (Minneapolis: Fortress, 2005). In his discussion of 1 Cor. 14:33b–36, Epp calls attention to the two dots in the left margin of this text in Codex Vaticanus that points to the doubts of the copier about this text. He also notes (14–20) the relocation of these verses, after 14:40 in several ancient texts. It is likely that Paul never wrote these verses since it would be rather difficult for women to pray or prophesy not only with their heads covered (1 Cor. 11:5) but also with their mouths shut (14:34–35)! In the case of 1 Tim. 2:8–15, most NT scholars rightly do not see this passage as a Pauline text, but coming instead from a later hand written in the name of Paul.

30. See my discussion in "Gospels in Early Christianity," 150–78.

31. Epp, "The Multivalence of the Term 'Original Text' in New Testament Textual Criticism," *HTR* 92 (1999): 274–79; repr. in Eldon J. Epp, *Perspectives on New Testament Textual Criticism: Collected Essays, 1962–2004* (Leiden: Brill, 2005), 584–90.

32. For discussion see Helmut Koester, *Ancient Christian Gospels: Their History and Development* (Philadelphia: Trinity Press International, 1990), 275–76 and 295–302. See also his "Text of the Synoptic Gospels," in *Gospel Traditions*, ed. Petersen, 19–21 and 30–31.

33. Ehrman, *Misquoting Jesus*, 84–89, has understood the seriousness of this problem and observes that the overwhelming number of variations in the surviving NT manuscripts actually outnumbers the words in the NT! While there is considerable agreement on most of the texts, there remain many unsolved issues regarding the original NT texts. See also Epp, "Multivalence," 245–81, who discusses the problem of determining an original text of the NT and draws attention to the implications of that inquiry (see 561).

34. See Metzger and Ehrman, *Text of the New Testament*, 142–49, for a more complete discussion of Erasmus's contribution to the stabilization of the Greek text of the NT.

35. Ehrman, *Misquoting Jesus*, 82–83, notes that the term "received text" (*textus receptus*) originates from Abraham and Bonaventure Elzevir, who produced an edition of the Greek NT in 1633 and told their readers: "You now have the text that is received by all, in which we have given nothing changed or corrupted" (82).

36. See Kent D. Clarke, "Original Text or Canonical Text? Questioning the Shape of the New Testament Text We Translate," in *Translating the Bible: Problems and Prospects*, ed. S. E. Porter and R. S. Hess, JSNTSup 173 (Sheffield: Sheffield Academic Press, 1999), 321–22.

37. Ehrman offers many examples of these kinds of changes in the biblical texts in his *Orthodox Corruption of Scripture*. The quotes above are on p. 280.

38. For further discussion of the NT text during that hundred or more years, see Koester, *Ancient Christian Gospels*, 275–76 and 295–302. See also his "Text of the Synoptic Gospels," in *Gospel Traditions*, ed. Petersen, 19–21 and 30–31.

39. Metzger and Ehrman, *Text of the New Testament*, 272–74.

40. Ibid., 274.

41. Koester, "Text of the Synoptic Gospels," 37.

42. Philip Wesley Comfort, *The Quest for the Original Text of the New Testament* (Grand Rapids: Baker Book House, 1992), contends that this goal is attainable, but his arguments on pp. 19–40 are not convincing and appear more theologically motivated than carefully constructed. He does not deal adequately with the numerous intentional changes that the early copyists made in the biblical text.

43. Schnabel, "Textual Criticism: Recent Developments," 75, makes this observation.

44. See Hyeon Woo Shin, *Textual Criticism and the Synoptic Problem in Historical Jesus Research: The Search for Valid Criteria*, Contributions to Biblical Exegesis amd Theology (Leuven: Peeters, 2004), 4–9. Throughout this study the usual criteria are challenged and additional criteria are employed to determine the authentic biblical text and consequently the authentic Jesus in the Synoptic Gospels. Brevard Childs also raises important questions about the criteria employed by text critics. See Excursus I, "The Hermeneutical Problem of New Testament Criticism," in *The New Testament as Canon: An Introduction* (Philadelphia: Fortress, 1985), 518–30. He concludes that there is no "neutral text" from which one can draw a "pure textual stream" because "the early period reflects highly complex recensional activity from the outset" (525). He is no doubt correct that the NT text "reflects a pattern of much fluidity with multiple competing traditions at its earliest stage which only slowly over several centuries reached a certain level of textual stability" (526). See also the challenges to the methodologies by J. K. Elliott, "Thoroughgoing Eclecticism," 139–45; Stanley E. Porter, "Why So Many Holes in the Papyrological Evidence?" 167–86; and B. M. Metzger, "The Future of New Testament Textual Studies," 201–8, in *Bible as Book: Transmission of the Greek Text*, ed. McKendrick and O'Sullivan.

45. E. E. Epp, "Issues in New Testament Textual Criticism," in *Rethinking New Testament Textual Criticism*, ed. D. A. Black (Grand Rapids: Baker, 2002), 75. He also challenges the notion that the original NT text can be discovered in "Multivalence," 264–65. See also Clarke, "Original Text or Canonical Text?" 281–322, especially 285–95, who raises important questions about the ability of scholars to retrieve the original text.

46. "Issues in New Testament Textual Criticism," 76.

47. Gordon D. Fee, "Textual Criticism of the New Testament," in Eldon J. Epp and Gordon D. Fee, *Studies in the Theory and Method of New Testament Textual Criticism*, Studies and Documents 45 (Grand Rapids: Eerdmans, 1993), 15.

48. Eldon Epp, "Decision Points in Past, Present, and Future New Testament Textual Criticism," in Epp and Fee, *Theory and Method*, 35.

49. For discussion see Eldon J. Epp, "Issues in New Testament Textual Criticism," in *Rethinking New Testament Textual Criticism*, ed. Black, 71–75. In the same volume, J. K. Elliott, "The Case for Thoroughgoing Eclecticism," 124, states: "It may well be that modern textual criticism is less confident about the need to, or its ability to, establish the original text and that its best contribution to biblical studies is to show how variations arose, ideally in what directions, and to explain the significance of all variants."

50. Both of these Greek NT texts are essentially the same and vary in the text rarely but often in the footnote apparatus.

51. These scholars' positions are explained in Michael Holmes, "The Case for Reasoned Eclecticism," and J. K. Elliott, "Case for Thoroughgoing Eclecticism," in *Rethinking New Testament Textual Criticism*, ed. Black, 77–100 and 101–24, respectively.

52. B. D. Ehrman, *TC: A Journal of Biblical Textual Criticism* (1998): par 22. Epp also expresses this same conclusion in "Multivalence," 245–81. See also his "Decision Points," in Epp and Fee, *Theory and Method*, 17–44; E. Epp, "Issues in New Testament Textual Criticism: Moving from the Nineteenth Century to the Twenty-First Century," in *Rethinking New Testament Textual Criticism*, ed. Black, 17–76, especially 70–76; and E. Epp, "Issues in the Interrelation," in *The Canon Debate*, ed. McDonald and Sanders, 485–515.

53. Thomas J. Kraus, *Ad Fontes: Original Manuscripts and Their Significance for Studying Early Christianity—Selected Essays*, Texts and Editions for New Testament Study 3 (Leiden: Brill, 2007), 25. See also three very useful articles on this subject that raise the question of what manuscript evidence to include in establishing the text of the NT: Gordon D. Fee, "The Use of the Greek Fathers for New Testament Textual Criticism," 191–207; J. Lionel North, "The Use of the Latin Fathers for New Testament Textual Criticism," 208–23; and Sebastian P. Brock, "The Use of the Syriac Fathers for New Testament Textual Criticism," 224–36, in *The Text of the New Testament in Contemporary Research: Essays on the Status Quaestionis*, ed. Bart D. Ehrman and Michael W. Holmes, Studies and Documents 46 (Grand Rapids: Eerdmans, 1995). All three of these scholars say that we should make use of these resources, but they also advise the reader to do a careful analysis and they provide helpful suggestions on how to do this.

54. Thomas J. Kraus, *Ad Fontes: Original Manuscripts*, 90–91.

55. Swanson also makes this point in the introduction to his *New Testament Greek Manuscripts: Romans*, xxv–xxx.

56. These figures come from Bruce M. Metzger, *The Bible in Translation: Ancient and English Versions* (Grand Rapids: Baker Academic, 2001), 8–9.

57. It is, of course, likely that some translation from Hebrew to Aramaic took place earlier when the returning remnant of Jews from Babylon heard the scriptures (the Law of Moses) from Ezra (Neh. 8:8).

58. See Nina Collins, *The Library in Alexandria and the Bible in Greek*, VTSup 82 (Leiden: Brill, 2000), 117–37, who argues this point cogently and also describes the Greek translation of the Law that was placed in the Alexandrian library.

59. The number "seventy-two" could have been rounded off to "seventy," hence "Septuagint," but it is also quite possible that the number LXX derives from the tradition of the seventy elders of Exod. 24:1, 9, who accompanied Moses and Joshua (hence 72?) to Mount Sinai, where Moses received the Law from Yahweh on tablets of stone. If this is the case, then the use of the term "Septuagint" by the Jews is likely an acknowledgment of an early Jewish and Christian

belief in the divinely inspired status of the translation, that is, that it authentically and faithfully conveyed the full intent of the divine Law given to Moses. The tradition related to this translation and the term "LXX" should technically be applied only to the Greek translation of the Pentateuch and not to the rest of the OT Scriptures, but the term eventually came to be used in reference to the other books of the Jewish Scriptures as well. According to the author of the prologue to Sirach (grandson of Sirach?) by around 130 BCE, the Prophets and some other sacred Jewish writings were likewise translated into the Greek language, a tacit implication of their sacredness.

60. The following information comes from Metzger, *Bible in Translation*, 25–51.
61. For a summary of this version, see ibid., 50–51.
62. Metzger and Ehrman, *Text of the New Testament*, 95.
63. Craig D. Allert, "Is Translation Inspired? The Problems of Verbal Inspiration for a Translation and a Proposed Solution," in *Translating the Bible*, ed. Porter and Hess, 85–113, discusses this issue and concludes that inspiration is not locked into any one translation. He calls for a redefinition of inspiration that more ably reflects the phenomena of Scripture and contends that inspiration is more appropriately related to the function of Scripture rather than to specific words of its text, as we see in 2 Tim. 3:16–17. He concludes that translations can be inspired, "because the community views them as accurately reflecting what the community as a whole believes. This reflection is preserved in the canon and is authoritative for the historic orthodox community of faith today" (112).
64. Swanson, *NT Greek Manuscripts: Romans*, xxv–xxx.

Chapter Ten

1. See the affirmation of this conclusion in Margalit Finkelberg and Guy G. Stroumsa, "Introduction: Before the Western Canon," in *Homer, the Bible, and Beyond: Literary and Religious Canons in the Ancient World*, ed. Finkelberg and Stroumsa, Jerusalem Studies in Religion and Culture (Leiden: Brill, 2003), 2–3. See especially the following chapters in that volume: Margalit Finkelberg, "Homer as a Foundation Text," 75–96; and H. Cancik, "Standardization and Ranking of Texts in Greek and Roman Institutions," 117–30.
2. See the very useful summary of the ancient noncanonical writings in C. A. Evans, *Ancient Texts for New Testament Studies: A Guide to the Background Literature* (Peabody, MA: Hendrickson, 2005). Evans is an evangelical scholar who rightly sees the value of these texts for understanding better both the meaning of the NT literature and the faith of the early Christians.

Chapter Eleven

1. Craig D. Allert, *A High View of Scripture? The Authority of the Bible and the Formation of the New Testament Canon* (Grand Rapids: Baker Academic, 2007), 147–72. He raises a number of relevant questions about traditional understandings of Scripture in the evangelical churches including the way that we define inspiration, inerrancy, error, and truth.
2. John J. Brogan, "Can I Have Your Autograph: Uses and Abuses of Textual Criticism in Formulating an Evangelical Doctrine of Inerrancy," in V. Bacote, L. C. Miguelez, and D. L. Okham, eds., *Evangelicals and Scripture: Tradition, Authority, and Hermeneutics* (Downers Grove, Ill: InterVarsity Press, 2004), 93–111.

3. Ibid., 110.
4. J. Daniel Hays, "Jeremiah, the Septuagint, the Dead Sea Scrolls, and Inerrancy: Just What Do We Mean by 'Original Autographs'?" in *Evangelicals and Scripture*, 133–49, claims that the LXX text of Jeremiah is likely closer to the original hand of Jeremiah than the MT, and the implications of this are not fully appreciated by those who are generally responsible for framing the various notions of the inspiration of Scripture.
5. I am aware of the distinction that some evangelical scholars make between "inerrant" and "infallible." The former has to do with inerrancy in all aspects in the original manuscripts, but the latter emphasizes that the Bible is true in all that it affirms. I find this both confusing to persons in the church and foolish wordplays that always need qualification. Why not use a term that our people understand and that needs no qualification?
6. Wrestling with this problem is at the heart of two recent volumes: Alan G. Padgett and Patrick R. Keifert, eds., *But Is It All True? The Bible and the Question of Truth* (Grand Rapids: Eerdmans, 2006); and William P. Brown, ed., *Engaging Biblical Authority: Perspectives on the Bible as Scripture* (Louisville, KY: Westminster John Knox, 2007).
7. The judgments of the scholars who constructed these texts are excellent but not infallible, and the members of those textual committees had doubts about several passages in their texts. The two current Greek New Testaments, namely the Nestle-Aland 27th edition of the *Novum Testamentum Graece* and the United Bible Society 4th edition of *The Greek New Testament*, which are almost (not exactly) alike in their text and form the basis for all modern translations, are eclectic texts that select various ancient texts to construct the text of the New Testament.
8. Eduard Schweizer, "θεόπνευστος," *TDNT*, 6:454–55. See also I. Howard Marshall, *The Pastoral Epistles*, ICC (Edinburgh: T & T Clark, 1999), 793–94, who correctly observes that the focus of the text is to emphasize "the authority of the Scriptures as coming from God and to indicate that they have a divinely-intended purpose related to his plan of salvation."
9. For this focus, see Martin Dibelius and Hans Conzelmann, *The Pastoral Epistles*, trans. Philip Buttolph and Adela Yarbro, Hermeneia (Philadelphia: Fortress, 1972), 120.
10. This observation comes from Jerome D. Quinn and William C. Walker, *The First and Second Letters to Timothy*, Eerdmans Critical Commentary (Grand Rapids: Eerdmans, 2000), 750–51.
11. E. J. Young, *Thy Word Is Truth* (Grand Rapids: Eerdmans, 1957), 27.
12. John Gerstner, *A Bible Inerrancy Primer*, 52 (privately published lectures without date).
13. He has also observed that by the word *canon* the early church simply meant the list of books that were acknowledged as Scripture (Barr, *Scripture*, 48). Barr's understanding of the traditional relationship of inspiration to the biblical canon is similar to that explained by Paul J. Achtemeier, *The Inspiration of Scripture*, 119, who says that "God inspired the canonical books with no exception, and no noncanonical books are inspired, with no exception."
14. Barr, *Scripture*, 57.
15. The understanding of inspiration in Origen is clearly different from that of Clement of Rome and Ignatius, but also from *all* of the church fathers who preceded him.
16. Take, for example, Clement of Alexandria, who cited the *Didache* as Scripture (*Strom.* 1.100.4) and regarded *1 Clement, Barnabas, Shepherd of Hermas*, the

Preaching of Peter, and the *Apocalypse of Peter* as inspired. See also Robert M. Grant, "The NT Canon," in *Cambridge History of the Bible,* vol. 1: *From the Beginnings to Jerome,* ed. P. R. Ackroyd and C. F. Evans (Cambridge: Cambridge University Press, 1970), 302.

17. Kalin, "The Inspired Community," 548.
18. Stendahl, "Apocalypse of John," 245.
19. Benjamin Breckenridge Warfield, *The Inspiration and Authority of the Bible* (Philadelphia: Presbyterian & Reformed, 1948; fourth printing, Grand Rapids: Baker Book House, 1964), 438. Warfield states, "These are often false—but they are a necessary part of human speech."
20. Ibid., 437–38.
21. Ibid., 439.
22. For a more complete listing of biblical passages with harmonization problems and apparent errors, see the dated but still relevant volume: Dewey M. Beegle, *Scripture, Tradition, and Infallibility* (Grand Rapids: Eerdmans, 1973).
23. Warfield, *Inspiration and Authority,* 438.
24. Hebrew *pesher* ("interpretation") is a style of commentary on sacred Scripture found especially among the Dead Sea Scrolls. The biblical text is explained in light of the interpreter's own day and circumstances, which are often seen as the last days, that is, eschatologically. The *Commentary on Habakkuk* is one of the best-known examples of this style of interpretation at Qumran. In the NT, see Acts 2:16–20 (cf. Joel 2:28–32); Acts 4:11 (cf. Ps. 118:22); and Eph. 5:31 (cf. Gen. 2:24). For a brief description of this practice, see Arthur G. Patzia and Anthony J. Petrotta, *Pocket Dictionary of Biblical Studies* (Downers Grove, Ill.: InterVarsity Press, 2002), 92. For a useful discussion of this practice, see Devorah Dimant, "Pesharim, Qumran," *ABD* 5:244–51; and for a more detailed discussion of this practice, see James H. Charlesworth, *The Pesharim and Qumran History: Chaos or Consensus?* (Grand Rapids: Eerdmans, 2002).
25. Craig A. Evans, "Textual Criticism and Textual Confidence: How Reliable Is Scripture?" in R. Stewart, ed., *Textual Reliability of the New Testament* (Minneapolis: Fortress, forthcoming), discusses this issue and cites other examples of the use of the size of the mustard seed. See *m. Nid.* 5:2: "even as little as a grain of mustard seed"; *y. Peah* 7:4: "I had a mustard plant . . . as (high) as a fig tree"; *b. Ber.* 31a: "they are so strict that if they see a drop of blood no bigger than a mustard seed they wait seven days." See these texts also in R. A. Guelich, *Mark 1–8:26,* WBC (Dallas: Word, 1989), 249–50; and R. H. Gundry, *Mark: A Commentary on His Apology for the Cross* (Grand Rapids: Eerdmans, 1993), 229.
26. See a discussion of this in my forthcoming article, "The Burial of Jesus in Light of Jewish Burial Practices and Roman Crucifixions," in J. H. Charlesworth, ed. [title not yet determined] (Grand Rapids: Eerdmans, 2009).
27. Peter Enns, *Inspiration and Incarnation: Evangelicals and the Problem of the Old Testament* (Grand Rapids: Baker Academic, 2005), 108.
28. Ibid., 109.

Bibliography

The following extended bibliography is intended to facilitate further research into the very important matter of how the ancient sacred texts tell an important story about the church's Scriptures in their formative development. All of the following works informed me at various stages as I developed this volume.

Abegg, Martin, Jr., Peter Flint, and Eugene Ulrich, eds. and trans. *The Dead Sea Scrolls Bible: The Oldest Known Bible Translated for the First Time into English*. San Francisco: HarperSanFrancisco, 1999.

Adler, W. "Pseudepigrapha in the Early Church." Pages 211–28 in *The Canon Debate*. Edited by L. M. McDonald and J. A. Sanders. Peabody, Mass.: Hendrickson, 2002.

Aichele, George. *The Control of Meaning: Canon as Semiotic Mechanism*. Harrisburg, Penn.: Trinity Press International, 2001.

Aland, Kurt, ed. *Repertorium der griechischen christlichen Papyri*. Vol. 1: *Biblische Papyri— Altes Testament, Neues Testament, Varia Apokryphen*. Berlin: Walter de Gruyter, 1976.

_____, and Hans-Udo Rosenbaum, eds. *Repertorium der griechischen christlichen Papyri*. Vol. 2: *Kirchenväter–Papyri*. Part 1: *Beschreibungen*. Berlin: Walter de Gruyter, 1995.

——, and Barbara Aland. *The Text of the New Testament: An Introduction to the Critical Editions and to the Theory and Practice of Modern Textual Criticism*. Translated by Erroll F. Rhodes. 2nd ed. Grand Rapids: Eerdmans, 1989.

Albl, Martin C. *'And Scripture Cannot Be Broken': The Form and Function of the Early Christian* Testimonia *Collections*. NovTSup 96. Leiden: Brill, 1999.

Alexander, Archibald. *The Canon of the Old and New Testaments Ascertained*. New York: Princeton Press, 1826.

Allert, Craig D. *A High View of Scripture? The Authority of the Bible and the Formation of the New Testament Canon*. Grand Rapids: Baker Academic, 2007.

_____. "Is Translation Inspired? The Problems of Verbal Inspiration for a Translation and a Proposed Solution." Pages 85–113 in *Translating the Bible: Problems and Prospects*. Edited by S. E. Porter and R. S. Hess. JSNTSup 173. Sheffield: Sheffield Academic Press, 1999.

_____. *Revelation, Truth, Canon and Interpretation: Studies in Justin Martyr's Dialogue with Trypho*. Supplements to VC 64. Leiden: Brill, 2002.

_____. "The State of the New Testament Canon in the Second Century: Putting Tatian's *Diatessaron* in Perspective." *BBR* 9 (1999): 1–18.

Anderson, G. W. "Canonical and Non-Canonical." Pages 113–58 in *The Cambridge History of the Bible*. Vol. 1: *From the Beginnings to Jerome*. Edited by P. R. Ackroyd and C. F. Evans. Cambridge: Cambridge University Press, 1970.

Armstrong, Jonathan J. "Victorinus of Pettau as the Author of the Canon Muratori." *Vigiliae christianae* 62 (2008): 1–34.

Avery-Peck, Alan J., Jacob Neusner, and Bruce Chilton, eds. *Judaism in Late Antiquity*. Part 5, vol. 2: *The Judaism of Qumran: A Systematic Reading of the Dead Sea Scrolls: World View, Comparing Judaisms*. Leiden: Brill, 2001.

Bacote, Vincent, L. C. Miguelez, and D. L. Okholm, eds. *Evangelicals and Scripture: Tradition, Authority and Hermeneutics*. Downers Grove, Ill.: InterVarsity Press, 2004.

Baehr, P., and M. O'Brien. "Founders, Classics and the Concept of a Canon." *Current Sociology* 42 (1994): 1–149.

Bagnall, Roger S. *Reading Papyri, Writing Ancient History: Approaching the Ancient World*. London: Routledge, 1995.

Baird, J. Arthur. *Holy Word: The Paradigm of New Testmaent Formation*. JSNTSup 224, CBTS 1. Sheffield: Sheffield Academic Press, 2002.

Balch, David L. "The Canon: Adaptable and Stable, Oral and Written. Critical Questions for Kelber and Riesner." *Forum* 7 (1991): 183–205.

Baldermann, I. "Didaktischer und »kanonischer« Zugang: Der Unterricht vor dem Problem des biblischen Kanons." *JBT* 3 (1988): 97–111.

Balz, H. R. "Anonymität und Pseudepigraphie im Urchristentum: Überlengungen zum literarischen und theologischen Problem der urchristlichen und gemeinantiken Pseudepigraphie." *ZTK* 66 (1969): 403–36.

Barr, James. *Holy Scripture: Canon, Authority, Criticism*. Philadelphia: Westminster, 1983.

Barrera, Julio Trebolle. *The Jewish Bible and the Christian Bible: An Introduction to the History of the Bible*. Translated by W. G. E. Watson. Grand Rapids: Eerdmans, 1998.

Barthélemy, Dominique. "La Critique Canonique." *Revue de l'Institut Catholique de Paris* 36 (1991): 191–220.

Barton, John. "Canon." Pages 101–5 in *A Dictionary of Biblical Interpretation*. Edited by R. J. Coggins and J. L. Houlden. Philadelphia: Trinity Press International, 1990.

_____. *Holy Writings, Sacred Text: The Canon in Early Christianity*. Louisville: Westminster John Knox, 1997.

_____. *How the Bible Came to Be*. Louisville: Westminster John Knox, 1997.

_____. *People of the Book? The Authority of the Bible in Christianity*. Louisville: Westminster John Knox, 1988.

_____. "The Significance of a Fixed Canon of the Hebrew Bible." Pages 67–83 in vol. I/1 of *Hebrew Bible/Old Testament: The History of Its Interpretation*. Edited by Magne Saebo. Göttingen: Vandenhoeck & Ruprecht, 1996.

_____. *The Spirit and the Letter: Studies in the Biblical Canon*. London: SPCK, 1997.

Bauckham, Richard. "For Whom Were the Gospels Written?" Pages 9–48 in *The Gospels for All Christians: Rethinking the Gospel Audiences*. Edited by R. Bauckham. Grand Rapids: Eerdmans, 1998.

_____. *Jesus and the Eyewitnesses: The Gospels as Eyewitness Testimony*. Grand Rapids: Eerdmans, 2006.

Beckwith, Roger T. "Canon of the Hebrew Bible and the Old Testament." Pages 102–4 in *The Oxford Companion to the Bible*. Edited by Bruce M. Metzger and M. D. Coogan. New York: Oxford University Press, 1993.

_____. "Formation of the Hebrew Bible." Pages 39–86 in *Mikra: Text, Translation, Reading and Interpretation of the Hebrew Bible in Ancient Judaism and Early Christianity*. Edited by M. J. Mulder and H. Sysling. CRINT II/1. Minneapolis: Fortress, 1990.

_____. *The Old Testament Canon of the New Testament Church*. Grand Rapids: Eerdmans, 1985.

_____. "'We Pay Heed to Heavenly Voices': The 'End of Prophecy' and the Formation of the Canon." Pages 19–31 in *Biblical and Humane: A Festschrift for John F. Priest*. Edited by Linda Bennett Elder, David L. Barr, and Elizabeth Struthers Malbon. Atlanta: Scholars Press, 1996.

Beegle, Dewey M. *Scripture, Tradition, and Infallibility*. Grand Rapids: Eerdmans, 1973.

Bergren, Theodore A. *Fifth Ezra: The Text, Origin and Early History*. SBLSCS 35. Altanta: Scholars Press, 1990.

_____. *Sixth Ezra: The Text and Origin*. New York: Oxford University Press, 1998.

Berstein, Moshe. "'Rewritten Bible': A Generic Category Which Has Outlived Its Usefulness?" *Textus* 22 (2005): 169–96.

Bialik, Hayim Nahman, and Yehoshua Hana Ravnitzky, eds. *The Book of Legends: Sefer Ha-Aggadah—Legends from the Talmud and Midrash*. Translated by W. G. Braude. New York: Schocken, 1992.

Black, David Alan, ed. *Rethinking New Testament Textual Criticism*. Grand Rapids: Baker Academic, 2002.

_____, and David S. Dockery, eds. *New Testament Criticism and Interpretation*. Grand Rapids: Zondervan, 1991.

Blenkinsopp, Joseph. *Prophecy and Canon: A Contribution to the Study of Jewish Origins*. Notre Dame, Ind.: University of Notre Dame Press, 1977.

Bloom, Harold. *The Western Canon: The Books and Schools of the Age*. New York: Harcourt Brace, 1994.

Blowers, Paul M., ed. and trans. *The Bible in Greek Christian Antiquity*. Notre Dame, Ind.: University of Notre Dame Press, 1997.

Boccaccini, Gabriele, ed. *Enoch and Qumran Origins: New Light on a Forgotten Connection*. Grand Rapids: Eerdmans, 2005.

Boeft, J. Den, and M. L. Van Poll-van De Lisdonk, eds. *The Impact of Scripture in Early Christianity*. Supplements to VC 44. Leiden: Brill, 1999.

Bohak, Gideon. *Joseph and Aseneth and the Jewish Temple in Heliopolis*. SBL Early Judaism and Its Literature 10. Atlanta: Scholars Press, 1996.

Bokedal, Tomas. *The Scriptures and the Lord: Formation and Significance of the Christian Biblical Canon*. Lund: Lund University, 2005.

Bossman, D. M. "Canon and Culture: Realistic Possibilities for the Biblical Canon." *BTB* 23 (1993): 4–13.

Bovon, François. "Vers une nouvelle édition de la littérature apocryphe chrétienne." *Aug* 23 (1983): 373–78.

_____. "The Synoptic Gospels and the Non-canonical Acts of the Apostles." *HTR* 81 (1988): 19–36.

_____. Ann Graham Brock, and Christopher R. Matthews, eds. *The Apocryphal Acts of the Apostles*. HDSS. Cambridge: Harvard University Press, 1999.

Bowley, James E., ed. *Living Traditions of the Bible: Scripture in Jewish, Christian, and Muslim Practice*. St. Louis, Mo.: Chalice Press, 1999.

Bowman, A. K. "The Vindolanda Tablets and the Development of the Book Form." *Zeitschrift für Papyrologie und Epigraphik* 18 (1975): 237–52.

Brock, Sebastian P. "The Use of the Syriac Fathers for New Testament Textual Criticism." Pages 224–36 in *The Text of the New Testament in Contemporary Research: Essays on the Status Quaestionis. A Volume in Honor of Bruce M. Metzger*. Edited by Bart D. Ehrman and Michael W. Holmes. SD 46. Grand Rapids: Eerdmans, 1995.

Brogan, John J. "Another Look at Codex Sinaiticus." Pages 17–32 in *The Bible as Book: The Transmission of the Greek Text.* Edited by S. McKendrick and O. O'Sullivan. London: British Library; New Castle, Del.: Oak Knoll Press, 2003.

Brooke, George J. *The Dead Sea Scrolls and the New Testament.* Minneapolis: Fortress, 2005.

Brown, Michelle P. *A Guide to Western Historical Scripts from Antiquity to 1600.* Toronto: University of Toronto Press, 1993.

_____. *Understanding Illuminated Manuscripts: A Guide to Technical Terms.* London: British Library, 1994.

Brown, William P., ed. *Engaging Biblical Authority: Perspectives on the Bible as Scripture.* Louisville: Westminster John Knox, 2007.

Broyde, M. J. "Defilement of the Hands, Canonization of the Bible, and the Special Status of Esther, Ecclesiastes, and the Song of Songs." *Judaism* 44 (Winter 1995): 65–79.

Bruce, F. F. *The Canon of Scripture.* Downers Grove, Ill.: InterVarsity Press, 1988.

_____. "Scripture and Tradition in the New Testament." Pages 68–93 in *Holy Book and Holy Tradition.* Edited by F. F. Bruce and E. G. Rupp. Manchester: Manchester University Press, 1968.

_____. "Some Thoughts on the Beginning of the New Testament Canon." *BJRL* 65 (1983): 37–60.

_____. "Tradition and the Canon of Scripture." Pages 59–84 in *The Authoritative Word: Essays on the Nature of Scripture.* Edited by Donald K. McKim. Grand Rapids: Eerdmans, 1983.

Bruns, G. L. "Canon and Power in the Hebrew Scriptures." *Critical Inquiry* 10 (1984): 259–89.

Buchanan, E. S. "The Codex Muratorianus." *JTS* 8 (1907): 537–39.

Buhl, Frants P. W. *Kanon und Text des alten Testaments.* Leipzig: Akademische Buchhandlung, 1891.

Callaway, Philip R. "The Temple Scroll and the Canonization of the Old Testament." *RB* 13 (1988): 239–43.

Campenhausen, Hans von. *The Formation of the Christian Bible.* Translated by J. A. Baker. Philadelphia: Fortress, 1972.

Canfora, Luciano. *The Vanished Library: A Wonder of the Ancient World.* Translated by Martin Ryle. Berkeley: University of California Press, 1987.

Carr, David. "Canonization in the Context of Community: An Outline for the Formation of the Tanakh and the Christian Bible." Pages 22–64 in *A Gift of God in Due Season: Essays on Scripture and Community in Honor of James A. Sanders.* Edited by R. Weis and D. Carr. Sheffield: Sheffield Academic Press, 1996.

Casey, R. "The Armenian Marcionites and the Diatessaron." *JBL* 57 (1938): 185–94.

Chapman, S. B. "How the Biblical Canon Began: Working Models and Open Questions." Pages 29–52 in *Homer, the Bible, and Beyond: Literary and Religious Canons in the Ancient World.* Edited by M. Finkelberg and G. G. Stroumsa. Leiden: Brill, 2003.

_____. *The Law and the Prophets: A Study in Old Testament Canon Formation.* FAT 27. Tübingen: Mohr Siebeck, 2000.

_____. " 'The Law and the Words' as a Canonical Formula Within the Old Testament." Pages 26–74 in *The Interpretation of Scripture in Early Judaism and Christianity: Studies in Language and Traditions.* Edited by Craig A. Evans. JSPSup 33, SSEJC 7. Sheffield: Sheffield Academic Press, 2000.

_____. "Reclaiming Inspiration for the Bible." Pages 167–206 in *Canon and Biblical Interpretation.* Edited by C. G. Bartholomew, S. Hahn, R. Parry, C. Seitz, and Al Wolters. Scripture and Hermeneutics Series 7. Grand Rapids: Zondervan, 2006.

Charlesworth, James H. "The Books of Enoch or 1 Enoch Matters: New Paradigms for Understanding Pre–70 Judaism." Pages 436–54 in *Enoch and Qumran Origins: New Light on a Forgotten Connection.* Edited by Gabrielle Boccaccini. Grand Rapids: Eerdmans, 2005.

_____. *The Old Testament Pseudepigrapha and the New Testament: Prolegomena for the Study of Christian Origins.* Cambridge: Cambridge University Press, 1985.

_____. *The Pesharim and Qumran History: Chaos or Consensus?* Grand Rapids: Eerdmans, 2002.

_____, ed. *The Bible and the Dead Sea Scrolls.* 3 vols. Waco: Baylor University Press, 2006.

_____, ed. *The Old Testament Pseudepigrapha.* 2 vols. Garden City, N.Y.: Doubleday, 1983–85.

_____, and Craig A. Evans. "Jesus in the Agrapha and Apocryphal Gospels." Pages 479–533 in *Studying the Historical Jesus: Evaluations of the State of Current Research.* Edited by B. Chilton and C. Evans. Leiden: Brill, 1994.

Charteris, A. H. *Canonicity: A Collection of Early Testimonies to the Canonical Books of the New Testament.* Edinburgh: William Blackwood and Sons, 1880.

Chazon, Esther G., Devorah Dimant, and Ruth A. Clements, eds. *Reworking the Bible: Apocryphal and Related Texts at Qumran.* Studies on the Texts of the Desert of Judah 58. Leiden: Brill, 2005.

Chazon, Esther G., and Michael E. Stone, eds. *Pseudepigraphic Perspectives: The Apocrypha and Pseudepigrapha in Light of the Dead Sea Scrolls—Proceedings of the International Symposium of the Orion Center, 12–14 January 1997.* Leiden: Brill, 1999.

Childs, Brevard. "The Hermeneutical Problem of New Testament Criticism." Pages 518–30 in *The New Testament as Canon: An Introduction.* Philadelphia: Fortress, 1985.

Chilton, Bruce, and Craig A. Evans. "Jesus and Israel's Scriptures." Pages 281–336 in *Studying the Historical Jesus: Evaluations of the State of Current Research.* Edited by B. Chilton and C. A. Evans. NTTS 19. Leiden: Brill, 1998.

Clarke, Kent D. "Original Text or Canonical Text? Questioning the Shape of the New Testament We Translate." Pages 281–322 in *Issues in Biblical Translation: Responses to Eugene A. Nida.* Edited by S. E. Porter and R. Hess. JSNTSup 173. Sheffield: Sheffield Academic Press, 1998.

Clemens, Raymond, and Timothy Graham. *Introduction to Manuscript Studies.* Ithaca, N.Y.: Cornell University Press, 2007.

Collins, J. J. "Before the Canon: Scriptures in Second Temple Judaism." Pages 225–41 in *Old Testament Interpretation: Past, Present, and Future.* Edited by James Luther Mays, David L. Petersen, and Kent Harold Richards. Nashville: Abingdon, 1995.

Collins, Nina L. *The Library in Alexandria & the Bible in Greek.* Supplements to Vetus Testamentum 82. Leiden: Brill, 2000.

Comfort, Philip Wesley. *Early Manuscripts and Modern Translations of the New Testament.* Grand Rapids: Baker Books, 1990.

_____. *The Quest for the Original Text of the New Testament.* Grand Rapids: Baker Book House, 1992.

_____, and David P. Barrett, eds. *The Text of the Earliest New Manuscripts: A Corrected, Enlarged Edition of The Complete Text of the Earliest New Testament Manuscripts.* Wheaton, Ill: Tyndale House, 2001.

Cosgrove, Charles H. "Justin Martyr and the Emerging Christian Canon: Observations on the Purpose and Destination of the Dialogue with Trypho." *VC* 36 (1982): 209–32.

Cowley, R. W. "The Biblical Canon of the Ethiopian Orthodox Church Today." *Ostkirchliche Studien* 23 (1974): 318–24.

Crawford, Sidnie White. *Rewriting Scripture in Second Temple Times.* Grand Rapids: Eerdmans, 2008.

Cribiore, Raffaella. *Writing, Teachers, and Students in Greco-Roman Egypt.* Atlanta: Scholars Press, 1996.

Cross, F. L. "History and Fiction in the African Canons." *JTS* 12 (1961): 227–47.

Cross, F. M. *From Epic to Canon: History and Literature in Ancient Israel.* Baltimore: Johns Hopkins University Press, 1998.

_____. *The Ancient Library at Qumran.* 3rd ed. Minneapolis: Fortress, 1995.

_____. "The History of the Biblical Text in the Light of the Discoveries in the Judean Desert." *HTR* 57 (1964): 281–99.

_____. "The Text Behind the Text of the Hebrew Bible." Pages 139–55 in *Understanding the Dead Sea Scrolls.* Edited by Hershel Shanks. New York: Random House, 1992.

Croy, N. Clayton. *The Mutilation of Mark's Gospel.* Nashville: Abingdon, 2003.

Crüsemann, F. "Das 'portative Vaterland': Struktur und Genese des alttestamentlichen Kanons." Pages 63–79 in vol. 2 of *Kanon und Zensur: Beiträge zur Archäologie der literarischen Kommunikation.* Edited by A. Assmann and J. Assmann. Munich: Wilhelm Fink, 1987.

Cullmann, O. "The Plurality of the Gospels as a Theological Problem in Antiquity." Pages 39–54 in *The Early Church.* Edited by A. J. B. Higgins. Philadelphia: Westminster, 1956.

Cunningham, Philip J. *Exploring Scripture: How the Bible Came to Be.* New York: Paulist Press, 1992.

Daniélou, Jean. *A History of Early Christian Doctrine Before the Council of Nicaea.* Vol. 1: *The Theology of Jewish Christianity.* Translated and edited by J. A. Baker. Philadelphia: Westminster, 1964.

_____. *A History of Early Christian Doctrine Before the Council of Nicaea.* Vol. 3: *The Origins of Latin Christianity.* Translated by David Smith and John A. Baker. Philadelphia: Westminster, 1977.

Davidson, Samuel. *The Canon of the Bible: Its Formation, History, and Fluctuations.* London: Henry S. King, 1877.

Davies, Philip R. *Scribes and Schools: The Canonization of the Hebrew Scriptures.* Louisville: Westminster John Knox, 1988.

De Boer, Esther A. *The Gospel of Mary: Listening to the Beloved Disciple.* London: T & T Clark International, 2004.

De Hamel, Christopher. *The Book: A History of the Bible.* London: Phaidon, 2001.

de Jonge, M. "The Authority of the 'Old Testament' in the Early Church: The Witness of the 'Pseudepigrapha of the Old Testament.'" Pages 459–86 in *The Biblical Canons.* Edited by J.-M. Auwers and H. J. de Jonge. BETL 163. Leuven: Leuven University Press, 2003.

De Troyer, Kristin. *Rewriting the Sacred Text: What the Old Greek Texts Tell Us about the Literary Growth of the Bible.* Text-Critical Studies 4. Atlanta: Society of Biblical Literature, 2003.

Dempster, Stephen G. "An 'Extraordinary Fact': Torah and Temple and the Contours of the Hebrew Canon." *TynB* 48 (1997): 23–56, 191–218.

_____. "The Prophets, the Canon and a Canonical Approach: No Empty Word." Pages 293–332 in *Canon and Biblical Interpretation.* Edited by C. G. Bartholomew, S. Hahn, R. Parry, C. Seitz, and A. Wolters. Scripture and Hermeneutics Series 7. Grand Rapids: Zondervan, 2006.

Denaux, A., ed. *New Testament Textual Criticism and Exegesis: Festschrift J. Delobel.* BETL 161. Leuven: Leuven University Press, 2002.

Derolez, Albert. *The Palaeography of Gothic Manuscript Books from the Twelfth to the Early Sixteenth Century.* Cambridge: Cambridge University Press, 2003.

Dimant, Devorah. "Pesharim, Qumran." *ABD* 5:244–51.

Dobschütz, E. von. "The Abandonment of the Canonical Ideal." *AJT* 19 (1915): 416–29.

Dohmen, C. "Der biblische Kanon in der Diskussion." *ThRv* 6 (1995): 452–60.

_____, and M. Oeming. *Biblischer Kanon, warum and wozu? Eine Kanontheologie.* QD 137. Freiburg: Herder, 1992.

Donelson, L. R. *Pseudepigraphy and Ethical Argument in the Pastoral Epistles.* HUT 22. Tübingen: Mohr, 1986.

DuBois, J.-D. "L'exégèse gnostique et l'histoire du canon des écritures." Pages 89–97 in *Les regles de l'intepretation.* Edited by M. Tardieu. Paris: Cerf, 1987.

Duff, Jeremy. "A Reconsideration of Pseudepigraphy in Early Christianity." D.Phil. diss. St. Cross College, Oxford, 1998.

_____. "P[46] and the Pastorals: A Misleading Consensus?" *NTS* 44 (1998): 581–82.

Duncker, P. G. "The Canon of the Old Testament at the Council of Trent." *CBQ* 15 (1953): 277–99.

Dungan, David L. *Constantine's Bible: Politics and the Making of the New Testament.* Minneapolis: Fortress, 2007.

Dunn, J. D. G. *The Living Word.* Philadelphia: Fortress, 1987.

_____. "How the New Testament Canon Began." Pages 122–37 in *From Biblical Criticism to Biblical Faith: Essays in Honor of Lee Martin McDonald.* Edited by W. Brackney and C. A. Evans. Macon, Ga.: Mercer University Press, 2006.

Dyck, E. "What Do We Mean By Canon?" *Crux* 25 (1989): 17–22.

Edrei, Arye, and Doron Mendels. "A Split Jewish Diaspora: Its Dramatic Consequences." *JSP* 16, no. 2 (2007): 91–137.

Ehrman, Bart D. *Lost Christianities: The Battles for Scripture and the Faiths We Never Knew.* Oxford: Oxford University Press, 2003.

_____. *Lost Scriptures: Books that Did Not Make It into the New Testament.* Oxford: Oxford University Press, 2003.

_____. "Methodological Developments in the Analysis and Classification of New Testament Documentary Evidence." *NovT* 29, no. 1 (1987): 22–45.

_____. *The Orthodox Corruption of Scripture: The Effect of Early Christological Controversies on the Text of the New Testament.* Oxford: Oxford University Press, 1993.

_____. *Studies in the Textual Criticism of the New Testament.* NTTS 33. Leiden: Brill, 2006.

_____. "The Text as Window: New Testament Manuscripts and the Social History of Early Christianity." Pages 361–79 in *The Text of the New Testament in Contemporary Research: Essays on the Status Quaestionis. A Volume in Honor of Bruce M. Metzger.* Edited by Bart D. Ehrman and Michael W. Holmes. SD 46. Grand Rapids: Eerdmans, 1995.

_____. "The Text of the Gospels at the End of the Second Century." Pages 95–122 in *Codex Bezae: Studies from the Lunel Colloquium, June 1994.* Edited by D. C. Parker and C.-B. Amphoux. NTTS 22. Leiden: Brill, 1996.

_____. "The New Testament Canon of Didymus the Blind." *VC* 37 (1983): 1–21.

_____. TC [1998]: par 22 = an online journal = *A Journal of Biblical Textual Criticism.*

_____, and M. A. Plunkett. "The Angel and the Agony: The Textual Problem of Luke 22:43–44." *CBQ* 45 (1983): 401–16.

_____, and Michael W. Holmes, eds. *The Text of the New Testament in Contemporary Research: Essays on the Status Quaestionis. A Volume in Honor of Bruce M. Metzger.* Grand Rapids: Eerdmans, 1995.

Ellege, C. D. *The Bible and the Dead Sea Scrolls.* Archaeology and Biblical Studies 14. Atlanta: Society of Biblical Literature, 2005.

_____. *The Statutes of the King: The Temple Scroll's Legislation on Kingship* (11Q19 LVI 12–LIX 21). Cahiers de la Revue biblique 56. Paris: Gabalda, 2004. (See especially pp. 1–69.)

274   Bibliography

Elliott, J. K. "The Case for Thoroughgoing Eclecticism." Pages 101–24 in *Rethinking New Testament Textual Criticism*. Grand Rapids: Baker Academic, 2002.
_____. "Manuscripts, the Codex, and the Canon." *JSNT* 63 (1996): 105–23.
_____. *A Survey of Manuscripts Used in Editions of the Greek New Testament*. NovTSup 57. Leiden: Brill, 1987.
_____, ed. *The Collected Biblical Essays of T. C. Skeat*. NovTSup 113. Leiden: Brill, 2004.
Ellis, E. Earle. *The Making of the New Testament Documents*. Boston: Brill, 2002.
_____. "The Old Testament Canon in the Early Church." Pages 653–90 in *Mikra: Text, Translation, Reading and Interpretation of the Hebrew Bible in Ancient Judaism and Early Christianity*. Edited by M. J. Mulder and H. Sysling. CRINT II/1. Minneapolis: Fortress, 1990.
_____. "Pseudonymity and Canonicity of New Testament Documents." Pages 212–24 in *Worship, Theology, and Ministry in the Early Church: Essays in Honor of Ralph P. Martin*. Edited by M. J. Wilkins and T. Paige. JSNTSup 87. Sheffield: JSOT Press, 1992.
Enns, Peter. *Inspiration and Incarnation: Evangelicals and the Problem of the Old Testament*. Grand Rapids: Baker Academic, 2005.
Epp, E. J. "The Codex and Literacy in Early Christianity and at Oxyrhynchus: Issues Raised by Harry Y. Gamble's Books and Readers in the Early Church." *CR* 10 (1997): 15–37.
_____. "Issues in the Interrelation of New Testament Textual Criticism and Canon." Pages 485–515 in *The Canon Debate*. Edited by L. M. McDonald and J. A. Sanders. Peabody, Mass.: Hendrickson, 2002.
_____. *Junia: The First Woman Apostle*. Minneapolis: Fortress, 2005.
_____. "The Multivalence of the Term 'Original Text' in New Testament Textual Criticism." *HTR* 92 (1999): 245–81.
_____. "The New Testament Papyri at Oxyrhynchus in Their Social and Intellectual Context." Pages 47–68 in *Sayings of Jesus: Canonical and Non-Canonical: Essays in Honor of Tjitze Baarda*. Edited by W. L. Petersen et al. Leiden: Brill, 1997.
_____. "The Oxyrhynchus New Testament Papyri: 'Not without Honor Except in Their Hometown'?" *JBL* 123, no. 1 (2004): 5–55.
_____. *Perspectives on New Testament Textual Criticism: Collected Essays, 1962–2004*. NovTSup 116. Leiden: Brill, 2005.
_____. "The Significance of the Papyri for Determining the Nature of the New Testament Text in the Second Century: A Dynamic View of Textual Transmission." Pages 71–103 in *Gospel Traditions in the Second Century*. Edited by W. L. Petersen. Notre Dame, Ind.: University of Notre Dame Press, 1989.
_____. "Textual Criticism in the Exegesis of the New Testament, with an Excursus on Canon." Pages 73–91 in *Handbook to Exegesis of the New Testament*. Edited by S. E. Porter. NTTS 25. Leiden: Brill, 1997.
Ernest, James D. *The Bible in Athanasius of Alexandria*. Bible in Ancient Christianity 2. Boston: Brill Academic, 2004.
Evans, Christopher F. *Is Holy Scripture Christian?* London: SCM Press, 1971.
Evans, Craig, A. *Ancient Texts for New Testament Studies: A Guide to the Background Literature*. Peabody, Mass.: Hendrickson, 2005.
_____. "The Scriptures of Jesus and His Earliest Followers." Pages 185–95 in *The Canon Debate*. Edited by L. M. McDonald and J. A. Sanders. Peabody, Mass.: Hendrickson, 2002.
_____. "Textual Criticism and Textual Confidence: How Reliable Is Scripture?" In *Textual Reliability of the New Testament*. Edited by R. Stewart. Minneapolis: Fortress, forthcoming.

_____, ed. *The Interpretation of Scripture in Early Judaism and Christianity: Studies in Language and Tradition.* JSPSup 33, SSEJC 7. Sheffield: Sheffield Academic Press, 2000.

Falk, Daniel K. *The Parabiblical Texts: Strategies for Extending the Scriptures among the Dead Sea Scrolls.* Library of Second Temple Studies 63. London: T & T Clark, 2007.

Fee, Gordon. "Codex Sinaiticus in the Gospel of John: A Contribution to Methodology in Establishing Textual Relationships." *NTS* 15 (1968–69): 23–44.

_____. "The Use of the Greek Fathers for New Testament Textual Criticism." Pages 191–207 in *The Text of the New Testament in Contemporary Research: Essays on the Status Quaestionis. A Volume in Honor of Bruce M. Metzger.* Edited by Bart D. Ehrman and Michael W. Holmes. SD 46. Grand Rapids: Eerdmans, 1995.

Feldman, Louis H. *Studies in Josephus' Rewritten Bible.* JSJSup. Leiden: Brill, 1998.

Finkelberg, Margalit, and Guy G. Stroumsa, eds. *Homer, the Bible, and Beyond: Literary and Religious Canons in the Ancient World.* Jerusalem Studies in Religion and Culture 2. Leiden: Brill, 2003.

Fitzmyer, Joseph A. *The Dead Sea Scrolls and Christian Origins.* SDSSRL. Grand Rapids: Eerdmans, 2000.

_____. "Scripture in the Catholic Tradition." Pages 145–62 in *Living Traditions of the Bible: Scripture in Jewish, Christian, and Muslim Practice.* Edited by James E. Bowley. St. Louis, Mo.: Chalice Press, 1999.

Flint, Peter W. *The Dead Sea Psalms Scrolls and the Book of Psalms.* Studies on the Texts of the Desert of Judah 17. Leiden: Brill, 1997.

Folkert, K. W. "The 'Canons' of Scripture." Pages 170–79 in *Rethinking Scripture: Essays from a Comparative Perspective.* Edited by M. Levering. Albany: SUNY Press, 1989.

Freedman, David Noel. "The Earliest Bible." Pages in 29–37 in *Backgrounds for the Bible.* Edited by M. P. O'Connor and D. N. Freedman. Winona Lake, Ind.: Eisenbrauns, 1987.

_____, general ed. *The Leningrad Codex: A Facsimile Edition.* Grand Rapids: Eerdmans, 1998.

Frowde, Henry. *The New Testament in the Apostolic Fathers.* Oxford Society of Historical Theology. Oxford: Clarendon, 1905.

Funk, Robert W. *Honest to Jesus.* San Francisco: HarperSanFrancisco, 1996. (See especially pp. 77–120.)

_____. "The Incredible Canon." Pages 24–46 in *Christianity in the 21st Century.* Edited by D. A. Brown. New York: Crossroad, 2000.

_____. "The New Testament as Tradition and Canon." Pages 151–86 in *Parables and Presence.* Philadelphia: Fortress, 1982.

_____, et al. *The Once and Future Jesus.* Santa Rosa, Calif.: Polebridge, 2000.

Friedman, S. "The Holy Scriptures Defile the Hands—The Transformation of a Biblical Concept in Rabbinic Theology." Pages 115–32 in *Biblical and Other Studies Presented to Nahum M. Sarna in Honor of His 70th Birthday.* Edited by M. Bretler and M. Fishbane. JSOTSup 154. Sheffield: Sheffield Academic Press, 1993.

Gafni, Israel M. *Land, Center and Diaspora: Jewish Constructs in Late Antiquity.* JSPSup 21. Sheffield: Sheffield Academic Press, 1997.

Gamble, Harry Y. *Books and Readers in the Early Church: A History of Early Christian Texts.* New Haven: Yale University Press, 1995.

_____. "Canon. New Testament." *ABD* 1:852–61.

_____. "The Canon of the New Testament." Pages 201–43 in *The New Testament and Its Modern Interpreters.* Edited by E. J. Epp and G. W. MacRae. Society of

Biblical Literature The Bible and Its Modern Interpreters 3. Philadelphia: Fortress; Atlanta: Scholars Press, 1989.

_____. "Christianity: Scripture and Canon." Pages 36–62 in *The Holy Book in Comparative Perspective*. Edited by F. M. Denney and R. L. Taylor. SCR. Columbia: University of South Carolina Press, 1985.

_____. *The New Testament Canon: Its Making and Meaning*. Guides to Biblical Scholarship. Philadelphia: Fortress, 1985.

_____. "The Pauline Corpus and the Early Christian Book." Pages 265–80 in *Paul and the Legacies of Paul*. Edited by William S. Babcock. Dallas: SMU Press, 1990.

Gerhardsson, Birger. *Tradition and Memory in Early Christianity*. Rev. ed. Biblical Resource Series. Grand Rapids: Eerdmans, 1998.

Gnuse, Robert. *The Authority of the Bible: Theories of Inspiration, Revelation and the Canon of Scripture*. New York: Paulist Press, 1985.

Gonis, N., D. Obbink, D. Colomo, G. B. D'Alessio, and A. Nodar, eds. and trans. *The Oxyrhynchus Papyri*. Vol. 69. Greco-Roman Memoirs, No. 89. London: British Academy, Egypt Exploration Society, 2005.

Gorak, J. *The Making of the Modern Canon: Genesis and Crisis of a Literary Idea*. London: Athlone, 1991.

Grafton, Anthony, and Megan Williams. *Christianity and the Transformation of the Book: Origen, Eusebius, and the Library of Caesarea*. Cambridge: Belknap Press of Harvard University Press, 2006.

Graham, William A. *Beyond the Written Word: Oral Aspects of Scripture in the History of Religion*. Cambridge: Cambridge University Press, 1987.

_____. "Scripture." Pages 133–45 in vol. 13 of *Encyclopaedia of Religion*. Edited by Mircea Eliade. New York: Macmillan, 1987.

Grant, Robert. The *Formation of the New Testament*. New York: Harper & Row, 1965.

Gregory, Caspar René. *Canon and Text of the New Testament*. ITL. Edinburgh: T & T Clark, 1907.

Griggs, C. Wilfred. *Early Egyptian Christianity from Its Origins to 451 CE*. Leiden: Brill, 1989.

Groh, Dennis E. "Hans von Campenhausen on Canon: Positions and Problems." *Int* 28 (1974): 331–43.

Grosheide, F. W., ed. *Some Early Lists of the Books of the New Testament*. Vol. 1: *Textus Minores*. Leiden: Brill, 1948.

Guillory, John. "Canon." Pages 233–49 in *Critical Terms for Literary Study*. Edited by F. Lentricchia and T. McLaughlin. Chicago: University of Chicago Press, 1987.

Haelst, Joseph van. *Catalogue des papyrus littéraires juifs et chrétiens*. Université de Paris IV. Serie Papyrologie 1. Paris: Publications de la Sorbonne, 1976.

Haines-Eitzen, Kim. *Guardians of Letters: Literacy, Power, and the Transmitters of Early Christian Literature*. Oxford: Oxford University Press, 2000.

Hallberg, Robert von, ed. *Canons*. Chicago: University of Chicago Press, 1983.

Harnack, Adolf von. *The Origin of the New Testament and the Most Important Consequences of the New Creation*. Translated by J. R. Wilkinson. New York: Macmillan, 1925. Translation of *Das Neue Testament um das Jahr 200*. Freiburg: Mohr [Siebeck], 1889.

Harrington, Daniel J. "Introduction to the Canon." Pages 7–21 in vol. 1 of *The New Interpreter's Bible*. Edited by Leander E. Keck. Nashville: Abingdon, 1994.

_____. "The Old Testament Apocrypha in the Early Church and Today." Pages 196–210 in *The Canon Debate*. Edited by L. M. McDonald and J. A. Sanders. Peabody, Mass.: Hendrickson, 2002.

Harris, William. "Why Did the Codex Supplant the Book-Roll?" Pages 71–85 in *Renaissance Society and Culture: Essays in Honor of Eugene F. Rice, Jr.* Edited by John Monfasani and Ronald G. Musto. New York: Italica, 1991.

Hay, David M. *Glory at the Right Hand: Psalm 110 in Early Christianity.* Nashville: Abingdon, 1973.

Head, Peter M. *The Early Greek Bible Manuscript Project: New Testament Uncial Manuscripts.* http://www.tyndale.cam.ac.uk/Tyndale/staff/Head/NTUncials.htm

Helmer, Christine, and Christof Lanmesser, eds. *One Scripture or Many? Canon from Biblical, Theological and Philosophical Perspectives.* Oxford: Oxford University Press, 2004.

Hengel, Martin. *The Four Gospels and the One Gospel of Jesus Christ: An Investigation of the Collection and Origin of the Canonical Gospels.* Translated by John Bowden. Harrisburg, Penn.: Trinity Press International, 2000.

_____. *The Septuagint as Christian Scripture: Its Prehistory and the Problem of Its Canon.* Translated by Mark E. Biddle. Edinburgh: T & T Clark, 2002.

Herbert, Edward D., and Emanuel Tov. *The Bible As Book: The Hebrew Bible and the Judaean Desert Discoveries.* London: British Library and Oak Knoll Press, 2002.

Holmes, Michael. "The Case for Reasoned Eclecticism." Pages 77–100 in *Rethinking New Testament Textual Criticism.* Edited by David A. Black. Grand Rapids: Baker Academic, 2002.

_____. "Textual Criticism." Pages 101–34 in *New Testament Criticism & Interpretation.* Edited by D. A. Black and D. S. Dockery. Grand Rapids: Zondervan, 1991.

Hooker, J. T., et al. *Reading the Past: Ancient Writing from Cuneiform to the Alphabet.* London: British Museum of the Past, 1990.

Horbury, W. "The Wisdom of Solomon in the Muratorian Fragment." *JTS* 45 (1994): 149–59.

Hübner, H. "Vetus Testamentum und Vetus Testamentum in Novo receptum: Die Frage nach dem Kanon des Alten Testaments aus neutestamentlicher Sicht." *JBT* 3 (1988): 147–62.

Hunt, H. "An Examination of the Current Emphasis on the Canon in Old Testament Studies." *SwJT* 23 (1980): 55–70.

Hurtado, Larry W. *The Earliest Christian Artifacts: Manuscripts and Christian Origins.* Grand Rapids: Eerdmans, 2006.

_____. *Lord Jesus Christ: Devotion to Jesus in Earliest Christianity.* Grand Rapids: Eerdmans, 2003.

_____, ed. *The Freer Biblical Manuscripts: Fresh Studies of an American Treasure Trove.* Text-Critical Studies 6. Atlanta: Society of Biblical Literature, 2006.

James, Montague Rhodes. *The Lost Apocrypha of the Old Testament: Their Titles and Fragments.* London: SPCK, 1920.

Jepsen, A. "Kanon und Text des Alten Testaments." *ThLZ* 74 (1949): 65–74.

Jinbachian, Manuel M. "The Bible the Apostles Used: Reflections from a Bible Translator." Pages 455–70 in *The Changing Face of Judaism, Christianity, and Other Greco-Roman Religions in Antiquity.* Edited by I. H. Henderson and G. S. Oegema. Studien zu den Jüdischen Schriften aus hellenistisch-römischer Zeit 2. Gütersloh: Gütersloher Verlaghaus, 2006.

Jones, Barry Alan. *The Formation of the Book of the Twelve: A Study in Text and Canon.* SBLDS 149. Atlanta: Scholars Press, 1995.

Kalin, Everett R. "Argument from Inspiration in the Canonization of the New Testament." Th.D. diss. Harvard University, 1967.

_____. "A Book Worth Discussing: *Canon and Community: A Guide to Canonical Criticism.*" *CTM* 12 (1985): 310–12.

_____. "Early Traditions About Mark's Gospel: Canonical Status Emerges, the Story Grows." *CTM* 2 (1975): 332–41.

_____. "The Inspired Community: A Glance at Canon History." *CTM* 42 (1971): 541–49.

_____. "Re-examining New Testament Canon History: 1. The Canon of Origen." *CTM* 17 (1990): 274–82.

Kampen, Kimberly van, and Paul Saenger, eds. *The Bible as Book: The First Printed Editions*. London: British Library and Oak Knoll Press, 1999.

Käsemann, Ernst. "The Canon of the New Testament and the Unity of the Church." Pages 95–107 in *Essays on New Testament Themes*. London: SCM Press, 1968.

_____. *Das Neue Testament als Kanon: Dokumentation und kritische Analyse zur gegenwärtgen Discussion*. Göttingen: Vandenhoeck & Ruprecht, 1970.

Katz, Peter. "Justin's Old Testament Quotations and the Greek Dodekapropheten Scroll." *StPatr* 1 (1957): 343–53.

_____. "The Old Testament Canon in Palestine and Alexandria." *ZNW* 47 (1956): 191–217.

_____. *Philo's Bible: The Aberrant Text of Bible Quotations in Some Philonic Writings and Its Place in the Textual History of the Greek Bible*. Cambridge: Cambridge University Press, 1950.

Kee, Howard Clark, ed. *The Bible in the Twenty-First Century—Symposium Papers*. Philadelphia: Trinity Press International, 1993.

Kenyon, Frederic G. *The Chester Beatty Biblical Papyri Descriptions and Texts of Twelve Manuscripts on Papyrus of the Greek Bible*. Vols. 1–3. London: Emery Walker, 1935–37.

Klauck, Hans-Josef. *Apocryphal Gospels: An Introduction*. Translated by Brian McNeil. London: T & T Clark, 2003.

Koester, Helmut. "Apocryphal and Canonical Gospels." *HTR* 73 (1980): 105–30.

_____. "*Gnomai Diaphoroi*: The Origin and Nature of Diversification in the History of Early Christianity." Pages 114–57 in *Trajectories through Early Christianity*. Edited by James M. Robinson and Helmut Koester. Philadelphia: Fortress, 1971.

_____. "The Intention and Scope of Trajectories." Pages 269–79 in *Trajectories through Early Christianity*. Edited by James M. Robinson and Helmut Koester. Philadelphia: Fortress, 1971.

_____. *Synoptische Überlieferung bei den apostolischen Vätern*. TU 65. Berlin: Akadamie Verlag, 1957.

_____. "The Text of the Synoptic Gospels in the Second Century." Pages 19–37 in *Gospel Traditions in the Second Century: Origins, Recensions, Text, and Transmission*. Edited by W. L. Petersen. Notre Dame, Ind.: University of Notre Dame Press, 1989.

_____. "Writings and the Spirit: Authority and Politics in Ancient Christianity." *HTR* 84 (1991): 353–72.

Kofoed, Jens Bruun. *Text History: Historiography and the Study of the Biblical Text*. Winona Lake, Ind: Eisenbrauns, 2005.

Kohler, W.-D. *Die Rezeption des Matthausevangeliums in der Zeit vor Irenaeus*. WUNT 2/24. Tübingen: Mohr/Siebeck, 1987.

Kooij, A. van der. "The Canonization of Ancient Books Kept in the Temple of Jerusalem." Pages 17–40 in *Canonization and Decanonization: Papers Presented to the International Conference of the Leiden Institute for the Study of Religions (LISOR) Held at Leiden 9–10 January 1997*. Edited by A. van der Kooij and K. van der Toorn. SHR 82. Leiden: Brill, 1998.

Kort, Wesley A. *Story, Text, and Scripture: Literary Interests in Biblical Narrative*. University Park: University of Pennsylvania Press, 1988.

Kraemer, David. "The Formation of the Rabbinic Canon: Authority and Boundaries." *JBL* 110, no. 4 (1991): 613–30.

Kraemer, Ross Shepherd. *When Aseneth Met Joseph: A Late Antique Tale of the Biblical Patriarch and His Egyptian Wife, Reconsidered.* New York: Oxford University Press, 1998.

Kraft, Robert. "Para-mania: Beside, Before and Beyond Bible Studies." *JBL* 126, no. 1 (2007): 5–27.

Krans, Jan. *Beyond What Is Written: Erasmus and Beza as Conjectural Critics of the New Testament.* MT Tools and Studies 35. Leiden: Brill, 2006.

Kraus, Thomas J. *Ad fontes: Original Manuscripts and Their Significance for Studying Early Christianity—Selected Essays.* TENTS 3. Leiden: Brill, 2007.

_____, and Tobias Nicklas, eds. *New Testament Manuscripts: Their Texts and Their World.* TENTS 2. Leiden: Brill, 2006.

Kraus, Wolfgang, and R. Glenn Wooden, eds. *Septuagint Research: Issues and Challenges in the Study of the Greek Jewish Scriptures.* SBLSCS 53. Atlanta: Society of Biblical Literature, 2006.

Kruger, Michael J. *The Gospel of the Savior: Analysis of P.Oxy 840 and Its Place in the Gospel Traditions of Early Christianity.* TENTS 1. Leiden: Brill, 2005.

Lake, Kirsopp. "The Sinaitic and Vaticanus Manuscripts and the Copies Sent by Eusebius to Constantine." *HTR* 11 (1918): 32–35.

Le Boulluec, Alain. "The Bible in Use among the Marginally Orthodox in the Second and Third Centuries." Pages 197–216 in *The Bible in Greek Christian Antiquity.* Edited by P. M. Blowers. Notre Dame, Ind.: University of Notre Dame Press, 1997.

Lea, T. D. "The Early Christian View of Pseudepigraphic Writings." *JETS* 27 (1984): 65–75.

Leiman, Sid Z. *The Canon and Masorah of the Hebrew Bible: An Introductory Reader.* New York: Ktav, 1974.

_____. *The Canonization of the Hebrew Scripture: The Talmudic and Midrashic Evidence.* Hamden, Conn: Archon, 1976.

_____. "Inspiration and Canonicity: Reflections on the Formation of the Biblical Canon." Pages 56–63 in vol. 2 of *Jewish and Christian Self-Definition.* Edited by E. P. Sanders, A. I. Baumgarten, and Alan Mendelson. Philadelphia: Fortress, 1981.

_____. "Josephus and the Canon of the Bible." Pages in 50–58 in *Josephus, the Bible, and History.* Edited by Louis H. Feldman and Gohei Hata. Detroit: Wayne State University Press, 1989.

Lentricchia, F., and Thomas McLaughlin, eds. *Critical Terms for Literary Study.* Chicago: University of Chicago Press, 1990.

Levy, B. Barry. *Fixing God's Torah: The Accuracy of the Hebrew Bible Text in Jewish Law.* Oxford: Oxford University Press, 2001.

Lichtenberger, Hermann. "Apocrypha." Pages 97–102 in vol. 1 of *The Encyclopedia of Early Christianity.* Edited by Erwin Fahlbusch et al. Translated by Geoffrey Bromiley. Grand Rapids: Eerdmans, 1999.

Lim, Timothy H. *Holy Scripture in the Qumran Commentaries and Pauline Letters.* Oxford: Clarendon, 1997.

Louw, Johannes P., ed. *Meaningful Translation: Its Implications for the Reader.* UBS Monograph Series 5. New York: United Bible Societies, 1991.

Lovering, E. H. "The Collection, Redaction, and Early Circulation of the Corpus Paulinum." Ph.D. diss. Southern Methodist University, 1988.

Lüdemann, Gerd. *The Unholy in Holy Scripture: The Dark Side of the Bible.* Translated by John Bowden. Louisville: Westminster John Knox, 1996.

Luijendijk, AnneMarie. *"Greetings in the Lord": Early Christians and the Oxyrhynchus Papyri.* HTS 59. Cambridge: Harvard University Press, 2009.

MacDonald, Dennis R. *Does the New Testament Imitate Homer? Four Cases from the Acts of the Apostles.* New Haven: Yale University Press, 2003.

Magness, Jodi. *Debating Qumran: Collected Essays on Its Archaeology*. Interdisciplinary Students in Ancient Culture and Religion 4. Leuven: Peeters, 2004.

Maier, J. "Zur Frage des biblischen Kanons im Frühjudentum im Licht der Qumranfunde." *JBT* 3 (1988): 135–46.

Malamat, Abraham. *Mari and the Bible*. Studies in the History and Culture of the Ancient Near East 12. Leiden: Brill, 1998.

Marcos, Natalio Fernandez. *The Septuagint in Context: Introduction to the Greek Versions of the Bible*. Translated by W. G. E. Watson. Leiden: Brill, 2000.

Martínez, Florentino García, and Eibert J. C. Tigchelaar, eds. *The Dead Sea Scrolls: Study Edition*. 2 vols. Grand Rapids: Eerdmans, 1997.

Mason, Steve. "Josephus on Canon and Scriptures." Pages 217–35 in vol. 1, part 1 of *Hebrew Bible/Old Testament: The History of Its Interpretation*. Edited by Magne Saebo. Göttingen: Vandenhoeck & Ruprecht, 1996.

Massaux, Edouard. *The Influence of the Gospel of Saint Matthew on Christian Literature before Saint Irenaeus*. Translated by Norman Belval and Suzanne Hecht. New Gospel Studies 5/3. Leuven: Peeters, 1993.

McDonald, Lee Martin. "Bible: Christian Scripture and Other Writings." In *Encyclopedia of Ancient Greece and Rome*. Edited by Steve Friesen. Oxford: Oxford University Press, 2009.

_____. "The Biblical Canon: Its Origin and Provenance." In *Non-Canonical Writings in Early Judaism and Early Christianity*. Edited by J. H. Charlesworth and L. M. McDonald. Leiden: Brill, 2009.

_____. *The Biblical Canon: Its Origin, Transmission, and Authority*. Peabody, Mass.: Hendrickson, 2006.

_____. "Canon." Pages 777–809 in *The Oxford Handbook of Biblical Studies*. Edited by J. W. Rogerson and J. M. Lieu. Oxford: Oxford University Press, 2006.

_____. "Canon of the New Testament." Pages 536–47 in vol. 1 of *The New Interpreter's Dictionary of the Bible*. Edited by K. D. Sakenfeld. Nashville: Abingdon, 2006.

_____. "The Gospels in Early Christianity: Their Origin, Use, and Authority." Pages 150–78 in *Reading the Gospels Today*. Edited by S. E. Porter. Grand Rapids: Eerdmans, 2004.

_____. "The New Testament Manuscripts: What Is in Them and What Do They Mean?" In *The Origin of the Bible*. Edited by Craig A. Evans and Emanuel Tov. Acadia Studies in Bible and Theology 4. Grand Rapids: Baker Academic, 2008.

_____. "The Scriptures of Jesus." In *Princeton-Prague Symposium on Jesus*. Edited by James H. Charlesworth. Edinburgh: T & T Clark, 2009.

_____. "What Ancient Manuscripts Tell Us about the New Testament Canon." In *The Pseudepigrapha and Christian Origins: Essays from the Studiorum Novi Testamenti Societas*. Edited by James H. Charlesworth and Gerbern S. Oegema. Edinburgh: T & T Clark, 2009.

_____. "What Do We Mean by Canon? Ancient and Modern Questions." In *Non-Canonical Writings in Early Judaism and Early Christianity*. Edited by J. A. Charlesworth and L. M. McDonald. New York: T & T Clark, 2009.

_____, and James Sanders, eds. *The Canon Debate*. Peabody, Mass.: Hendrickson, 2002.

McGrath, Alister. *In the Beginning: The Story of the King James Bible and How It Changed a Nation, a Language, and a Culture*. New York: Random House, 2001.

McKendrick, Scott, and Orlaith O'Sullivan, eds. *The Bible as Book: The Transmission of the Greet Text*. London: British Library and Oak Knoll Press, 2003.

McLay, R. Timothy. *The Use of the Septuagint in New Testament Research*. Grand Rapids: Eerdmans, 2003.

Meade, David G. *Pseudonymity and Canon: An Investigation into the Relationship of Authorship and Authority in Jewish and Earliest Christian Tradition*. Grand Rapids: Eerdmans, 1986.

Menken, Maarten J. J. *Matthew's Bible: The Old Testament Text of the Evangelist.* BETL 173. Leuven: Leuven University Press, 2004.

Metzger, Bruce M. *The Bible in Translation: Ancient and English Versions.* Grand Rapids: Baker Academic, 2001.

_____. *The Canon of the New Testament: Its Origin, Development, and Significance.* Oxford: Clarendon, 1987.

_____. "The Context and Development of the Christian Canon." Pages 85–102 in *Living Traditions of the Bible: Scripture in Jewish, Christian, and Muslim Practice.* Edited by James E. Bowley. St. Louis: Chalice Press, 1999.

_____. "Explicit References in the Works of Origen to Variant Readings in New Testament Manuscripts." Pages 78–95 in *Biblical and Patristic Studies in Memory of Robert Pierce Casey.* Edited by J. N. Birdsell and R. W. Thomson. Freiberg: Herder, 1963. [Repr. pages 88–103 in B. M. Metzger, *Historical and Literary Studies.* Grand Rapids: Eerdmans, 1968.]

_____. "The Future of New Testament Textual Studies." Pages 201–8 in *The Bible as Book: The Transmission of the Greek Text.* Edited by Scot McKendrick and Orlaith O'Sullivan. London: British Library and Oak Knoll Press, 2003.

_____. "Literary Forgeries and Canonical Pseudepigrapha." *JBL* 91, no. 1 (1972): 3–24.

_____. *Manuscripts of the Greek Bible: An Introduction to Greek Palaeography.* New York: Oxford University Press, 1981.

_____. "St Jerome's Explicit References to Variant Readings in Manuscripts of the New Testament." Pages 179–90 in *Text and Interpretation: Studies in the New Testament Presented to Matthew Black.* Edited by E. Best and R. McL. Wilson. Cambridge: Cambridge University Press, 1979.

_____. *A Textual Commentary on the Greek New Testament.* 2nd ed. Stuttgart: Deutsche Bibelgesellschaft/United Bible Societies, 1994.

_____, Robert C. Dentan, and Walter Harrelson. *The Making of the New Revised Standard Version of the Bible.* Grand Rapids: Eerdmans, 1991.

_____, and Bart D. Ehrman. *The Text of the New Testament: Its Transmission, Corruption, and Restoration.* 4th ed. Oxford: Oxford University Press, 2005.

Milik, J. T. *The Books of Enoch: Aramaic Fragments of Qumran Cave 4.* Oxford: Clarendon, 1976.

Millard, Alan. *Reading and Writing in the Time of Jesus.* Sheffield: Sheffield Academic Press, 2000.

Miller, John W. *How the Bible Came to Be: Exploring the Narrative and Message.* New York: Paulist Press, 2004.

_____. *The Origins of the Bible: Rethinking Canon History.* Theological Inquiries. New York: Paulist Press, 1994.

Morgan, R. L. "Let's Be Honest about the Canon: A Plea to Reconsider a Question the Reformers Failed to Answer." *ChrCent* 84 (1967): 717–19.

Moyise, Steve. *The Old Testament in the New: An Introduction.* CBSS. London: Continuum, 2001.

Mullen, Roderic L. *The New Testament Text of Cyril of Jerusalem.* The NT in the Greek Fathers 7. Atlanta: Scholars Press, 1997.

Müller, Mogens. *The First Bible of the Church: A Plea for the Septuagint.* JSOTSup 206. Sheffield: Sheffield Academic Press, 1996.

Nagy, Gregory. *Pindar's Homer: The Lyric Possession of an Epic Past.* Baltimore: Johns Hopkins University Press, 1990.

Neusner, Jacob. *Judaism and Scripture: The Evidence of Leviticus Rabbah.* Chicago: University of Chicago Press, 1986.

Nigosian, S. A. *From Ancient Writings to Sacred Texts: The Old Testament and Apocrypha.* Baltimore: Johns Hopkins University Press, 2004.

North, J. Lionel. "The Use of the Latin Fathers for New Testament Textual Criticism." Pages 208–23 in *The Text of the New Testament in Contemporary Research: Essays on the Status Quaestionis. A Volume in Honor of Bruce M. Metzger.* Edited by Bart D. Ehrman and Michael W. Holmes. Grand Rapids: Eerdmans, 1995.

Oepke, Albrecht. "κρύπτω." *TDNT* 3:957–1000.

Ofer, Yosef. "The Shattered Crown: The Aleppo Codex 60 Years After the Riots." *BAR* 34, no. 5 (2008): 39–49.

Omanson, Roger L. *A Textual Guide to the Greek New Testament: An Adaptation of Bruce M. Metzger's Textual Commentary for the Needs of Translators.* Stuttgart: Deutsche Bibelgesellschaft, 2006.

Osiek, C. "The Shepherd of Hermas: An Early Tale that Almost Made It into the New Testament." *BibRev* 10 (1994): 48–54.

O'Sullivan, Orlath, ed. *The Bible as Book: The Reformation.* London: British Library and Oak Knoll Press, 2000.

Outler, A. C. "The 'Logic' of Canon Making and the Tasks of Canon-Criticism." Pages 263–76 in *Texts and Testaments: Critical Essays on the Bible and the Early Church Fathers.* Edited by W. E. March. San Antonio: Trinity University Press, 1980.

Padgett, Alan G., and Patrick R. Keifert, eds. *But Is It All True? The Bible and the Question of Truth.* Grand Rapids: Eerdmans, 2006.

Parker, David C. *The Living Text of the Gospels.* Cambridge: Cambridge University Press, 1997.

Patterson, L. G. "Irenaeus and the Valentinians: The Emergence of the Christian Scriptures." *StPatr* 18, no. 3 (1989): 189–220.

Pattie, T. S. *Manuscripts of the Bible: Greek Bibles in the British Library.* Rev. ed. London: British Library, 1995.

Patzia, Arthur G. *The Making of the New Testament: Origin, Collection, Text & Canon.* Downers Grove, Ill.: InterVarsity Press, 1995.

Paulsen, David L. "Are Christians Mormon? Reassessing Joseph Smith's Theology in His Bicentennial." *BYU Studies* 45, no. 1 (2006): 35–128; see especially pp. 45–55.

Pelikan, Jaroslav. *Whose Bible Is It? A History of the Scriptures through the Ages.* New York: Viking Penguin, 2005.

Perrin, Nicholas. *Thomas and Tatian: The Relationship between* The Gospel of Thomas *and the* Diatessaron. Academia Biblica 5. Atlanta: Society of Biblical Literature, 2002.

Petersen, W. L. "The Diatessaron of Tatian." Pages 512–34 in *The Text of the New Testament in Contemporary Recent Research: Essays on the Status Quaestionis. A Volume in Honor of Bruce M. Metzger.* Edited by Bart D. Ehrman and Michael W. Holmes. SD 46. Grand Rapids: Eerdmans, 1995.

———. *Tatian's Diatessaron: Its Creation, Dissemination, Significance and History in Scholarship.* Leiden: Brill, 1994.

———. "Textual Evidence of Tatian's Dependence upon Justin's 'APOMNEMONEUMATA.'" *NTS* 36 (1990): 512–34.

———, Johan S. Vos, and Henk J. de Jonge, eds. *Sayings of Jesus: Canonical and Non-Canonical—Essays in Honor of Tjitze Baarda.* NovTSup 89. Leiden: Brill, 1997.

Pfeiffer, Rudolf. *History of Classical Scholarship: From the Beginnings to the End of the Hellenistic Age.* Oxford: Clarendon, 1968.

Pietersma, Albert, and Benjamin G. Wright, eds. *A New English Translation of the Septuagint.* New York: Oxford University Press, 2007.

Porter, Stanley E., ed. "When and How Was the Pauline Canon Compiled?" Pages 113–27 in *The Pauline Canon.* Edited by S. E. Porter. Pauline Studies 1. Leiden: Brill, 2004.

———. "Why So Many Holes in the Papyrological Evidence?" Pages 167–86 in *The Bible as Book: The Transmission of the Greek Text.* Edited by Scot McKendrick and Orlaith O'Sullivan. London: British Library and Oak Knoll Press, 2003.

_____, and Richard S. Hess. *Translating the Bible: Problems and Prospects.* JSNTSup 173. Sheffield: Sheffield Academic Press, 1999.

Powery, Emerson B. *Jesus Read Scripture: The Function of Jesus' Use of Scripture in the Synoptic Gospels.* Biblical Interpretation Series. Leiden: Brill, 2003.

Rahlfs, Alfred, and Robert Hanhart, eds. *Septuaginta.* Rev. ed. Stuttgart: Deutsche Bibelgesellschaft, 2006.

Resnick, Irven M. "The Codex in Early Jewish and Christian Communities." *JRH* 17 (1992): 1–17.

Reuss, Edward W. *History of the Canon of the Holy Scriptures in the Christian Church.* Translated by David Hunter. Edinburgh: R. W. Hunter, 1891.

Richards, E. Randolph. "The Codex and the Early Collection of Paul's Letters." *BBR* 8 (1998): 151–66.

_____. *The Secretary in the Letters of Paul.* WUNT 2/42. Tübingen: Mohr/Siebeck, 1991.

Rist, M. "Pseudepigraphy and the Early Christians." Pages 75–91 in *Studies in New Testament and Early Christian Literature: Essays in Honor of Allen P. Wikgren.* Edited by D. E. Aune. NovTSup 33. Leiden: Brill, 1972.

Rix, H. J., and P. J. Parsons. "Pseudepigraphic Literature." Page 1270 in *The Oxford Classical Dictionary.* Edited by S. Hornblower and A. Spawforth. 3rd ed. Oxford: Oxford University Press, 1996.

Roberts, C. H. "Books in the Greco-Roman World and in the New Testament." Pages 48–66 in *The Cambridge History of the Bible.* Vol. 1: *From the Beginnings to Jerome.* Edited by P. R. Ackroyd and C. F. Evans. Cambridge: Cambridge University Press, 1970.

_____. "The Christian Book and the Greek Papyri." *JTS* 50 (1949): 155–68.

_____. *Manuscript, Society and Belief in Early Christian Egypt.* London: Oxford University Press, 1979.

_____, and T. C. Skeat. *The Birth of the Codex.* Oxford: Oxford University Press, 1983.

Robinson, James M., ed. *The Nag Hammadi Library in English.* Rev. ed. San Francisco: HarperSanFrancisco, 1990.

Römer, Corneila. *Christian Papyri: A Supplement to van Haelst's Catalogue.* http://www.ucl.ac.uk/GrandLat/research/christianpapyri.htm.

Rüger, H. P. "The Extent of the Old Testament Canon." *Bible Translator* 40 (1989): 301–8.

Rutgers, L. V., P. W. van der Horst, H. W. Havelaar, and L. Teugels, eds. *The Use of Sacred Books in the Ancient World.* BET 22. Leuven: Peeters, 1998.

Ruwet, J. "Clement d'Alexandrie: Canon des écritures et apocryphes." *Bib* 29 (1948): 77–99, 240–68, 391–408.

Ryle, H. E. *The Canon of the Old Testament.* 2nd ed. London: Macmillan, 1904.

Sanders, James A. "Adaptable for Life: The Nature and Function of Canon." Pages 531–60 in *Magnalia Dei: The Mighty Acts of God: Essays on the Bible and Archaeology in Memory of G. E. Wright.* Edited by Frank Moore Cross, Werner E. Lemke, and Patrick D. Miller Jr. New York: Doubleday, 1976.

_____. "Cave 11 Surprises and the Question of Canon." *McCQ* 21 (1968): 284–317.

_____. *From Sacred Story to Sacred Text.* Philadelphia: Fortress, 1987.

_____. "Intertexuality and Canon." Pages 316–33 in *On the Way to Nineveh: Studies in Honor of George M. Landes.* Edited by S. Cook and S. Winter. Atlanta: Scholars Press, 1999.

_____. "Palestinian Manuscripts 1947–72." *JJS* 24 (1973): 74–83.

_____. "The Scrolls and the Canonical Process." Pages 1–23 in vol. 2 of *The Dead Sea Scrolls after Fifty Years: A Comprehensive Assessment.* Edited by P. Flint and J. VanderKam. Leiden: Brill, 1999.

_____. "Spinning the Bible." *BR* (June 1998): 22–29, 44–45.

_____. "Stability and Fluidity in Text and Canon." Pages 203–17 in *Traditions of the Text: Studies Offered to Dominique Barthélemy in Celebration of His 70th Birthday*. Edited by G. Norton and S. Pisano. Göttingen: Vandenhoeck & Ruprecht, 1991.

_____. "Text and Canon: Concepts and Method." *JBL* 98 (1979): 1–20.

_____. "Text and Canon: Old Testament and New." Pages 373–94 in *Mélanges Dominique Barthélemy: Études bibliques*. Edited by Pierre Casetti, Othmar Keel, and Adrian Scheuber. Orbis Biblicus et Orientalis 38. Fribourg: Editions Universitaires, 1981.

_____, J. H. Charlesworth, and H. Rietz. "Non-Masoretic Psalms." In *Pseudepigraphic and Non-Masoretic Psalms and Prayers*. Edited by J. H. Charlesworth with H. Rietz. PTSDSSP 4A. Louisville: Westminster John Knox, 1997.

Sarna, N. M. "Canon, Text, and Editions." *EncJud* 1:816–36.

Sawyer, John F. A. *Sacred Languages and Sacred Texts: Religion in the First Christian Centuries*. New York: Routledge, 1999.

Scanlin, Harold P. "What Is the Canonical Shape of the Old Testament Text We Translate?" Pages 207–20 in *Issues in Bible Translation*. Edited by Philip C. Stine. UBS Monograph Series 3. London: United Bible Societies, 1988.

Schechter, Salomon. "The Quotations from Ecclesiasticus in Rabbinic Literature." *Jewish Quarterly Review* 3 (1890–91): 682–706.

Schenker, Adrian. *The Earliest Text of the Hebrew Bible: The Relationship Between the Masoretic Text and the Hebrew Base of the Septuagint Reconsidered*. SBLSCS 52. Atlanta: Society of Biblical Literature, 2003.

Schlossnikel, R. F. *Bedeutung im Rahmen von Text- und Kanongeschichte*. VL 20. Freiburg: Herder, 1991.

Schmidt, Daryl. "The Greek New Testament as a Codex." Pages 469–84 in *The Canon Debate*. Edited by L. M. McDonald and J. A. Sanders. Peabody, Mass.: Hendrickson, 2002.

Schnabel, Eckhard J. "Textual Criticism: Recent Developments." Pages 59–75 in *The Face of New Testament Studies: A Survey of Recent Research*. Edited by Scott McKnight and Grant Osborne. Grand Rapids: Baker Academic, 2004.

Schneemelcher, Wilhelm, ed. *New Testament Apocrypha*. Translated by R. McL. Wilson. 2nd ed. 2 vols. Louisville: Westminster/John Knox, 1991–92.

Schniedewind, William M. *How the Bible Became a Book: The Textualization of Ancient Israel*. Cambridge: Cambridge University Press, 2004.

Schuller, Eileen M. "The Use of Biblical Terms as Designations for Non-Biblical Hymnic and Prayer Compositions." Pages 207–22 in *Biblical Perspectives: Early Use of the Bible in Light of the Dead Sea Scrolls—Proceedings of the First International Symposium of the Orion Center, 12–14 January 1996*. Edited by M. E. Stone and E. G. Chazon. Leiden: Brill, 1998.

Schürer, Emil. *The History of the Jewish People in the Age of Jesus Christ 175 B.C.–A.D. 135*. Revised and edited by Geza Vermes, Fergus Millar, and Matthew Black. 4 vols. Edinburgh: T & T Clark, 1973–87.

Segal, M. H. "The Promulgation of the Authoritative Text of the Hebrew Bible." *JBL* 72, no. 1 (1953): 35–47.

Sharpe, John L., III, and Kimberly van Kampen, eds. *The Bible as Book: The Manuscript Tradition*. London: British Library and Oak Knoll Press, 1998.

Sheler, Jeffrey L. *Is the Bible True? How Modern Debates and Discoveries Affirm the Essence of the Scriptures*. San Francisco: HarperSanFrancisco, 1989.

Shinn, Hyeon Woo. *Textual Criticism and the Synoptic Problem in Historical Jesus Research: The Search for Valid Criteria*. BET 36. Leuven: Peeters, 2004.

Silver, Daniel Jeremy. *The Story of Scripture: From Oral Tradition to the Written Word*. New York: Basic, 1990.

Skeat, T. C. "The Codex Sinaiticus, the Codex Vaticanus, and Constantine." *JTS* 50 (1999): 583–625.

_____. "A Codicological Analysis of the Chester Beatty Papyrus Codex of Gospels and Acts (P⁴⁵)." *Hermathena* 155 (1993): 27–43.

_____. "Irenaeus and the Four-Gospel Canon." *NovT* 34 (1992): 194–99.

_____. "The Oldest Manuscript of the Four Gospels." *NTS* 43 (1997): 1–34.

_____. "The Origin of the Christian Codex." *ZPE* 102 (1994): 263–68.

Skemp, Vincent T. M. *The Vulgate of Tobit Compared with Other Ancient Witnesses.* SBLDS 180. Atlanta: Society of Biblical Literature, 1999.

Smith, D. Moody. "When Did the Gospels Become Scripture?" *JBL* 119, no. 1 (2000): 3–20.

_____. "Why Approaching the New Testament as Canon Matters." *Int* 40 (1986): 407–11.

Snyder, H. Gregory. *Teachers and Texts in the Ancient World: Philosophers, Jews and Christians.* Religion in the First Christian Centuries. London: Routledge, 2000.

Souter, Alexander. *The Text and Canon of the New Testament.* Revised by C. S. C. Williams. London: Gerald Duckworth, 1954.

Steck, O. H. *Der Abschluss der Prophetie im Alten Testament: Ein Versuch zur Frage der Vorgeschichte des Kanons.* BThSt 17. Neukirchen-Vluyn: Neukirchener Verlag, 1991.

_____. "Der Kanon des hebräischen Alten Testaments." Pages 231–52 in *Vernunft des Glaubens: Wissenschaftliche Theologie und kirchliche Lehre.* Edited by J. Rohls and G. Wenz. Göttingen: Vandenhoeck & Ruprecht, 1988.

Steinmann, Andrew E. *Oracles of God: The Old Testament Canon.* St. Louis: Concordia, 1999.

Stern, David. "Sacred Text and Canon." Pages 841–47 in *Contemporary Jewish Religious Thought: Original Essays on Critical Concepts, Movements, and Beliefs.* Edited by Arthur A. Cohen and Paul Mendes-Flohr. New York: Charles Scribner's Sons, 1987.

Stonehouse, Ned Bernard. *The Apocalypse in the Ancient Church: A Study in the History of the New Testament Canon.* Goes: Oosterbaan & Le Cointre, 1929.

Stott, Katherine M. *Why Did They Write This Way? Reflections on References to Written Documents in the Hebrew Bible and Ancient Literature.* LHB/OTS. Edinburgh: T & T Clark International, 2008.

Strack, H. L., and G. Stemberger. *Introduction to the Talmud and Midrash.* Translated by Markus Bockmuehl. Minneapolis: Fortress, 1992.

Stroker, William D. *Extracanonical Sayings of Jesus.* SBLRBS 18. Atlanta: Scholars Press, 1989.

Stuart, Moses. *A Critical History of the Old Testament Canon.* London: George Routledge, 1849.

Stuhlhofer, Franz. *Der Gebrauch der Bibel von Jesus bis Euseb: Eine statistische Untersuchung zur Kanongeschichte.* Wuppertal: R. Brockhaus, 1988.

Stuhlmacher, Peter. "The Significance of the Old Testament Apocrypha and Pseudepigrapha for the Understanding of Jesus and Christology." Pages 1–15 in *The Apocrypha in Ecumenical Perspective.* Edited by Siegfried Meuer. UBS Monograph Series 6. New York: United Bible Societies, 1991.

Sundberg, Albert C., Jr. "The Bible Canon and the Christian Doctrine of Inspiration." *Int* 29, no. 4 (1975): 352–71.

_____. "Canon Muratori: A Fourth-Century List." *HTR* 66, no. 1 (1973): 1–41.

_____. "Canon of the NT." Pages 136–40 in *Interpreter's Dictionary of the Bible, Supplement Volume.* Edited by Keith Crim. Nashville: Abingdon, 1976.

_____. *The Old Testament of the Early Church.* Cambridge: Harvard University Press, 1964.

286 Bibliography

_____. "A Symposium on the Canon of Scripture: 2. The Protestant Old Testament Canon: Should It Be Re-examined?" *CBQ* 28 (1966): 194–203.

Swanson, Reuben, ed. *New Testament Greek Manuscripts: Variant Readings Arranged in Horizontal Lines Against Codex Vaticanus.* (Volumes on Matthew, Mark, Luke, John, Acts, 1 Corinthians, Galatians, and Romans.) Wheaton, Ill.: Tyndale House Publishers, 1995–2005.

Swete, H. B. *Introduction to the Old Testament in Greek.* Revised by Richard R. Ottley and appendix by H. St. J. Thackeray. Cambridge: Cambridge University Press, 1914.

Talmon, Shemaryahu. "The Crystallization of the 'Canon of Hebrew Scriptures.'" Pages 5–20 in *The Bible as Book: The Hebrew Bible and the Judaean Desert Discoveries.* Edited by E. D. Herbert and E. Tov. London: British Library and Oak Knoll Press, 2002.

Theron, Daniel J. *Evidence of Tradition.* Grand Rapids: Baker, 1980.

Tobin, Paul. *Manuscript Fallacies.* 7/18/08. www.geocities.com/paulntobin/manufall.html.

_____. *New Testament Manuscripts and Text Types.* 7/18/07. http://www.geocities.com/paulntobin/ntmanuscript.html.

Tov, Emanuel. *The Greek and Hebrew Bible: Collected Essays on the Septuagint.* Supplements to Vetus Testamentum 72. Leiden: Brill, 1999.

_____. *The Greek Minor Prophets Scroll from Nahal Hever (8HevXIIgr.).* DJD 8. Oxford: Clarendon, 1990.

_____. "Groups of Biblical Texts Found at Qumran." Pages 85–102 in *Time to Prepare the Way in the Wilderness: Papers on the Qumran Scrolls by Fellows of the Institute for Advanced Studies of the Hebrew University.* Edited by D. Dimant and L. H. Schiffman. Jerusalem: Jerusalem University, 1989–90.

_____. "Hebrew Biblical Manuscripts from the Judaean Desert: Their Contribution to Textual Criticism." *JJS* 39 (1988): 5–37.

_____. "The History and Significance of a Standard Text of the Hebrew Bible." Pages 49–66 in *Hebrew Bible/Old Testament: The History of Its Interpretation.* Vol. 1: *From the Beginnings to the Middle Ages (until 1300).* Göttingen: Vandenhoeck & Ruprecht, 1996.

_____. "The Nature of the Large-Scale Differences between the LXX and MT STV, Compared with Similar Evidence in Other Sources." Pages 121–44 in *The Earliest Text of the Hebrew Bible: The Relationship between the Masoretic Text and the Hebrew Base of the Septuagint Reconsidered.* Edited by Adrian Schenker. SBLSCS 52. Atlanta: Society of Biblical Literature, 2003.

_____. "The Rewritten Book of Joshua as Found at Qumran and Masada." Pages 233–56 in *Biblical Perspectives: Early Use of the Bible in Light of the Dead Sea Scrolls—Proceedings of the First International Symposium of the Orion Center, 12–14 January 1996.* Edited by M. E. Stone and E. G. Chazon. Leiden: Brill, 1998.

_____. "Scribal Practices and Physical Aspects of the Dead Sea Scrolls." Pages 45–60 in *The Bible as Book.* Edited by J. L. Sharpe and K. van Kampen. London: Oak Knoll, 1998.

_____. *The Septuagint Translation of Jeremiah and Baruch.* Harvard Semitic Monograph 8. Missoula, Mont.: Scholars Press, 1976.

_____. "The Status of the Masoretic Text in Modern Text Editions of the Hebrew Bible: The Relevance of the Canon." Pages 234–51 in *The Canon Debate.* Edited by L. M. McDonald and J. A. Sanders. Peabody, Mass.: Hendrickson, 2002.

_____. *Textual Criticism of the Hebrew Bible.* 2nd ed. Minneapolis: Fortress, 2001.

Trobisch, David. *Die Endredaktion des Neuen Testaments: Eine Untersuchung zur Entstehung der christlichen Bibel.* NTOA 31. Freiburg: Universitätsverlag, 1996.

_____. *Die Entstehung des Paulusbriefsammlung: Studien zu den Anfangen christlicher Publizistik.* NTOA 10. Göttingen: Vandenhoeck & Ruprecht, 1989.

_____. *The First Edition of the New Testament.* Oxford: Oxford University Press, 2000.

_____. *The Oldest Extant Editions of the Letters of Paul.* 1999. http://www.bts.edu/faculty/trobisch.htm.

_____. *Paul's Letter Collection: Tracing the Origins.* Philadelphia: Fortress, 1994.

_____. "The Status of the Masoretic Text Editions of the Hebrew Bible: The Relevance of Canon." Pages 234–51 in *The Canon Debate.* Edited by L. M. McDonald and J. A. Sanders. Peabody, Mass.: Hendrickson, 2000.

Tuckett, C. M. *The Scriptures in the Gospels.* BETL 131. Leuven: Leuven University Press, 1997.

Turner, C. H. "Appendix to W. Sanday's Article: 'The Cheltenham List of the Canonical Books, and the Writings of Cyprian.'" *StudBib* 3 (1891): 304–25.

_____. "Latin Lists of the Canonical Books: 3. From Pope Innocent's Epistle to Exsuperius of Toulouse (A.D. 405)." *JTS* 13 (1911–12): 77–82.

Ulrich, Ernst. "Inspiration, Normativeness, Canonicity, and the Unique Sacred Character of the Bible." *CBQ* 44 (1982): 447–69.

Ulrich, Eugene. "The Bible in the Making: The Scriptures at Qumran." Pages 77–93 in *The Community of the Renewed Covenant.* Edited by E. Ulrich and J. VanderKam. Christianity and Judaism in Antiquity 10. Notre Dame, Ind.: University of Notre Dame Press, 1994.

_____. "The Canonical Process, Textual Criticism, and Latter Stages in the Composition of the Bible." Pages 267–91 in *'Sha'arei Talmon': Studies in the Bible, Qumran, and the Ancient Near East Presented to Shemaryahu Talmon.* Edited by M. Fishbane and E. Tov with the assistance of W. W. Fields. Winona Lake, Ind.: Eisenbrauns, 1992.

_____. "The Community of Israel and the Composition of Scriptures." Pages 327–42 in *Studies in Biblical Intertextuality in Honor of James A Sanders.* Edited by C. A. Evans and S. Talmon. Biblical Interpretation Series 18. Leiden: Brill, 1997.

_____. "The Dead Sea Scrolls and the Biblical Text." Pages 79–100 in vol. 1 of *The Dead Sea Scrolls after Fifty Years: A Comprehensive Assessment.* Edited by P. Flint and J. VanderKam. Leiden: Brill, 1998.

_____. *The Dead Sea Scrolls and the Origins of the Bible.* SDSSRL. Grand Rapids: Eerdmans, 1999.

VanderKam, J. C. "Authoritative Literature in the Dead Sea Scrolls." *DSD* 5 (1998): 382–402.

_____. *From Revelation to Canon: Studies in the Hebrew Bible and Second Temple Literature.* JSJSup 62. Leiden: Brill, 2000.

_____. "1 Enoch, Enochic Motifs, and Enoch in Early Christian Literature." Pages 33–101 in *The Jewish Apocalyptic Heritage in Early Christianity.* Edited by James C. VanderKam and William Adler. CRINT. Minneapolis: Fortress, 1996.

_____, and J. T. Milik. "The First *Jubilees* Manuscript from Qumran Cave 4: A Preliminary Publication." *JBL* 110, no. 2 (1991): 243–70.

VanElderen, Bastiaan. "Early Christian Libraries." Pages 45–59 in *The Bible as Book: The Manuscript Tradition.* Edited by J. Sharpe and K. van Kampen. London: British Library; Newcastle, Del.: Oak Knoll Press, 1998.

Veltri, Giuseppe. *Libraries, Translations, and 'Canonic' Texts: The Septuagint, Aquila and Ben Sira in the Jewish and Christian Traditions.* JSJSup 109. Leiden: Brill, 2006.

Verheyden, J. "The Canon Muratori: A Matter of Dispute." Pages 487–556 in *The Biblical Canons.* Edited by J.-M. Auwers and H. J. de Jonge. BETL 163. Leuven: Leuven University Press, 2003.

Vokes, F. E. "The Didache and the Canon of the New Testament." *SE* 3 (1964): 427–36.

Vööbus, Arthur. *Early Versions of the New Testament: Manuscript Studies.* Stockholm: Estonian Theological Society in Exile, 1954.

Warfield, Benjamin Breckenridge. *The Inspiration and Authority of the Bible.* Philadelphia: Presbyterian & Reformed, 1948; fourth printing, Grand Rapids: Baker Book House, 1964.

Washburn, David L. *A Catalogue of Biblical Passages in the Dead Sea Scrolls.* Text-Critical Studies 2. Atlanta: Society of Biblical Literature, 2002.

Wasserstein, Abraham, and David J. Wasserstein. *The Legend of the Septuagint: From Classical Antiquity to Today.* Cambridge: Cambridge University Press, 2006.

Weitzman, M. P. *The Syriac Version of the Old Testament: An Introduction.* Cambridge: Cambridge University Press, 1999.

Wieland, Willker. Greek New Testament Papyri [Recent update of Kurt Aland] online at http://www-uner.uni-bremen.de/~wie/texte/Papyri-list.html.

Wise, Michael. "The Dead Sea Scrolls: Non-Biblical Manuscripts, Part 2." *BA* 49 (December 1986): 228–39.

Würthwein, Ernst. *The Text of the Old Testament: An Introduction to the Biblia Hebraica.* Translated by Erroll F. Rhodes. 2nd ed. Grand Rapids: Eerdmans, 1995.

Wyrick, Jed. *The Ascension of Authorship: Attribution and Canon Formation in Jewish, Hellenistic, and Christian Traditions.* Cambridge: Harvard University Press, 2004.

Yadin, Yigael. "The Temple Scroll—The Longest and Most Recently Discovered Dead Sea Scroll." Pages 161–77 in vol. 2 of *Archaeology and the Bible: The Best of BAR. Archaeology in the World of Herod, Jesus, and Paul.* Edited by Hershel Shanks and D. P. Cole. Washington, DC: Biblical Archaeology Society, 1990.

———, ed. *The Temple Scroll.* 3 vols. Jerusalem: Israel Exploration Society, 1983.

Young, Frances, Lewis Ayres, and Andrew Louth, eds. *The Cambridge History of Early Christian Literature.* Cambridge: Cambridge University Press, 2004.

Zahn, Theodore. *Forschungen zur Geschichte des neutestamentlichen Kanons und der altkirchlichen Literatur.* 10 vols. Leipzig: A. Deichert, 1881–1929.

———. *Geschichte des neutestamentlichen Kanons.* 2 vols. Erlangen: A. Deichert, 1888–92.

Zenger, E., ed. *Die Tora als Kanon für Juden und Christen.* HBS 10. Freiburg: Herder, 1996.

Zevit, Z. "The Second-Third Century Canonization of the Hebrew Bible and Its Influence on Christian Canonizing." Pages 133–60 in *Canonization and Decanonization.* Edited by A. van der Kooij and K. van der Toorn. Leiden: Brill, 1998.

Zuntz, G. *The Text of the Epistles: A Disquisition upon the Corpus Paulinium.* Schweich Lectures 1946. Eugene, OR: Wipf & Stock, 1946, 1953.

Ancient Sources Index

289

4:48	150	10:4	148	19:36	148	
5:2	148	10:9	148	19:37	149	
5:5	148	10:11	148	19:38–42	217	
5:10	148	10:16	148	20	183, 184, 217	
5:18	150	10:20	150	20:1	217	
5:21	148	10:22	80, 149	20:11–18	217	
5:22	150	10:33	148	20:12–13	217	
5:30	148	10:34	44, 90,	20:17	148, 218	
5:35	148, 150		133, 148	20:17–19	218	
5:37	148	10:36	148	20:18–19	218	
5:39	186	11:50	148	20:22	150, 250n19	
5:44	148	11:51	148	20:27	218	
5:46	148	11:54	148	20:28	148, 250n19	
6:21	148	12:12–15	214	20:29	149	
6:31	148	12:13	148, 149	20:30–31	124, 183	
6:32	148	12:15	148	21	183, 184, 217	
6:35	150	12:26	149	21:16	148	
6:45	148	12:27	148	21:24–25	184	
6:49	148	12:29	148			

Acts
6:53	148	12:34	148	1:6–9	218	
7:2	148	12:38	148	1:8	45	
7:17	148	12:40	148	2:1–21	139	
7:18	148	12:41	148	2:16–20	266n24	
7:22	148	13:18	90, 148	2:17–18	211	
7:34	148	13:19	148	2:17–36	45	
7:37	148	13:23	250n19	4:11	266n24	
7:38	148, 149, 150	13:34	26	6:1	115	
7:42	148, 150	14:1	148	7:2–53	215	
7:49	148	14:6	220	7:4	215	
7:51	148	14:15	129, 150	13:15	133	
7:52	148	14:27	148	13:27	43	
7:53–8:11	174, 181	15:1	150	15:36–41	219	
8:3	148	15:6	148	17:28	126	
8:5	148	15:9–10	150	24:14	133	
8:7	148	15:15	148	28:23	43, 90, 133	
8:12	148	15:19	26			

Romans
8:21	148	15:25	148, 150	1:3	216	
8:28	148	16:13	148	1:24–32	134	
8:32	148, 220	16:21	148	3:10–19	44, 133	
8:34	148	16:22	148	3:21	43, 133	
8:40	148	16:32	149	4	54	
8:44	150	17:3	150	5:12–21	135	
8:49	149	17:12	148	7:7	135	
8:52	149	17:17	148	14	184	
8:53	150	18:20	148	15	184	
8:58	148	18:22	148	16	184	
9:4	148	18:31–33	162	16:7	180	
9:7	148	18:33–38	115			
9:24	148	18:36–19:7	162			

1 Corinthians
9:29	148	18:37–38	162	1:21–24	28	
9:31	148	19:24	148	1:27	206	
9:34	148	19:28	148	2:1–2	28	
10:3	148	19:31	148			

Author/Name Index

on changes in biblical manuscripts, 174
citing deliberate changes to New Testament
    texts, 179
on current practice of textual criticism, 185
on difficulties of translating Greek syntax
    and vocabulary, 189
doubting possibility of recovering original
    New Testament text, 183
explaining why early New Testament manu-
    scripts were more prone to error, 176
influence of, 223n1
on limited influence of orthodoxy, 13
on loyalty to orthodoxy affecting transmis-
    sion of text, 182
on proto-orthodoxy in early church, 30
on textual variants, 155
Eleazar, 87
Elliott, J. K., 117, 185, 186
Ellis, E. Earle, 138
Elzevir, Abraham, 261n35
Elzevir, Bonaventure, 261n35
Enns, Peter, 219
Epictetus, 14
Epicurus, 14
Epimenides, 126
Epiphanius, 228n42
Epp, Eldon, 164, 166–67, 180, 184, 185
Erasmus of Rotterdam, 179–80, 181
Eusebius, 26, 89, 142, 160, 228n42
    on Irenaeus's warning to people copying his
        work, 177
    offering first datable catalogue of sacred New
        Testament writings, 170
    using "encovenanted" to refer to accepted
        sacred scripture, 16
Evans, Craig, 65, 66, 174

Falk, Daniel, 102
Fee, Gordon, 184–85
Ferguson, Everett, 228n42
Finkelberg, Margalit, 194
Flint, Peter, 56, 71
Frumentius, 95
Funk, Robert, 198

Gamble, Harry, 29, 158
Gelasius (pope), 68
Grant, Robert, 30, 138
Gregory the Illuminator, 95

Haelst, Joseph van, 67
Hahneman, Geoffrey Mark, 26, 228n42
Harnack, Adolf von, 20–21, 22

Harrington, Daniel J., 251n27
Hays, J. Daniel, 203
Hippolytus, 30, 81, 142
Holmes, Michael, 160, 175, 185
Homer, 87–88
Hort, F. J. A., 168
Hurtado, Larry, 162–63, 164, 176
Hyeon Woo Shin, 262n44
Hyrcanus, John, 76

Ignatius of Antioch, 30, 209
Irenaeus, 26, 30, 89, 138, 142, 228n42
    acknowledging errors made when copying
        manuscripts, 177
    arguing for acceptance only of four
        Gospels, 15
    on Christian faith, 15–16
    influence of teaching about apostolic
        succession, 13
    use of "canon," 15
    views on four Gospels, not universally
        held, 32
    warning against deliberate changes in sacred
        texts, 177

Jerome, 81, 89, 93, 94, 110, 114, 139, 177,
    189
Jesus
    apocryphal and pseudepigraphal texts attrib-
        uted to, parallels in Synoptic Gospels, 149
    apocryphal and pseudepigraphal texts attrib-
        uted to, parallels in Gospel of John, 150
    drawing from many sources of material, 145
    endorsing a biblical canon, as anachronistic
        concept, 123
    establishing database for citations of biblical
        texts, difficulty of, 124–25
    familiarity of, with religious texts not in
        Hebrew Bible, 124
    as final authority in early Christianity, 28
    languages of, 115
    not inheriting or passing along a fixed
        canon, 196
    scriptures cited by, 65, 66, 83–84, 127–28,
        133, 146–48
    sources of knowledge about, 125
    statements of, informed by wide variety of
        Jewish religious writings, 66
    thought of, informed by other religious lit-
        erature, 128
    Torah as core of sacred scripture for, 135–36
    using texts to support specific teachings, 124
Johanan (rabbi), 79, 80

Subject Index

CPSIA information can be obtained at www.ICGtesting.com
Printed in the USA
LVOW06s1919090813

347195LV00001B/153/P